Developmentally Ap
and Instruction

This timely and accessible volume explores how our understanding of research in child development can help cultivate the knowledge, skills, and attitudes children need for informed and thoughtful participation in society by viewing the curriculum through a developmental lens.

Biddle and Garcia-Nevarez cover a range of key topics including characteristics of physical, cognitive, and psychosocial development of children; heritable and environmental influences on children's developing self; language and literacy development; mathematical cognition; growth mindsets; and evidence-based positive behavioral interventions and supports. The expert team of contributors offers an advanced exploration of developmental science and how this applies to learning and education in order to create inclusive environments that support children with a range of abilities, including those with the most significant medical, intellectual, and developmental delays. Each chapter contains boxes exploring how the topic relates to the themes of "Promoting Social and Emotional Competence Theory," "Research to Practice Connection," "Common Core and Other Standards," and "Social Justice and Diversity," ensuring comprehensive and consistent coverage across the volume.

Developmentally Appropriate Curriculum and Instruction will be essential reading for students of child development and education, as well as educators and those in teacher training who are interested in how theory and research can be effectively harnessed to improve children's outcomes.

Ana Garcia-Nevarez is Professor of Child and Adolescent Development in the College of Education at California State University, Sacramento.

Kimberly A. Gordon Biddle is Professor Emeritus at California State University, Sacramento.

Developmentally Appropriate Curriculum and Instruction

Pedagogy for Knowledge, Attitudes, and Values

Edited by Ana Garcia-Nevarez and Kimberly A. Gordon Biddle

NEW YORK AND LONDON

First published 2021
by Routledge
52 Vanderbilt Avenue, New York, NY 10017

and by Routledge
2 Park Square, Milton Park, Abingdon, Oxon, OX14 4RN

Routledge is an imprint of the Taylor & Francis Group, an informa business

Library of Congress Cataloging-in-Publication Data
Names: Garcia-Nevarez, Ana, editor. | Gordon, Kimberly A. (Kimberly Ann), 1965- editor.
Title: Developmentally appropriate curriculum and instruction : pedagogy for knowledge, attitudes and values / Ana Garcia-Nevarez and Kimberly A. Gordon Biddle.
Description: New York, NY : Routledge, 2021. | Includes bibliographical references and index. |
Identifiers: LCCN 2020044661 | ISBN 9780367373269 (hbk) | ISBN 9780367373290 (pbk) | ISBN 9780429353147 (ebk)
Subjects: LCSH: Child psychology. | Child development. | Inclusive education.
Classification: LCC BF721 .D458 2021 | DDC 155.4--dc23
LC record available at https://lccn.loc.gov/2020044661

ISBN: 978-0-367-37326-9 (hbk)
ISBN: 978-0-367-37329-0 (pbk)
ISBN: 978-0-429-35314-7 (ebk)

Typeset in Garamond
by Deanta Global Publishing Services, Chennai, India

Contents

About the Authors

Ana Garcia-Nevarez is Professor of Child and Adolescent Development in the College of Education at California State University, Sacramento. She has a double BA in Psychology and Child Development from California State University, Northridge, an MA in School Psychology from Arizona State, and a Ph.D. in Curriculum and Instruction (emphasis elementary education) from Arizona State University. She was a Regents' graduate academic scholar at Arizona State University. She has more than 18 years of experience as a college professor and has numerous accomplishments and awards. She has published numerous publications and has presented at national and international conferences. Dr. Garcia-Nevarez's recent research studies have examined the attitudes of pre-service teachers toward teaching as a career and working with culturally and linguistically diverse students. Specifically, she has studied the impact of early field experiences on prospective teachers' career goal orientations, the relationship between school classification (Title I, non-Title I) and participant outcomes, and the relationship between participants' facility in a second language and their response to early field experiences. Previous research studies have focused on the attitudes and perceptions that foreign-trained teachers and bilingual education teachers have toward their education training and the promising prospects these teachers have in the United States.

Kimberly A. Gordon Biddle has a Ph.D. from Stanford University in Child and Adolescent Development. She is an American Psychological Association MFP Fellow. She is a retired college professor of 28 years, now Emeritus Professor at California State University, Sacramento. She is the author or co-author of over 15 peer-reviewed articles and some book chapters. She is a presenter or co-presenter of more than 35 peer-reviewed presentations. She has obtained approximately $1,000,000 in grants. She won Outstanding Teaching and Service Awards at Sacramento State. She is also the winner of one of the Stanford GSE Alumni Awards for Excellence in Education for 2018, and she won one of the Alumni Career Awards from the University of Redlands in 2019.

Contributors

Eric B. Claravall, Ph.D., is Assistant Professor of Literacy and Special Education at California State University, Sacramento. His main research interest falls within the intersection of multiple source use and digital literacies across the discipline.

Cindy Collado, Ph.D., is Assistant Professor of Special Education at California State University, Sacramento. She conducts research and trains preservice and current teachers on evidence-based practices in Early Childhood Special Education (ECSE), inclusive education, assessment, and engagement of families raising children with disabilities. Her work is grounded in her experiences as an ECSE teacher co-teaching in inclusive preschool programs in Chicago.

Elizabeth Ferry-Perata is a lecturer at Sacramento State University where she teaches Child Development courses. Elizabeth is an Infant Toddler Specialist and does consulting work with early care and education programs throughout the state of California. Elizabeth enjoys spending time with her family, friends, and loved ones.

Sayonita Ghosh Hajra is Assistant Professor in the Department of Mathematics and Statistics at California State University, Sacramento. She has a Ph.D. in Mathematics and an MA in Mathematics Education from the University of Georgia. She has 6 years of college teaching experience. She has been involved with mathematics and mathematics education research, and has published her research in peer-reviewed journals. She has also presented at multiple peer-reviewed conferences.

Jean Gonsier-Gerdin, Ph.D., is a professor in the Teaching Credentials Department at California State University, Sacramento. Her teaching and research interests include: inclusive education practices, peer supports and social relationships of students with extensive support needs, positive behavioral supports, evidence-based practices for students with autism spectrum disorders, and special education teacher preparation to promote advocacy, leadership, and systems-change.

Aletha Harven is a professor, global teacher educator and humanitarian, and Diversity Equity & Inclusion (DEI) Strategist. Dr. Harven holds a Ph.D. in Education from the University of California, Los Angeles. As an associate professor of Psychology and Child Development at California State University Stanislaus, she coaches STEM faculty in inclusive and culturally sustaining pedagogical practices through her multi-year National Science Foundation (NSF) Grant, CIENCIA.

Alicia Herrera is a lecturer of Child Development at California State University, Sacramento. She received her Master's degree in Education from the University of California, Berkeley. She is a doctoral candidate in Educational Leadership at University of California, Davis, after holding a variety of educational positions both nationally and internationally in K-12 systems for nearly two decades.

Erin Miranda Morrison is a California Middle School teacher specializing in the Visual Arts. She recently received her Master of Arts in Teaching from San Diego Christian College.

Arlene Ortiz is Assistant Professor of School Psychology in the department of Graduate and Professional Studies in Education, College of Education, California State University, Sacramento. She holds a Ph.D. in School Psychology from The Pennsylvania State University.

Wanda J. Roundtree has an Ed.D. in Early Education. She has also co-authored a textbook in Early Childhood Education. She has experience as a consultant, grant writer, and lecturer at the college level. Currently, she is an administrator in Twin Rivers School District in the Sacramento Area.

Lindy Valdez, Ed.D. is a professor of Kinesiology at California State University, Sacramento. Professor Valdez is an international scholar who has presented around the world. His professional endeavors include teaching of physical education in K-12 settings and authoring of textbooks in this field.

Chapter 1

Developmental Learning Theories

Wanda J. Roundtree

In memory of my soulmate... whose perpetual smile always lifted me.
Dr. Darryl O. Henderson
1961-2017

Introduction

Imagine, if you will, a scenario that portrays a teacher–student *dyad* engaged in an intersubjective teaching-learning task that involves stringing beads of different sizes, shapes, and colors. This relatively popular learning task has been proven to be instrumental in assisting young students' development of their fine motor skills, including their acquisition of a range of other skills vital to students' successful reading, letter recognition, story-sequencing, writing, etc. Hence, a four-year-old Transitional Kindergarten (TK) student, otherwise known as "the less expert other," must refer to a series of picture cards, each depicting a specific stringing pattern or sequence. The teacher, often referred to as the "more expert other" within the context of the classroom, attempts to *scaffold* the student's development within the *Zone of Proximal Development (ZPD).* Working in collaboration with the teacher, the student attempts to string the beads according to the specific sequence depicted on each card.

As a teacher of elementary school-age students, you are probably quite familiar with the deployment of scaffolding strategies during student–teacher interactions. The countless teacher–student transactions that you have experienced or witnessed at some point in your teaching career demonstrate the very essence of what constitutes a successful teaching-learning episode. Every exchange between the teacher and student underscores the very crucial role that parents, guardians, teachers, and significant others play in bolstering children's (cognitive) development. The teacher carefully scaffolds the student's development within her respective zone of mastery. Ultimately, the process results in an intersubjective experience in which the pair, having begun the task with varying ideas as to how to complete it, eventually arrives at a shared understanding of the task at hand. And while scaffolding scenarios within the classroom primarily focus on bolstering the student's cognitive abilities, it is impossible to ignore the elements of social-emotional and physical functioning on behalf of the student. Each domain of development works both independently and in concert with other developmental domains to spur students' motivation and varied approaches to learning. This understanding should, therefore, pique our interests about the importance of carefully considering individual students' gifts, talents, propensities, multiple intelligences, temperament styles, cultural, personal/familial, and linguistic attributes when planning for students. What we have come to understand is that the three broad domains of development—cognitive, physical, social-emotional—must never be viewed in isolation or as distinct aspects of development, separate and apart from each other, but rather the three broad domains must be seen as a holistic, well-integrated and dynamic system, each contributing individually and collectively to the child's overall functioning within any given context in which development or growth is occurring.

To be an effective teacher, it is necessary to have a rather sophisticated view of development. So, how should we as educators view development? It is important to note that investigations into developmental science, especially as it relates to child development, have centered on whether development should be viewed as continuous or discontinuous. While some developmental theorists believe that human development is *continuous*, which is a view that attributes variations in developmental abilities among the immature vis-a-vis the mature as a matter of amount or complexity, other theorists simply maintain that developmental changes or novel ways of behaving or responding to the world at specific stages across the early phase of the lifespan is *discontinuous*. Thus, these two opposing views simply come down to viewing developmental changes or constancy, at any point in growth, as either quantitatively or qualitatively different. Equally debatable has been the question of biological determinants and their impact on individuals' development and to what extent we can attribute the environment and/or the *whole* range of human experience to a person's development. Nevertheless, we can find solace in the fact that extreme views concerning these questions are no longer in vogue. Today, most recent theorists assume a middle-of-the-ground stance on these issues, recognizing that development can be both continuous and discontinuous and that human development is much more plastic than originally thought. Most theorists today recognize that the impact of an individual's life experiences may wax and wane across domains and over the course of the lifespan, and that both environmental and genetic factors have been found to have an indelible impact on development (Berk & Myers, 2016).

While most critical questions regarding learning and development have already been answered by theorists during the early to mid-twentieth century, there are some questions concerning development that still warrant further observation and study. Nevertheless, this chapter seeks to provide the teaching professional with answers to some of the most fundamental questions about how young students come to "know" and provides a basic overview of the quintessential theories of learning and development that we uphold today. The theories discussed below are "blueprints" of the human change process and provide a sound basis for our understanding of how and why humans change as they age.

The Constructivist View of Learning

Most learning and developmental theories underscore the vital role that a child's environment and significant adults (mother, father, teacher, and/or other consistent caregivers) play in the life of a developing child. Young children are constantly interacting with their physical and social worlds; it is how they come to know and understand the people and things around them. Children are active and persistent in their approach to construct their own meaning of their world; they have a natural ability to think about their actions and social interactions. Children's motivation to understand the inner workings of the world around them is the very essence of the *constructivist* view of learning. Structural changes in the way children come to think about their world are a direct result of their myriad of experiences. They seem to be always about the business of framing and reframing their mental structures (altering their thought processes) as they derive meaning from their daily experiences and interactions. Children are like "little construction engineers"; in much the same way that construction workers need tools, nails, and steel to build a building, young children need people, places, and things in order to construct their knowledge of their personal world.

Knowledge is not simply floating around in space somewhere waiting for someone to come along and grab it. In fact, the only *true* knowledge that exists is the knowledge we construct for ourselves. Constructivists believe that knowledge cannot simply be "spoon-fed" to children. Children's learning process must consist of hands-on experiences that engage both their bodies and minds; children must have the opportunity to experience the world through their many senses as well as to process that sensory data. Educators who uphold a constructivist view of learning facilitate children's thinking by seeking varied opportunities to engage them. They encourage collaborative and peer learning among children, organize stimulating and challenging classroom environments, and provide numerous opportunities for children to problem solve on their own. These teachers facilitate children's learning by focusing their attention to details, modeling, guiding children's behavior, asking questions, and getting children to think "a head above", sort to speak, their developmental capacity.

Box 1.1 Theory and Research to Practice Connection

The Benefits of Social Constructivist Classrooms for Both Students and Teachers

Carefully researched and well-crafted theories can certainly persist over time. Such is the case with regard to the theories developed by both Piaget and Vygotsky. Indeed, their theories, which have stood the test of time, have contributed considerably to developmental scientists' and educators' understanding of the intricacies of human development and cognition. Sharkins et al. (2017), in their research article entitled "Flipping Theory: Ways in Which Children's Experiences in the 21st-Century Classroom Can Provide Insight into the Theories of Piaget and Vygotsky," discuss ways in which the two theories converge to promote teachers' pedagogy and knowledge about students in today's classroom contexts.

Located within a large metropolitan area, a first-grade classroom in a small community school, utilizing the principles of Charlotte Mason (2008), portrayed a vivid demonstration of constructivist principles at work as children examined themselves and developed high moral standards. Teachers regularly provided guidance by asking students open-ended questions that encouraged imagination and the construction of knowledge, and teachers provided gentle guidance aimed at helping students to derive their own solutions to real-life and academic challenges. Students were given time to work at their own pace, to explain their thought processes, and to engage in self-correction. Similarly, in a suburban, more traditional elementary kindergarten classroom, located on the opposite side of town, constructivist principles were also at work, as evidenced by the transactions between the teacher and students as well as among peers. During a shared storybook reading, the teacher employed distancing strategies and open-ended questioning techniques in order to get students to think more comprehensively about their responses. Students were encouraged to think about the "things that they noticed" and to share these observations with their peers and teacher. They were also afforded the "right" to change or correct their answer to a response and to defend their respective viewpoints, etc. Furthermore, students were encouraged to write their own stories with illustrations; phonetic spelling was supported so that students could focus on the story.

Math tasks in both of these settings indicated that youngsters were functioning in both Piaget's preoperational and concrete operational stage of development. Teachers' flexibility in allowing the students to use their fingers or counting markers as they constructed concepts of number ordinality and cardinality further underscored the importance of connecting theory to classroom practice. Students' understanding was verified by the teacher asking the question, "Tell me how you thought about that…". Also, as students engaged in casual conversations while completing math exercises, teachers had the unique opportunity to observe students' language development and use of private/egocentric speech. Students' egocentric and private speech was quite evident throughout their engagement in learning tasks. As task difficulty moved from low to moderate, students' private speech increased. Furthermore, the intentionality of the teaching processes as well as the learning environment afforded the children numerous opportunities to construct and co-construct (with peers and the classroom teacher) their own knowledge.

Hence, in both of these settings, students were expected to derive their own answers, which were often scaffolded by their teacher and peers. And when the students worked conjointly (more "expert others" working collaboratively with less "expert others"), they displayed higher levels of cognitive functioning. Furthermore, the teachers' questions related to children's thinking processes, i.e., "Tell me how you thought about that…"—followed by pregnant pauses to allow ample time for students to think and respond—were very instrumental in promoting increased meta-cognitive skills among the young students. Students were encouraged to operate in the *Zone of Proximal Development (ZPD)*, or within their scope of mastery (Berk & Meyers, 2013). Moreover, in both settings, social-emotional learning and self-regulation behavioral strategies were interwoven into the lesson plans and were an evidentiary part of the teachers' repertoires of behaviors. Finally, teachers at both settings were consistently engaged in reflective thought during common planning time and within the classroom setting itself.

Both of the settings described above provide concrete examples of the convergence of theory and practice in the classroom. This article validates the compatibility of Piaget's and Vygotsky's theories; principles from both theories can be successfully woven together. The teachers' understanding, endorsement, and implementation of Piaget's and Vygotsky's theories resulted in intentional teaching practices that bolstered children's construction of knowledge and independent thought. Rather than focusing on practice to assist student teachers with understanding abstract theory, teacher education and professional learning programs must flip this pedagogical practice and begin to employ novice teachers' *intentional* reflections to help them to better interpret classroom practice (Sharkins et al., 2017).

Piaget's Theory of Cognitive Development

Piaget can be credited with making the most appreciable advances in our understanding of children's thought processes, thanks to his thorough investigation into the *epigenesis* of human intelligence (the study of how one's interactions in the environment influence development). According to Piaget, as children increase in age, so do their cognitive abilities. Thus, adults, unlike children, demonstrate both reasoned and logical thought processes. Some psychologists revere Piaget as the "giant in developmental psychology in the area of cognition" (Weber, 1984, p. 1951). Before Piaget introduced his theory, children were considered to be passive beings, molded and shaped by their surroundings (DeVries & Kohlberg, 1987). Much of Piaget's research in child cognition was based on his very meticulous observations of his three children; he spent years watching them, carefully observing the use and function of their eyes, ears, arms, and legs during their very early development. A constructivist at heart, Piaget firmly believed that children construct their knowledge of the world by using what they already know to interpret novel experiences and events. Piaget was not so much concerned about what children knew as he was about how they processed problems and devised solutions to challenging tasks.

According to constructivists like Piaget, cognitive development constitutes qualitative *and* quantitative changes in the way children reason and think about their worlds. A three-year-old is not a miniature version of a ten-year-old who simply lacks the experience and knowledge of his older peer. Not only are there *quantitative* differences—variations in the *amount* or *degree* of knowledge that each child possesses, but also there are *qualitative* differences too, or variations in how they know what they know. There are differences in the *type* and *form* of knowledge that each child possesses (Bjorlund, 2005).

Piaget's work in intelligence testing spurred his interest in children's thought processes. For example, two children may agree that a tree is alive, but offer very different explanations for their response; one child might reply that it is because the tree moves and another child might say that it is because it makes seeds. Piaget's work revealed many surprising ways in which children think (DeVries & Kohlberg, 1987, p. 17). He contended that children's "incorrect" views about the world are subjective—reflecting a very unique personal perspective (De Vries & Kohlberg, 1987). In other words, each child's unique interactions in the world precipitate his or her thoughts and reactions.

Piaget is also considered to be a *stage theorist*. He believed that children's cognitive development consists of four distinct stages, with each stage of development to be qualitatively and quantitatively different than the one that preceded it and the one that will follow. According to Piaget's theory, all children's cognitive processes proceed in the same sequential manner; it is not possible for a child to miss a stage nor is it possible for children to regress to an earlier stage of reasoning or cognitive functioning. Changes in children's thought processes and their progression from one stage to the next occur rather abruptly and over relatively brief periods. However, Piaget emphasized that there is evidence of continuity in the development of cognition, which facilitates the child's relatively easy transition from one stage of cognitive development to the next. According to Bjorklund (2005), continuity is achieved due to brief "preparatory phases" between stages in which the developing child withstands a dual existence in two qualitatively different cognitive worlds. Thus, a seven-year-old child may demonstrate some aspects of concrete operational thought (e.g., the ability to classify objects and reverse operations) but may, at times, show signs of egocentric thought, which is prevalent at the preoperational stage of development.

Before examining Piaget's stages of cognitive development, it is necessary to explicate a key term that is central to his theory: *schemata*.

Table 1.1 Piaget's Stages of Cognitive Development

Developmental Stage/Age Range	Stage Characteristics	Major Milestones
Sensorimotor Birth to 2 years	Infants knowledge of the world is derived primarilly from their senses & motor abilities.	Infants begin to think through mental actions & acquire the skill of object permanence. People/things still exist even when they are not in the infants sight.
Preoperational 2 to 6 years	Children's thinking is primarilly egocentric; they tend to view the world from their own perspective.	Imaginative thought, vocabulary, & language explosion lead to young children's self-expression & increased sociability.
Concrete Operational 6 to 11 years	Children's thinking is limited to concrete experiences, what they can see, hear, touch, & directly experience. They begin the process of applying logical operations & principles to interpret the world.	Children are able to comprehend concepts of conservation, number classification, & scientific theory through the application of logical thought
Formal Operations 12 Years Through Adulthood	Adults & adolescents enter into the realm of analytical thinking; their reasoning ability is characterized by abstractions, hypothetical ideas/thoughts.	Adults & adolescents think broadly & theorectically about ethical/moral issues & politics.

Schemata

People of all ages, including babies, have a tendency to organize knowledge of their environment into what Piaget refers to as *schemata* or *schemes*. Schemes consist of physical actions, concepts, and theories that children use to gain information about their world. They are *mental structures* in the brain that underlie an individual's intelligence. For example, young infants have particular schemes for interacting with their favorite rattle; they know how to grab it and thrust it in their month. A five-year-old child who has had both urban and suburban experiences might possess a broad scheme that includes knowledge of both domestic animals (cats and dogs) and farm animals (cows and sheep). By the same token, an eight-year-old child might possess a particular scheme for writing that includes both print and cursive letters.

Piaget believed that when learning occurs, unobservable changes in an individual's cognition occur as well; e.g., a person's schemes are modified and refined. It is logical to assume that the older an individual becomes and the more experiences he gains, the more extensive his mental structures become. However, it is also important to remember that the schemes of very young children are primarily comprised of physical actions. Children between birth and age two learn about the world primarily through their senses and motor abilities. As children develop, their schemes expand to include a range of mental operations, concepts, and theories that are largely facilitated by language. For instance, children become increasingly more adept at using symbol systems (e.g., language, numbers, sign language, etc.) to organize schemes of an abstract and complex nature.

Cognitive Equilibrium/Disequilibrium

The concept of *adaptation*, which is a very important concept in human biology, is also central to Piaget's theory of cognitive development. With regard to human biology, adaptation is the evolutionary or change process whereby an organism becomes better suited or adjusts to its habitat. And in much the same way that our bodies adapt to our immediate environment, our mental structures adapt in order to better represent our external world. Also, through a process referred to as *organization*, children reorder and connect new schemes to other schemes in order to create a more elaborate schemata or cognitive system.

As a cognitive theorist, Piaget believed that individuals are always engaged in the process of achieving some degree of *cognitive equilibrium*, or mental balance. The tendency for people to achieve some balance among their mental structures or schemes is innate, and it is the state of *disequilibrium*, or imbalance, that continuously motivates us to adapt our cognitive structures in order to restore balance. The state of disequilibrium is a most dissatisfying and undesirable mental state. Piaget, therefore, maintains that individuals use two complementary processes to achieve a state cognitive balance: *assimilation* and *accommodation*. Through the process of *assimilation*, children utilize new experiences to fit preexisting schemes. In assimilation, children interpret novel or new experiences through old lenses, so to speak. For example, a young child who has never seen a cow may refer to the cow as a big dog with funny spots. The process of assimilation is not a passive one; the child is earnestly trying to modify or reinterpret the new experience to fit his or her existing mental scheme.

On the other hand, when children encounter a new task or experience that does not fit into their existing scheme, they are compelled to alter their old way of thinking and acting in order to *accommodate* or fit the new information into an already existing scheme—or they may be forced to create a brand-new scheme. Thus, in the case provided above, children may simply expand their existing scheme to include "cow," or they might create a brand-new scheme (e.g. farm animals) once they figure out that the farm animal is not a dog but a cow. Accommodation requires more mental activity and energy than assimilation because new concepts and experiences may not always fit into preexisting cognitive structures. Accommodation can only occur if the new idea or task that the child is confronting is only slightly discrepant with his or her existing mental scheme; an idea or a task that is too discrepant will not be accommodated. Under these circumstances, the child does not have an available mental structure to interpret the new information or experience (Meece & Daniels, 2008). When accommodation does occur, intellectual growth advances, and the child is promoted to the next stage of cognitive development. In short, *cognitive equilibrium* is the ongoing process of striking a balance between assimilation and accommodation.

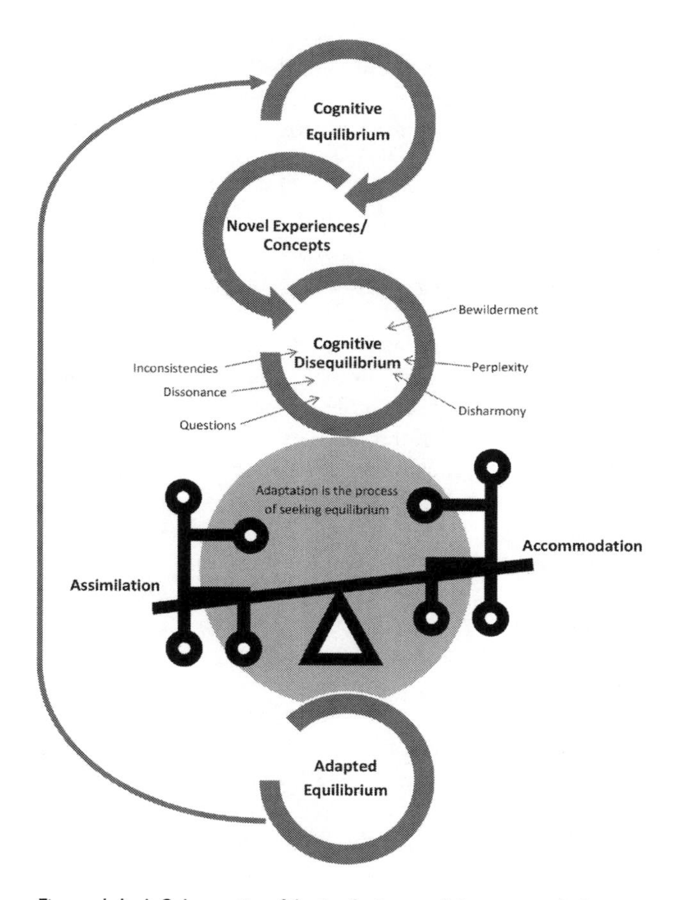

Figure 1.1 A Schematic of Assimilation and Accommodation

Piaget's Stages of Cognitive Development

Piaget proposed that cognitive development progresses in a predictable sequence from infancy through adolescence for all human beings. The periods or stages are age-related, and each period promotes a particular way of thinking and behaving (Inhelder & Piaget, 1958; Piaget, 1952b). Additionally, children meet important developmental benchmarks at each stage of cognitive development. According to Piaget, there are four stages of cognitive development: (1) sensorimotor, (2) preoperational, (3) concrete, and (4) formal operational.

Sensorimotor Stage

The first stage, *sensorimotor*, spans the first two years of a child's life. This is the period when children's mental structures are developed largely through their senses and motor reflexes. The range of children's reflexive behaviors assists them in building their knowledge and understanding of the world. Infants have an extensive repertoire of reflexes (a total of 18 in all), some of which are absolutely necessary for their survival (e.g., sucking and breathing). Young infants, for example, use their sucking reflex not just for feeding, but to learn about the world. Initially, everything fits the child's existing "suckable scheme." As the child grows and is introduced to table food, it is likely that she will need to create a brand-new scheme in order to gain nourishment, since chewing requires different, specific mouth and tongue movements.

The period of sensorimotor development is so rife with developmental changes that Piaget found it necessary to divide the period into six substages: (1) reflexive schemes; (2) primary circular reactions; (3) secondary circular reactions; (4) coordination of secondary circular reactions; (5) tertiary circular reactions; and (6) mental representation. Each substage provides evidence of continuous interaction between the child's brain, senses, and motor functions; the child is viewed as an active being. Over time, young infants become increasingly adept at coordinating a variety of movements to learn about the world around them.

The first 24 months is an exciting time for young infants. By the end of the child's first year of development, they often appear as "little scientists," regularly flirting with the method of "trial-and-error." Also, these children are just beginning to participate in *deferred imitation*, the ability to imitate the behaviors of others who are not present, and *make-believe play*, the process of acting out common, everyday experiences and imaginary activities. By the end of the sensorimotor period, children achieve two major competencies: (1) *goal-directed behavior* and (2) *object permanence*. When young infants engage in goal-directed behavior, they are more expansive, creative, and intentional—meaning they are deliberate in their coordination of behavioral schemes as a means to an end. They will intentionally and repeatedly use their coordinated schemes (e.g., hand and arm movements) to manipulate a favorite toy, just to hear its interesting sounds and see its blinking lights. Children's goal-directed behavior comes as a result of their awareness of cause and effect, improved memory, and an increased understanding of people's intentions (Behne et al., 2005; Willatts, 1999). *Object permanence*, on the other hand, which begins to emerge around the time a child is eight months old, entails children's basic understanding that objects or people still exist even when they can no longer see them. The child who achieves an understanding of object permanence is unlike his or her younger peers who relate to objects and people in an out-of-sight, out-of-mind fashion. Thus, a 22-month-old will intentionally use a number of coordinated schemes to search for a ball that has rolled under the bed until he or she finds it. This type of action conveys both goal-directed behavior and the child's acquisition of object permanence.

Early childhood professionals providing care for infants and toddlers during the sensorimotor stage of development can foster children's learning by playing games like peek-a-boo, pat-a-cake, and hide-and-go-seek with them, and by providing them with wide open, stimulating, and safe environments that foster active exploration.

Preoperational Stage

Children between the ages of two and six are said to possess what Piaget referred to as *preoperational intelligence*. The *preoperational stage* of development is an exciting period, marked by significant childhood competencies such as, increased language facility, *representational thought*, (the young child's ability to internalize visual experiences and maintain mental imagery of things not present), and an enhanced ability to engage in both deferred imitation and make-believe play. However, there are also limits to children's thinking during this stage of development. Children tend to be quite *egocentric* (self-centered) with regard to their thinking ability. Egocentric thinking is often defined as children's inability to consider other perspectives. Children at this phase of development will, undoubtedly, focus on a particular aspect of a situation without taking other aspects of the situation under consideration. For example, it is hard for a child at this stage to understand that daddy can be a brother or husband because the child is singularly focused on the role that father plays in his or her life. Children's thinking during this stage is focused on appearance to the exclusion of other factors.

Children also engage in *static reasoning*; they think that nothing ever changes. Therefore, whatever exists today constitutes what it was yesterday and what it will be tomorrow. So, for example, a child might contend that mommy was never a little girl and that she will never be a grandmother. One final characteristic of preoperational thought is *irreversibility*, the ability to understand that reversing an action or process restores it to its original state. A four-year-old child who doesn't like his or her sandwich cut in two will have an absolute fit when he or she sees the two halves. Any attempt to place the two halves closely together on his or her plate in order to create the illusion of wholeness is futile. Preoperational children focus on one feature: "the divided sandwich." They do not think reversibly or consider the fact that by simply putting the sandwich halves back together again that the sandwich is now whole once again!

In order to test the limitations of children's preoperational thinking, Piaget devised several experiments in *conservation* (the fact that something remains the same regardless of changes in its form or appearance). These classic landmark studies in conservation have greatly enhanced our understanding of children's reasoning abilities during the preoperational stage of development. Young children centered their thoughts exclusively on appearance, the immediate condition or state of the quantity, liquid, and mass. They never considered the possibility of reversing the process (static reasoning) or the changes made in real-time to the substances.

Nevertheless, children's use of language and symbolic thought processes is a hallmark of the preoperational stage of cognitive development. Teachers who work with children in the preoperational stage of development can best promote their learning by providing numerous opportunities for language development, such as reading, writing, and speaking activities, experiences in exploration as well as opportunities in creative art expression and working with a range of manipulative materials.

Concrete Operations Stage

During the *concrete operational period*, which usually occurs between the ages of 6 and 11, children tend to use increasingly more mental operations that involve symbols and images, and they are even capable of reversing operations. In other words, at this stage in children's cognitive development, they recognize that things can return to their original state. So, let's say that during a classic conservation experiment, the child is asked to observe two identical glasses with the exact amount of water. The water from one glass is then poured into a wider, shorter glass. The concrete operational student recognizes that the amount of liquid does not change by one simply pouring the liquid from one of the identical taller glasses into a wider, shorter glass. Mentally, children during this phase of development are able to reverse the operations in their head to provide a correct response to the question of which glass has more. The student is likely to respond: "Both glasses have the same about of liquid."

During this crucial developmental period, children are also less egocentric and are able to apply logical thinking to operations that are concrete, or visible and tangible. One important logical concept that children master during this stage of development is *classification*, the organization of things into some group or class based on a certain characteristic. As children grow older, they are more precise and flexible when engaged in classification tasks. During middle childhood, children use mental categories and subcategories flexibly, inductively, and simultaneously (Hayes & Younger, 2004). Children become adept at using many subcategories when categorizing or classifying. For example, food can be separated into various categories such as fruits, vegetables, meats, grains, and/or textures.

Some *pedagogical techniques* (teaching methods) that teachers can use when instructing children who are in the early stages of concrete operations might include experiences in classification that are increasingly more sophisticated and multi-faceted, providing children tangible examples to explain complex phenomena and opportunities for children to engage in the scientific exploration and manipulation of various objects and materials.

Formal Operations

Piaget's fourth and final stage of development, *formal operations*, begins at age 12 and continues throughout the life span. During this period, adolescents and adults effectively consider abstractions and hypothetical situations and are able to reason analytically—as opposed to children in the stage of concrete operations who reason logically, but only about direct experiences and perceptions. This is the stage in which you currently find yourself and where most of your mental operations are executed. All of us, however, at times revert to the use of mental processes that are characteristic of previous stages. For example, adults may use their sensorimotor intelligence (sense of touch) to feel a sweater's fabric in order to determine its suitability for their wardrobe. Still others may engage in concrete operations by using their fingers to count the days remaining in a given month.

Over the years, according to *Neo-Piagetians*, Piaget's work in cognitive development theory has ignited both criticism and praise from developmentalists and other researchers in related fields, i.e., education, psychology, etc. (Bjorklund, 2005). Nevertheless, regardless of the limitations of Piaget's theory such as his highly subjective investigative technique, and his underestimation of children's cognitive functioning at different stages of development, Piaget remains a giant in the field of developmental psychology. Piaget's fascination with children's thought processes and their acquisition of knowledge sustained his expansive work in developmental psychology for almost 60 years, giving rise to a very prolific career, and our enhanced understanding of "how children come to know."

Vygotsky's Sociocultural Theory of Development

Western educators have only recently embraced Lev Semenovich Vygotsky's pioneering work from the 1920s and 1930s in the area of sociocultural theory and his theory. Over the past 20 years, Vygotsky's theory has been gaining popularity among early childhood educators and researchers alike. Vygotsky's *sociocultural theory* asserts that an individual's development can only be understood in the context of his or her social and cultural experiences; there is always a dynamic interplay between one's sociocultural context and one's personal development (Rogoff, 2003). According to Vygotsky's theory, also referred to as the sociogenesis of cognitive development (Yu & Bain, 1980, p. 2), knowledge, or how it is that we come to know things, is socially constructed. "What we know is inextricably bound to when and where we know it" (Grave, 1993, p. 2). In other words, cognition, or the development of mental structures, is consummately social in nature. Hence, Jean Piaget is often described as being a cognitive (individual) constructivist theorist, and Vygotsky is typically viewed as a social constructivist theorist.

According to Vygotsky, "Any function in the individual's psychological development appears twice, initially on the *interpsychological*, or social plane [between people] and then on the *intrapsychological* plane [within the individual]" (Vygotsky, 1978, p. 57). In other words, learning first occurs between people; it is an externalized social process. Then, the learning is internalized. This process applies across the board in all areas of the child's intellectual functioning, such as voluntary attention, logical memory, and the formulation of concepts.

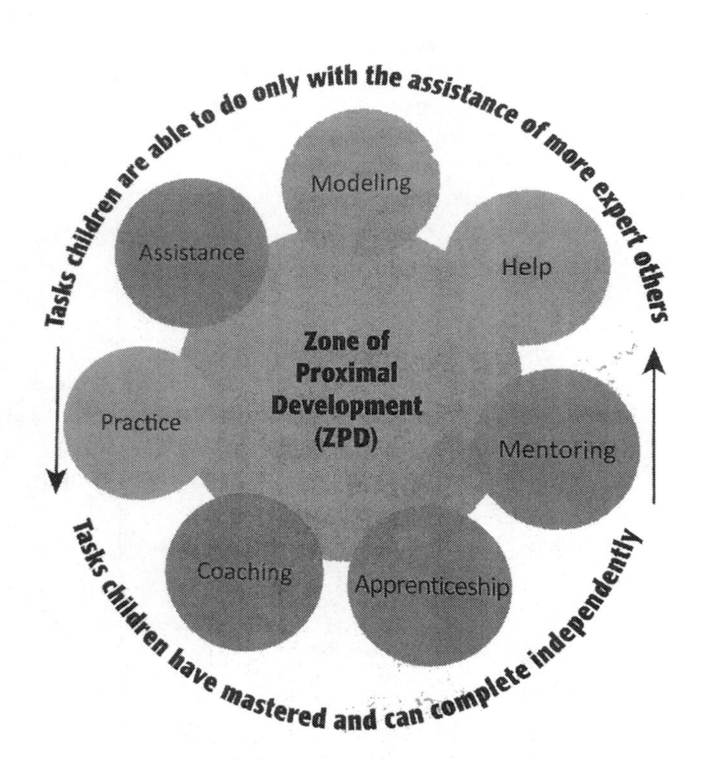

Figure 1.2 Vygotsky's Zone of Proximal Development (ZPD)

Learning in the ZPD

Vygotsky coined the term, "*zone of proximal development*" (ZPD) to further explain the internalization process. The *ZPD* is the distance between the child's actual developmental level as determined by what the child is able to do independently and the child's potential level of development, as determined by what the child can master under adult guidance or in collaboration with a more capable peer. Within the ZPD, intrapsychological functioning represents mental processes that are mature. Such mental processes constitute tasks that children can do independently or concepts that they fully understand. With regard to the interpsychological plane, mental processes are not fully mature, but still unfolding. Therefore, children functioning on this psychological or social plane will require adult assistance or guidance in order to fully engage in a task or to acquire an understanding of a particular concept. For example, a five-year-old who is just learning how to tie her sneaker laces will need the assistance of an adult or a more expert (capable) other. The child might need to see the adult or expert other model the task several times, and/or she may need several practice runs with the adult before she can tie her sneaker laces independently.

When engaged around problem-solving tasks or operating in the ZPD, both the child and the more capable other must arrive at a place of *intersubjectivity*, which is a shared understanding, or "a meeting of the minds" as to how best to approach the task. When a mutual understanding of a targeted goal is achieved between the child and a more capable other, learning is facilitated.

The amount of assistance and support that the adult provides the child within the ZPD is always changing because the adult is sensitive to the abilities of the learner and responds accordingly. This changing level of support during a teaching-learning situation is called *scaffolding*. The more capable other provides more assistance and support during the initial phase of the task (when the task is new) and begins to gradually withdraw support as the child becomes increasingly more capable. For example, a father who is teaching his young daughter how to ride a bike will initially assist the child by holding on to the child's handlebars in order to help her maintain her balance. As he provides support by encouraging her to pedal, he begins to roll her along more swiftly. It may take several trials before he can safely remove his hands from the handlebars altogether. Eventually, the father removes his hands from the handlebars after witnessing his daughter's increased mastery in balancing her weight and pedaling. This process, which may take several trials before the child fully masters the technique of bike riding, requires patience and flexibility on behalf of the more capable or expert other.

In scaffolding, the child is seen as the edifice under construction and the child's social environment and experiences (more experienced others, teaching tools/materials) scaffold or build the child up so that he or she can achieve new and improved competencies. The term "scaffolding" is also recognized in the research as a "*tutorial intervention*" (Wood et al., 1976, p. 89), *guided participation*, and *apprenticeship learning*.

Teachers of elementary-age students who understand the importance of scaffolding children's development are warm and responsive to the students' needs and strengths; flexible and willing to allow students to self-regulate during the joint problem-solving task as much as possible; willing to assume the role of "learner" rather than "teacher" at appropriate times; assume the role of facilitator or coach; deploy a range of distancing strategies (questioning techniques) and other techniques, such as gesturing (e.g., prompting, pointing) and modeling; administer authentic assessments; and engage students in group projects, task analysis, and peer group evaluations to assess student progress (Berk & Winsler, 1995). Needless to say, scaffolding students' development and engaging students in *collaborative learning* are effective in bolstering student achievement. Students are quite influential at impacting each other's cognitive structures; they support one another and encourage new ways of thinking and generating ideas in response to novel material.

Box 1.2 Common Core and Other Standards

The Balanced Literacy Approach: A Catalyst for the Effective Learning of English Language Arts (ELA)/Common Core State Standards

The belief that language and literacy are foundational to *all* learning is one de facto truism adopted by most educators. In most schools, language and literacy growth among students, notwithstanding the acquisition of math skills, are tantamount to determining teacher accountability, student success, and achievement. In 2010, the adoption of the Common Core State Standards by the majority of states in the U.S. resulted in accountability becoming an even weightier issue for school personnel across this nation. Over the course of the past few years, schools have carefully considered a compendium of curricular, pedagogical, and assessment approaches to bolster and subsequently gauge student progress, particularly in the domains of English Language Arts (ELA) and Math.

Balanced literacy was one such curricular approach adopted by a very large urban school district in Northern California as a means of addressing the abysmal reading scores of specific student subgroups. The disparities in the areas of cognitive, oral language, and literacy functioning that existed among certain student populations vis-a-vis other student groups from more affluent backgrounds with less at-risk markers necessitated the delivery of a more balanced and holistic approach to teaching literacy to the district's youngest constituents (TK–grade 3). The balanced literacy approach includes all of the quintessential components of emergent literacy—in a word, "the whole package" of emergent literacy skills (Bialystok, 1996; Whitehurst & Lonigan, 1998).

Needless to say, the initiative allowed for a more explicit, cogent, and integrative approach to teaching English Language Arts (ELA). The equal emphasis on reading and writing endemic to the balanced literacy approach; the focus on metacognitive skills or "deep thinking about text and students' exposure to various types of texts"; the explicit teaching of phonics and the use of whole language strategies; and allowing students significant practice deriving meaning from text via a variety of methods (discussion, drawings/sketches, writing, etc.) render the balanced literacy approach and Common Core ELA State Standards highly compatible. Even English Language Learners (ELLs) can flourish from the approach. Like their English-speaking peers, ELLs can benefit from explicit teaching of the components of literacy such as phonemic awareness, phonics, vocabulary, comprehension, and writing (Goldenberg, 2008). Hence, the balanced literacy approach, which includes essential components such as: word study, shared reading, guided reading, interactive read-aloud, independent reading, interactive writing, and independent writing workshop has been found to be quite efficacious in teaching reading and writing and in bolstering *all* students' literacy and language development.

Vygotsky's sociocultural theory and its related concepts have made appreciable advances in our understanding of the interconnectedness between students' engagement in legitimate socio-cultural activities and their subsequent development

Bronfenbrenner's Bioecological Theory of Development

Urie Bronfenbrenner, like the theorists before him, was acutely aware of the importance of caring adults in the lives of young children when he developed his theory in the late 1970s. Bronfenbrenner's early experiences working alongside his father at a mental institution for young children provided the seminal seeds for his theory of the *ecology of human behavior* and his later work as a staunch advocate for the obliteration of social and political practices that negatively impact children and families. Recently, Bronfenbrenner's theory has been renamed "*bioecological systems theory*" in order to emphasize the importance of the child's own biology as a primary factor in the interplay between the child and her environment, and the environment's crucial role in fueling the child's development.

One might agree that the popular cliché "It takes a village to raise a child" underscores the very essence of Bronfenbrenner's theory. According to him,

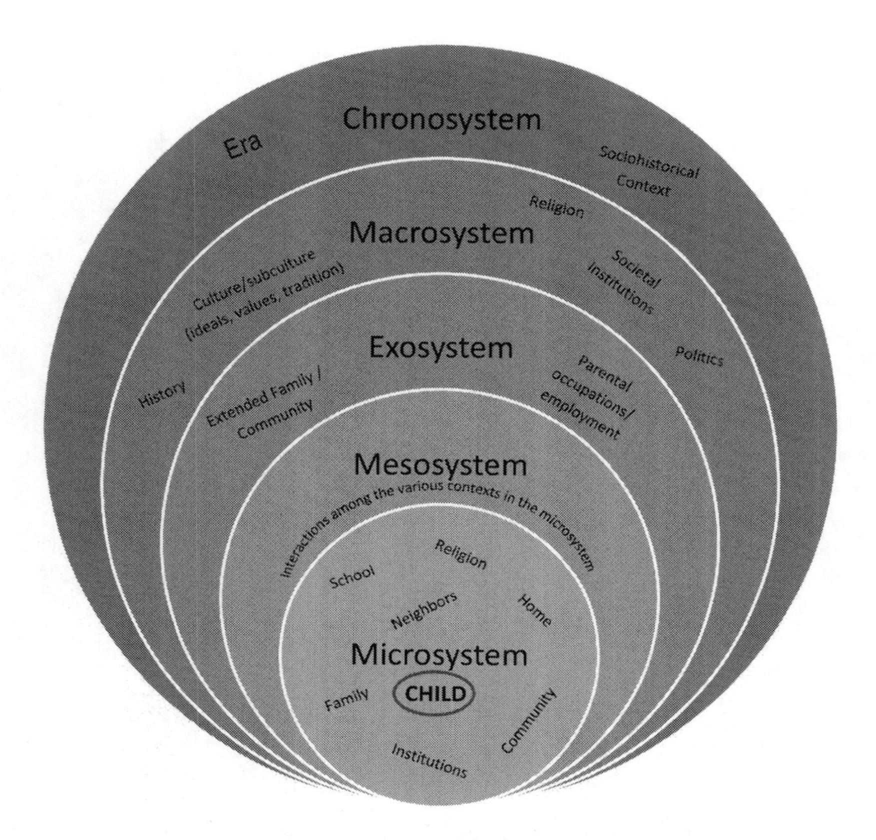

Figure 1.3 Bronfenbrenner's Bioecological System of Development

educators and developmentalists need to fully consider all of the various systems that surround the development of the child. For instance, a child's ability to read may be just as contingent upon the teacher's pedagogical skills as it is upon the quality of the relationship between the child's school and home. These environmental systems, according to Bronfenbrenner, are constantly unfolding over the course of the child's development and impacting his/her total being, as well as the existence of those adults around the child.

Bronfenbrenner's theory consists of three major nested systems: (1) microsystem, (2) mesosystem, and (3) exosystem. The *microsystem* is the innermost level and comprises the child's immediate environment—the child's home, family, peer group, kindergarten classroom, religious institution, etc. These are the settings in which the child has direct, personal experience. The *mesosystem*, on the other hand, constitutes the interactions or connections between and among the various settings at this and other levels, as well as the interactions between and among the various elements or settings belonging to the three systems. For example, an aggressive seven-year-old child might be required by the school psychologist to participate in a special after-school program aimed at averting bullying behavior in young elementary school students. Bullying concerns evident in the larger social context (at the local school) can impact children who may be already primed for aggressive behavior, in one way or another. The *exosystem* consists of formal and informal entities such as employment agencies, community resource organizations, and parental networks that might influence the child's development, but only indirectly. For instance, a single parent who is either underemployed or unemployed might drift into a state of depression, which may ultimately impact his or her parenting skills. The *macrosytem* represents the culture and subcultures in which the child lives, including its ideals, values, and traditions, as well as regional identity. For example, some children growing up in the infamous town of Juarez, Mexico today, which has been referred to by many as the "murder capital of the world," might grow to be very indifferent to pain, suffering, and death over time. Bronfenbrenner also recognized that familial interrelationships are modified with the passage of time and that societal and sociohistorical trends can impact family life. The *chronosystem* recognizes the timing of these adjustments and the relative position of the child during these periods, including the impact of these changes on the developing child (Bronfenbrenner, 2005). For instance, during the housing boom at the turn of the twenty-first century, many working-class families realized the "American Dream" and were able to buy houses, thereby bolstering the family's socio-economic status. However, by 2006, the incomes of many families plummeted due to the "great recession" and many of these same families lost their homes. Scores of children and their families became homeless for the very first time. When children lack secure housing and are forced to double-up with other family members and change schools, such major transitions can have a deleterious effect on their growth and development over time. Thus, the child's well-being is closely tied to the various systems of which he or she is a part.

According to Bronfenbrenner, there are many influences that can impact the development of the child; however, being aware of these environmental influences is simply not enough. Careful consideration of the impact of these various systems on the child and his or her family should propel all professionals to work in conjunction with families in creating public policy and practices that lead to the creation of social landscapes that clearly support and protect the sanctity of family life.

Box 1.3 Social Justice and Diversity

Deconstructing the U.S. Immigration Paradox Conundrum: Implications for Research, Policy, and Practice

The United States of America has experienced a watershed period with regard to the unprecedented number of immigrant families that have entered the United States over the course of the past several decades. For example, the wave of immigrant families seeking refuge in the United States (U.S.)—fleeing war and persecution in their homelands—has resulted in a disproportinate number of immigrant children. As a matter of fact, immigrant youth are the fastest-growing demographic in the U.S. According to Marks et al. (2014), data regarding the number of immigrant children living in America reveal that at least 25 percent of youngsters under the age of ten are either first-generation (born in a foreign country) or second-generation (U.S.-born to foreign-born parents). It is important to note that the "great emigration" to the U.S. over the past few decades does not merely consist of families escaping extreme conditions such as the perils of war, famine, or fears associated with the horrific crimes of ethnic cleansing—notwithstanding the gradual stripping away of human dignity and sense of agency due to the disallowance of religious and civic freedom. Many immigrant parents began their sojourn to America with the hope of finding a better way of life for themselves and their children. Needless to say, a significant portion of the monolith of immigrants simply seeking improved living conditions over the past few decades has consisted of *Latinx* (a gender-neutral alternative [more recently] used when referring to persons of Latin origin) families (Gonzalez, 2019).

Not too long ago (over 50 years), research on Latinx families yielded rather disparaging reports relative to their familial and social contexts as well as the growth and development of their offspring, especially when juxtaposed with white middle-class families. Hence, like their African American counterparts, Latinx families have been subjected to the same or similar fate—the tendency on behalf of earlier researchers to cast an entire race of people as inherently culturally and socially bankrupted. Needless to say, the fall-out from this earlier and rather myopic view of Latinx families has resulted in the perpetuation of social justice issues and some unhealthy notions about diversity that are rather difficult to dispel. These newer perspectives about the plight of immigrant children and adolescents—for both first and second generations—have done more than simply enhance our understanding of the age-old U.S. immigration paradox. These new understandings can serve as a catalyst for deep and impenetrable systems change. Seeing Latinx families through an asset-focused prism can mitigate inequities and result in appreciable advances in the creation and implementation of social policy and related processes that are beneficial for *all* U.S. citizens.

However, more recently, research on Latinx families in general has been quite revolutionary! Researchers like Marks et al. (2014) illuminate extant research, which is aimed at moving us away from the view of Latinx experiences (and eventual outcomes) in the U.S. as monolithic in scope. Current studies seek to debunk and more fully explore the common phenomenon known as the *U.S. Immigration Paradox*, which is the tendency for immigrant children and adolescents who have acculturated in the U.S. to demonstrate less optimal outcomes over time—which is quite antithetical to earlier beliefs about assimilation. Earlier held notions about assimilation posit that the longer immigrant families remain in America and become more socially, culturally, and economically entrenched, the better off they will be in the long run (Alba, 1997). While it is true that the U.S. immigrant paradox continues to persist, researchers Fuller & Garcia Coll (2010) cite that current research on Latinx families, for example, calls our attention to "the strengths of Latinx families and the resulting benefits for their children" (Fuller & Garcia Coll, 2010, p. 559). Trends in related research highlight the diversity and complexity of children's bounded contexts, the nuanced multiple settings that immigrant children must negotiate each day, and the critical role that sociocultural histories (and not just individual differences) play in determining children's growth and development. The degree to which the paradox rings true is inextricably tied to a number of very important factors, e.g., age of the child; variations in Latinx children's and adolescents' respective contexts/households within subgroups; and the diversity that exists within these subgroups. Other factors include the link between children's/adolescents' approaches/motivations to learn and the specific contexts from these notions about learning emerge; how children are "apprenticed for competence" (Fuller & Garcia Coll, 2010, p. 561); the parenting goals and practices of more or less acculturated individuals; and immigrant parents' insistence that children and adolescents adapt to novel experiences, which can result in both benefits and risks for today's youths, etc. Today, contemporary research on Latinx families utilizes a compendium of methodologies such as extended ethnographic methods; a "forensic-like" uncovering of Latinx familial and social contexts with the goal of making very clear connections to specific child outcomes; and a compilation of large-scale data sets by interdisciplinary teams that reveal the assets of heritage cultures and parenting styles (Fuller & Garcia Coll, 2010).

Erikson's Theory of Psychosocial Development

Erik Erikson (1902–1994) contributed significantly to the field of human development. Erikson, a follower of Sigmund Freud, the father of Psychosexual Development who posited that the child's inner drives, urges, and unconscious wishes are the basis for children's thinking and behavior over their extended life, extended Freud's theory to include children's social context. Erikson viewed the human lifespan as consisting of various stages, each one involving a psychological crisis or conflict that requires a resolution. And while the crisis at each stage is presented in an either-or fashion, Erikson recognized that the resolution of the crisis at each stage did not necessarily lead to one extreme or the other, but somewhere in the middle. According to Erikson, there are eight stages of psychosocial development, which begin at birth and end in the twilight years of the adult's life. (Please note that the table delineates Erikson's theory in its totality but for our purposes here, only Erikson's first four stages apply.)

The first stage, *trust vs. mistrust*, is the period between birth and one year old. During this period, children learn to trust their primary caregivers to address their basic need for nourishment, consolation, warmth, etc. Infants and toddlers who are not afforded responsive caregiving soon learn to mistrust (the care of) others over time.

Table 1.2 Erikson's Stages of Psychosocial Development

Age	*Psychological Stage*	*Psychological Conflict/Dilemma*
Birth to 1 year	Basic Trust vs Mistrust	Infants learn to trust others to meet their basic needs OR Mistrust develops
1 to 3 years	Autonomy vs Shame & Doubt	Children learn to make choices and aquire agency OR Become uncertain and doubtful about their abilities
3 to 6 years	Initiative vs Guilt	Children learn to initiate activites and acquire a sense of purpose OR They begin to feel guilty about their efforts at independence
6 years to Adolescence	Industry vs Inferiority	Children are eager and curious OR They begin to feel inferior and become disenchanted
Adolescence	Identity vs Role Confusion	Adolescence begin the process of aquiring their personal identity OR They become confused, misguided and misdirected
Young Adulthood	Intimacy vs Isolation	Young adults enter into commited relationships OR They become isolative and disenfranchised
Middle Adulthood	Generativity vs Stagnation	Adults proliferate and nurture others OR They become self-centered and disengaged
Old Age	Integrity vs Despair	Older adults engage in introspaction about their life and emanate pride OR They feel regretful and resentful about how thier life has transpired

During stage two, the child, who is usually between the ages of one and three years old must resolve the conflict of *autonomy vs. shame and doubt*. Children either gain a sense of self-efficacy—they began to feel self-confident about engaging in a variety of activities such as toileting, feeding, walking, exploring, etc.— or they begin to doubt their abilities.

Children entering Erikson's third stage of psychosocial development, *initiative vs. guilt*, are interested in adult activities. These are your preschool, TK, and kindergarten students, children between the ages of three and six. Hence, they are often interested in engaging in activities that exceed their abilities or the boundaries established by adults, which is spurred by their need to gain a sense of ambition and responsibility. For example, children at this age will put their shoes on the wrong feet, concoct messy sandwiches, make breakfast for mommy, or jump into the swimming pool. Children's initiation of tasks at this stage may be a source of pride or failure, with failure leading to guilt.

Erikson's fourth stage of psychosocial development is *industry vs. inferiority* and includes children between the ages of about 6 and 11 (adolescence). At this phase of development, the outcome of the prior stage is paramount. The child will either seek independence, becoming increasingly competent and productive at mastering certain tasks over time, or the child will experience feelings of inadequacy.

Erikson recognized that the child's resolution of the crisis at each stage of development is predicated on such factors as the child's sociocultural and economical contexts, the parents' childrearing practices, and both the individual child's and family's temperament.

Box 1.4 How Might Educators Help Students to Get the Most out of Digital Technology Use in the Classroom and Avert the Deleterious Impact of Its Use on Students' Social, Emotional, and Moral Development?

- Consistently support and reinforce students in their efforts to control impulsive behaviors and to delay immediate gratification. Social-emotional learning should be pervasive throughout all curriculum domains.
- As early as transitional kindergarten, assist students in developing their self-concept by calling specific attention to their unique gifts, attributes, talents, and propensities. Help students to draw a distinction between their "true self" and idealized self, which will later loom large on Instagram and Facebook (for example), or some other social media genre yet to be created. Remember that helping students to live with and seek ways to overcome their vulnerabilities, imperfections, and setbacks builds character.
- Bolster students' self-esteem by offering intermittent praise—calling specific attention to those things that students are doing well.

- Provide numerous opportunities for students to *construct* knowledge independently, as well as collaboratively with their peers.
- Encourage face-to-face dialogue among students as much as possible and consistently call students' attention to other individuals' body language, facial expressions, tone of voice, etc. Promoting emotional literacy among students by calling attention to their inner feelings and that of others is the *sin quo none* of healthy relationships.
- In an effort to encourage empathy, cultivate a positive classroom climate that endorses collectivist values rather than individualism. Remember that students, like the adults in their lives, are "uniquely human" and social beings that desperately need others to create a sense of both community and agency.
- Discourage multitasking among students and insist on students' focused attention on one task at a time.
- During the formal years, teach youngsters to be *ethically* responsible when using digital media; students must learn early about the importance of respecting and valuing the intellectual property of others (Schaffer & Kipp, 2014).
- Finally, recognizing the internet's limitations in conveying passion or eros, teachers must do everything in their power to exude *creative passion* whenever they approach the teaching platform.

Maslow's Hierarchy of Human Needs

Maslow conceptualized and devised a pyramid scheme to convey a *hierarchy of human needs*, which was prompted by his earlier work with primates (see Figure 1.4). One of the things that stood out for Maslow during his research with the monkeys was that certain needs of the monkeys trumped others, meaning that certain needs took precedence over others.

At the very basest level of the pyramid are the *needs addressing human survival*. These needs consist of food, water, and sleep. Maslow contended that the individual's primary needs must be met first before the person can even consider the challenges of addressing the needs presented at the next level. Thus, the assumption is that when a young child is hungry, it is impossible for him or her to concentrate in school or to learn effectively. When considering the logic of Maslow's hierarchy of needs, we can now fully understand why schools implement free breakfast programs for children from low socioeconomic (LSES) backgrounds. Everywhere today, schools provide a range of nutritional programs for children because these schools recognize that children need nourishment before they can successfully engage in learning activities.

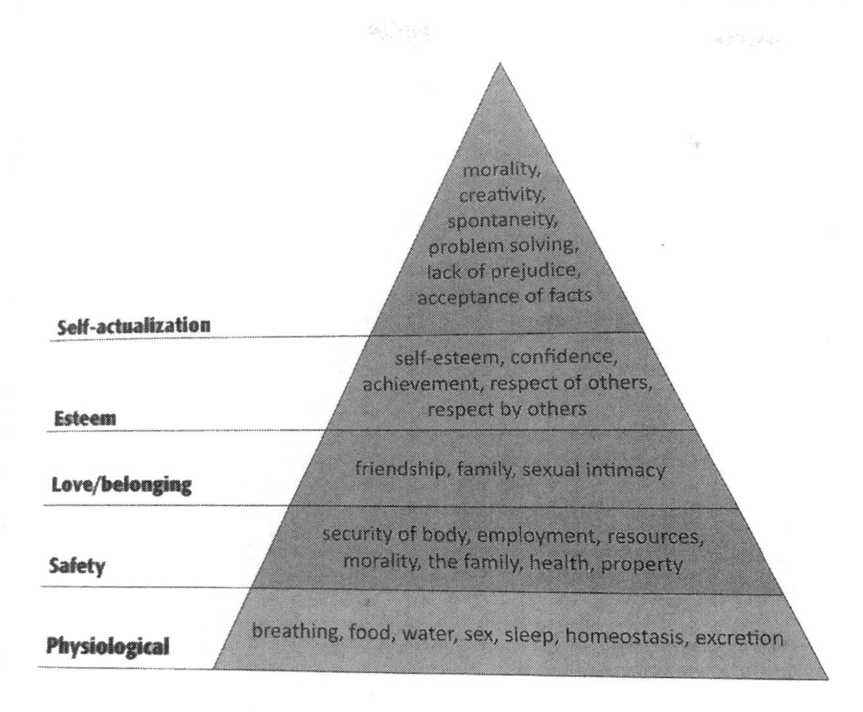

Figure 1.4 Maslow's Hierarchy of Needs

Maslow's second level on the pyramid addresses the human *need for security and safety*. People of all ages need shelter, a sanctuary, or a home that makes them feel safe. Even infants and toddlers need to feel secure enough to use their range of sensory-motor skills to explore their immediate environment. As children grow older and become adults, their basic needs for safety and security can also become threatened. After the aftermath of Hurricane Katrina in New Orleans, Louisiana in 2005, the situation grew even more chaotic as people dealt with the lack of basic shelter and safety.

Maslow's third level on the pyramid deals with the social needs of people, the *need for belonging and love*. Both children and adults need to know that they matter and that someone cares. Urie Bronfenbrenner once said that children need the irrational involvement of people in their lives in order to become human; somebody has to be crazy about them (Bronfenbrenner, 1971). Children who feel rejected internalize their pain and feelings of worthlessness and begin to act out these emotions in a number of ways. These are the children that later become bullies and juvenile delinquents. In our day-to-day lives, we exhibit the need for belonging in our desire to marry, have a family, or become a member of a community, church, fraternity, or bowling league, or even a member of a gang!

Stage four of Maslow's hierarchy of needs addresses the *need for achievement and prestige*. In our day-to-day life, the need for achievement and prestige is manifested in a number of ways, such as pursuing an academic degree, purchasing a house, or writing a book. This elevated level of human need in Maslow's scheme represents our desire for self-respect and the respect of others. The young father who boasts about his recent promotion on the job and the school-aged girl who points out to her mother her "perfect" spelling test pinned to the bulletin board are both experiencing the joys resulting from the recognition of others.

At the very top of Maslow's hierarchy of human needs is *the need for self-actualization*. Children and adults who are self-actualized recognize their full potential and are motivated to become the very best that they can be. They have an enhanced sense of self-efficacy and self-worth. These are the children who are typically very excited about learning; they demonstrate what is referred to as *intrinsically motivated scholarship*. In such cases, children across the developmental spectrum learn for learning's sake and begin to rely increasingly less on external reinforcements in order to engage in learning.

While Maslow's theory has become incredibly popular, it has been criticized for its lack of empirical support; the theory was predicated mostly on his observations and intuitions about the human experience (Sheldon et al., 2001; Smither, 1998). Maslow's theory also yields some discrepant themes throughout in that it is plausible for individuals to demonstrate needs from two or more levels simultaneously. Also, people who have had their basic needs met may not care to address their higher needs, and those whose basic needs have gone unmet may not always be destined to act out or to behave poorly. Furthermore, higher needs may, at times, supersede lower ones. For example, people who have dared to climb Mount Everest or who may have hiked across the country have obviously dismissed their need to be safe at home.

Behaviorism and Social Learning Theory

B.F. Skinner referred to his theory of *operant conditioning* as "*radical behaviorism*" because he wanted to distinguish it from John B. Watson's behaviorism, known as *classical conditioning*. Classical conditioning is the learning process by which a meaningful stimulus (food) becomes connected to a neutral stimulus (bell) again and again, until such time as the bell alone triggers the behavior, i.e., salivation in a dog. On the other hand, Skinner's *operant conditioning* is a type of behaviorism that is best described as a learning process by which a certain action is followed by either something that causes the behavior to be repeated or by something negative, which makes the action less likely to be repeated. This concept constitutes one of the basic laws of learning—that behavior is less likely or more likely to occur depending on the consequences that follow it. Skinner argued that when it comes to behavior, we must focus our attention on the external consequences of an action. In other words, in order to explain behavior, we must first look outside the individual, not within.

In operant conditioning, pleasant consequences are "*rewards*" and unpleasant ones are called "*punishments*." But for some people, a punishment might actually be considered a reward, and the converse is also true. For example, for a child who is craving attention, spanking may be welcomed—a means of gaining his parents' attention. On the other hand, withholding dessert from a child who does not eat all of his food may not constitute punishment for the child, because the child might not care for the dessert in the first place. According to Skinner, any consequence that follows a behavior and increases the likelihood of the behavior being repeated is referred to as a *reinforcement*. Hence, *reinforcement* can be either *positive or negative*. Thus, a student will consistently submit his homework because he is given a ticket for each submission (positive reinforcement) that can be used to purchase treats and toys at the end of the month. Similarly, a ball is taken away from a student to avert problematic behavior (negative reinforcement). Operant responses are typically non-reflexive, compared to classical conditioning responses, which are usually reflexive in nature. Operant responses include complex behaviors like riding a skateboard or scooter, writing a letter, or throwing a tantrum.

We witness operant conditioning played out in the grocery store all of the time. A child puts a favorite food in the shopping cart and throws a fit when the mother doesn't buy the item. To avoid further embarrassment, the mother eventually gives in and purchases the item, which causes the child to end his tantrum. When the child and mother visit the grocery store again, the same scenario is repeated. The child has obviously learned that crying and throwing a tantrum is instrumental in obtaining his favorite food. Operant conditioning has also been called *instrumental conditioning*.

Skinner's contributions to the field of early childhood education stem from his work in operant conditioning. As illustrated in his book, *Walden Two*, Skinner described the idea of using consistent, positive reinforcement to shape the behavior of individuals within society. The book is a well-written treatise on humans living in a carefully controlled society (utopia), and how to establish desirable behavior among them (Weber, 1984). His theories on reinforcing desired behaviors guided parents and teachers alike to influence and shape school-age children's behavior by using appropriate environmental reinforcements. The ideas set forth in Skinner's book represent an alternative method for shaping human behavior instead of resorting to the use of threat or punishment. Skinner's landmark research on the effects of reinforcement helped to shift society's focus from restricting undesirable behaviors (punishment) to a greater emphasis on supporting desirable behaviors.

Chapter Summary

The range of major developmental theories discussed in the aforementioned pages helps to crystallize educators' understanding of the evolution of children's learning experiences—and the role of *learning* in shaping students' growth and development. The theories discussed above provide a comprehensive view of human development during youngsters' most formative schooling years and beyond. It is critically important for teachers of young children to have an evolved understanding of the development of children and what various theorists have to say about learning and the interplay between nature and nurture in the lives of children. Teachers' in-depth understanding of children's development and their deliberate and focused (intentional) teaching strategies translate into effective practices and engagement of young students. Hence, effective elementary school teachers typically possess a real grasp of developmental learning theory, and such teachers capitalize on students' interests and interactions in an effort to bolster their academic achievement and success. Learning theories unlock the secret of how children begin to discover both what they can do and who they can become—in other words, how children begin to develop both their range of abilities and their unique identity as individuals (Bronfenbrenner, 1971).

Bibliography

Alba, R. (1997). Rethinking assimilation theory for a new era of immigration. *International Migration Review*, *31*, 826–874.

Behne, T., Malinda, Call, J., & Tomasello, M. (2005). Unwilling versus unable: Infant's understanding of intentional action. *Developmental Psychology*, *41*, 328–337.

Berk, L. (2012). *Infants, children and adolescents*, 7th ed. Boston, MA: Allyn & Bacon.

Berk, L., & Myers, A. (2016). *Infants, children and adolescents*, 8th ed. New York, New York: US: Pearson Education.

Berk, L. E., & Winsler, A. (1995). *Scaffolding children's learning: Vygotsky and early childhood education*. Washington, DC: National Association for the Education of Young Children.

Bialystok, E. (1996). Preparing to read: The foundations of literacy. In H. W. Reese (Ed.), *Advances in child development and behavior*, Vol. 26, pp. 1–34. San Diego, CA: Academic.

Bjorklund, D. F. (2005). *Children's thinking: Cognitive development and individual differences.* , Belmont, CA: ThomsonWadsworth.

Bodrova, E., and Leong, D. (2007). *Tools of the mind*: *The Vygotskian approach to early childhood education*, 2nd ed. Upper Saddle River, NJ: Merrill/ Prentice Hall.

Bornstein, M. H., Arterberry, M. E., & Mash, C. (2005). Perceptual development. In M. H. Bornstein & M. Lamb (Eds.), *Developmental science: An advanced textbook* (5th ed., pp. 283–325). Mahwah, NJ: Erlbaum.

Bronfenbrenner, U. (1971). Who cares for America's children? *Young Children*, *26*, 157–163.

Bronfenbrenner, U. (2005). *Making human beings human*. Thousand Oaks, CA: SAGE.

DeVries, R. (2001). *Developing constructivist early curriculum: Practical principles and activities*. New York: Teachers College Press.

DeVries, R.& Kohlberg, L. (1987). *Constructivist early education: Overview and comparison with other programs*. Washington, DC: National Association for the Education of Young Children

Dewey, J. (1916). *Democracy and education*. New York: Macmillan Company.

Dupont, H. (1994). *Emotional development, theory and applications: A neo-piagetian perspective*. Westport, CT: Praeger.

Fisher, K. W., & Bidell, T. (1998). Dynamic development of psychological structures in action and thought. In M. Lerner (Ed.), *Theoretical models of human development* (Vol. 1) (pp. 467–561), in W. Damon (Gen. Ed.), *Handbook of child psychology* (5th ed.) New York: Wiley.

Fuller, B. & Coll C.G., (2010). Learning From Latinos: Contexts, Families and Child Development in Motion. *Developmental Psychology*.Vol. 46. No. 3 pp. 559–565

Galimberti, U. (2010). *Grozlijivi gost:nihilizem in mladi*. Ljubljana: Modrijan, 36.

Galimberto, U. (2018). *La parola ai giovani: dialogo con la generazione del nichilismo attivo*. Milano: Feltrinelli, 16–17.

Garcia, I. (2019). What does "Latinx" mean? Exactly everything you need to know about the gender inclusive term. https://www.oprahmag.com August 11, 2020.

Globakar, R. (2018). Impact of digital media on emotional, social and moral development of children. *Nova Prisutnost*, *16*(3), 545–560. doi: 10.31192/np.16.3.8.

Goldenberg, C. (2008). Teaching English language Learners: What the research does— and does not—say. *American Educator,* Summer 2008.

Goleman, D. (1995). *Emotional intelligence. Why it can matter more than IQ*. New York: Bantum Books.

Gonzalez I., (2020). What Does Latinx Mean, Exactly? Everything you need to know about the gender-inclusive term. Aug. 11, 2020 :*The Oprah Magazine*

Grave, E. M. (1993). *Ready for what/constructing meanings of readiness for kindergarten*. Albany, NY: State University of New York Press.

Hartmann, D. P., & Pelzel, K. E. (2005). Design, measurement, and analysis in developmental research. In M. H. Bornstein & M. E. Lamb (Eds.), *Developmental science: An advanced textbook* (5th ed., pp. 103–184). Mahwah, NJ: Erlbaum.

Hayes, B. K., & Younger, K. (2004). Category-use effects in children. *Child Development*, *75*, 1719–1732.

Inhelder, B., & Piaget, J. (1958). *The growth of logical thinking form childhood to adolescence: An essay on the construction of formal operational structures*. New York: Basic Books.

Karmiloff-Smith, A. (1991). Beyond modularity: Innate constraints and developmental change. In S. Carey & R. Gelman (Eds.), *The epigenesist of mind: Essays on biology and cognition* (pp. 171–197). Hillsdale, NJ: Erlbaum.

Konrath, S. H., O'Brien, E., & Hsing, C. (2011). Changes in dispositional empathy in America college students over time: A meta-analysis. *Personality and Social Psychology Review*, *15*(2), 180–198.

Mandler, J. M. (2004). *The foundations of mind. Origins of conceptional thought*. Oxford, England: Oxford University Press.

Marks, A. K., Ejesi, K., & Coll, C. G. (2014). Understanding the U.S. immigrant paradox in childhood and adolescence. *Child Development Perspectives*, *8*, 59–64. doi: 10.1111// cdep.12071

Mason, C., (2008). *Home Education: A Homeschooling Classic*. Radford, VA: Wilder Publications, LLC.

Meece, J., & Daniels, D. H. (2008). *Child & adolescent development for educators*, 3rd ed. New York: Mcgraw Hill.

Munakata, Y. (2006). Information processing approaches to development. In W. Damon & R. M. Lerner (Series Eds.) & Deanna Khun & Robert S. Siegler (Vol. Eds.) *Handbook of child psychology: Vol. 2. Cognition, perception and language* (6th ed. pp. 426–4630). Hoboken, NJ: Wiley.

O'Donohue, W. T., & Ferguson, K. E. (2001). *The psychology of B.F. Skinner*. Thousand Oaks, CA: SAGE.

Pence, A. R. (1988). *Ecological research with children and families*. New York: Teachers College Press.

Piaget, J. (1952). *The origins of intelligence*. Oxford, England: International Universities Press.

Puckett, M. B., Black, J., Wittmer, D. S., & Petersen, S. H. (2009). *Young children: The development from pre-birth to age 8*. Upper Saddle River, NJ: Merrill/Pearson

Quinn, P. C. (2004). Development of subordinate-level categorization in 3–7-month- old infants. *Child Development, 75*, 886–899.

Rideout, V. (2017). The common sense census: *Media use by kids age zero to eight*. San Francisco, CA: Common Sense Media. https://www.commonsensemedia.org/research/the-common-sense-census-mediause-by-kids-age-zero-to-eight-2017 (28. 03. 2018), 3.

Rogoff, B. (1990). *Apprenticeship in thinking: Cognitive development in social context*. New York: Oxford University Press.

Rogoff, B. (1998). Cognition as a collaborative process. In Williams Damon (Series Ed.) & Deanna Kuhn & Robert S. Seigler (Vol. Eds.) *Handbook of child psychology: Vol. 2. Cognition, perception, and language* (5th ed., pp. 679–744). New York: Wiley.

Rogoff, B. (2003). *The cultural nature of human development*. New York: Oxford University Press.

Rogoff, B., Mistry, J., Goncu, A., & Mosier, C. (1993). Guided participation in cultural activity by toddlers and caregivers. *Monographs of the Society for Research in Child Development, 58* (Serial No. 236, No 8.) The Society for Research in Child Development, Inc. Reprinted with permission.

Roundtree, W. J. (2000). *A case study analysis of parental scaffolding among three mother-child dyads participating in the Home Instruction Program for Preschool Youngsters.* Submitted in partial fulfillment of the requirements for the degree of doctor of education: Teachers College, Columbia University.

Russell, D. (1956). *Children's thinking*. Boston, MA: Ginn.

Shaffer, D. R., Kipp, K. (2014). *Developmental psychology: Childhood and adolescence*, 9 ed. Belmont: Wadsworth Centage Learning, 513–526.

Sharkins, K. N., Causey, A. C., & Ernest, J. M. (2017). Flipping theory: Ways in which children's experiences in the 21st century classroom can provide insight into theories of Piaget and Vygotsky. *International Journal of Early Childhood Education Care, 6*, 11–18. ISSN 2289-3156/eISSN 2550-1763.

Sheldon, K. M., Elliot, A. J., Kim, Y., & Kasser, T. (2001). What is satisfying about events? Testing 10 candidate psychological needs. *Journal of Personality and Social Psychology, 80*, 325–339.

Smither, R. D. (1998). *The psychology of work and human performance*, 3rd ed. New York: Longman.

Spelke, E. S., & Newport, E. L. (1998). *Nativism, empiricism, and the developmental of knowledge*. In R. Learner (Vol. Ed.), *Theoretical models of human development*, Vol. 1. In W. Damon (Gen. Ed.), *Handbook of child psychology* (pp. 181–200). New York: Wiley.

Vygotsky, L. (1934/1978). *Mind in Society: The development of higher psychologoical processes*. Cambridge, MA: Harvard University Press

Vygotsky, L. S. (1994). *Thought and language* (Rev. ed., trans. Alex Kozulin). Cambridge, MA: MIT Press.

Wade, C., & Travis, C. (2008). *Psychology*, 9th ed. Merrill/Pearson: Upper Saddle River, NJ.

Weber, E. (1984). *Ideas influencing early childhood education*. New York: Teachers College Press.

Whitehurst, G. J., & Lonigan, C. J. (1998). Child development and emergent literacy. *Child Development*. Wiley Online Library 1999–2017. Hoboken, New Jersey: John Wiley & Sons, Inc.

Willatts, P. (1999). Development of means-end behavior in young infants: Pulling a support to retrieve a distant object. *Developmental Psychology, 35*, 651–667.

Wood, D. J., Bruner, J. S., & Ross, G. (1976). The role of tutoring in problem solving. *Journal of Child Psychology and Psychiatry, 17*, 89–100.

Yamamoto, J., & Ananou, S. (2015). Humanity in the digital age: Cognitive, social, emotional, and ethical implications. *Contemporary Educational Technology*, 6(1), 1–18, 2.

Yu, A., & Bain, B. (1980). *Language, class and cultural implications on the first and second language acquisition: A cross-cultural study of cognitive consequences*. Paper presented at the Los Angeles Second Language Research Forum. October 1980

Chapter 2

Positive Behavioral Interventions and Supports

Jean Gonsier-Gerdin

Introduction

> If a child doesn't know how to read, we teach.
> If a child doesn't know how to swim, we teach.
> If a child doesn't know how to multiply, we teach.
> If a child doesn't know how to drive, we teach.
> If a child doesn't know how to behave, we ... teach? ... punish?
> Why can't we finish the last sentence as automatically as we do the others?
>
> (Herner, T. (1998) Counterpoint. *NASDE*, p. 2.)

In schools across the United States, educators are increasingly responding to that last question with "teach." More and more schools are implementing positive behavioral interventions and supports (PBIS) as part of a multi-tiered system of support (MTSS) to provide universal academic and behavioral instruction to all students, selected group supports, and specialized individual supports. This chapter will address positive behavioral interventions and supports as an evidence-based framework that elementary teachers can use to proactively teach students appropriate academic, social, emotional, and behavioral skills. The chapter introduction will provide an overview of PBIS as a part of a multi-tiered system (MTSS) to create safe and effective learning environments, and will describe the key principles and features of PBIS that have emerged from three decades of research and practice at both individual and school-wide levels. Next, the chapter will focus on how PBIS can be implemented by teachers in diverse, inclusive, elementary school classrooms. Specific evidence-based practices will be shared that can be used to establish culturally responsive physical environments (e.g., classroom space, time, routines, and materials), and teaching strategies that provide structure and predictability, to teach behavior routines and expectations to students explicitly, to adapt instruction and curriculum to engage students in active learning, to acknowledge and reinforce students' appropriate behaviors consistently, and to respond to students' inappropriate behaviors meaningfully.

What Are Multi-Tiered Systems of Support?

Over the last decade, multi-tiered systems of support (MTSS) have emerged as an educational model or framework to provide academic and behavioral instruction and support to all students in schools. MTSS has been defined as "the integration of a number of multiple-tiered systems into one coherent, strategically combined system meant to address multiple domains or content areas in education" (McIntosh & Goodman, 2016, p. 5). One overarching goal of MTSS is to improve the culture of schools and its classrooms to prevent academic and behavioral problems, and to increase academic and social success for all students.

Two particular approaches have been identified as multi-tiered systems of support (MTSS): academic response to intervention (RTI) (Brown-Chidsey & Steege, 2010; National Center on Response to Intervention, 2010) and positive behavioral interventions and supports (PBIS) (Center on Positive Behavioral Interventions and Supports, 2020; Sugai & Horner, 2009). One purpose of each is to provide early identification of students struggling with either learning and behavior or both and to proactively offer a continuum of supports to meet the needs of these students. RTI and PBIS are often represented as two halves of a multi-tiered triangle with RTI focusing on academic instruction and PBIS focusing on behavioral instruction. The majority of MTSS models utilize three tiers of support—Tier One, universal or primary school-wide intervention for the majority or approximately 80 to 90 percent of students, Tier Two, secondary, targeted for small groups of students or approximately 5 to 10 percent of students, and finally, Tier Three, tertiary, intensive, and specialized individual support for a few or approximately 1 to 5 percent of students. See Figure 2.1 for a visual of RTI and PBIS.

Within the MTSS framework, teachers, school staff, and administrators collaborate to provide and monitor evidence-based academic and behavioral prevention and interventions across the tiers. Another important component of the MTSS model is that there is ongoing and frequent measuring and monitoring of student progress and assessing students' responses to instruction and interventions (Brown-Chidsey & Bickford, 2016). For the purposes of this chapter, we will focus on PBIS, although it is important to note that the MTSS framework acknowledges the relationship between academic skills and behavior and the importance of RTI and PBIS as complementary approaches (McIntosh & Goodman, 2016).

What Are the Origins of PBIS?

While PBIS is more recently associated with the schoolwide, multi-tiered applications of positive behavior support principles (SWPBIS), its origins were at the individual student level. In fact, PBIS was first developed as a set of strategies for individual children and youth who demonstrated significant behavioral challenges in schools, homes, and the community. In the

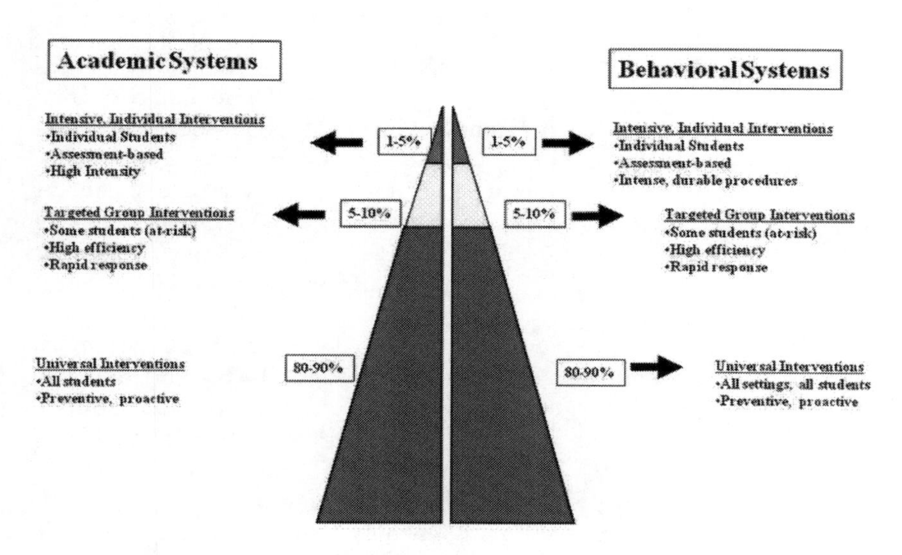

Figure 2.1 Visual of MTSS—RTI and PBIS

mid-1980s, PBIS emerged as an alternative to punitive, aversive intervention techniques (e.g., contingent electric shock, water mist in the face, hot sauce on the tongue) that caused pain, physical discomfort, humiliation, or loss of dignity. These forms of punishment were frequently used with students who had developmental disabilities and exhibited aggressive and/or self-injurious behaviors that impeded their own learning or the learning of other students (Lucyshyn, Dunlap, & Freeman, 2015). PBIS differs greatly from traditional reactive approaches to discipline which often focus on the short-term reduction of problem behaviors and the use of punishment as a consequence for these problem behaviors, without taking into consideration the motivation for or function of the problem behavior (Sailor, Dunlap, Sugai, & Horner, 2011). With PBIS, problem behaviors are seen as the consequences of students not having the appropriate skills to obtain what they need or want so teaching and reinforcing the expected skills are an important part of effective interventions. Furthermore, there is an understanding that teachers should focus on preventing the problem behaviors and improving student outcomes by organizing responsive learning environments, teaching appropriate behaviors, and providing students with meaningful consequences for their behaviors (i.e., reinforcement and natural consequences). While the reduction of problem behaviors is important, improvements in student's quality of life, gains in academic, social, and emotional skills, and access to valued activities are critical outcomes to be expected from behavioral support (Brown & Anderson, 2015). PBIS is considered a person-centered approach that emphasizes the importance of taking a look at a student's whole life and making improvements to their quality of life in school and in their home and community. This approach also involves considering the values, preferences, and environment of the student and their family, as well as of the teachers.

The roots of PBIS are within the application of applied behavior analysis (ABA) principles (Lewis, 2015). Accordingly, key assumptions of PBIS, which stem from ABA, include the following: 1) most behavior is learned; 2) behavior serves a function; 3) behavior is influenced by the environment and context in which it occurs; 4) problem behavior exists because it has been effective for the individual; 5) appropriate new behaviors that serve the same function (i.e., replacement behavior) need to be taught and reinforced; and 6) it is important not to reinforce the problem behavior (Brown & Anderson, 2015). Typically, a problem behavior serves one of the following functions: access to a desired object or activity, access to attention from adults or peers, escape or avoidance of demands or undesired social situations, and access to sensory input/stimulation or an escape from sensory input/stimulation. Multiple functions could also be at play at once (Brown & Anderson, 2015).

PBIS also relies on a competing behavioral pathway model/approach to understanding behavior also derived from ABA (Crone & Horner, 2003; O'Neill, Horner, Albin, Sprague, Storey, & Newton, 1997). This competing behavior pathway model/approach demonstrates that for every problem behavior, there is an antecedent (i.e., the trigger for the behavior) and consequence (i.e., the response by people in the environment to the behavior), and there is an alternative behavior or replacement skill that could be taught to serve the same function and a desired behavior for the situation. There may also be a setting event that makes it more likely that when the antecedent occurs, the challenging behavior will occur. The setting event can be something internal to the individual, such as the student not feeling well, lacking sleep, missing a medication dose, or something external such as an argument with a classmate, or being teased by a peer. See Figure 2.2 for the Competing Behavior Pathway Model.

In order to develop positive interventions and supports to effectively increase student's appropriate and adaptive behavior and thereby, decrease the problem behavior, there must be an understanding of what the "function" of the student's problem behavior may be. The formal process by which the function of a student's problem behavior is determined is known as functional behavioral assessment (FBA). A teacher will work in collaboration with school counselors and psychologists and the student's family to conduct an FBA through direct observations, interviews with the student and family members, and other rating scales (e.g., Motivation Assessment Scale, Social Skills Rating, learning style questionnaire). The purpose of the FBA is to determine the setting events (if any), antecedents, and maintaining consequences (i.e., the function[s]) of the student's problem behavior and to be able to complete the competing behavioral pathway. Once these are identified,

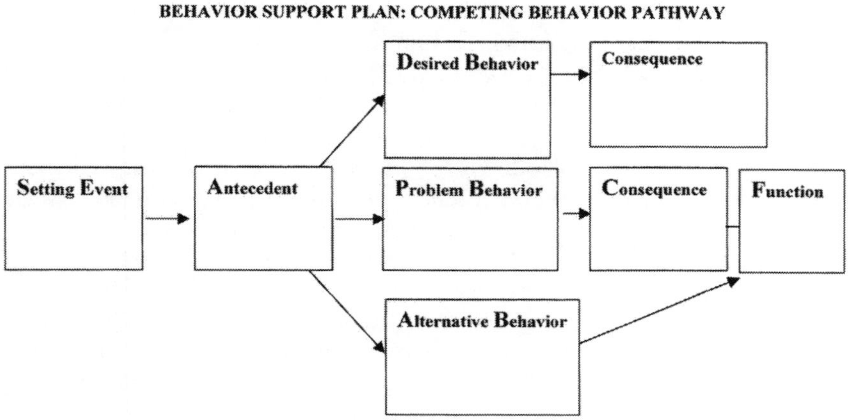

BEHAVIOR SUPPORT PLAN: COMPETING BEHAVIOR PATHWAY

Desired Behavior
Consequence
Setting Event
Antecedent
Problem Behavior
Consequence
Function
Alternative Behavior

Figure 2.2 Competing Behavior Pathway Model (adapted from Crone & Horner, 2003; O'Neill, Horner, Albin, Sprague, Storey, & Newton, 1997)

then a multi-component positive intervention and support plan will be developed and implemented to mitigate and/or, if possible, remove setting events and antecedents of the problem behavior, to teach adaptive and coping skills, including the expected behaviors and the replacement behavior, to increase reinforcement of expected, desired behavior, and to remove or reduce reinforcement of the problem behavior. In short, the individualized PBIS plan will be proactive, educative, and reinforcement-based. This approach assumes that environmental factors, such as teacher practices, are influences on student behavior, and changes in these practices can support change in students' behaviors.

Box 2.1 Theory to Practice: How Can Teachers Apply the Competing Behavioral Pathway and Function-Based Thinking (FBT) in the Classroom?

The core elements involved in the process of conducting an FBA, using the competing behavioral pathway model, and developing individual behavioral support plans can be used by teachers through implementing function-based thinking (FBT) (Hershfeldt, Rosenberg, & Bradshaw, 2010). This systematic, problem-solving approach to explore factors possibly contributing to a student's problem behavior in the classroom can be used to intervene early and prevent further behavioral problems that would necessitate a more time-consuming FBA process. Hershfeldt and her colleagues (2010) noted that "FBT is not designed as a replacement for FBA. Rather it is intended to be a preliminary, proactive, and user-friendly examination of how student behavior problems relate to their environments. The ultimate goal of FBT is for a teacher to independently think functionally about problematic student behavior and select an intervention that serves the same function without the support of multiple team meeting" (p. 14). This process starts with gathering information about the problem behavior that can be naturally collected in the course of a school day. Teachers can ask themselves the following questions: When does the problem behavior occur? What happens directly before the behavior (i.e., the antecedent or trigger)? What happens directly after the behavior occurs (i.e., the consequence)? Are there events or circumstances that may make it more likely for the antecedent to trigger the behavior?

Recall the competing behavior pathway model described earlier in the chapter and how it provided a link between FBA information and developing a positive behavioral support plan for an individual student. Let's consider the following example. Derek is a second grader in Ms. R.'s classroom. During large group phonics lessons, he has begun to yell out, "This is boring!" When this occurs, Ms. R. has stopped the lesson and asked him a question, such as "What...?" At the end of the day, Ms. R. remembers what she has learned about PBIS and the competing behavior pathway. Firstly, she brainstorms about what has been going on in Derek's life that may serve as a setting event. For instance, she remembers that his mom just had a baby girl. Possibly Derek has less attention from his parents since he is not the only child anymore, or he could be tired since the baby may wake him up crying in the middle of the night. Ms. R. also reflects on the lessons during which Derek has called out and recalls the consequences of his calling out have been her stopping the lesson and asking him questions or trying to point out interesting aspects of the lesson to him. As a result of this function-based thinking, she has begun to complete the competing behavior pathway and continues to ask herself the following questions: What can she do to change the environment to support positive behavior? Are there any skills to teach? How can she respond so that the challenging behavior is not reinforced, but the desired behaviors are? See Figure 2.3 for the competing behavior pathway completed for Derek by Ms. R. by using function-based thinking.

In this case, Ms. R. decides that seeking adult attention is the function of Derek's behavior, and she believes that settings events include less adult attention at home and being tired due to less sleep. She then brainstorms strategies to address the setting events and antecedents. She identifies times during the school day when Derek can receive more positive interactions from her and other adults. For example, Ms. R. starts to check in with Derek at various points in the day, when he arrives in the morning, at recess, etc., and she asks him to share about the new baby at home. She also begins to prompt the replacement

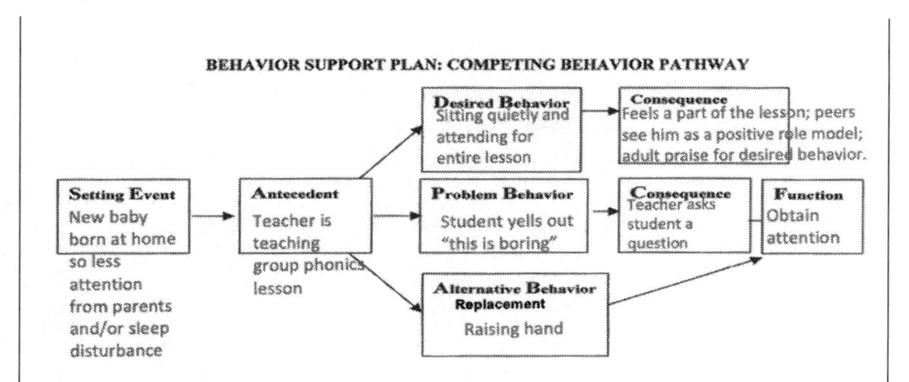

Figure 2.3 Competing Behavior Pathway Completed through Function-Based Thinking

behavior of raising his hand to be called on and to shape the behavior of sitting quietly and attending to the lesson. Before a lesson, she quietly reminds Derek to raise his hand and provides him with a preview of upcoming questions. Then, during the lesson, Ms. R. makes sure that she calls on Derek as soon as he raises his hand to answer the question and offers positive encouragement for participating in the lesson. Last but not least, she tries to not respond if Derek does yell out.

How Did Individual PBIS Evolve into School-Wide PBIS?

In the 1990s, as schools became more inclusive of students with a variety of abilities and needs (see Chapter 9 for further discussion of inclusive schools), PBIS started to be extended to all students in schools in order to prevent challenging behavior from developing in these students as well as to effectively address the challenging behavior of students at risk for or with behavioral disorders (Lucyshyn, Dunlap, & Freeman, 2015). There also came to be an understanding that educators (e.g., teachers, other school personnel) could more effectively develop and implement individual behavior support plans in a context (i.e., schools, classrooms) where a similar approach to behavioral support was being utilized. Moreover, as practitioners and researchers came to recognize that reactive, punitive strategies to manage and discipline were inefficient and unproductive with individual students who had aggressive and/or self-injurious behaviors, they came to realize that the same was true for working with small and large groups of students. Similar to the desire to replace the use of reactive, aversive practices with individuals who had aggressive and self-injurious behaviors, the development of effective procedures for SWIPBIS was driven by the interest in replacing the use of reactive, exclusionary discipline practices (Sugai & Horner, 2020). Rather than send students to detention or suspend and even expel students whose behavior is perceived as troubling and disruptive, adopting SWPBIS requires educators to value these students, and to work with them to develop student-directed or regulated behavior.

In 1998, the Office of Special Education Programs (OSEP) provided funding for a research and national technical assistance center on positive behavioral support. Today, this Center on Positive Behavioral Interventions and Support (2020) continues to be funded through both the U.S. Department of Education's OSEP and the Office of Elementary and Secondary Education (OESE) to improve the capacity of schools to establish and maintain the implementation of the PBIS framework to improve social, emotional and academic outcomes for all students, including students with disabilities and students from underrepresented groups. Over the last three decades, research has demonstrated compelling outcomes associated with the implementation of SWPBIS, including not only the reduction of problem behavior, but also reduction in rates in office discipline referrals and out-of-school suspensions, improvements in social competence, emotional regulation, and academic performance, and improvements in perceptions of school safety and teacher efficacy (McIntosh & Goodman, 2016). Clearly, PBIS has expanded and is no longer viewed as an approach just for students with disabilities who receive special education services. As of August 27, 2019, there were 27,294 schools in the United States (approximately 30 percent of all schools) are actively implementing PBIS to support 15,284,640 students (Sugai, 2019).

What Is School-Wide PBIS?

When implementing SWPBIS, administrators, teachers, and other school staff agree to a formalized approach to discipline that is positive, comprehensive, and ongoing, and that aligns with their school's mission. Each school creates a local, school-site team to support the implementation of the three-tiered model and to regularly analyze the school-wide data. Tier One of SWPBIS involves a set of universal or primary interventions to foster a positive, safe school culture for all students, school staff, and community members across all school settings. In other words, Tier One interventions teach and reinforce pro-social behavior, maximize opportunities for teaching and learning, and prevent the occurrences of problem behavior (Sugai & Horner, 2009). Accordingly, a set of three to five positively stated school-wide behavioral expectations are identified by the school-site team, including teachers, school administrators, students, family members, and then these expectations are taught across school environments. For example, Leataata Floyd Elementary School in Northern California has the mission "to provide a safe environment and challenging curriculum which will enable all students to become independent life-long learners and responsible citizens" (Leataata Floyd

Elementary School, 2020), and their school-wide-expectations that align with this mission are: "Be Responsible, Be Respectful, Be Hardworking." Since their school mascot is a panther, following these school-wide expectations is considered "The Panther Way." Specific behaviors that demonstrate each of these expectations have been detailed for a variety of school locations, such as hallways/breezeways, classroom, cafeteria, library, computer lab, bathrooms, office, and for particular activities, such as arrival to school, recess, physical education, and dismissal. See Figure 2.4 for a visual with the rules of expected behaviors and how they are to be demonstrated at recess. At the beginning of the year, these behavioral expectations are explicitly taught and modeled for students in each of the environments and activities and throughout the year are reviewed and retaught if necessary.

Other key components of Tier One SWPBIS are that school staff consistently acknowledge and reinforce students for engaging in appropriate, expected behaviors and also consistently respond when rule violations or other problem behaviors occur. The school establishes systems to provide this feedback across both classroom and non-classroom settings and across school staff (e.g., teachers, principal, office staff, counselors, cafeteria staff, playground supervision staff, etc.). At Leataata Floyd Elementary, students receive Panther Way tickets on the back of which the staff person giving the student the ticket writes what the student demonstrated to be either responsible, respectful, or

Recess		
Be Responsible	**Be Respectful**	**Be Hardworking**
• Follow directions first time asked. 	• Say and do only kind things to others. 	• Tell an adult if there is a problem you can't solve. 
• Follow whistle, game, and specific area procedures. 	• Share and take turns. 	• Put all equipment away when finished. 
• Accept responsibility for your choices or actions. 	• Keep your hands and feet to yourself. 	• Use the bathroom and get a drink of water during recess. 

Figure 2.4 Visual Display of School-Wide Expectations for Recess

hardworking. These tickets are placed into a classroom lottery to be drawn one or more times per week to receive privileges (e.g., go straight to the head of the lunch line, eat lunch with a staff member of choice, receive a positive note home from teacher or principal), and then into a school-wide drawing to occur on average once a week for other privileges (e.g., help principal sort and count Panther way tickets, assist the vice principal during recess or lunch, announce the winner of next week's school-wide drawing). These privileges are easily accessible and are usually no or low cost. In addition, to be motivating and reinforcing, there need to be privileges that are valued by the students of all grades and ages at the school.

Schools that practice PBIS also develop clear guidelines for responses to occurrences of problem behavior. Possible rule violations or problem behavior are clearly defined and there usually are distinctions made between behaviors that the teacher or staff person manage (e.g., engaging in "rough play;" talking back to the teacher; laughing at others), and those that the principal or office staff manage (e.g., physical contact with intent to harm, such as hitting, punching, kicking; deliberate damage of property). Examples of consequences to problem behavior may include loss of a privilege, a written assignment to reflect on behavior, a parent contact, or suspension if deemed appropriate. There are also procedures for reporting and documenting these problem behaviors and the responses taken as well as for when a problem behavior becomes reoccurring and the student may receive a referral for a Tier Two intervention.

SWPBIS may also integrate other programs and approaches into Tier One to further support students' academic, social and emotional growth and to address school safety, bullying, trauma, and other mental health issues (Good, McIntosh, & Gietz, 2011; Sugai & Horner, 2020). For example, Leataata Floyd Elementary employs the *Second Step* social-emotional learning curriculum to teach and provide opportunities to practice skills for learning, empathy, self-regulation and emotional management, friendship, executive functioning skills (e.g., attention, working memory, self-awareness, inhibition), and problem-solving (Committee for Children, 2011). This classroom-based program contains separate sets of curricular units and lessons that research has shown to be effective for use in preschool through middle school (Espelage, Low, Polanin, & Brown, 2013; Low, Cook, Smolkowski, & Buntain-Ricklefs, 2015; Upshur, Heyman, &Wenz-Gross, 2017). In recent years, Leataata Floyd Elementary has also adopted mindfulness practices to assist students to regulate their emotions and to direct their attention to and focus on learning. Teachers select videos from free web-based libraries, such as Mind Yeti and Go Noodle, to provide students with exercises for guided meditation and brain breaks at various times during the school day (e.g., before independent work, when coming in from recess, etc.). Research on mindfulness-based programs in schools has shown promise for improvements in attention and executive functioning, social-emotional resiliency, and management of school-related stress (Semple, Droutman, & Reid, 2017).

As previously noted, Tier Two interventions and supports are intended for a smaller percentage of students, approximately 5 to 10 percent, who are not successful with Tier One supports alone and at risk for developing more serious behavioral challenges. Schools develop and implement these additional interventions for students who are referred by their teachers. These interventions are consistent with the school-wide expectations, flexible so as to be modified for the specific needs of the student population, are available continuously so a student can have quick access when needed, and incorporate home school communication and linkages. Tier Two practices focus on increased opportunities for the instruction of social and self-regulation skills, adult supervision, positive reinforcement of appropriate behavior, pre-corrections for possible problem behavior, and access to academic supports (Hawken, Adolphson, MacLeod, & Schumann, 2011). Examples of Tier Two interventions include Check-in/Check-out (CICO), tutoring (adult or peer), mentoring (adult or peer), a behavioral contract, small group social skills instruction, homework club, and study skills programs.

Check-in/Check-out (CICO) is an evidence-based Tier Two intervention commonly used at the elementary and secondary level (Filter, Mckenna, Benedict, Horner, & Todd, 2007; Maggin, Zurheide, Pickett, & Baillie, 2015), and more recently modified for use with preschool children (LaBrot, Dufrene, Radley, & Pasqua, 2016). The procedures for CICO include the following key components: 1) the student checks in with an assigned mentor (e.g., teacher, counselor, principal, paraprofessional, etc.) to review the behavioral expectations for the day and to receive positive attention and coaching to meet these expectations; 2) a daily behavioral rating/ point card is given to the student during the morning check-in and serves as a means for monitoring the student's behavior; 3) the student's teacher(s) provides feedback to the student in relation to the behavioral expectations throughout the school day at regularly scheduled intervals (e.g., before morning recess, before lunch, after lunch, before dismissal) using the behavioral rating/point card; 4) the student checks in with the mentor at the end of the school day to review the daily behavior rating/point card, to determine if the student has met the goal, and to receive verbal encouragement and/or a tangible reward if the goal is met; and 5) home–school communication which involves the student taking home the behavioral rating/point card to a parent(s) or guardian(s) who reviews it with the student, provides additional feedback and reinforcement, and then signs so the card can be brought back to school the next day (Crone, Hawken, & Horner, 2010). The CICO program also involves teaching the student to self-monitor using the daily behavior rating/point cards so that the structured program can be gradually phased out. Not surprisingly, since CICO provides students with a number of structured opportunities to have positive contact with adults throughout the school day, it has been found to be beneficial with students who seek adult attention or find adult attention reinforcing (Crone, Hawken, & Horner, 2010)

At Leataata Floyd Elementary School, the CICO program aligns with the school-wide expectations of being responsible, respectful, and hardworking and uses Panther PAWS cards as the daily behavioral rating/point card. See Figure 2.5 for an example of a Panther PAWS card.

The school site team reviews the effectiveness of the CICO program for students about every eight weeks. If there is significant progress, then the team in collaboration with the student and parent(s) or guardian(s) may determine to phase out the program. If the intervention is not effective, the CICO program may be modified, additional Tier Two interventions may be tried, or a more intensive, individualized intervention (i.e., Tier Three) may be developed and implemented.

Finally, Tier Three interventions of SWPBIS are individualized, comprehensive PBIS plans for 1 to 5 percent of students who demonstrate significant problem behaviors (e.g., aggressive behavior towards peers and/or adults, self-injurious behavior, property destruction, etc.), and who have not been responsive to Tier One and Tier Two interventions and supports. As previously described, Tier Three interventions are developed for a student based on

PANTHER PAWS CARD

_________'S goal is to earn 20 points.

2 = WOW!	1 = OK	0 = Hard Time

	Responsible	Respectful	Hardworking		
Time	*Accept Responsibility for Choices or Actions*	*Allow Others to Work Without Interruption*	*Keep Your Voice at an Appropriate Level*	Teacher's Initials	Comments
Before 1st Recess (9:00 – 10:35)	☺ 😐 ☹	☺ 😐 ☹	☺ 😐 ☹		
Before Lunch (10:50 – 11:50)	☺ 😐 ☹	☺ 😐 ☹	☺ 😐 ☹		
After Lunch (12:30 – 2:00)	☺ 😐 ☹	☺ 😐 ☹	☺ 😐 ☹		
Before dismissal (2:15 – 3:00)	☺ 😐 ☹	☺ 😐 ☹	☺ 😐 ☹		
Today you earned _________ points. Goal met? Y/N					
Boys and Girls Club 3:00 – 6:00	☺ 😐 ☹	☺ 😐 ☹	☺ 😐 ☹		

Parent Signature ______________________________ Returned ☺

Figure 2.5 Example of CICO Daily Point Card

a functional behavioral assessment (FBA). These students continue to take part in the Tier One and Tier Two interventions.

What Does PBIS in a Classroom Look Like?

Within schools that utilize SWPBIS, each teacher works to translate the three-tiered model of proactive, positive practices to the classroom level. In other words, teachers use approaches to support expected behaviors for all students (Tier One), some strategies for a smaller group of students who are at risk for behavioral challenges (Tier Two), and then other more individualized, intensive supports for the one or two students in the classroom who demonstrate ongoing problem behaviors (Tier Three).

Tier One in the Classroom: Creating a Calm, Safe, Responsive, and Inclusive Classroom

The foundation for Tier One classroom behavioral support is a calm, safe, and responsive environment that is thoughtfully arranged to maximize opportunities for effective and efficient teaching, active academic engagement, and positive social interactions for all students. In order to lay this foundation, a teacher needs to organize the physical space, create and teach predictable routines, establish and teach classroom rules and expected behaviors, regularly supervise and reinforce student behavior, provide corrective feedback, and plan and implement high-quality academic instruction that actively engages all students in learning (Bambara, Janney, & Snell, 2015).

Well Organized Physical Space

Creating a calm, safe, and responsive environment begins with the organization and arrangement of the classroom's furniture, materials, and displays to enhance learning, minimize crowding and distraction, and support independence and positive interdependence.

The layout of a classroom should ensure that all students can see the teacher and instructional displays (e.g., the Smartboard, word wall, etc.) as well as ensure they can be seen and supervised by the teacher from all parts of the room. All necessary supplies and work areas (i.e., desks, tables, carpet) need to be easily identified by and accessible to all students and be appropriate to the number of students and adults in the classroom. High traffic areas (e.g., the aisles between desks, the doorway) should be easy to navigate. The teacher can promote a community by posting student work and photographs of students on the walls. When necessary, it also should be clear what areas of the classroom are not available for use by students. For instance, there may be a 'teachers-only' area, such as the teacher's desk, or at certain times, a teacher may signal to students that a computer station in the classroom is not available by placing a sign or cover over the computer.

It is also important to designate an area where students can go if they need to calm or cool down. Such a place may be a "calming corner" (or any designated quiet space) with soft furnishings and calming materials where students can go to self-regulate, take a break from instruction, etc. In this area, there can be visuals and instructions for different strategies to practice self-regulation skills and to calm down and prepare to learn. These strategies can be introduced and practiced with students during class lessons. Time in this space should not be used as a punishment or consequence for problematic behavior (Porter, 2003).

Organization of Schedule and Routines

A calm, safe, and responsive classroom also has a predictable daily schedule, along with routines and procedures that are clear, consistent, cued, taught, practiced, and reinforced regularly. The daily schedule will be posted so all students can see and understand. Additionally, there may be routines for how to enter the classroom, where to put personal belongings, how to transition between activities/centers, class jobs that students are assigned, what signals the teacher will give to get or regain the attention of students, etc. One routine that teachers may have is to greet their students at the door of the classroom as a way to make positive contact with each one at the start of the day.

Another common classroom routine is the class meeting. Class meetings in a variety of formats and for a number of purposes can be implemented across grade levels. Examples include morning meetings, problem-solving meetings, harm/conflict (restorative justice) circles, community-building circles, and planning and goal setting meetings (Nelson & Gfroerer, 2017; California Conference for Equality and Justice, 2013). A key practice of both the responsive classroom approach and the positive discipline approach that use evidence-based practices to engage students and create positive classroom culture is having morning meeting to assist students to prepare for the day's events (Nelson & Gfroerer, 2017; Responsive Classroom, 2020). These meetings facilitate and nurture trusting relationships between the students as well as between the teacher and students. At Leataata Floyd Elementary, every morning for the first 20 to 25 minutes of the school day, Ms. R. gathers all her second-grade students on the carpet area for a morning meeting. This meeting starts with everyone greeting each other and is followed by a share time with a prompt based on a social-emotional learning concept (e.g., How are you feeling this morning?) the class may be practicing from the *Second Step* curriculum. Next, they may play a group game and then have the "problem box" discussion. This problem-solving discussion revolves around an issue that a student may be having with one or more classmates. Students submit these issues by completing a form with the following "I" message statement, "I feel ________ when you ________ and I would like you to stop please," and putting the completed form into a box labeled, "Problem Box." The student has a choice to discuss privately or to discuss with the class during a morning meeting. Finally, the morning meeting ends with a morning message from Ms. R written on the board or chart paper. This message may integrate social-emotional learning and academic concepts (e.g., looking for all the contractions in the message, doing a math problem from the day before).

Establishing, Teaching, and Reinforcing Classroom Rules and Expected Behaviors

Another Tier One component of classroom PBIS is having three to five rules clearly posted, defined, and explicitly taught to all students. These classroom expectations should reflect and align with the school-wide expectations. See Figure 2.6 for a visual with the rules and expected classroom behaviors posted in Ms. R.'s second-grade classroom at Leataata Floyd Elementary. In each classroom, the teacher and students will then apply these rules to their classroom community. In fact, students are encouraged to have a voice in creating the classroom rules and routines in order for them to have buy-in and ownership. For example, students at any grade level can be part of developing the classroom expectations, brainstorming examples of the expected behaviors, and even be part of implementing classroom expectations. To apply the school-wide expectations, "Be Responsible, Be Respectful, Be Hardworking" to their second-grade classroom, the students

In the Classroom		
Be Responsible	**Be Respectful**	**Be Hardworking**
• Follow directions first time asked. 	• Say and do only kind things to others. 	• Begin work immediately. 
• Follow classroom procedures. 	• Be an active listener. 	• Be on task during work times. 
• Accept responsibility for your choices or actions. 	• Allow others to work without interruption. 	• Keep your voice at an appropriate level. 

Figure 2.6 Visual Display of Classroom Expectations

with Ms. R.'s guidance created the following Class Constitution signed by all the students:

> We the kids of Room 16 have decided to show our best selves. First, we will be kind to others. Second, we will show how to sit crisscross. Third, we will be leaders. Fourth, we will follow directions quickly [the] first time [we are] asked. Fifth, we will do our work. Sixth, we will treat others the same as we want to be treated. Seventh, we will help other[s] when they fall down.

Each of the classroom expectations, like school-wide expectations, are taught, modeled, and practiced in real-life situations, and reviewed when necessary, such as when returning from school breaks, and reinforced so that students maintain and generalize the skills. Similar to how school-wide expectations are delineated for the various locations in the school (i.e., hallways, cafeteria, and playground), these rules or expectations will be delineated for each area of the classroom. See Figure 2.7 for an image of the rules and expected behaviors posted in the area in a fifth-grade classroom at Leataata Floyd Elementary where students can go for time away to calm down or refocus.

In addition to establishing and teaching expected behaviors, the teacher will monitor and reinforce these behaviors on a consistent basis. Positive attending to students' appropriate behaviors with specific praise and encouragement is one evidence-based practice found to be associated with the promotion and maintenance of students' positive classroom behavior (Perle, 2016). To be effective, teachers who implement positive attending should provide this direct feedback as soon as the desired behavior occurs and on a

Time Away		
Be Responsible	**Be Respectful**	**Be Hardworking**
• Follow time away and calming caddy procedures. • Put materials away when finished. • Be sure you are using time away only when you really need to.	• Use calming caddy materials appropriately. • Be considerate of others when they are in time away.	• Focus on calming down and using SEL strategies. • Select items in the calming caddy with purpose.

Figure 2.7 Visual Display of Expectations for Time Away/Calming Caddy

frequent, consistent basis. Another important component of positive attending is to focus on the student's performance or process (e.g., "You worked hard on the assignment.") and not on ability (e.g., "You are so smart.") (Corpus & Lepper, 2007; Dweck, 2007). Teachers can "catch a student being good" instead of waiting to correct problem behavior. Positive attending can also be used to prompt appropriate behavior, rather than focusing on corrective feedback. Instead of telling students what not to do, teachers can provide positive attending to the students who are doing what is expected. For example, if a few students are calling out loudly without raising their hands, the teacher can acknowledge the students who are sitting quietly and raising their hands.

In her second-grade class, Ms. R. has several strategies for positively attending to and rewarding appropriate behaviors for the whole class, groups of students, and/or individual students. She attempts to recognize and acknowledge appropriate behavior more than inappropriate behavior (i.e., a four-to-one ratio of positive reinforcement to corrective feedback). For the whole class, there is a jewel jar in which a "jewel" is placed when Ms. R. observes the whole class being on task at any time in the day. On the jewel jar, different pieces of tape indicate a privilege (e.g., extra recess, class party, pajama and movie day) that the class will earn when the jewels reach the level of the piece of tape. During language arts workshop time, when groups of students are working independently or with an adult, Ms. R. randomly selects a group to be the "secret group." She observes this group and if the group works well, then the whole class earns a letter in the word, "PANTHER." Once the whole word is spelled, each student in the class can pick a privilege (e.g., no shoes for a day, time to play with class rabbit, or use a special pen or pencil).

One of the class jobs in Ms. R.'s second-grade classroom is "Work Manager" —a student who is responsible for passing out "Panther Way" tickets to classmates who are observed being responsible, respectful, or hardworking. These tickets, along with any other tickets a student may receive from Ms. R. or another adult on campus, are placed into a classroom lottery to be drawn one or more times per week to receive privileges and then entered into a schoolwide draw (to occur on average once a week) for other privileges. At the end of the day, Ms. R. also has the students reflect on how they feel they did that day and what they can improve on the next day. At this time, students individually may earn a sticker to put on a sticker chart. The students are encouraged to try to earn as many stickers per month as they can.

Active Adult Supervision and Corrective Feedback

Clearly, the classroom teacher plays a critical role in organizing classroom time and space and in teaching and reinforcing expected behaviors. However, the teacher also actively supervises and provides redirection and corrective feedback to students who may not be exhibiting the expected behaviors. In order to effectively do so, the teacher needs to hone the ability to be aware of what is happening in all parts of the classroom by moving around and visually and auditorily scanning frequently and systematically. This ability, coined as "withitness" by Kounin (1977), enables the teacher to notice students' non-verbal and verbal reactions. It also allows them to see if students are maintaining interest and involvement in the class's activity, and identify if one or more need assistance, reminders, or encouragement to continue. Moreover, the teacher is able to respond quickly to unexpected events. Whenever a teacher does need to redirect or correct a student, it is important for the teacher to provide positive reinforcement as soon as the same student follows the direction or rules. For example, if a student is redirected for calling out instead of raising her hand, the teacher will want to be sure to call on her as soon as she does raise her hand without calling out.

A classroom teacher can use a variety of strategies to respond to minor disruptive problem behaviors that may be expected and occur on a regular basis, such as minor rule infractions or disruptions and off-task behaviors (e.g., whispering, calling out, passing notes, doing other work, etc.). Larrivee (2009) referred to these strategies as "surface management techniques" that serve to redirect a student's behavior before escalation and in the moment without interrupting the flow of instruction. These techniques may include, but are not limited to, the following: a) planned ignoring—do not respond to certain behaviors, particularly if the behavior is not likely to escalate or spread to other students and is attempting to get attention from the teacher and/or peers; b) signal interference—use a non-verbal cue, such as clearing one's throat, making eye-contact, or using a hand gesture, to redirect the student and communicate expected behavior; c) proximity control—stand near the student who is exhibiting the problem behavior to help student control impulses; d) interest boosting—when a student is showing signs of boredom, disinterest, or restlessness, engage in a conversation about a topic of interest to the student or display interest in the student's work; e) use of humor—make a funny comment to ease a tense situation and make students feel comfortable, but be sure it is not perceived that the student is the focus of the comment; f) hurdle help—assist a student who may be overwhelmed, frustrated by, and/or unmotivated to help them get started on a task (i.e., remove the hurdle); g) removal of distracting object—politely ask the student to put away a distracting object (e.g., small toy, cell phone); and h) antiseptic bouncing—find a way to have the student go to another setting (e.g., deliver a message to another classroom or the office; take the lunch count to the cafeteria) for a short time to give the student time to regroup, but not to be seen as a punishment.

Planning and Implementing High-Quality Instruction

Another essential part of classroom PBIS is the use of effective, high-quality instructional practices that create varied, motivating contexts and maximize the active engagement of all learners (Scheuermann & Hall, 2016). When developing units and lesson plans for literacy, mathematics, social studies, science, the arts, or physical education, teachers will want to ensure that all students have ways to access the curricular materials, to engage with the materials and information, and to show what they have learned. These instructional practices may include providing individualized accommodations or modifications to learning materials, environment, and/or expectations based on the needs of students and possible barriers that might exist. The particular interests, motivations, and cultural backgrounds and experiences of the students in the classroom should also be taken into consideration. In short, teachers should follow the principles of Universal Design for Learning (UDL) to ensure that all students have access to learning content and instruction (see Chapter 9 for further discussion of UDL).

Box 2.2 Common Core: Linking PBIS to Academic Common Core Standards

At times, teachers may feel that they are too occupied with teaching their students the Common Core English language arts (ELA)/literacy and mathematics curriculum to focus on teaching social-emotional skills and other prosocial behaviors. However, these skills are often essential for students to engage in academic work and, thereby, reach the high expectations of the Common Core standards. For example, a number of social, emotional, and behavioral skills can be seen in ELA Standards for Speaking and Listening (SL) across the elementary school grades. The Kindergarten ELA Standard for SL includes the following expected social behaviors for students: "participate in collaborative conversations with [a] diverse partner," "follow agreed-upon rules for discussions," and "listening to others and taking turns speaking." In the Grade 5 ELA Standard for SL, students are expected to "engage effectively in a range of collaborative discussions," "come to discussions prepared," "follow agreed-upon rules for discussion and carry out assigned roles," and "pose and respond to specific questions by making comments that contribute to the discussion and elaborate on the remarks of others." Therefore, teachers need to be prepared to teach and reinforce these behavioral skills along with the academic content and curriculum since students may lack these appropriate behaviors or inconsistently display the behaviors. The school- and class-wide behavioral expectations that are established, taught, and reinforced through SWPBIS include self-management and -regulation skills and resilience which in turn support students in accessing academic content and engaging in productive academic work to meet Common Core State Standards. In short, positive behavioral support in schools and classrooms is not implemented independently of academic instruction.

Tier Two and Tier Three in the Classroom

As with SWPBIS, there may be students in a classroom who may need additional support to learn and consistently use adaptive and prosocial behaviors. These students may require, for a short-term basis, one or more of the Tier Two interventions described earlier in this chapter. For example, in Ms. R.'s second-grade class of 24 students, two students are part of the school's Check-in/Check-out (CICO) program. These students also benefit from sixth-grade buddies who spend about 20 minutes per day with them, particularly to mentor during writing time. Finally, in any classroom, there may be a student who requires a functional behavioral assessment (FBA) to develop and implement an individualized PBIS plan (i.e., Tier Three intervention) in addition to the interventions and supports at the Tier One and Two levels. One of Ms. R.'s students had previously not attended school since preschool and demonstrated challenging behaviors, such as throwing materials and running out of the classroom when given instructional demands, and hitting and kicking peers during social interactions. Ms. R., in collaboration with the student's family and the school PBIS team, conducted an FBA and developed an individualized PBIS plan for this student. This multi-component plan included altering how instructional tasks were presented to him (e.g., fewer items on a worksheet), teaching how to ask for help and to initiate and respond to peers, teaching peers how to interact with him, and reinforcing more frequently with an individual token chart (i.e., earn stars for listening to the teacher, keeping hands to self, using "big boy" voice, and staying safe; five stars earned a privilege). Ms. R. continues to take data so that the team can monitor if the plan is effective in terms of increasing the students' adaptive skills and decreasing the problem behaviors.

Within the PBIS framework, teachers are encouraged to self-evaluate and determine which effective general classroom behavioral support practices are in place and to develop an action plan to make improvements based on their findings (Center on Positive Behavioral Interventions & Support, 2006) While classrooms where PBIS is implemented will have similar, key practices and strategies in place, every classroom is unique and should reflect the culture and community of the students who attend that classroom. As such, diversity in ability, culture, language, gender, sexual orientation, religion, socio-economic status, etc. must be taken into consideration when creating and maintaining the classroom environment.

Box 2.3 Social Justice and Diversity: Need for Culturally Responsive and Relevant PBIS Practices

As school populations in the United States have become increasingly diverse in terms of race, ethnicity, language, and culture, research findings have demonstrated disproportionate discipline outcomes for students from culturally and linguistically diverse backgrounds (Vincent, Randall, Cartledge, Tobin, & Swain-Bradway, 2011). In particular, African-American students are two to four times more likely to receive an office referral than white students (Kaufman et al., 2010), and receive severe school discipline, including suspension and expulsion, more frequently and for longer durations (Gregory & Weinstein, 2008; Krezmien, Leone, & Achilles, 2006). Furthermore, students from culturally and linguistically diverse backgrounds are disproportionality referred to be evaluated for special education services and found eligible in different special education categories, including behavioral disorders, than white students (Harry & Klingner, 2014).

These findings indicate that teachers and school personnel may be implementing practices that inadvertently discriminate against and marginalize students from racial and ethnic minority backgrounds while privileging others. Teachers may tend to interpret and respond to students' behaviors through the lens of mainstream socio-cultural norms. For example, a teacher may interpret a student who talks back as being disrespectful, while to the student this may be an expression of their culture's communication style. Not surprisingly, there have been calls for culturally responsive and relevant PBIS at school, classroom, and individual levels (Bal, King, Thorius, & Kozleski, 2012; Fallon, O'Keeffe, & Sugai, 2012; Sugai, O'Keeffe, & Fallon, 2012; Vincent, Randall, Cartledge, Tobin, & Swain-Bradway, 2011).

According to Weinstein, Curran, and Tomlinson-Clarke (2003), in order to be able to implement culturally responsive classroom management and behavioral support, teachers need to first recognize that everyone belongs to a culture with its own assumptions, beliefs, and biases about human behavior. Next, teachers must acknowledge the cultural, linguistic, ethnic, racial, class, and gender differences that exist in their classrooms. In other words, to be culturally responsive, teachers should not strive to be "color-blind," but instead should learn about their students' family backgrounds, previous learning histories or educational experiences, the cultural norms for interpersonal relationships, parental expectations for discipline, etc. Moreover, teachers can demonstrate openness and willingness to learn about what students and their families consider to be important aspects of their culture. Lastly, teachers need to reflect on ways that their schools may perpetuate discriminatory practices and on the ways that their own classroom behavioral support practices serve to promote or hinder equity in access to learning. Weinstein et al. (2003) stressed that teachers should view all the tasks involved in classroom behavioral support, such as creating the physical space, establishing expectations for behavior, communicating with students, and working with families, through the lens of cultural diversity in order to enhance equity.

Box 2.4 Social-Emotional Competence: PBIS as Framework for Teaching Social-Emotional Competencies

As there has been tremendous growth over the last decade in the use of PBIS in schools across the United States, so too has there been growth in use of interventions focused on social-emotional learning (Weissberg, Durlak, Domitrovich, & Gullotta, 2015). The Collaborative for Academic, Social and Emotional Learning (CASEL) defines social and emotional learning (SEL) as

> the process through which children and adults acquire and effectively apply the knowledge, attitudes, and skills necessary to understand and manage emotions, set and achieve positive goals, feel and show empathy for others, establish and maintain positive relationships, and make responsible decisions.
>
> (CASEL, 2013)

The SEL approach emphasizes the development of social, emotional, and behavioral competencies in the contexts of supportive relationships between teachers and students (Bear, Whitcomb, Elias, & Blank, 2015). Social-emotional competencies involve the skills, behaviors, and attitudes that are necessary to effectively manage cognitive, affective, and social behavior. These competencies involve self-awareness, self-management of emotions and behavior, social awareness, relationship skills, and responsible decision-making in school, home, and community (Collaborative for Academic, Social, and Emotional Learning, 2013.). Unsurprisingly, these competencies are also essential for students to meet the behavioral expectations at their schools and to effectively engage in learning of academic material.

Evidently, SEL and PBIS have a number of similarities and are considered to be complementary approaches (Bear et al., 2015; Rimm-Kaufman & Hulleman, 2015). Barrett, Eber, McIntosh, Perales, and Romer (2018) go further to recommend that PBIS be viewed as a framework for promoting social-emotional competencies. Rather than adopting a social-emotional learning curriculum as a separate intervention and perhaps even implemented by a different school team than the one that is responsible for implementing PBIS, social-emotional learning can be embedded into all three tiers of PBIS. Examples of how to embed instruction of social and emotional competencies within classroom PBIS include organizing activities that involve student interdependency, collaboration, and cooperation, sharing examples of what successful collaboration looks like in books read and other curricular materials used, and coaching during an activity and reinforcing appropriate cooperative behaviors immediately.

Chapter Summary

This chapter has presented the concept of positive behavioral interventions and supports (PBIS) as a multi-tiered system of support (MTSS) and provided an overview of the origins and key principles and features of PBIS at the school and classroom levels. Throughout the chapter, strategies and interventions at all three tiers of school and classroom PBIS were illustrated through examples from one elementary school in Northern California. The importance of culturally responsive PBIS that meets the needs of an increasingly diverse population of students was explored. Finally, PBIS as a framework for teaching social-emotional learning and facilitating equitable access to academic instruction to meet the rigorous Common Core State Standards was presented.

References

Bal, A., King Thorius, K., & Kozleski, E. (2012). *Culturally responsive positive behavioral support matters*. Tempe, AZ: Equity Alliance. Retrieved July 15, 2020, from www.equityallianceatasu.org/sites/default/files/CRPBIS_Matters.pdf

Bambara, L. M., Janney, R., & Snell, M. E. (2015). *Teachers' guides to inclusive practices: Behavior support*, 3rd ed. Baltimore, MD: Paul H. Brookes.

Barrett, S., Eber, L., McIntosh, K., Perales, K., & Romer, N. (2018). *Teaching social-emotional competencies within a PBIS Framework*. Retrieved July 15, 2020, from www.pbis.org

Bear, G. G., Whitcomb, S. A., Elias, M. J., & Blank, J. C. (2015). SEL and schoolwide positive behavioral interventions and supports. In J. A. Durlak, C. E. Domitrovich, R. P. Weissberg, & T. P. Gullotta (Eds.), *Handbook of social and emotional learning: Research and practice* (pp. 453–467). New York: Guilford Publications.

Brown, F., & Anderson, J. L., (2015). Foundational assumptions about challenging behavior and behavior interventions. In F. Brown, J. L. Anderson, & R. L. De Pry (Eds.), *Individual positive behavioral supports: A standards-based guide to practices in school and community settings* (pp. 27–46). Baltimore, MD: Paul H. Brookes.

Brown-Chidsey, R., & Bickford, R. (2016). *Practical handbook of multi-tiered systems of support: Building academic and behavioral success in schools*. New York: Guilford Publications.

Brown-Chidsey, R., & Steege, M. (2010). *Response to intervention: Principles and strategies for effective practice*, 2nd ed. New York: Guilford Publications.

California Conference for Equality and Justice. (2013). Using restorative justice practices and positive behavior interventions and supports (PBIS) together. Retrieved July 15, 2020, from http://wh1.oet.udel.edu/pbs/wp-content/uploads/2015/05/Restorative-Justice-PBIS.pdf

Center on Positive Behavioral Interventions and Supports. (2006). Classroom management: Self-assessment revised. Retrieved July 15, 2020, from www.pbis.org/resource/positive-behavior-support-classroom-management-self-assessment

Center on Positive Behavioral Interventions and Supports. (2020). Getting started. Retrieved July 15, 2020, from www.pbis.org/getting-started.

Collaborative for Academic Social and Emotional Learning (CASEL). (2013). The CASEL guide to schoolwide social and emotional learning. Retrieved July 15, 2020, from https://schoolguide.casel.org/

Committee for Children. (2011). *Second Step: Social emotional learning curriculum*. Seattle, WA: Author.

Corpus, J. H., & Lepper, M. R. (2007). The effects of person versus performance praise on children's motivation: Gender and age as moderating factors. *Educational Psychology, 27*, 487–508.

Crone, D. A., Hawken, L. S., & Horner, R. H. (2010). *Responding to problem behavior in schools: The behavior education program*, 2nd ed. New York: Guilford Publications.

Crone, D. A., & Horner, R. H. (2003). *Building positive behavior support systems in schools*. New York: Guilford Publications.

Dweck, C. S. (2007). The perils and promises of praise. *Educational Leadership, 65*, 34–39.

Espelage, D. L., Low, S., Polanin, J. R., & Brown, E. C. (2013). The impact of a middle school program to reduce aggression, victimization, and sexual violence. *Journal of Adolescent Health, 53*(2), 180–186.

Fallon, L. M., O'Keeffe, B. V., & Sugai, G. (2012). Consideration of culture and context in school-wide positive behavior support: A review of current literature. *Journal of Positive Behavior Interventions, 14*, 209–219. doi: 10.1177/1098300712442242

Filter, K. J., McKenna, M. K., Benedict, E. A., Horner, R. H., & Todd, A. W. (2007). Check-in/Check-out: A post hoc evaluation of an efficient, secondary-level targeted intervention for reducing problem behaviors in schools. *Education and Treatment of Children, 30*, 69–84.

Good, C. P., McIntosh, K., & Gietz, C. (2011). Integrating bullying prevention into schoolwide positive behavior support. *Teaching Exceptional Children, 44*, 48–56.

Gregory, A., & Weinstein, R. (2008). The discipline gap and African Americans: Defiance or cooperation in the high school classroom. *Journal of School Psychology, 46*, 455–475.

Harry, B., & Klingner, J. (2014). *Why are so many minority students in special education? Understanding race & disability in schools*. New York: Teachers College Press.

Hawken, L. S., Adolphson, S. L., Macleod, K. S., & Schumann, J. (2011). Secondary-tier interventions and supports. In W. Sailor, G. Dunlap, G. Sugai, & R. Horner, R. (Eds.), *Handbook of positive behavioral support* (pp. 395–420). New York: Springer.

Hershfeldt, P. A., Rosenberg, M. S., & Bradshaw, C. P. (2010). Function-based thinking: A systematic way of thinking about function and its role in changing student behavior problems. *Beyond Behavior, 19*, 12–21.

Kaufman, J. S., Jaser, S. S., Vaughan, E. L., Reynolds, J. S., Di Donato, J., Bernard, S. N., et al. (2010). Patterns in office discipline referral data by grade, race/ethnicity, and gender. *Journal of Positive Behavior Interventions, 12*, 44–54.

Kounin, J. (1977). *Discipline and group management in classrooms*. New York: Holt, Rinehart, & Winston.

Krezmien, M. P., Leone, P. E., & Achilles, G. M. (2006). Suspension, race, and disability: Analysis of statewide practices and reporting. *Journal of Emotional and Behavioral Disorders, 14*, 217–226.

LaBrot, Z., Dufrene, B., Radley, K., & Pasqua, J. (2016). Evaluation of a modified check-in/check-out intervention for young children. *Perspectives on Early Childhood Psychology and Education 1*, 143–165.

Larrivee, B. (2009). *Authentic classroom management: Creating a learning community and building reflective practice* (3rd ed.). Upper Saddle River, NJ: Pearson.

Leataata Floyd Elementary School. (2020). About Leataata Floyd Elementary. Retrieved July 15, 2020, from https://leataata.scusd.edu/about

Lewis, T. (2015). Applied behavior analysis as a conceptual framework for understanding positive behavior support. In F. Brown, J. L. Anderson, & R. L. De Pry (Eds.), *Individual positive behavioral supports: A standards-based guide to practices in school and community settings* (pp. 107–122). Baltimore, MD: Paul H. Brookes.

Low, S., Cook, C. R., Smolkowski, K., & Buntain-Ricklefs, J. (2015). Promoting social–emotional competence: An evaluation of the elementary version of second step. *Journal of School Psychology*, *53*, 463–477.

Lucyshyn, J. M., Dunlap, G., & Freeman, R. (2015). The evolution of positive behavior support. In F. Brown, J. L. Anderson, & R. L. De Pry (Eds.), *Individual positive behavioral supports: A standards-based guide to practices in school and community settings* (pp. 3–25). Baltimore, MD: Paul H. Brookes.

Maggin, D. M., Zurheide, J., Pickett, K. C., & Baillie, S. J. (2015). A systematic evidence review of the check-in/check-out program for reducing student challenging behaviors. *Journal of Positive Behavior Interventions*, *17*, 197–208.

McIntosh, K., & Goodman, S. (2016). *Integrated multi-tiered systems of support: Blending RTI and PBIS*. New York: Guilford Publications.

National Center on Response to Intervention. (2010). *Essential components of RTI—A closer look at response to intervention*. Retrieved July 15, 2020, from https://rti4success.org/resource/essential-components-rti-closer-look-response-intervention

Nelson, J., & Gfroerer, K. (2017). *Positive discipline tools for teachers: Effective classroom management for social, emotional, and academic success*. New York: Penguin Random House.

O'Neill, R. E., Horner, R. H., Albin, R. W., Sprague, J. R., Storey, K., & Newton, J. S. (1997). *Functional assessment and program development for problem behavior: A practical handbook*. Pacific Grove, CA: Brooks/Cole.

Perle, J. G. (2016). Teacher-provided positive attending to improve student behavior. *Teaching Exceptional Children*, *48*, 250–257. doi: 10.1177/0040059916643707

Porter, D. (2003). A quiet place for rough moments. Retrieved July 15, 2020, from www.responsiveclassroom.org/a-quiet-place-for-rough-moments/

Responsive Classroom. (2020). *Principles and practices of responsive classroom*. Retrieved July 15, 2020, from www.responsiveclassroom.org/about/principles-practices/

Rimm-Kaufman, S. E., & Hulleman, C. S. (2015). SEL in elementary school settings: Identifying mechanisms that matter. In J. A. Durlak, C. E., Domitrovich, R. P. Weissberg, & T. P. Gullotta (Eds.), *Handbook of social and emotional learning: Research and practice* (pp. 151–166). New York: Guilford Publications.

Sailor, W., Dunlap, G., Sugai, G., & Horner, R. (2011). *Handbook of positive behavioral support*. New York: Springer.

Scheuermann, B. K., & Hall, J. A. (2016). *Positive behavioral supports for the classroom*, 3rd ed. New York: Pearson.

Semple, R. J., Droutman, V., & Reid, B. A. (2017). Mindfulness goes to school: Things learned (so far) from research and real-world experiences. *Psychology in the Schools*, *54*, 29–52.

Sugai, G. (2019, November). *Core MTSS & PBIS system features: Avoiding misrules*. Presentation, Traverse Bay Area Intermediate School District Regional Staff Development Day.

Sugai, G., & Horner, R. H. (2009). Responsiveness-to-intervention and school-wide positive behavior supports: Integration of multi-tiered system approaches. *Exceptionality*, *17*, 223–237.

Sugai, G., & Horner, R. H. (2020). Sustaining and scaling positive behavioral supports: Implementation drivers, outcomes, and considerations. *Exceptional Children*, *86*, 120–136. doi: 10.1177/0014402919855331

Sugai, G., O'Keeffe, B. V., & Fallon, L. M. (2012). A contextual consideration of culture and school-wide positive behavior support. *Journal of Positive Behavior Interventions*, *14*, 197–208. doi: 10.1177/1098300711426334

Upshur, C. C., Heyman, M., & Wenz-Gross, M. (2017). Efficacy trial of the *Second Step Early Learning* (SSEL) curriculum: Preliminary outcomes. *Journal of Applied Developmental Psychology*, *50*, 15–25.

Vincent, C. G., Randall, C., Cartledge, G., Tobin, T. J., & Swain-Bradway, J. (2011). Toward a conceptual integration of cultural responsiveness and school-wide positive behavior support. *Journal of Positive Behavior Interventions*, *13*, 219–229.

Weinstein, C., Curran, M., & Tomlinson-Clarke, S. (2003). Culturally responsive classroom management: Awareness into action. *Theory into Action*, *42*, 269–276.

Weissberg, R. P., Durlak, J. A., Domitrovich, C. E., & Gullotta, T. P. (2015). Social and emotional learning: Past, present, and future. In J. A. Durlak, C. E. Domitrovich, R. P. Weissberg, & T. P. Gullotta (Eds.), *Handbook of social and emotional learning: Research and practice* (pp. 3–19). New York: Guilford Publications.

Chapter 3

Engaging Students' Learning and Thinking Through Reading

Eric B. Claravall

Vignette

Mr. Nguyen is developing a poetry unit using Langston Hughes's poems for his 5th-grade language arts class. He realizes that Hughes's poems can provide a deeper understanding of the state of race relations in the United States, decades after slavery had been abolished. However, he understands that teaching poetry can be challenging because of his students' limited reading exposure to this genre. He also finds it challenging because he seldom uses poetry to anchor his students' literacy development. In designing his poetry unit, he aims to develop students' intellectual engagement with the text. He expects them to remain on-task when working in small group activities and sustain their interest in Langston Hughes's poems and social justice issues beyond this unit. As Mr. Nguyen explores, he finds a short film clip about the life of Langston Hughes online. He collects four poems that deal with African racial identity development. He also gathers news clippings, photos, political cartoons, and diary excerpts to develop his students' background knowledge of the Jim Crow era. The hurdle for Mr. Nguyen is not the development of his poetry unit. The challenge is how he can engage his students in learning the social justice theme in Langston Hughes' poems and writing an expository essay—analyzing the metaphor, allusion, and symbolism found in the texts.

This chapter situates the concept of academic engagement in students' learning and thinking through reading poetry. First, I define academic engagement as a multifaceted construct. Then, I ground the discussion of engagement using motivational theories and socio-cultural models. Finally, I demonstrate an instructional model that focuses on reading poetry as one of the ways to engage students in learning and thinking.

Engagement

Engagement, as a construct, has been defined in many different ways depending on the context (Bundick, Quaglia, Corso, & Haywood, 2014). In this chapter, I frame the understanding of student engagement as a multifaceted construct (Appleton, Christenson, & Furlong, 2008; Bundick, Quaglia,

Corso, & Haywood, 2014), within the context of academic learning in the classroom. Bundick et al. (2014) define academic engagement as having three components: behavioral, affective, and cognitive. When students are behaviorally engaged in their learning, they show sustained effort to understand the text and participate in different classroom activities (Chapman, 2003; Libby, 2004). On an affective level, students have a positive attitude toward learning, and they are committed to finish the assigned academic tasks (Jimerson, Campos, & Grief, 2003; Marks, 2000). Cognitively, engaged students develop short- and long-term plans to accomplish the task, self-regulate their thought to effectively and efficiently implement the plans, and exert mental effort to understand the concepts and master skills (Frederick, Blumenfeld, & Paris, 2004; Newman, Wehlage, & Lamborn, 1992).

Student engagement has been linked to academic achievement and subjective well-being (Finn & Rock, 1997; Newmann, 1992; Suldo, Friedrich, White, Farmer, Minch, & Michalowski, 2009). From a developmental perspective, classroom dynamics influence students' engagement in learning. At the core of this developmental process is the interactions between the three classroom elements—student, teacher, and content—that promote student engagement (Bundick, Quaglia, Corso, & Haywood, 2014). In elementary school classrooms, teachers exert influence on students' cognitive and affective engagement. When students perceive their teachers as caring, accepting, and supportive, students' levels of academic engagement increase (Weyns, Colpin, De Laet, Engels, & Verschueren, 2018). Also, providing authentic work and high expectations motivates students to learn (Marks, 2000). As students approach late childhood, adults' influence on students' cognitive and socio-emotional learning wanes, and peer influences increase over time (Buhrmester & Furman, 1987). This shift from teacher support to peer acceptance affects how engagement is enacted in the classroom. Hence, peer relationships influence the development of students' academic engagement in later elementary grades (Kindermann, 2007).

Teachers play an important role in keeping students' engagement in the classroom and developing lifelong learners. Over the last decade, we have learned enough about the nature of classroom engagement and effective interventions to keep students engaged in their academic development and optimize their learning potential. This chapter situates the multidimensionality of academic engagement in the classroom through teaching poetry. Central to the understanding of academic engagement is how context influences students' cognitive, affective, and behavioral engagement in learning. But first, it is important to understand the theoretical foundations of academic engagement.

Theoretical Underpinnings of Academic Engagement

Motivation

The word motivation comes from the Latin word *movere*, which means to move. How do we make students move to learn and develop academic skills? When you ask students what they do in their spare time, you want to know what motivates them to do this activity. Motivation is a theoretical construct that explains why an individual initiates, directs, persists, and maintains a quality of behavior to achieve a specific goal (Murphy & Alexander, 2000). Motivation is essential to keep students engaged in their academic work in the classroom. It is the machine that provides power to sustain the mental effort, directs the path to achieve the goal, and develops the disposition to frame the reasons for doing the task (Rubin et al., 2006). The first step a teacher takes when planning a lesson is to determine what the students are trying to accomplish when working on an academic task. Some students might need extrinsic motivation to initiate the task. This kind of motivation involves external rewards and contingencies necessary for students to complete the academic task. External motivation is common in younger children. Food and other tangible objects are powerful behavior reinforcers for many elementary school children. However, the use of tangible rewards can sometimes limit the students' motivation for learning. The rewards control the behavior of doing the task and do not necessarily drive the student to genuinely learn the task (Nichols & Berliner, 2008). Motivation is then attributed to extrinsic factors that led to the students' academic engagement. The use of external rewards to motivate students undermines the value of intrinsic motivation (Wentzel & Brophy, 2014). To temper the problem of behavior control in extrinsic motivation, providing genuine praise to students can enhance intrinsic motivation and promote perseverance and engagement in academic tasks (Henderlong & Lepper, 2002). When students are intrinsically motived to do the task, they see the value in learning, which can lead to long-term academic engagement in the classroom and beyond.

Flow and Optimal Learning Environment

Associated with intrinsic motivation is a psychological experience that involves an intense concentration while performing a certain skilled task. Imagine an artist working on his canvas for hours, attending to his brushstrokes that create lines, shapes, and colors. A pianist performs on stage with elegance and virtuosity, as his fingers magically touch the piano to recreate the music of Vivaldi. An Olympic swimmer glides in the water, seemingly unaware of the crowd's cacophony of cheers on the poolside. A child reads the book *The Lion, the Witch, and the Wardrobe* for hours uninterrupted, inhabiting the world of Narnia in her mind. All these individuals share a common experience that led to an optimal level of performance despite all the challenges and external factors that can constrain their achievement. Csikszentmihalyi (1990) called this optimal experience a flow. According to Csikszentmihalyi, the person who is in the state of flow is goal-directed and mentally focused; everything else external is irrelevant while the task is being performed.

Every time an individual engages in a task—learning the skills and practicing the steps to achieve mastery—the individual enters the state of flow at some point in his/her performance. The individual finds joy in doing the task, and thus, any challenges are overcome because of the intrinsic drive to perform the task with dexterity and elegance. This is common among painters, dancers, singers, athletes, and surgeons. Many accomplished artists, writers, doctors, lawyers, musicians, and athletes are deeply engaged in mastering their professional craft (Csikszentmihalyi, 1990). The hours and energy they put in to practice their skills have led to achieving the optimal level of performance. When performing their craft, they enjoy what they do despite the external pressure—be it the presence of an audience, an expectation from the public, or a life/death situation. As they practice their craft, they became oblivious of time and space. This is the flow moment.

When applied to classroom learning, the state of flow can be achieved when the skills are developed through multiple practices within a challenging and complex task. To achieve the state of flow, the student has to feel responsible for his or her growth and enjoy the different tasks the teacher provides. Students are more likely to be engaged in a task when this is novel, mentally stimulating, and relevant to their own life. This is an initial step to classroom engagement. Once the students are engaged, they add personal value to what they do and enter the state of flow (Csikszentmihalyi, 1997).

The Zone of Proximal Development

Engagement in learning can lead to the development of students' academic skills, and with multiple practices, these skills mature to a point of performing the task with efficiency, fluency, and accuracy without any support from adults. However, Vygotsky (1978) argues that the most important part of development is when a student is given a challenging academic task that necessarily needs an adult's support because it is beyond the student's capacity to accomplish the task independently. This transition space, from the stage of immature skills to the stage of approximating skills when done together with mature adults or peers, is the developmental stage called the zone of proximal development (ZPD), "the distance between the actual developmental level as determined by independent problem solving and the level of potential development as determined through problem-solving under adult guidance or in collaboration with more capable peers" (Vygotsky, 1978, p. 86).

While it is beyond Vygotsky's conceptualization of intellectual development, the role of academic engagement within the ZPD is hard to ignore. The process of mental maturation that happens within the zone interacts with the students' ability to sustain mental effort notwithstanding the challenging task and to keep that positive attitude toward learning intact. As the teacher models and scaffolds the steps involved in completing the task, the students' engagement can lead to the internalization of skills and builds on the foundation for doing the task independently.

How Do We Engage Students' Thinking Using Poetry?

Poetry is an underrated literary genre in the teaching of language arts, and the road that is seldom taken in literacy instruction to develop reading and writing skills (Elster & Hanauer, 2002; Henkin, Harmon, Pate, & Moorman, 2009; Hughes & John, 2009). Among the literary genres, teachers privilege fiction and non-fiction texts more when teaching literacy skills in the classrooms. Even though the popularity of the use of poetry in elementary and middle school classrooms is growing (Elster, 2010; Heard, 2009; Marcell & Ferraro, 2013), it remains disproportionately underutilized due to the Common Core Standards' emphasis on informational texts. The less we use poetry in the classroom, the more students think that poetry is mysterious, inaccessible, obscure, and complex (Andrews, 1991), or at worst, boring (Arenson & Kretschmer, 2010).

After a year of incorporating poetry in Mr. Nguyen's language arts class, many of his students have shown engagement in reading and writing. One day in spring, he received an e-mail from a parent:

> We were so excited to see Rajeev recite Fallen Leaf in the car back home with awesome expressions. It's fabulous how his voice could just rise and drop in the right places. It's great how the expressions bring so much meaning into the poem. He is very excited and wants to play Fallen Leaf on the piano. We are very glad that you teach Rajeev poetry and he loves it to heart. Thank you for reinforcing it to the kids.

This note from a parent has motivated Mr. Nguyen to engage students in developing their literacy skills through poetry. Reading poetry provides students with rich vocabulary words that emanate from the deepest part of their human emotion—sadness, anger, joy, exhilaration, and loneliness (Fletcher, 2002). As Robin Williams's character in the movie *The Dead Poets Society* emphatically describes:

> We don't read and write poetry because it's cute. We read and write poetry because we are members of the human race. And the human race is filled with passion. And medicine, law, business, engineering, these are noble pursuits and necessary to sustain life. But poetry, beauty, romance, love, these are what we stay alive for.

Although some books have been published related to the teaching of poetry to young children (e.g., Carter, 1998; Keyworth & Robison, 2015; Savren, 2016), research on how poetry is read in the classroom and how teachers use this genre in literacy learning provides limited empirical data (Elster & Hanauer, 2002). Yet, scholars and practitioners agree that poetry engages readers in developing their fluency, word-recognition ability, and confidence (Elster & Hanauer, 2002; Rasinski & Zimmerman, 2013; Wilfong, 2008).

Poems are also useful texts to use to support the literacy development of students with special needs. The relative brevity of words and plenty of spaces on the page seem less daunting for students who struggle in reading. Using one poem multiple times in a week, the reading teacher or reading specialist can focus on developing students' vocabulary knowledge, decoding skills, word identification, reading fluency, reading comprehension, written expression, and academic discourse.

To introduce students to poetry, the teacher begins by reading a poem aloud, letting them wonder, engaging them to create images in their mind, and suspending their textual interpretations and analysis. Then, this follows the explicit instruction of the basic elements of poetry: form (e.g., lines and stanzas), sound (e.g., rhyme, rhythm, alliteration, or onomatopoeia), language (e.g., metaphor, simile, personification, or symbolism), tone (e.g., emotion and attitude), and imagery (e.g., concreteness and meaning).

Consider the poem "Stopping By Woods on a Snowy Evening" by Robert Frost (Figure 3.1). The teacher tells the students that all poems have stanzas and lines. This can be explicitly taught by creating a box around the first stanza and underlining the four lines in this stanza. Then the students do the same for the remaining three stanzas. This provides multiple means of input for students to remember the structure of a poem. These steps can be repeated

Whose woods these are I think I know.
His house is in the village though;
He will not see me stopping here
To watch his woods fill up with snow.

My little horse must think it queer
To stop without a farmhouse near
Between the woods and frozen lake
The darkest evening of the year.

He gives his harness bells a shake
To ask if there is some mistake.
The only other sound's the sweep
Of easy wind and downy flake.

The woods are lovely, dark and deep,
But I have promises to keep,
And miles to go before I sleep,
And miles to go before I sleep.

Figure 3.1 "Stopping by Woods on a Snowy Evening" by Robert Frost

using another poem until the students can verbally identify the stanzas and the lines in the poem.

The elements of sound and language can be embedded in the teaching of vocabulary. Right at the beginning of the poetry lesson, the students learn the meaning of rhyme, rhythm, alliteration, onomatopoeia, metaphor, simile, personification, and symbolism. These vocabulary words can be revisited throughout the intervention period depending on the poem students read. For example, the rhyming scheme can be discussed in Frost's poem; direct students' attention to rhyming words like "queer/near" and "shake/mistake."

The teaching of tone is best learned within the context of reading comprehension and written expression. This adds another layer to students' inferential understanding of the author's attitude and emotion. For example, the teacher can lead the discussion on what feeling the lines evoke to the students when they read the following:

Between the woods and frozen lake
The darkest evening of the year.

When focusing on sensory details, the teacher can direct the students' attention to line 4 (*To watch his woods fill up with snow*) and line 12 (*Of easy wind and downy flake*). This provides a discussion point on imagery that the poet creates in the minds of the readers. The words in the text invite the readers to grapple with the concreteness of the idea and go deeper with meaning according to their experiential interpretation (Rosenblatt, 1978). Later on, the teacher can come back to the idea of sensory details when the students are ready to write a sentence that appeals to the students' sense of sight, sound, touch, smell, or taste.

Benefits of Using Poetry: Developing Literacy Skills

As mentioned earlier, teachers can use poetry to develop students' literacy skills. By reading a poem, students can learn new vocabulary, practice decoding multisyllabic or sight words, improve upon their reading fluency, use different reading comprehension strategies, and write a sentence or a paragraph. To explore more on teaching poetry see Box 3.1.

Box 3.1 Teaching Poetry

More to Explore

- Teaching poetry in primary school (Carter, 1998). This presents a comprehensive framework for teaching poetry to young children. Of significant importance to the RTI model, chapter three provides different strategies when planning a lesson and assessing children's poetry-making.

- Welcome to poetryland: Teaching poetry writing to young children (Savren, 2016). Written by a poet, this book describes the process of teaching students the process of writing poems using exemplar texts. In chapter two, the author provides sample writing exercises for students with special needs.
- Poetryfoundation.org. This website contains a wide collection of poems written by classical and contemporary poets. Visitors can listen to the audio recording of the poem, and educators will find this site rich with information and resources relevant to the teaching of poetry in the classroom.

Vocabulary

Poetry is rich with semantic networks that deepen and widen students' understanding of words (Sekeres & Greg, 2007). For instance, when we think of words associated with poems, a web of words can be created to reflect its relationship to the overall understanding of poetry (Figure 3.2). Words like metaphor, simile, onomatopoeia, rhyme, rhythm, personification, symbolism, and alliteration can be treated as specialized academic vocabulary words when learning the elements of poetry. In the succeeding lessons, the teacher can create a thematic unit where students can expand their understanding of these vocabulary words by reading a set of poems that focus on one poetic device—metaphor, simile, onomatopoeia, or personification.

Alternatively, depending on the length of the poem, the teacher can select three to five semantically complex words and front-load these vocabulary words before reading the poem. When using the poem "Stopping by Woods on a Snowy Evening" to 2nd and 3rd-graders, words like *farmhouse*, *harness*, *downy*, and *flake* can be used to create a vocabulary word map (Figure 3.3). Any of these quadrants can be changed to rhyming words, homonyms, antonyms, or polysemy, contingent upon the teacher's focus for each lesson. Then as the teacher reads the poem aloud, the students highlight these words on their

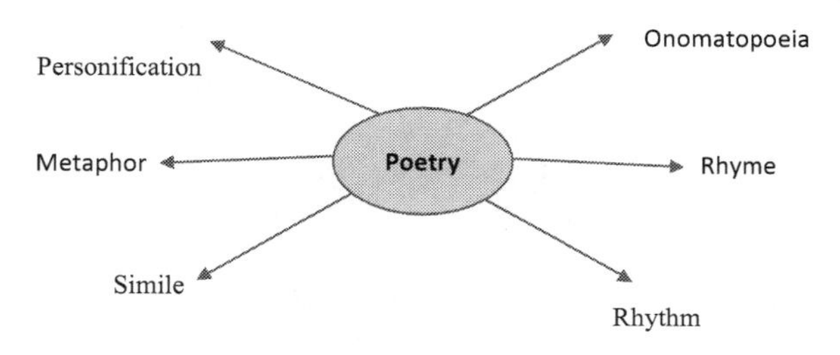

Figure 3.2 Word Web

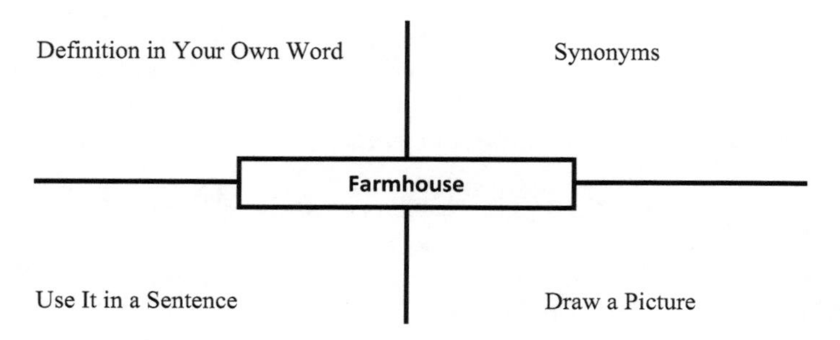

Figure 3.3 Vocabulary Word Map

copy. Using the margin, the students write a synonym for each vocabulary word or a denotative meaning taken from an online dictionary. These words will then be used later when the students are ready to write a sentence or two, describing the poem.

For upper-grade students, highlighting semantic anomalies (Elster & Hanauer, 2002) in poetry can be a good way to make the vocabulary lesson fun and engaging. For example, using the third stanza of Ingrid Michaelson's song "Be OK" demonstrates an example of a semantic anomaly (i.e., a gallery of broken hearts).

> *Open me up and you will see*
> *I'm a* ***gallery of broken hearts***
> *I'm beyond repair, let me be*
> *And* ***give me back my broken parts***

Decoding and Word Recognition

Reading poems is an excellent avenue to contextualize students' development of decoding skills and word recognition. Rather than practicing word-reading in isolation, students learn more in the meaning-making process when given continuous texts (Ehri & McCormick, 1998). Going back to Robert Frost's poem, teachers can prepare a word hunt activity after reading the poem aloud. Students in the primary grades can highlight words with a long vowel sound (e.g., woods, sleep, deep, near, between, frozen), compound words (e.g., farmhouse, without), words with inflectional morphemes (e.g., stopping, darkest, downy, lovely), or basic sight-words (e.g., these, his, he, to, my, the, and, but). This can be done parallel to their lessons on phonics or word study. Then, after highlighting the target words, students attempt to read the poem, while the teacher is on stand-by to provide a scaffold for other words that might be challenging to the reader.

Reading Fluency

One of the benefits of using poetry with students in tier 2 intervention is the affordances that the poems provide in the development of reading fluency. Reading poems is meant to be read aloud in the classroom (Lenz, 1992). As students practice reading the poem, the focus of instruction is on the accuracy of decoding words and automaticity of word recognition. Students get the chance to have multiple exposures to words that were taught as part of their decoding and word identification practice. Also, when reading a poem multiple times, the teacher can direct students' conscious effort of transforming the read-aloud strategy into a conveyance of emotion through changing the pitch, varying the intonation, or phrasing the lines. The teacher models the reading of each line of the poem in the beginning, and then the student mimics the way the teacher delivers the recitation of the poem. Also, students can practice reading poems aloud to each other. They can use this opportunity to help each other develop prosody—reading with expression through proper pacing, line by line. Classic poems, like the ones written by Shakespeare, are good exemplars to use to develop students' prosody. After a series of repeated readings, the students internalize the rhythm and the cadence in poetry (Marcell & Ferraro, 2013). In the long run, this can be a fertile ground for transferring the learning of prosody to the reading of narrative texts.

Frost's poem exemplifies rhythm and cadence when students read the last two lines of the fourth stanza:

And miles to go before I sleep,
And miles to go before I sleep.

The teacher can highlight the repetition of the lines as a poetic technique used by the author and the effect of punctuation marks on the overall cadence. These techniques affect students' delivery of the poem and, certainly, influence the mood of the poem towards the end.

Reading Comprehension

Reading poetry is not like reading a news article or a textbook where the reader's main purpose is to ferret out information. To appreciate poetry as a literary text, the teacher needs to build the student's "linguistic-experiential reservoir" (Rosenblatt, 1978). This experience is personal to the reader, and the validity of students' interpretation depends on what they bring to the text using their past experience and present personality (Rosenblatt, 1978). The reader's prior knowledge or background experience plays a significant role in the meaning-making process of reading poetry.

One way of enhancing students' prior sensory experience is through the use of a video. For example, to introduce Frost's poem, the teacher can show a video on YouTube that can anchor the students' visual and auditory experience as they think about the walk in the woods on a snowy night. In this video, the students listen to the poem read aloud while hearing someone's steps on crisp fresh snow, and seeing the ground and the naked trees enveloped with easy white downy flakes. Then the teacher can ask students to describe what they see and hear in the video. This discussion further amplifies students' visualization when they read the text the second time. This is how the teacher can mediate the challenging task of understanding imagery, figurative language, and poetic structure (Elster & Hanauer, 2002).

Close reading is another strategy that teachers can use to mediate understanding of the poems. As the teacher models the unpacking of symbolism and metaphors in poetry through the analysis of words and phrases, the students learn to read with a critical eye on the text. In addition, the teacher models close reading by finding significant details or patterns in the text through the analysis of poetic structure, form, and writing craft. For example, in Frost's poem, the teacher can use the following prompts to unpack the meaning of the first stanza:

- Describe the setting.
- What is going on in the speaker's mind when he passes through the woods?
- What is happening in the first stanza?

These prompts stir students' sensory images and propel them to make inferences based on their reading of the poetic world. Students share their ideas and the teacher writes these ideas on the board. The students, then, write these ideas on the margins as annotations. Later, these annotations will then be useful to students when discussing the main idea of the poem.

Focusing on the author's use of language is another strategy that the teacher can use to understand and appreciate poetry. For instance, in the second stanza of Frost's poem, ask students to highlight line 8. The poet alludes to the changing of the season when he says "the darkest evening of the year." This can be a good discussion point about the winter solstice. How does this affect the mood of the poem? How does this contribute to the overall understanding of the poem?

Reading and Writing Connection

After multiple exposures to the text and a deeper understanding of the language structure, syntactic patterns, and lexical density (Elster & Hanauer, 2002), the students are now ready to write a summary and analysis of the poem. Students' use of sentence frames provides a scaffold to their writing of a paragraph (Box 3.2). Initially, the teacher models the use of these sentence frames, emphasizing that each sentence has a specific focus. For example, the students start with a topic sentence. Then, they develop this idea further in the second sentence. In the third sentence, the students add their interpretation or analysis. Finally, the students write a conclusion in the fourth sentence. This four-sentence paragraph becomes an exemplar text for the next round of writing a poetry analysis.

This reading-to-writing cycle continues through 10 to 12 weeks of intervention. As students learn the structure of the paragraph, the teacher encourages the students to veer away from the use of sentence frames. This is the time the teacher encourages students to be creative or to expand their writing into two paragraphs. In the first paragraph, students can write an introduction about the poet's background based on the information they gather using online resources such as poetryfoundation.com, biography.com, and readingrockets.org. The second paragraph is the analysis of the poem.

Box 3.2 Differentiation of Instruction for English Language Learners

Four-Sentence Paragraph for Writing Poetry Analysis

First Sentence	The main idea of the poem ___________ is about ___________.
Topic Sentence	The poem _________ by _________ reminds me of ________.
	The central theme of this poem revolves around _____________.
	___________________ is the main thesis of the poem.
	_________________ wrote this poem to describe ____________.
Second Sentence	The poet used (what literary device?) to describe ____________.
Developing the Idea Further	It provides rich image of ________________.
	The use of words like _______ gives us clues to ___________.
	It talks about /describes the ______________.
Third Sentence	This reminds me of _____________.
Adding Your Own Interpretation	I like this poem because ________________.
	I learn that ___________________.
	What makes this an interesting poem is that _____________.
Fourth Sentence	I recommend this poem to other students who ______________.
Conclusion	If you like ______, then you will find this poem ____________.
	This poem is suited for those students who _____________.
	You will enjoy reading this poem because of _________.

Assessment

In a 12-week tier 2 intervention, running records can be collected four times to monitor students' progress. The teacher pre-selects four poems with an approximately similar number of words and level of complexity. These poems should not be part of the set of poems used for instruction. When introducing each poem, the teacher should provide a biographical sketch about the poet and front load at least three vocabulary words taken from the poem. Then, read this aloud before assessing the student's oral reading accuracy and fluency.

To calibrate the quantitative level of complexity, it is recommended to use online free Lexile analyzers. For example, "Stopping by Woods on a Snowy Evening" has 108 words with a Lexile measure between 800L–900L. Like any running records, the teacher collects data on accuracy and fluency rate, as well as qualitative data describing the student's prosodic reading of the poem.

Prosody is an important component of oral language that is relevant to poetry when reading aloud. To express emotion and tone, the reader needs to vary the recitation in loudness, duration, pitch, and pausing. While it is unrealistic to quantitatively assess students' prosodic development, I recommend using a scale or a rubric to gauge the student's qualitative development of prosody (Pinnell, Pikulski, Wixson, Campbell, Gough, & Beatty, 1995). Box 3.3 shows an example of an oral reading prosody scale that is based on Benjamin and Schwanenflugel's (2010) definition: placing stress on a particular word, phrase, or exclamation (loudness); lengthening vowels or the entire word for emphasis (duration); reading word phrases with proper pausing in commas (pausing). This scale is purely descriptive and dependent on the teacher's informed decision. Just like any scale, some students might fall between two levels.

Understanding poetry is different from understanding fiction and non-fiction texts. The reader plays an important role in comprehending the text. When using poetry to assess students' reading comprehension, avoid the pitfall of hunting for messages in the text (Brooks & Warren, as cited in Carillo, 2016). The text-centric way of understanding poems makes it even more difficult for struggling readers to fully appreciate the beauty of poetry. Instead, teachers need to privilege the role of the reader's "personality traits, memories of past events, present needs and preoccupations, and a particular physical condition" (Rosenblatt, 1978, p. 30) when assessing students' understanding of the poem.

To assess a student's comprehension of the poem, the following questions can be raised:

- What are some of the sensory words in the poem that conjure images of yourself or your life?
- How do you feel about reading this poem?
- Is this poem interesting to you? Why or why not?
- If the poet was right in front of you, what questions would you ask?

While these questions are subjective, they encourage students to think critically and interpret the poem within the context of a student's life experience. These questions are suggestive and not exhaustive. Teachers can create some comprehension questions that are tailored to the socio-cultural characteristics and demographics of the students they serve. For students who continue to struggle in understanding the text, rather than giving them open-ended queries, provide options that they can choose to answer these questions.

Teachers can also collect samples of a poetry analysis to demonstrate a student's writing progress in 12 weeks. These collections of writing samples will be part of the student's writing portfolio that the teacher reviews at the end of the intervention period. Alternatively, the teacher can administer an on-demand writing task after giving the running records and reading comprehension test. Students compose a one-paragraph summary and analysis for 15 to 30 minutes (Mackie & Dockrell, 2004). A rubric for scoring can be created using the following criteria (Koutsoftas & Gray, 2012): writing fluency, conventions, organization. For more details, see Box 3.4 for the on-demand writing rubric.

In summary, the assessment process involves collecting varied qualitative and quantitative data that represent students' development in the different literacy skills areas—reading accuracy, fluency rate, prosody, reading comprehension, spelling, writing fluency, and written expression. The teacher can collect these data on four different occasions over the 12 weeks of intervention. These data can be the basis for deciding whether the students respond to the intervention or a more intensive tier 3 intervention is needed.

Box 3.3 Assessment

Oral Reading Prosody Scale

Level	*Description*
Level 3	Reads at least two or three-word phrases with proper pausing in commas; consistently places stress on a particular word, phrase, or exclamation; rhythm is established; lengthening of vowels or the entire word for emphasis is consistent throughout the reading.
Level 2	Reads word for word with proper pausing in commas; occasionally places stress on a particular word, phrase, or exclamation; and rhythm and lengthening of vowels or words for emphasis is inconsistent.
Level 1	Reads word for word without proper pausing in commas; placing stress on a particular word, phrase, or exclamation is not observed; and rhythm and lengthening of vowels or words for emphasis is unobservable.

Box 3.4 Writing Assessment

On-Demand Writing Rubric

Criteria	Meets the Criteria *5 Points*	Developing Skills *3 Points*	Needs Improvement *1 Point*
Organization	Writes a paragraph with a topic sentence, two to three supporting sentences, a concluding sentence.	Writes a paragraph but missing one of the following criteria: topic sentence, two to three supporting sentences, or concluding the sentence.	Writes a paragraph but lacks coherence and missing at least two of the following criteria: topic sentence, two to three supporting sentences, or concluding the sentence.
Writing Fluency	Writes at least 100 words	Writes between 80 to 99 words	Writes 79 words or less
Convention	Writes strong grammatical conventions, and correct punctuations and capitalization; commits one or two spelling errors.	Writes weak grammatical conventions, makes one or two punctuation and capitalization errors, commits three or four spelling errors.	Writes weak grammatical conventions, makes three or more punctuation and capitalization errors, commits more than five spelling errors.

One Poem A Week: An Intervention Framework

In a 12-week intervention, students are exposed to the complexity of language in poetry and grapple with the lexical meaning the author used in creating images and evoking emotion in the poem. Through this process, the teacher plays a pivotal role in bridging the difficulty level of the text with the students' reading and writing skills. In the first five weeks, the teacher provides explicit instruction by scaffolding the different skills and modeling the strategies described in the previous sections of this article. Reading one poem a week for 30 minutes each day, students receive multiple exposures to the text. For five days, the teacher uses the poem with a different instructional focus as exemplified in the following examples.

Background Knowledge

On the first day, develop or activate students' background knowledge by giving a brief biographical background of the poet and the context in which s/he wrote the poem. Then, read the poem aloud as the students follow along with their text.

Vocabulary Development and Word Study

Pre-select three to five vocabulary words before reintroducing the poem to the students on the second day. Print these vocabulary words each on a white strip and present them to the students. Students highlight the words on their copy. Use the word web or word map to elaborate on the students' knowledge of the words. For students who need to expand their sight word reading, choose 10 sight words and ask them to highlight these words and write each word on a strip of paper. Alternatively, the student can use a small whiteboard—write the word, say it out loud, erase the word, and write it again. Then read the word in context.

Making Sense of the Language and Close Reading

On day three, ask the students to read the poem silently. As they read the poem, encourage the students to write annotations on the margin. Initially, this is done explicitly as the teacher models how to annotate the text. The teacher also models the think-aloud process, focusing on the specific target language element (e.g., metaphor, symbolism, onomatopoeia, imagery, simile, mood, or emotion). From modeling the strategies, the teacher can then provide activities that encourage students to talk about the poem and help each other write an annotation. Then, as students gain skills and confidence, a gradual release of responsibility can be implemented after week six or seven.

Poetry Recitation and Developing Fluency

Day four is devoted to reading the poem multiple times, encouraging students to recite the poem with a partner, and then in unison with the group. This is also a good time to administer running records and collect data on their fluency and accuracy rate. While collecting data, students can record their recitation and create a poetry podcast; the details are discussed in the next section.

Writing Exercise

On day five, review what has been discussed on day three. For example, provide an open-ended discussion related to the aesthetics of the poem. The writing exercises can be differentiated depending on the readiness of the student. Some students can write words and add pictures to complete this activity. Some can write a sentence and others can write a four-sentence summary using the sentence frame as a scaffold. At some point, allow students to write a paragraph without using the sentence frame.

Poetry Podcast

At the end of the intervention period, to celebrate students' hard work, the teacher can integrate technology and help students create their poetry podcasts (Box 3.5). The students get to choose a poem they read in the last 12 weeks. In preparation for the podcast project, students do online research about the poet's life and work, and based on the gathered information, they write a brief paragraph about the poet and a reflection on why they choose the poem. This preparatory activity leads to the writing of their script for their podcast. The students write the draft and then go through peer editing and revision.

A mini-lesson on the use of recording technology is recommended if this is the first time the students create a podcast. Mac users can use GarageBand. Alternatively, especially if the school uses Chromebook or PC, an online platform such as Huffduffer or Soundcloud can be used. A week-long lesson for about 30 minutes each day can be allocated to explore and learn the use of technology.

The poetry podcast provides students with engagement in reading poetry (Tarasiuk, 2009). It also motivates students to learn the different tools of digital literacy by connecting music, images, symbols, mood, and tone as they process information to create multi-modal online content (Alvermann, 2008).

Box 3.5 Technology

A Poetry Podcast

You can use any available recording device that you have in the classroom. However, I highly recommend the free version of Garage Band—if students have an iPhone, iPod, or Apple computer—because it has a complete sound library that students can embed as a background to their podcast and be creative in the process. To guide students in making their poetry podcast, create a simple protocol with a sentence frame to initially scaffold the writing of the script. Below is an example:

1. Introduce your name and the focus of your poetry podcast: Hi, my name is ________. This month, our poetry podcast focuses on the work of ________.

2. Tell brief biographical information about the poet. Students can read the paragraph that they wrote about the poet.
3. Describe the poem and what is it all about and share your analysis of the poem. Students can read the analytical paragraph that they wrote.

For more ideas on the use of podcasts in the classroom, I recommend the following articles:

- Bull, G. (November, 2005). Podcasting and the long trail. *Learning & Leading with Technology*, 24–25.
- Dlott, A. M. (April, 2007). A (pod)cast of thousands. *Educational Leadership*, 80–82.
- Smythe, S., & Neufeld, P. (2010). "Podcast time": Negotiating digital literacies and communities of learning in a middle years ELL classroom. *Journal of Adolescent & Adult Literacy, 53*(6), 488–496.

Chapter Summary

Engaging students in critical thinking and learning goes beyond cognition. When planning a lesson, one important question to ask is how to develop students' intrinsic motivation to learn literacy skills. In a poetry unit lesson, it is important to understand what students value in learning and how this affects the development of their literacy skills. The use of technology and multimedia can tap into students' intrinsic motivation and engage them in reading and writing about poetry. As you learned in this chapter, teachers play a significant role in engaging students to learn. Students find joy in learning when teachers plan activities and provide materials that are meaningful to them. When students find joy in learning, they achieve their optimal level of performance and improve academic achievement.

References

Alvermann, D. E. (2008). Why bother theorizing adolescents' online literacies for classroom practice and research? *Journal of Adolescent and Adult Literacy*, *52*, 8–19.

Andrews, R. (1991). *The problem with poetry*. Milton Keynes: Open University Press.

Appleton, J. J., Christenson, S. I., & Furlong, M. J. (2008). Student engagement with school: Critical conceptual and methodological issues of the construct. *Psychology in the Schools*, *45*(5), 369–386.

Arenson, R., & Kretschmer, R. E. (2010). Teaching poetry: A descriptive case study of a poetry unit in a classroom of urban deaf adolescents. *American Annals of the Deaf*, *155*(2), 110–117.

Balfanz, R., Herzog, L., & Mac Iver, D. (2007). Preventing student disengagement and keeping students on the graduation path in urban middle-grades schools: Early identification and effective intervention. *Educational Psychologist, 42*(4), 223–235.

Benjamin, R. B., & Schwanenflugel, R. J. (2010). Text complexity and oral reading prosody in young readers. *Reading Research Quarterly, 45*(4), 388–404.

Buhrmester, D., & Furman, W. (1987). The development of companionship and intimacy. *Child Development, 58*, 1101–1113.

Bundick, M. J., Quaglia, R. J., Corso, M. J., & Haywood D. E. (2014). Promoting student engagement in the classroom. *Teachers College Record, 116*, 1–43.

Carillo, E. (2016). Reimagining the role of the reader in the Common Core State Standards. *English Journal, 105*(3), 29–35.

Carter, D. (1998). *Teaching poetry in the primary school*. London, UK: David Fulton Publishers.

Chapman, E. (2003). Alternative approaches to assessing student engagement rate [Online]. *Practical Assessment, Research and Evaluation, 8*(13). Retrieved November 20, 2019, from http://PAREonline.net/getvn.asp?v=8&n=13

Csikszentmihalyi, M. (1990). *Flow: The psychology of optimal experience*. New York: Harper & Row.

Csikszentmihalyi, M. (1997). *Finding flow: The psychology of engagement with everyday life*. New York: Perseus Books Group.

Ehri, L. C., & McCormick, S. (1998). Phases of word learning: Implications for instruction with delayed and disabled readers. *Reading & Writing Quarterly: Overcoming Learning Difficulties, 14*(2), 135–163.

Elster, C. A. (2010). "Snow on my eyelashes": Language awareness through age-appropriate poetry experiences. *YC: Young Children, 65*(5), 48–50.

Elster, C. A., & Hanauer, D. I. (2002). Voicing texts, voices around texts: Reading poems in elementary school classrooms. *Research in the Teaching of English, 37*, 89–134.

Finn, J. D., & Rock, D. A. (1997). Academic success among students at risk for school failure. *Journal of Applied Psychology, 82*, 221–234.

Fletcher, R. (2002). *Poetry matters*. New York: Harper Collins.

Fredericks, J. A., Blumenfeld, P. C., & Paris, A. H. (2004). School engagement: Potential of the concept, state of the evidence. *Review of Educational Research, 74*, 59–109.

Fuchs, D., Fuchs, L. S., & Vaughn, S. (2008). *Response to intervention: A framework for reading educators*. Newark, DE: International Literacy Association.

Heard, G. (2009). Celestino: A tribute to the healing power of poetry. *Voices from the Middle, 16*(3), 9–14.

Henderlong, J., & Lepper, M. R. (2002). The effects of praise on children's intrinsic motivation: A review and synthesis. *Psychological Bulletin, 128*(5), 774–795. https://doi.org/10.1037/0033-2909.128.5.774

Henkin, R., Harmon, J., Pate, E., & Moorman, H. (2009). The road seldom taken: Poetry. *Voices from the Middle, 16*(3), 7–9.

Hughes, J., & John, A. (2009). From page to digital stage: Creating digital performances of poetry. *Voices from the Middle, 16*(3), 15–22.

Jimmerson, S. R., Campos, E., & Greif, J. L. (2003). Toward an understanding of definitions and measures of school engagement and related terms. *California School Psychologist, 8*, 7–27.

Keyworth, S., & Robison, C. (2015). *Writing and understanding poetry for teachers and students: A heart's craft*. Lanham, MD: Rowman & Littlefield.

Kinderman, T. A. (2007). Effects of naturally existing peer groups on changes in academic engagement in a cohort of sixth graders. *Child Development, 78*(4), 1186–1203.

Klem, A. M., & Connell, J. P. (2004). Relationships matter: Linking teadcher support to student engagement an achievement and related terms. *California School Psychologist*, *8*, 7–27.

Koutsoftas, A. D., & Gray, S. (2012). Comparison of narrative and expository writing in students with and without language learning disabilities. *Language, Speech, and Hearing Services in Schools*, *43*, 395–409.

Lenz, L. (1992). Crossroads of literacy and orality: Reading poetry aloud. *Language Arts*, *69*(8), 597–603.

Libby, H. P. (2004). Measuring students' relationship to school: Attachment, bonding, connectedness, and engagement. *Journal of School Health*, *74*, 274–283.

Mackie, C., & Dockrell, J. E. (2004). The nature of written language deficits in children with SLI. *Journal of Speech, Language, and Hearing Research*, *47*, 1469–1483.

Marcell, B., & Ferraro, C. (2013). So long robot reader: A superhero intervention plan for improving fluency. *The Reading Teacher*, *66*(8), 607–614.

Marks, H. M. (2000). Student engagement in instructional activity: Patterns in the elementary, middle, and high school years. *American Educational Research Journal*, *37*, 153–184.

Murphy, P., & Alexander, P. (2000). A motivated exploration of motivation terminology. *Contemporary Education Psychology*, *25*, 3–53.

Newman, F. M. (1992). Higher-order thinking and prospects for classroom thoughtfulness. In F. Newman (Ed.), *Student engagement and achievement in American secondary schools* (pp. 62–91). New York: Teachers College Press.

Newman, F. M., Wehlage, G. G., & Lamborn, S. D. (1992). The significance and sources of student engagement. In F. M. Newman (Ed.), *Student engagement and achievement in American secondary schools* (pp. 11–39). New York: Teachers College Press.

Nichold, S. L., & Berliner, D. C. (2008). Testing the joy out of learning. *Educational Leadership*, *65*(6), 14–18.

Pinnell, G. S., Pikulski, J. J., Wixson, K. K., Campbell, J. R., Gough, P. B., & Beatty, A. S. (1995). *Listening to children read aloud: Data from NAEP's Integrated Reading Performance Record (IRPR) at grade 4 (NCES 95-726)*. Washington, DC: National Center for Education Statistics, U.S. Department of Education.

Rasinski, T., & Zimmerman, B. (2013). What's the perfect text for struggling readers?: Try poetry! *Reading Today*, April/May, 15–16.

Rosenblatt, L. M. (1978). *The reader, the text, the poem: The transactional theory of the literary work*. Edwardsville, IL: Southern Illinois University Press.

Rubin, K. H., Bukowski, W. M., & Parker, J. G. (2006). Peer interactions, relationships, and groups. In N. Eisenberg, (Ed.), *Handbook of child psychology*, Vol. 3: *Social, emotional, and personality development* (6th ed., pp. 571–645). New York: Wiley.

Savren, S. (2016). *Welcome to poetryland: Teaching poetry writing to young children*. Lanham, MD: Rowman & Littlefield.

Sekeres, D. C., & Gregg, M. (2007). Poetry in thirds grade: Getting started. *The Reading Teacher*, *60*(5), 466–475.

Skelton, S. (2006). Finding a place for poetry in the classroom every day. *English Journal*, *96*(1), 25–29.

Suldo, S. M., Friedrich, A. A., White, T. N., Farmer, J., Minch, D., & Michalowski, J. (2009). Teacher support and adolescents' subjective well-being: A mixed-methods investigation. *School Psychology Review*, *38*(1), 67–85.

Tarasiuk, T. (2009). Extreme poetry: Making meaning through words, images, and music. *Voices from the Middle*, *14*(3), 50–51.

Vygotsky, L. (1978). *Mind in society*. Cambridge, MA: Harvard University Press.

Wentzel, K. R., & Brophy, J. E. (2014). *Motivating students to learn*. New York: Routledge.

Weyns, T., Colpin, H., De Laet, S., Engels, M., & Verschueren, K. (2018). Teacher support, peer acceptance, and engagement in the classroom: A three-wave longitudinal study in late childhood. *Journal of Youth and Adolescence*, *47*(6), 1139–1150.

Wilfong, L. G. (2008). Building fluency, word-recognition ability, and confidence in struggling readers: The poetry academy. *The Reading Teacher*, *62*(1), 4–13.

Chapter 4

Language and Literacy Development

Ana Garcia-Nevarez

Oral language development is the foundation for later literacy development (reading and writing). Young children will start by listening to the sounds of speech, and later they will begin to imitate them unless there are developmental delays that would impede children from developing normal language acquisition. In this chapter, we provide a broad spectrum to the study of language development and it will provide you with an understanding of how children acquire their first and second languages. We also explore the importance of literacy development, emergent literacy, and different methods for teaching young children reading. In addition, we will emphasize how parents and teachers can support young children's language and literacy development.

Language allows children, at a very young age, to learn and express their needs, emotions, and desires, to give and receive information. We, as humans, use language to communicate, to express our emotions and beliefs with one another. The most common tool to express this communication is oral and written language. In summary, it allows children to better comprehend the world in which they live.

As an innate process of human development, children learn such skills as listening and speaking without any formal instruction. Children learn these language skills by socially interacting with others in a verbal environment. Researchers have found that children as young as four or five years of age (preschool age) can understand and use sentences and grammar of their native language (Neuman & Roskos, 1993). The following section presents the theories that support language development.

The Theories of Language Development

Behaviorist Theory

Behavioral theorists believe that actions are shaped by responses to other individuals' performances so that behaviors that are reinforced become reinforced, and behaviors that are punished become inhibited. Therefore, humans stimulate language and children learn language as adults reinforce their speech. Through constant reinforcement, children recognize language as a means of gaining autonomy over their spoken utterances (Yaacob, 2016). The child behaves as though she/he had learned the structures of oral speech as a result of this imitation reinforced or inhibited processes. Language development continues as children grow older and learn the more complex structures of language which parents and teachers continually reinforce.

The Nativist Theory

A strong advocate of the nativist theory (also known as the innate hypothesis) is Noam Chomsky (1965), who believed that children are "prewired" for language, and that language is a process of normal human development. Chomsky explained children's ability to produce and understand new and novel sentences as an innate capacity – known as the *language acquisition device* (LAD) – dedicated to language and not to other forms of learning. Nativists try to investigate the internal logic of language structure and seek to explain how language is acquired (van der Walt, 1991). Children do not just imitate language they have learned, but test the rules they have verbalized. Through early trial and error, children formulate the rules for transforming the basic structures of sentences into all sentence types.

To compare these two theories, the behaviorist and the nativist, one would say that Chomsky would focus on the learner, in this case, the child. The behaviorist, on the other hand, would put the situation or the environment as its main focus.

The Interactionist Theory

The interactionist contemplates certain functions of language to be a combination of maturational and genetically determined. In other words, there is an interaction between the child's innate language abilities and the child's environment in order for language development and reasoning to occur. The nativist maintained that language development was biologically determined. The interactionist also believes that language development is innately determined; the difference, however, is that language development is also dependent on the age of the child. This interaction allows the child to formulate rules for communicating in that environment.

Box 4.1 Theory and Research to Practice Connection: ***Who are the two research proponents that support the interaction theory?***

Two proponents of the interaction theory are Vygotsky (1962) and Piaget (1955) who saw language and cognition as related components that occur during different stages of development: sensorimotor, preoperational, concrete operational, and formal operational.

Piaget argued that children developed language with the capacity for logical thought and reasoning, and that language reflects these capacities. He further advocated that children have innate cognitive abilities for language learning but, as these internal abilities grow and develop, children must interact with their environment and absorb these elements into their internal structure before moving into the next developmental stage. Children need a language-rich environment in order to be able to construct the phonetic, morphemic, syntactic, pragmatic, and semantic rules of language. They also need to practice language in a variety of ways for a variety of purposes.

Social interaction is a term coined by Vygotsky which happens between an infant and parents, siblings, teachers, and/or peers. This social interaction is a critical mechanism for children's language acquisition. Vygotsky viewed language as a uniquely human ability that exists independently of the child's cognition. Starting at about two years of age, general cognition and language are interconnected, and as the child gets older, these two processes begin to develop as separate entities. According to Vygotsky, children develop external speech, apart from thought, during the sensorimotor stage. During this stage, speech is followed by an action, but it is not connected to an understanding of speech as communication. Vygotsky maintains that human consciousness develops through words. During the preoperational stage, egocentric speech becomes inner speech, a sort of isolated talk that one hears in one's head. At the same time, children become conscious that through speech they can communicate ideas and concepts to others. This awareness becomes apparent in children's language development as they become interested in learning the names of things and constantly ask to be informed.

Vygotsky emphasized the importance of the adults' role in children's language development. He maintained that children develop their understanding of the rules and function of language from the adults who use that language in a regular and constant manner. At a young age, children have some concept of the meanings of adults' language even before they can pronounce the words. These vague concepts come closer to adult meanings in a series of more complex ways (not unlike Piaget's stages) as children interact with the adults. During these stages, adults supply more context for concepts as children build and refine their own meaning. Though the children construct meaning, the adults determine the direction of their thinking process.

Researchers emphasized how the adult language styles can affect the development of a child's language, and thus the child's capacity for more complex thinking processes (Hazan, Tuomainen, & Pettinato, 2016). Chapman (2000) has revealed that different parental language styles and interactions result in differing scores on children's intellectual and language tests. Parental styles that include such characteristics as reading to children, mealtime conversations, role-playing in pretend games, expanding children's language, and engaging children in different verbal interchanges are related to children's more extensive use of language and increased problem-solving ability (Lynch, Anderson, Anderson, & Shapiro, 2006).

In addition, studies have revealed that children learn the five general language structures before entering school: phonology (sound system), morphology (rules regarding words), syntax (grammatical structure), semantics (meaning of words), and pragmatics (appropriate usage). We will discuss these five language structures in the section to follow.

Language Structures

Phonology

Phonology is the study of sounds that deals with the delivery and sequencing of speech sounds. Infants, for example, have the ability to produce a broad range of sounds. The sounds infants make, during what is called the babbling stage, develop into the sounds heard in adult language. The sounds infants hear in the adult language are the sounds they put together to make sense of their surroundings; some examples of words infants put together based on what they hear are "coo," and "ahh" (which later develops to be "ma"). These sounds are indicators of the beginning of a child's mastery of the phonetic rules of language.

Morphology

Morphology is the study of the formation of words, the arrangement and content of words. In other words, morphologists examine the patterns of word-formation such as the root of the words, prefixes, and suffixes. Words are considered the smallest grammatical unit, called morphemes. Children learn new words and word forms when they start to understand that combinations of sounds have structural meaning. For example, they can correctly make words past tense, such as "fell" for "fall," and words in plural tense, "cats" for "cat." Children are able to understand the rules of morphemes before they enter school. They are not thinking of the rules of words as adults might be; however, they demonstrate their awareness of them when they overgeneralize and say "bited" instead of "bit." Overgeneralization is when we draw conclusions that are very general and are without facts. Children are capable of learning the rules for changing words early in their development. Researchers argue, however, that some words are not learned until six to ten years of age (Wood, 1976, p. 124).

Semantics

Semantics is the study of the meaning of words and word combinations. When children learn and store the sounds and patterns of a new word, they are learning to express the meaning; of course, this is all dependent on the situation in which the words are used. Consider Gabriela, a 24-month-old toddler who sees outside the window and notices that it is raining and says "raining." This word corresponds to a situation (event or thing) that is happening in her environment.

Syntax

Syntax refers to word order that suggests how words are combined to create sentences, for example, "it + is + raining + outside." As children's language develops, they learn that word order is important in producing meaning and understanding other people's messages. The rules of using grammar are said to be "in the heads" of native speakers, a "mental grammar," allowing children to create and understand grammar with extraordinary ease and speed (Jacobs, 1995, p. 4).

Pragmatics

Pragmatics is a set of rules concerned with the way language is used within different social contexts. Heath (1983), Labov (1970), Tizard and Hughes (1984), and Vygotsky (1962) pointed out that children learn from the conversations they have with others, from the community in which they live. Different social and cultural practices will be taught to children based on the specific rules of conversation of their home, social, or cultural customs. For example, the U.S. public school system uses the syntactic rules of Standard English and the politeness rules of a middle-class society. Other types of syntactic rules pertain to telephone conversations, classrooms, doctor–patient

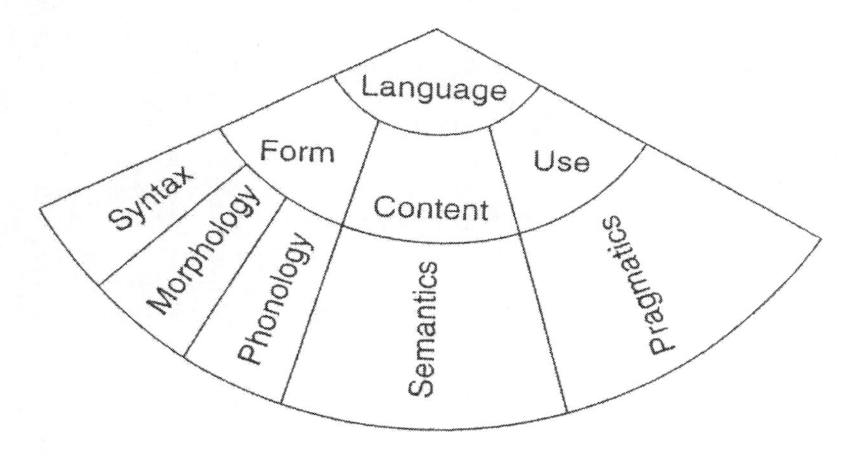

Figure 4.1 Relationship of Language Structures and Linguistic Components

relationships, jokes, and rituals (Otto, 2006). Children, early on, begin to learn that there are "polite and proper" ways to say things depending on where they are. For example, a five-year-old boy may use the polite convention of saying "please" whenever he is at school, but not at home where it may not be used as much. When school language practices are too different from a child's at-home language, teachers must respect that child's language and teach the child new sets of rules for different social contexts.

Language learning is an ongoing process. The verbal and rule development of phonology, morphology, syntax, semantics, and pragmatics are learned early as children socially interact with adults in their environment. As children progress in school, new learning will be built upon the basic language structures that children learn in their own social and cultural community of speakers. Figure 4.1 provides you with the pragmatics of language development that children go through.

Language Comprehension

Parents and teachers tend to speak differently to children than they do to adults. New language is being introduced by parents and teachers as the child gets older. When informal language is being used by young children, the conversation focuses on the here and now or on the direct type of activity or situation; this is referred to as context-dependent (Sousa, 2005). On the other hand, formal speech is more complex or content-independent (Sousa, 2005), which means that the individual may be referencing different possible conclusions to their story. Sometimes people say one thing but really mean something else, and they hope that the listener will grab those subtleties within the sentences.

These different language forms are a recognition that there are several types and levels of spoken language and language comprehension.

Unambiguous Communication

Unambiguous communication is the most basic type of language comprehension. The speaker is talking and creating sentences that are clear and unambiguous to the listener. The listener knows exactly what the speaker means and does not need to create any inferences. For example, when someone says, "drink your milk" or "sit on this chair," the interpretations are clear and unmistakable. Parents and teachers tend to use this type of language to young children when communicating for easy understanding and to get things done. As children get older, adults start using more reasoning and inferred language.

Inferred Communication

Inferred communication is a type of filtered form of speech. The speaker is talking and creating sentences that make inferences about meanings that go beyond what they said. This type of communication requires the listener to use their prior knowledge and experiences based on the information they heard to draw a conclusion. This is what some would call "reading between the lines" to come up with the conclusions. For example, when a parent tells a child that "milk contains calcium which is an essential nutrient for strong bones and teeth," what they are really telling the child is "drink your milk because it is good for you."

Young children have difficulty with inferred comprehension. Inferred language has to be taught and it takes practice. Teachers teach inferences through observation, predictions, and reading a text. If you are outside and notice that it is cloudy and windy, you can predict that it will rain. When reading, children should form questions about the character, setting, or anything they just read. After they have their questions, children should review their text to find evidence to answer their questions. Students usually use their prior knowledge about the character or topic which helps them with their answers and to make their own conclusions. Language comprehension involves different styles of speech that reflects the formality of the conversation, the context in which it occurs, the explicitness, and the underlying intent of the speaker. When all of this is obtained and children gain a good understanding of these patterns of speech, they will be better able to comprehend what they hear and read.

The Foundation for Literacy Development

Young children's oral or expressive language develops in stages, beginning with cooing around six to eight weeks of age. At around four to six months, most infants will begin to babble. Later on, their babbling reflects or echoes the intonation and expressive prosody (the rhythm of spoken language), such as the intonation of speech of their home language (echolalic babbling). At around one year of age, most infants will use single words and then develop two- to three-word utterances, known as telegraphic speech. In order to create developmentally appropriate learning activities for both infants and toddlers, the early childhood teacher needs to be aware of each child's level of oral language.

The development of spoken language competencies is a major accomplishment during the preschool years. All children will become relatively fluent in their primary language during the first four years unless there are developmental delays, cognitive impairment, or physical speech impediments. The ability to use language to communicate affects children's learning and their daily social interactions. Understanding spoken language gives children the foundation for later development of reading and writing skills. According to Moats (2000) "what children bring to the printed page and to the task of writing is knowledge of spoken language" (p. 16).

Literacy awareness begins right after birth. Even though the infant is unable to read or write, exposure to reading at an early age is critical for talking, reading, and, later, writing skills.

The eight-month-old child who cuddles up on her mother's lap to look at a picture book is developing early literacy understandings. Reading to young children on a regular basis is important for the developing sense of understanding that pictures and text have meaning and that they represent the spoken language. The 18-month-old scribbling on a piece of paper is preparing for writing in later childhood. Through these and other early learning experiences and practices, very young children slowly expand their knowledge of literacy concepts such as starting to see pictures and words in the front cover of the book and moving sequentially to the back, reading each line of print from left to right, and being aware that print has meaning (Bobys, 2000).

Emergent Literacy

The belief that learning to read and write has much in common with spoken language development is called emergent literacy. Emergent literacy has also been referred to as early literacy development. This approach endorses the belief that children begin learning about reading and writing as early as infancy. With appropriate materials and supportive adults, young children construct knowledge about print and gradually become more literate (Rhyner, 2007). Adults can help young children grow into readers and writers if they involve children in a print-rich environment and provide guidance during their developmental process.

Emergent literacy is the foundation for children's spoken language and their knowledge of written language. As a teacher, one can observe preschoolers engaged in emergent literacy behavior when they participate in literacy-related activities with others as well as when they interact with reading and writing on their own. When they are engaged in these practices, such as participating in book sharing, interpreting environmental print, and attempting to write and read what they write, they are using their spoken language abilities.

Implementing and Encouraging Emergent Literacy in the Curriculum

1. *Listening*. Children will develop the ability to listen so they can make meaning of their environment. They will be able to vary their listening strategies appropriately.

   Children will listen to the words and see the pictures as you read to them, and will come to an understanding that words have meaning.
2. *Speaking*. Children need to learn that the manner in which they speak depends on the situation. Informal speech is appropriate with friends and family, but more precise speech is appropriate at school. Children recognize that very clear and often formal speech is required in school when the teacher employs this language in giving directions for a classroom assignment.
3. *Reading*. Young children first learn to gain information and interpret picture signs from the environment. It may be that children first notice changes in the faces of their caregivers and interpret their moods, or they may notice clouds in the sky and know they may need a raincoat. For infants and toddlers, picture books, movable books, pop-up books, toys, and coloring and songbooks tend to attract young children's interest. Further, in a print-rich environment, children learn to recognize letters and words and eventually become aware of the relationships of sounds to letters and words. Finally, they learn a system for figuring out the unknown parts of a passage and discover that they are reading, and they learn to read different types of texts and establish different reasons for reading.
4. *Writing*. Children will develop the ability to write in an increasingly complex and precise manner in order to show appreciation, share information, request things, and give pleasure and amusement. In school and home environments, children need experiences in making marks on paper and in pretending to write. As these scribbles become more like letters and the nonsense letters come closer to phonetic spellings, children discover that these marks have meaning. Children's first discovery of connecting words and concepts is often their own name, and they become fascinated with the results. From these beginnings, children learn the often difficult but exciting task of putting their words and thoughts on paper. They eventually learn that there are different purposes for writing and that the style of writing changes with the purpose.
5. *Visual Environmental Print*. Environmental images and logos are important aspects of emergent literacy. These environmental images provide

children with a rich print exposure to words which facilitates children's recognition and understanding that images have meaning before they enter school. Viewing visual images, labels, and logos from the environment may assist children with word reading. Zhao, Zhao, Weng, and Li (2014) found that children were able to read words from the environment based on the contextual cues that pertained to these images. Environmental images that are familiar to young children, such as the McDonald's arch sign, are logos that allow children to make connections between words and their meanings, and understand that signs and words around us are meant to convey a message.

Creating a Quality and Rich Literacy Environment

Parents and teachers should provide children with a rich literacy environment that consists of meaningful reading and written materials that will lead to literacy development. A variety of books are the most obvious types of literacy learning materials. Starting in the infant and toddler programs, preschool teachers should provide children with access to a wide variety of books and should read to individuals or small groups of children (Kupetz & Green, 1997). Christie, Enz, and Vukelich (2003) described several key elements of creating a print-rich environment:

- *A variety of reading and writing supplies.* In addition to books, classrooms should have many types of print that serve real-life functions (labels on food items, restaurant menus, road signs.).
- *Reading and writing centers.* A well-equipped writing center should be the focus of these activities, with materials available throughout the classroom that encourage children to record important written communications (title the artwork, label the materials around the classroom, describe a block structure, make stories to accompany flannel board figures, etc.).
- *Showcase children's written products.* Teachers help children see the importance of writing by displaying their stories, books, and letters to friends and families.
- *Make reading and writing part of the daily routines.* Literacy activities can be highlighted during the routines of the school day. Labeling the attendance charts and the daily schedule, and reading the Pledge of Allegiance and the weather chart can be used for meaningful reading and writing experiences.

In addition to infants and preschoolers, kindergartners and elementary school-age children need a setting that is print-rich. Teachers should select books that are functional and provide educational messages; children's work should be posted on bulletin boards, blackboards, and in play areas. Children's own messages, labels, lists, and beginning writings should be part of these postings.

Writing and art centers should contain a variety of papers, pencils, crayons, paintbrushes, and magic markers. And children should be given the time and opportunity to discover what makes reading and writing work for them.

A developmentally appropriate classroom provides a safe and secure environment for all children. In addition to providing supportive opportunities for physical growth, cognitive development, and emotional well-being, this environment also needs to provide opportunities to develop language competencies. A literacy-rich environment will have these five characteristics:

1. A special area of the room for book reading and sharing,
2. A variety of language and literacy-related activities embedded throughout each day,
3. Opportunities for collaboration and communication,
4. Opportunities to explore and interact, and
5. Materials that are developmentally appropriate for the age group of the classroom.

Learning Materials and Activities

A language- and literacy-rich classroom will have materials that are age-appropriate and have been chosen to fit the developmental needs of the children in the classroom. For example, in an infant and toddler classroom, the books need to be picture books with large print; they should be sturdy and heavy-duty, such as cardboard, or be laminated because young children are just learning how to manipulate objects and often will mouth or chew on the object as they explore its features. Having pictures and big print is necessary since the children will be viewing and not reading at this age. As children get older, toddler or preschool age, they will begin to show interest in drawing and writing. With this age group, they will need to have materials that fit their developmental needs. For example, toddlers will need large and thick pieces of paper for fine motor skills, which refer to the control of movement in the arms and hands, particularly in the wrists, small joints, and muscles of the fingers (Beil & Peske, 2005), for their endeavors in early writing since they are in the process of developing small-muscle coordination. Other materials such as water markers, which are washable and non-toxic, and chalk should be available to them for practicing their writing and scribbling.

Young children's reading materials should be engaging and interesting; this will strengthen children's curiosity and motivate them to seek these kinds of reading activities. In addition to a wide variety of appropriate books, stuffed animals and puppets that resemble storybook characters will add interest to picture-book sharing and will encourage children to participate and use their language to express their understanding from viewing the images from the book (Soundy, 1997).

A quality preschool and elementary classroom curriculum provides learning opportunities that enhance the attainment of phonetic, syntactic, semantic, morphemic, and pragmatic language understanding. After teachers have established the individual needs of their children in the classroom, a more exclusive curriculum and language goals should be developed for those children. These language goals or objectives are often guided by each state with their state standards.

Box 4.2 Common Core Standards: *What is the purpose of the English Language Arts standards?*

The English Language Arts (ELA) standards are guidelines that define what students should learn and understand at a specific grade level. Learning to read, write, speak, listen, and use language effectively in a variety of content areas is what the ELA standard is endorsing as literacy skills required for college and career readiness. The ELA/literacy standards are designed to prepare students with the necessary skills and knowledge in literacy for life outside the classroom. These skills consist of critical thinking and the ability to carefully and thoughtfully read texts in a way that will help students understand and enjoy complex works of literature. Students will learn and apply persuasive thinking and research skills that are essential for success in college, career, and life. The Common Core standards vision is preparing students to be literate people in the 21st century.

Ultimately, the curriculum and lesson plans should have activities that are clear, coherent, and purposeful. Many sources of curriculum ideas and activities describe how to conduct specific activities but do not indicate why these activities should be used. As a result, teachers may implement activities without a full awareness of the potential of curriculum and language goals to foster language development. When teachers have a strong educational rationale for each learning activity, implementation of each activity is more focused and assessment of the learning outcome is more direct. When activities are implanted without a clear rationale or objective, the focus may simply be on keeping the children busy.

School-age learning activities and their potential for fostering language development are described in four categories of activities: read aloud, technology-based interactive educational tools, teacher-guided group activities, and daily routine.

1. *Read aloud*. Parents and teachers should encourage school-age children to read aloud. Reading aloud encourages independent reading. This gives

parents and teachers the opportunity to listen to the child's ability to read fluently, pronounce the words, and express with emotions what they are reading. Children are building the cognitive skills that reading aloud carries. Such skills consist of listening, thinking, making comments, and asking questions.

2. *Technology-based interactive educational tools.* The use of technology in elementary classrooms is growing in popularity. The internet and software programs are having a positive impact on children's reading skills. The Reporter Project conducted by Kinzer and Leu (1997) found that 6th-grade students' writing skills were better overall than those of same-age peers not using similar technology. Similarly, Moran, Ferdig, Pearson, Wardrop, and Blomeyer's (2008) study on middle school-age students found that both reading comprehension and the development of vocabulary were typically enhanced by the use of technology. The technology used in this study included media images, video, audio, hypermedia, and websites to assist reading and literacy. When students are allowed to conduct their own online research for homework or classwork, for example, this can give the students a sense of control, ownership, and agency in their own reading and writing development. However, it is important to maintain a balance between time typing and looking at a screen and time writing by hand and developing listening skills. Something to keep in mind is that certain elements of technology have the potential to impact reading and writing literacy in negative ways. The concern has not been whether computers should be in the classroom, but how they should be used (Smith, 1988; Mambretti, 1999). As teachers, we should keep in mind that computers and other software are tools to *facilitate learning.*
3. *Teacher-guided group activities.* Both large and small group activities are designed and directed by the teacher, and group size is an important factor to consider when deciding which type will be appropriate. It is easier for teachers to plan for an entire class group, but small groups are more suitable for young children because they provide greater intimacy, opportunity for conversation, and feedback. The length and frequency of whole-class activities should be limited with very young children due to the wide range of attention spans among this age group. They will vary in their listening comprehension skills and some may not be able to attend to speech that is directed to the whole group. Teachers should encourage children to participate in large group activities, but participation should be voluntary, and children should not be disciplined for choosing not to join in with the large group. Storybook reading has been shown to be crucial for emergent literacy and language acquisition. Rice felt that storybook reading "bridges the development of oral language skills and the emergence of print literacy" (Rice, 1995, p. 8). It has been reported that children who have had familiarity with early story sharing also have "greater success in

learning to read and write" (Slaughter, 1993, p. 4). Morrow (1989) has noted these benefits to children from storybook sharing:

1) Increased interest in reading,
2) Increased familiarity with written language,
3) Increased vocabulary development, and
4) Awareness of story structure.

Language-related goals for storybook activities include increasing children's listening comprehension and vocabulary, helping children become aware of the relation between speech and print, and encouraging children to learn and to recall how to sequence events.

4. *Daily routine.* Routine activities are those activities that happen on a normal basis and serve the institution's needs, such as taking attendance or taking care of children's physical needs (recess and snack time, dressing to go outside), and paying attention (listening to instructions). Routines often go unnoticed because they are not credited with any opportunity for important learning. However, routine activities provide opportunities for acquiring important language knowledge, such as conversational skills (during snack or lunchtime), and listening skills (when children listen to each other speak). Establishing specific language objectives for daily, routine activities can help to encourage developing conversational skills (pragmatic knowledge) as well as to enhance the other four forms of language knowledge: phonetic, semantic, morphemic, and syntactic.

Children's Books

Every classroom should have a book collection that invites children into its library center. Books covers should be at the child's eye-level. The International Reading Association (1998) recommended that elementary classrooms should have library centers for students to access at least five books for every child. Some of these books can remain in the center throughout the year, but rotating the books by removing or storing some from time to time and supplying different books will make the area more motivating and eager to return. The classrooms should develop guidelines that outline the rules and responsibilities of book handling. These rules should be designed to encourage children to return books to shelves, turn pages carefully, and respect quietness in the area.

There are many types of children's books available that are developmentally appropriate. For infants and toddlers, novelty books are fun, short, and entertaining: bath-time floating books, bedtime books that are soft; pocket-sized books, jumbo board and easel books; lift-the-flap books, movie-like flip-books, glow-in-the-dark books, potty training books, and sing-a-story books. Additional types of books appropriate for infants and toddlers are described by Kupetz and Green (1997):

- *Rhyme books*. Classical rhyme books (e.g., *Hickory Dickory Dock*) are fun books to read to very young children.
- *Listen and point books*. These books contain pictures or photos of familiar animals, toys, and/or family members. These books allow parents and teachers to say the names of the items and point to the pictures. Eventually, children can do the pointing and become more involved in the reading.
- *Touch-and-smell books*. Books that address the five senses introduce children to different textures and a variety of smells. This will get them actively involved in exploring the senses.
- *Board books*. These durable books are made with safe board-like materials that resist the pounding and chewing of young children. Many of the classical books are also bound as board books for infants and toddlers.
- *Early picture storybooks*. Many children are ready for books with simple storylines and clear illustrations that help tell the story.

Older children may require different types of books and Neuman and Roskos (1993) suggested the following categories of books for preschool and early elementary school-age children.

- *Adventure and fantasy*. These books can be fictional or non-fictional. Some of these books can be inspiring stories or mystery books. Examples are the series of *Harry Potter*, or *If You Grew Up At The Time of Martin Luther King*.
- *Informational books*. Books that share specific content on topics of interest to young children through words and pictures fit this category. *A Very Hungry Caterpillar* and *Charlotte's Web* are examples of informational books.
- *Picture books*. Books of this type contain mostly pictures and have limited print. Preschool children can learn many of the conventions of reading books (e.g., reading each page from left to right and top to bottom) while enjoying the pictures.
- *Predictable books*. These books have repetitive patterns that make it easy for children to predict what comes next. Many of the Dr. Seuss books fit this category. Examples of predictable books are *Green Eggs and Ham*, *Are You My Mother*, and *Horton Hears a Who?*).
- *Storybooks*. Although containing pictures on most pages, these books also provide children with an interesting storyline to follow. Examples of storybooks for elementary children are *The Velveteen Rabbit*, *The Snow Queen*, and *Hansel and Gretel*.
- *Beginning chapter books*. These books are more adult-like. They have limited pictures, complex plots, and are organized into chapters. Parents or teachers often read these books to primary school-age children. Examples of chapter books are *Harriet the Spy*, *Elijah of Buxton*, and *Becoming Naomi Leon*.

Parental Involvement

Parents contribute to and nurture the literacy development of their children. At the same time, the elementary school setting provides a critical role in literacy-related experiences for children. The quality literacy interactions that children have with their parents and teachers are associated with reading and writing. Research has shown that early literacy exposure and supportive parental reading opportunities are effective practices for preparing children to be successful in school. The box below lists parental characteristics that support literacy development through social and emotional behaviors.

Box 4.3 Promoting Social and Emotional Competence: *What can parents do to help their children be ready to learn to read by the time they start school?*

Parents can provide a high-quality language environment and support once the infant is born. Here are some important characteristics to consider.

Parents find reading to children important.

1. Parents encourage and value children's early attempts to draw and write.
2. Parents engage children in frequent book sharing.
3. Parents encourage children to explore with books.
4. Parents allow children to ask questions and respond positively to children's questions.
5. Parents engage children in frequent conversations.
6. Parents are sensitive to their child's age and prior experiences.
7. Parents use scaffolding and mediation.

Senechal and Young (2008) reported that there are three types of parental involvement: 1) parents reading to their children, 2) parents listening to their children read, and 3) parents tutoring their children in reading. They found that numbers 2 and 3, parents listening to their children read and parents tutoring their children in reading, had a significant positive effect on their children's reading success and development (Fawcett, Padak, & Rasinski, 2013). Additionally, Postlethwaite and Ross (1992), found that parental involvement and the time they spend reading to their children was a positive indicator of reading achievement among 2nd-graders. Furthermore, parents reading to their children as a toddler and in the early years of schooling, for example, has been found to have beneficial outcomes on students' literacy development in both the 3rd and 4th grade (Senechal & Lefevre, 2002; Senechal, 2006b).

Other factors affecting the development of children's literacy are the setting and events, whether they are planned or unplanned (Machado, 1999). The setting is the home or school where books, toys, materials, supplies, and the space to read are made available. The family's socioeconomic status is a huge variable that may determine the opportunities and access to reading materials that are available to the child at home. However, parents' imagination and resourcefulness may overcome the lack of financial resources. Parents can promote literacy through devoting their time, attention, and passion to reading rather than on how much money they need to purchase reading materials (Mavrogenes, 1990).

Other interesting and unplanned places for literacy development include shopping at the grocery store, the post office, and the bank. Ask the children to make drawings of what they observed at the various places and talk about these places and their experiences. Finally, planning a field trip to the library, museum, or aquarium that involves reading and writing can make literacy development fun and entertaining.

The Approches to Teaching Reading and Writing

There has been a historical debate about what approach to use when teaching children how to read. Educators have focused on using one approach exclusively instead of using a combination. In order to understand what these approaches are, we must first compare each.

Phonics

This approach to teaching reading and writing means that the teacher is using the sounds of letters and words. The child decodes the new word being introduced and they read the word by sounding the word out. Phonics advocates argue that letter-sound leads children to make automatic connections between words and sounds; this helps children form letters and blend the sounds as they read words. Reading using the phonics method emphasizes the understanding that sounds and letters have a relationship. This relationship is a link between what we say and what we read and write. As children combine sounds and letters together, this is called blending sounds; for instance, sounding out each letter of the word "bat." Following this example, the child learns that the letter B has the sound of "*b*" as in "*bag*." Later, the child learns how to blend two-letter sounds to make words like *br*ing (br blend).

Sight Words

Sight words are high-frequency words that are recognized by sight and cannot be sounded out or decoded. Sight words are part of phonic instructions; they are introduced after children have learned how to decode words and are able to sound out the words when reading. Sight words are high frequency or the most commonly occurring words in children's books. Dolch (1936) and Fry (1999) recommended that a list of words be memorized so that children could immediately recognize the words they frequently encounter when reading. The sight words are presented in flashcards so that the child's attention is focused on the written word, which helps them to become familiar with and memorize the word and its correct spelling. High-frequency sight words for first grade include "were," "going," "every," and "again." Proponents of sight words instruction argue that teaching children sight words speeds up the reading process and increases the students' reading confidence (Hayes, 2016). The essence of sight word reading is noted to be a cognitive process in which it enables the reader to automatically retrieve the spoken and written word from their memory (Ehri, 2013). However, opponents of sight word instruction argue that this process is a combination of memorization and guessing, and children are not learning how to read.

Whole Language

The whole language approach is a philosophical view influenced by the Constructivist theory on how children learn to read. Learning to read and write is a holistic approach in which children do not learn to break down the sounds of the words or decode them individually, but instead take the entire word and associate it with prior knowledge. That is, children make connections between reading the word and real-life experiences. Children memorize the sight vocabulary words introduced when reading. The belief with the Whole Language Approach is that children will learn to read and write the same way they learn to speak. The reading fluency is built and strengthened with real-life reading practices. For example, if the child sees the word "cat" written enough times with a picture of a cat, the child will associate that word while being conscious of the picture of a cat. An example of what this approach would look like is: a teacher reads a story to the class that includes the children's experience, "the rainbow fish." Included in the story are some keywords, for example, "blue," "shining," "happy," "water," "share," and "beautiful." These keywords are put up on a board for the children to see. The teacher then discusses how the words are spelled and what they mean, and gets the children to practice writing them. This method focuses on children learning to read by picking and retaining words that interest them, much the same way as they develop oral language.

Whole-Word

The whole-word reading method teaches children to read at the word level, also referred to as sight-reading. This method is part of the whole language approach. It does not use the decoding process and students are not sounding out words but rather learning to say the word by recognizing its written form. Context is important and images of pictures that match the words are used. Familiar words may initially be presented on their own, then in short sentences, and eventually in longer sentences. As their vocabulary grows, children begin to extract rules and patterns that they can use to read new words. Whole-word instruction involves associating word names with printed words. By repeated exposure to words, especially in meaningful contexts, it is expected that children will learn to read the words without any conscious attention to single units. Therefore, whole-word recognition, or the development of a whole-word vocabulary, is a goal of whole-word instruction. The idea behind this approach is that children can learn to recognize words through repeated exposure. Children are taught to read whole words and then parts of the words, whereas phonics teaches children to read parts of the word then the whole word.

Selecting one method of teaching children how to read is not always the most effective approach. Learning how to read is grounded in a personalized style where the methods of teaching and learning will be different for every child. Teachers are encouraged to try employing more than one approach. Recognizing that individual children differ in ability, interest, and learning styles is crucial to determine the type of reading method to be taught. A combination of all the methods work together and the reading approaches do not conflict with, but rather, complement each other.

Cursive Writing

With the recent changes in curriculum and National Standards, cursive writing is a skill that has been phased out across the country. The increase of computers, tablets, and Chromebooks, coupled with the onset of rigorous Common Core standards and new demands on teachers, has led to a gradual disappearance of cursive instruction across the nation. Cursive is not part of the Common Core standards; instead, keyboarding has become part of the curriculum. Prior to Common Core standards, kindergarten and 1st-grade teachers would teach print, then in 2nd and 3rd grade, children would start learning cursive. Berninger et al.'s (2006) study revealed that the process of writing on a piece of paper has an effect on the brain. That is, writing by hand keeps the mind sharper than typing on the computer, especially as we get older. Berninger argues that handwriting aids children to connect the letters into word units, which benefits children with spelling words. Additionally, handwriting helps children stay focus, retain more information, and improve motor skills (James & Engelhardt, 2012).

Second Language Acquisition

Second language acquisition (SLA) is the study of how children learn and create a new language system with either structured or unstructured exposure to the second language. Second language learners (L2) are confronted with the challenge of learning a second and new language that has different characteristics from their primary language (L1). The syntactic, semantic, morphemic, phonetic, and pragmatic aspects of the two languages may be significantly different. Languages from the same "language family" have similar characteristics and features, whereas languages from different language families will be dissimilar (Crystal, 1987). For example, French and Italian are considered to be in the Indo-European (Romance) language family and have some similarities such as the use of an alphabetic writing system and similar word stems (Otto, 2006). The Indo-European language is divided into 12 branches. Two of the ten are extinct. There are two branches that are spoken worldwide, the Italic, whose root language is Latin, and Germanic, whose languages are from English, Central European, and Scandinavian languages. On the other hand, Italian and Chinese belong to different language families and are distinctly different in not only the writing system used, but in other aspects of language as well, including four of the five general rules of language – syntax, semantics, pragmatics, and morphemes. The similarities or differences between the two languages influence second language acquisition. Children who are attempting to learn a language from a different language family will find it more difficult than if they were attempting to learn another language from the same language family. As the second language is learned, children build on their understanding of language by making connections and comparisons between their first and second languages. A second language that is noticeably different from the first language will require more effort to learn.

Bilingualism and Multilingualism

Bilingualism is a term that depicts the process whereby children acquire and use two languages (whether it is fluently or not is debatable among researchers), whereas multilingualism is acquiring and using several languages with the same amount of fluency. If children learn more than two languages they are considered to be multilingual. When children acquire two or more languages from birth, the process of learning is called "simultaneous," whereas other children acquire additional languages in a "sequential" manner. DeHouwer (1995) argued that children develop a second language very similarly to how they learn the first language. Language transfer has argued that we can transfer grammar, vocabulary, syntax, semantics, and culture to the L2 language. However, SLA can be predicted by the number of similarities between L1 and L2 (Language Transfer: Definition, Types & Effects, 2018).

Simultaneous Bilingualism

The child that acquires two or more languages from birth acquires these languages simultaneously – simultaneous language acquisition. These children usually receive language input in two or more forms from their parents, grandparents, other close relatives, or child care providers. Simultaneous language acquisition occurs before the age of three. Children acquiring two languages simultaneously follow three developmental phases. The California Department of Education (2009) has characterized the following three phases.

First Phase (Birth to Age Three Years)

1. The young child progresses through each language structure (phonology, morphology, syntax, and semantics),
2. The young child combines elements of language and begins to code-switch,
3. At age three, the young child acquires the rules of grammar,
4. The young child begins to make overgeneralizations (e.g., "goed" for "went"),
5. The young child begins to understand at least 1,000 words,
6. The young child starts producing several hundred words, however, the vocabulary words are fewer in one language versus the other, and
7. The young child begins to use a variety of language for different purposes.

Second Phase (Three to Four Years)

1. The young child begins to accurately pronounce words,
2. The young child begins to use conjunctions by increasing the length and complexity of the sentences produced,
3. The young child begins to use the "wh" questions when constructing sentences,
4. The young child begins to use concepts for time, quantity, and relationships,
5. The young child begins to use private speech,
6. The young child begins to express vocabulary, but its comprehension is limited,
7. The young child begins to participate in effective, appropriate conversations and in certain situations will modify their speech if it's not understood, and
8. The young child begins to use polite words in their speech, for example, "please" and "thank you."

Third Phase (Five to Six Years)

1. The young child uses more than six words per sentence,
2. The young child begins to make indirect requests and comparisons,
3. The young child begins to expand their vocabulary in both languages,
4. The young child begins to understand which language is effective in specific settings and individuals,

5. The young child begins to adjust their speech to the listeners and adds more details to clarify its meaning, and
6. The young child begins to produce word sounds more accurately and explores more complex sounds such as *v* and *w*.

Sequential Bilingualism

Sequential bilingualism begins by having the child learn one language first and then later he/she learns the second language (L2). Parents may prefer to use just one language from the child's birth and wait to introduce the second language, or it may be that the second language input may not be available directly after birth. For example, the child may have a babysitter or start to attend childcare with a caretaker who speaks a different language than the child. This is the case for many immigrant children in the United States whose native language is Spanish and second language is American English. This sequential learning seems easiest for younger children in their accent and grammar, but there is no empirical evidence that younger children are any more successful with vocabulary and syntax.

After the age of three, sequential bilingual children develop one language at home and a second with peers or in school. Although humans are capable of acquiring a second language at any age, by the late teens it is difficult for a speaker to acquire native speakers' pronunciation in a second language. In part, this difficulty may be that adult speakers use the communication strategies of their native language to interpret or translate the second language (Tao & Healy, 1996, 2002).

Situational Code-Switching

Code-switching is the process of switching from one linguistic language to another depending on the social norms, situation, or conversational context an individual may be involved with. Bilingual or multilingual speakers often demonstrate evidence of code-switching from one language to another. Code-switching was once believed to be a deficiency by the speaker; however, it is the result of functional and grammatical principles and is a complex, rule-governed phenomenon. Code-switching is systematically influenced by the context and the situation in which the individual lives (Auer, 1984; McClure, 1981; Penalosa, 1981; Poplack, 1981; Sanchez, 1983). Children start by code-switching single words, switching from one language to another (Lanza, 1992). Adults, on the other hand, tend to replace whole sentences (Huerta-Macias, 1981). This typically occurs when a word concept is not available in the language being used (e.g., proper noun or new terminology, referring to latest technological terms), or if a specific meaning is needed (Baker, 1996; Bhatia & Ritchie, 1996; Cloud, Genesee, & Hamayan, 2000; Lessow-Hurley, 2000).

Cod-switching for children appears to be a function of the listener in a conversation (McClure, 1981). Three characteristics of the listeners in a conversation are essential: perceived language proficiency, language preference, and social identity (McClure, 1981). Children under age five use proficiency and preference decisions for code-switching. Older children make finer distinctions and will consider the individual they are addressing, making sure that the individual will understand before they code-switch.

It is unknown as to why people code-switch. However, it is believed to be controlled by social or psychological factors, such as to show ethnic unity (Cloud, Genesee, & Hamayan, 2000; Lessow-Hurley, 2000). Huerta-Macias (1981) provided two reasons: 1) it may sustain the retention of the first language while a second is acquired, and 2) once the two languages are acquired, code-switching may ensure that both are used.

Box 4.4 Social Justice and Diversity: *Is code-switching detrimental for bilingual speakers?*

People engage in code-switching to fill in grammatical gaps when they are speaking. When they do not know a translation equivalent for a word, no matter whether they are using their more proficient or less proficient language. That is, children draw on the strengths of their more proficient language when they lack a grammatical construction word in their less proficient language.

Previous studies on language attitudes towards code-switching have found that monolingual and multilingual speakers often felt guilty for code-switching and had negative attitudes toward it (Hale, 1995; Martin-Jones, 2000). Further, code-switching was looked down upon and seen as a deficiency even when used in informal conversation between bilingual speakers. All participants saw it as a negative aspect of bilingualism (Hale, 1995). Further, code-switching in young children was seen as an example of poor cognitive abilities and parents were concerned that code-switching impacted their child's language development (De Houwer, 2009).

Nonetheless, bilingual and multilingual education research have found that code-switching is a cognitive asset; it has shown to be a sign of linguistic creativity and provides higher levels of cognitive executive functioning, in that the child justifies his/her language choice to manage the communicative demand of their environment (Genesee, 2003; Zhu Hua & Li Wei, 2005). This level of cognitive functioning has been supported by researchers explaining this complex structure of code-switching. This is suggesting that the ability to switch between languages during social conversation requires sociolinguistic understandings as well as high levels of linguistic knowledge (Gardner-Chloros, 2009).

Brain Hemisphere in Bilingual and Multilingual Children

The left hemisphere of the brain is the area that controls language and speech in all humans. For bilinguals and multilinguals, however, it may be different. The brains of bilingual and multilingual speakers may be organized differently than those of monolingual speakers (Sousa, 2005). The brain is organized based on a number of variables, such as the age when the L2 is acquired, the process of learning and usage, and the similarity of characteristics of the languages (van Hell & de Groot, 2008; Paradis, 2004). Learning a second or third language may involve right-hemisphere brain functioning which may not be involved in monolinguals. For example, Paradis (2004) had argued that if a second language is learned before puberty, there may be symmetrical brain representation – balanced brain image – within the two hemispheres. If the second language is learned after puberty, it may result in more complex brain organization and thus less symmetrical lateralization – less balance in one side of the brain (Paradis, 2004).

However, not all researchers concur with Paradis. In contrast to what was just stated about the symmetry of the brain, there may be more right-hemisphere involvement if the second language is acquired later (after puberty) compared to the first, and if the exposure to the second language was learned after age six (Sussman, Franklin, & Simon, 1982; Paradis, 2004). In addition, the involvement of the right hemisphere is more likely if the languages differ greatly, e.g., have a different alphabetic principle. The more proficient children are in their second or third language, the more the left hemisphere is involved. Overall, the reported differences between monolinguals and bilinguals may reflect different approaches in processing language rather than distinctive brain organizational differences (Vaid, 1983). For example, in some languages, such as Chinese, comprehension of the language requires background knowledge of historical, social, and cultural understanding, and the right hemisphere plays a critical role in incorporating such knowledge (Li, 2015). The normal brain lateralization is formed by two hemispheres, the right and left, and each function interdependently (see Figure 4.2). The left hemisphere is known for language dominance, analytical thinking, and detailed mathematical functioning, whereas the right is known for creativity, intuition, and the ability to see the big picture.

Effects of Bilingualism and Cognition

There is a very strong relationship between bilingualism and cognitive development. This association has been found in research studies conducted on young children. For example, when a young bilingual child attempts to communicate, he/she must select and focus on one language; this requires the brain to be flexible (Bialystok & Martin-Rhee, 2004). The internal language interference that the brain must resolve provides the cognitive muscles to work harder and be strengthened. If the cognitive functions are regularly exercised they will become stronger. Similarly, a child who plays soccer

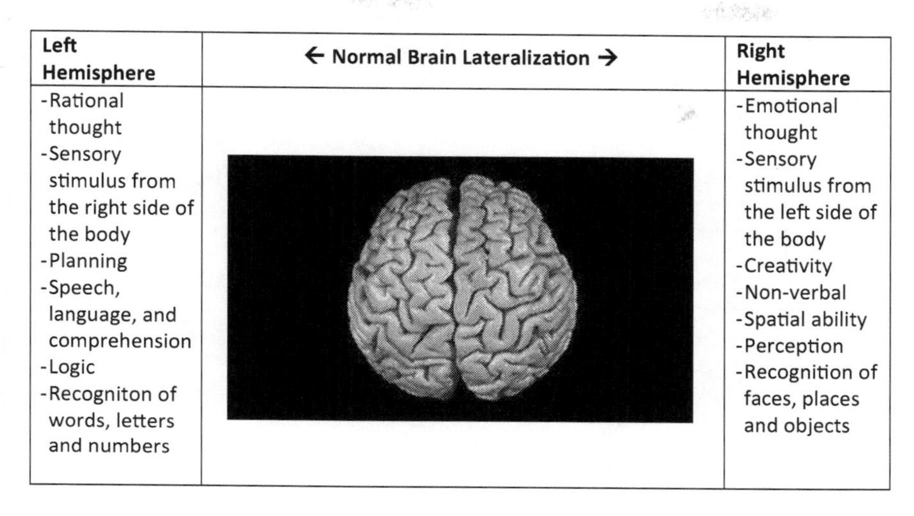

Left Hemisphere	← Normal Brain Lateralization →	Right Hemisphere
-Rational thought -Sensory stimulus from the right side of the body -Planning -Speech, language, and comprehension -Logic -Recogniton of words, letters and numbers		-Emotional thought -Sensory stimulus from the left side of the body -Creativity -Non-verbal -Spatial ability -Perception -Recognition of faces, places and objects

Figure 4.2 Brain Lateralization

regularly, for example, will become stronger, run faster, and be more agile compared to a child who doesn't play soccer. This is the same for a child who speaks and practices multiple languages regularly; he/she will develop a more powerful and flexible brain. The cognitive benefits of being multilingual are that these individuals are better at classifying objects, creativity, forming concepts, memory, metalinguistic awareness, problem-solving, role-taking, social sensitivity, and understanding complex instructions (Eckstein, 1986; Fang, 1985).

Chapter Summary

The young child will acquire language in the first three years of life. This is a period of intense language and speech development. Babies will begin recognizing their mother's language; then they will be producing speech sounds that they hear from their environments. Later, during the preschool years (three to five years of age), children will begin to read and write. Learning to read is a process that children must learn early on in their development to succeed in their later schooling. Parental involvement is critical in order to support a child's literacy environment, one that is rich with joint reading, drawing, singing, rhyming, storytelling, and playing games. Bilingualism and multilingualism are not a deficiency or a risk factor for delayed language acquisition. On the contrary, knowing two or more languages has multiple benefits so that children and adults can develop parts of their brain that help with cognitive skills. Research has also demonstrated that the bilingual brain uses both the left and right hemispheres for language processing.

References

Auer, J. C. P. (1984). *Bilingual conversation*. Amsterdam: Benjamins.

Baker, C. (1996). *Foundations of bilingual education and bilingualism* (2nd ed.). Philadelphia, PA: Multilingual Matters Ltd.

Beil, L., & Peske, N. (2005). *Raising a sensory smart child: The definitive handbook for helping your child with sensory integration issues*. New York, Penguin Group.

Berninger, R. D., Jones, A. J., Wolf, B. J., Gould, L., Anderson-Youngstrom, M., Shimada, S., & Apel, K. (2006). Early development of language by hand: Composing, reading, listening, and speaking connections; three letter-writing modes; and fast mapping in spelling. *Developmental Neuropsychology*, *29*(1), 61–92. doi: 10.1207/s15326942dn2901_5

Bhatia, T., & Ritchie, W. (1996). Bilingual language mixing, universal grammar, and second language acquisition. In W. Ritchie & T. Bhatia (Eds.), *Handbook of second language acquisition* (pp. 627–688). San Diego, CA: Academic Press.

Bialystok, E., & Martin-Rhee, M. M. (2004). Attention and inhibition in bilingual children: Evidence form the dimensional change card sort task. *Developmental Science*, 7, 325–339.

Bobys, A. (2000). What does emerging literacy look like? *Young Children*, *55*(4), 16–22.

California Department of Education. (2009). *Preschool English learners: Principles and practices to promote language, literacy and learning* (p. 36). Sacramento, CA: Author.

Chapman, R. S. (2000). Children's language learning: An interactionist perspective. *Journal of Child Psychology and Psychiatry*, *41*(1), 33–54.

Chomsky, N. (1965). *Aspects of the theory of syntax*. Cambridge: MIT Press.

Christie, J., Enz, B., & Vukelich, C. (2003). *Teaching language and literacy – Preschool through the elementary grades* (2nd ed.). New York: Longman.

Cloud, N., Genesee, F., & Hamayan, E. (2000). *Dual language instruction: A handbook for enriched education*. Boston, MA: Heinle & Heinle.

Crystal, D. (1987). *The Cambridge encyclopedia of language*. Cambridge: Cambridge University Press.

De Houwer, A. (1995). Bilingual language acquisition. In P. Fletcher & B. MacWhinney (Eds.), *Handbook of child language* (pp. 219–250). Cambridge, MA: Blackwell.

De Houwer, A. (2009). *Bilingual first language acquisition*. Bristol: Multilingual Matters.

Dolch, E. W. (1936). A basic sight vocabulary. *The Elementary School Journal*, *36*(6), 456–460. doi: 10.1086/457353

Eckstein, A. (1986). Effect of the bilingual program on English language and cognitive development. In M. Clyne (Ed.), *An early start: Second language at primary school* (pp. 82–89). Melbourne: River Seine Publications.

Ehri, L. (2013). Orthographic mapping in the acquisition of sight word reading, spelling memory, and vocabulary learning. *Scientific Studies of Reading*, *18*(1), 5–21.

Fang, F. (1985). An experiment on the use of classifiers by 4 to 6 years olds. *Acta Psychologica Sinica*, 17, 384–392.

Fawcett, G., Padak, N., & Rasinski, T. (2013). *Evidence-based instruction in reading: A professional development guide to family involvement*. Boston, MA: Pearson.

Fry, E. B. (1999). *1000 instant words: The most common words for teaching reading writing and spelling*. Westminster, CA: Teacher Created Resources.

Gardner-Chloros, P. (2009). *Code-switching*. Cambridge: Cambridge University Press.

Genesee, F. (2003). Rethinking bilingual acquisition. In J.-M. Dewaele, A. Housen, & Li Wei (Eds.), *Bilingualism: Beyond basic principles* (pp. 158–82). Clevedon: Multilingual Matters.

Hale, S. (1995). All those problems that bilinguals have: Codeswitching and the bilingual attitude. Paper presented at the Annual Congress of the Applied Linguistic Association of Australia, September 26-29, 1995, 20th Canberra, Australian Capital Territory, Australia.

Hayes, C. (2016). *The effects of sight word instruction on students' reading abilities*. Thesis. Fisher Digital Publications. https://fisherpub.sjfc.edu/education_ETD_masters/327.

Hazan, V., Tuomainen, O., & Pettinato, M. (2016). Suprasegmental characteristics of spontaneous speech produced in good and challenging commincative conditions by talkers age 9–14 years. *Journal of Speech, Language, and Hearing Research*, 59, 1596–1607.

Heath, S. (1983). *Ways with words: Language, life and work in communities and classrooms*. Cambridge: Cambridge University Press.

Huerta-Macias, A. (1981). Codeswitching: All in the family. In R. Duran (Ed.), *Latino language and communicative behavior*, 153–168. Norwood, NJ: Ablex.

International Reading Association. (1998). Learning to read and write: Developmentally appropriate practices for young children. A joint statement of the International Reading Association (IRA) and the National Association for the Education of Young Children (NAEYC). *Young Children*, *53*(4), 30–46.

Jacobs, R. A. (1995). *English syntax: A grammar for English language professionals*. Oxford, England: Oxford University Press.

James, K. H., & Engelhardt, L. (2012). The effects of handwriting experience on functional brain development in pre-literate children. *Trends in Neuroscience and Education*, *1*(1), 32–42. doi: 10.1016/j.tine.2012.08.001

Kinzer, C., & Leu, D. J. (1997). Focus on research the challenge of change: Exploring literacy and learning in electronic environments. *Language Arts*, *74*(2), 126–136.

Kupetz, B., & Green, E. (1997). Sharing books with infants and toddlers: Facing the challenges. *Young Children*, *52*(2), 22–27.

Labov, W. (1970). The logic of nonstandard English. In F. Williams (Ed.), *Language and poverty: Perspectives on a theme* (pp. 153–190). Chicago, IL: Markham.

Language transfer: Definition, types & effects. Ralica Rangelova, (2018, June 18). Retrieved from https://study.com/academy/lesson/language-transfer-definition-types-effects.html

Lanza, E. (1992). Can bilingual two year-olds code-switch? *Journal of Child Language*, *19*, 633–658.

Lessow-Hurley, J. (2000). *The foundations of dual language instruction* (3rd ed.). New York: Longman.

Li, P. (2015). Bilingualism as a dynamic process. In B. MacWhinney & W. O'Grady (Eds.), *Handbook of language emergence* (pp. 511–536). Malden, MA: John Wiley & Sons, Inc.

Lynch, J., Anderson, J., Anderson, A., & Shapiro, J. (2006). Parents' beliefs about young children's literacy development and parents' literacy behaviors. *Reading Psychology*, *27*, 1–20. doi: bmjqmb

Machado, J. M. (1999). *Early childhood experiences in language arts: Emerging literacy*. Albany, NY: Delmar Publishers.

Mambretti, C. (1999). Internet technology for schools. *Reference & User Services Quarterly*, *39*(1), 109–110.

Martin-Jones, M. (2000). Bilingual classroom interaction: A review of recent research. *Language Teaching*, *33*(1), 1–9. doi: 10.1017/S0261444800015123.

Mavrogenes, N. A. (1990). Helping parents help their children become literate. *Young Children*, *45*(4), 4–9.

McClure, F. (1981). Formal and functional aspects of the code-switched discourse of bilingual children. In R. Duran, (Ed.), *Latino language and communicative behavior*. Norwood, NJ: Ablex.

Moats, L. (2000). *Whole language lives on: The illusion of "balanced" reading instruction.* Washington, DC: Thomas B. Fordham Foundation. ERIC ED449465.

Moran, J., Ferdig, R. E., Pearson, P. D., Wardrop, J., & Blomeyer, R. L. (2008). Technology and reading performance in the middle-school grades: A meta-analysis with recommendations for policy and practice. *Journal of Literacy Research*, *40*, 6–58.

Morrow, L. (1989). *Literacy development in the early years.* Upper Saddler River, NJ: Prentice Hall.

Neuman, S., & Roskos, K. (1993). *Language and literacy learning in the early years.* Ft. Worth, TX: Harcourt Brace Jovanovich.

Otto, B. (2006). *Language development in early childhood.* Upper Saddle River, NJ: Pearson Prentice Hall.

Paradis, M. (2004). *A neurolinguistic theory of bilingualism.* Amsterdam,Philadelphia: John Benjamins Publishing.

Penalosa, F. (1981). *Introduction to the sociology of language.* Rowley, MA: Newbury House.

Piaget, J. (1955). *The language and thought of the child.* New York: World.

Poplack, S. (1981). Syntactic structure and social function of code switching. In R. Duran (Ed.), *Latino language and communicative behavior*, 169–184. Norwood, NJ: Ablex.

Postlethwaite, T. N., & Ross, K. N. (1992). *Effective schools in reading: Implications for policy planner.* The Hague: International Association for the Evaluation of educational Achievement.

Rhyner, P. M. (2007). An analysis of child caregivers' language during book sharing with toddler-age children. *Communication Disorders Quarterly*, *28*(3), 167–178.

Rice, M. (1995). Children's language acquisition. In B. Power & R. Hubbard (Eds.), *Language development: A reader for teachers.* Upper Saddle River, NJ: Merrill/Prentice Hall.

Sanchez, R. (1983). *Chicano discourse.* Rowley, MA: Newbury House.

Senechal, M. (2006). Testing the home literacy model: Parent involvement in kindergarten is differentially related to grade 4 reading comprehension, fluency, spelling, and reading for pleasure. *Scientific Studies of Reading*, *10*, 59–87. doi: 10.1207/s1532799xssr1001_4

Senechal, M., & Lefevre, J. (2002). Parental involvement in the development of children's reading skill: A five-year longitudinal study. *Child Development*, *73*, 445–460. doi: 10.1111/1467-8624.00417

Senechal, M., & Young, L. (2008). The effect of family literacy interventions on children's acquisition of reading from kindergarten to grade 3: A meta-analytic review. *Review of Educational Research*, *78*, 880–907. doi: 10.3102/0034654308320319

Slaughter, J. (1993). *Beyond storybooks: Young children and the shared book experience.* Newark, DE: International Reading Association.

Smith, F. (1988). *Joining the literacy club: Further essays into education.* Portsmouth, NH: Heinemann Educational Books.

Soundy, C. (1997). Nurturing literacy with infants and toddlers in group settings. *Childhood Education*, *73*, 149–153.

Sousa, D. A. (2005). *How the brain learns to read.* Corwin Press: Thousand Oaks, CA: A Sage Publications Company.

Sussman, H., Franklin, P., & Simon, T. (1982). Bilingual speech: Bilateral control? *Brain and Language*, *15*, 125–142.

Tao, L., & Healy, A. F. (1996). Cognitive strategies in discourse processing: A comparison of Chinese and English speakers. *Journal of Psycholinguistic Research*, 25, 597–616.

Tao, L., & Healy, A. F. (2002). The unitization effect in reading Chinese and English text. *Scientific Studies of Reading*, 6(2), 167–197.

Tizard, B., & Hughes, M. (1984). *Young children learning.* Cambridge: Harvard University Press.

Vaid, J. (1983). Bilingualism and brain lateralization. In S. Segalowitz (Ed.), *Language functions and brain organization*. New York: Academic Press.

Van der Walt, J. L. (1991). In search of a nativist theory of second language acquisition. In *Per Linguam*, 7(2), 3–11.

van Hell, J. G., & de Groot A. M. B. (2008). Sentence context modulates visual word recognition and translation in bilinguals. *Acta Psychologica*, *128*, 431–451.

Vygotsky, L. (1962). *Thought and language*. Cambridge: MIT Press. (Orig. pub. In 1934).

Wood, B. S. (1976). *Children and communication: Verbal and nonverbal language development*. Englewood Cliffs, NJ: Prentice-Hall.

Yaacob, S. (2016). Mentalist vs behaviorist: Chomsky's linguistic theory. *Global Journal Al-Thaqafah*, 6(1), 7–12.

Zhao, J., Zhao, P., Weng, X., & Li, S. (2014). Do preschool children learn to read words from environmental prints? *PloS ONE* 9(1), e85745. doi: 10.1371/journal

Zhu, H., & Li, W. (2005). Bi- and multi-lingual acquisition. In M. Ball (Ed.), *Clinical sociolinguistics* (pp. 165–179). Oxford: Blackwell.

Chapter 5

Mathematics

Sayonita Ghosh Hajra

Mathematics is everywhere! While growing up, children fail to see the beauty of mathematics, as rules and algorithms win over it. Thus, it is important to select tasks that engage children in mathematical thinking and conversation. Also, tasks must promote positive attitudes toward learning mathematics from a very early age. With this in mind, this chapter discusses three important elementary mathematical content areas: numbers and operations, geometry, and probability and statistics; task selections through the lens of a growth mindset; and strategies to foster positive mathematical identity in learners.

This chapter has four sections—mathematical content knowledge for TK–6 elementary pre-service teachers, tasks promoting right mathematical attitudes, selecting mathematical tasks with context, and cultivating successful mathematics learners.

Mathematical Content Knowledge for TK–6 Elementary Pre-Service Teachers

What are some important mathematical content areas for TK–6 elementary pre-service teachers? This section discusses three important elementary mathematical content areas: numbers and operations, geometry, and probability and statistics. It includes some recommendations of the National Association for the Education of Young Children (NAEYC) and the National Council of Teachers of Mathematics (NCTM) for mathematics education for three- to six-year-old children. This section also touches on specific Common Core State Standards for Mathematical Content, including Standards for Mathematical Practice for each content area.

Numbers and Operations

Putting it into Practice

"How many beans are scattered on the countertop?" Sami asked Mon, her four-year-old. Mon started picking one bean at a time and saying the number-name *"one, two, three, four, five, six, seven,..."*. Sami is wondering whether Mon understands the number-name "seven" represents seven beans.

Figure 5.1 Counting the Beans

Numbers and operations lay key foundations for children's mathematical learning. Numbers are used for quantification; for example, to describe "how many" of some objects or "how much" of something there are. There are different types of numbers: counting numbers, whole numbers, fractions, integers, decimals, etc. Young children first learn the counting numbers one, two, three, four, ... (Beckmann, 2014). Young children can identify number-names of counting numbers and their symbolic representations as early as two years of age (Gelman & Gallistel, 1978; Sella, Berteletti, Lucangeli, & Zorzi, 2017). The collection of counting numbers is an ordered sequence of numbers that starts at one, and each number has a unique successor and a unique predecessor except for one (Beckmann, 2014). Children need numbers to quantify how many of something there is. First, children must learn to recite the number-names in the correct order. Next, children need to connect the number-names with the process of counting objects; this requires children to associate each number-name with one and only one object in a collection. This process is known as "one-to-one correspondence" (Beckmann, 2014, p. 3). By four or five years of age, children understand the concept of one-to-one coordination for a collection of five or less than five objects (Baroody & Wilkins, 1999). At that age, children face challenges to track counted and uncounted objects in a large collection while counting objects (Fuson, 1988). Without effective tracking strategies, children might miss an object or might count an object multiple times (Baroody & Wilkins, 1999). Finally, a complete understanding of counting numbers entails connecting counting with the cardinality of a finite set (National Governors Association Center for Best Practices, 2010). The cardinality of a finite set is the total number of objects in the set. It is also the last recited number-name. For example, when counting one, two, three, and four, the last number-name "four" gives the total number of objects present in a particular set. Thus, for a complete understanding of counting numbers, children need to: a) recite the number-names in a particular order, b) develop one-to-one correspondence, and c) understand the cardinality of a set. This whole process, from reciting number names to the learning of cardinality, approximately takes one to two years (Sarnecka, Goldman, & Slusser, 2015). In another research study, Spaepen, Gunderson, Gibson, Goldin-Meadow, and Levine (2018) argue that understanding cardinality helps children conceptualize the ordering of the counting numbers and categorize number-names with lower and upper bounds, i.e., knowing the number-name "four" has exactly four objects, neither three nor five. This development process in children is crucial as it builds children's quantitative reasoning skills in terms of comparison of quantities; it helps children associate number-names appearing earlier in the counting list to smaller quantities and number-names appearing later to larger quantities.

Putting it into Practice

Reflection: Mon seems to recite the number-names and can associate a bean with a number-name. This suggests Mon has conceptualized one-to-one correspondence. To understand Mon's understanding of cardinality, Sami can ask Mon to give her seven beans. Mon gives her seven beans by associating each bean with a number-name. Then Sami can ask the same question again, "*So how many beans are here?*" If Mon starts counting from "*one*" again, then Mon has not conceptualized counting.

Once children progress from reciting and counting the number of objects in a collection, they learn how to write the numbers as symbols. The counting number symbols 1, 2, 3, 4... are merely symbols, and they could have been completely different sets of symbols (Beckmann, 2014). The representation of counting numbers as the base-ten system is one of the most powerful constructs of human history (Copeland, 1979). The base-ten system uses only ten distinct symbols, 0, 1, 2, 3, 4, 5, 6, 7, 8, 9, called the digits, and a specific way to position the digits in a number representing specific quantities called the place value of a digit (Beckmann, 2014). The meaning of the notation for "ten" is very crucial for understanding the base-ten system. For example, after exhausting all the nine digits 1, 2, …9, a collection of nine craft sticks along with an extra stick can be grouped to create a giant group of sticks, called a "bundle"(see Figures 5.2 and 5.3).

Conventionally, this bundle is called a "ten" and is denoted by 10. We read 10 from right to left; 0 refers to the place value for ones; 1 refers to the place value for tens. When a child understands the meaning of the digit 1 appearing in 10 as one bundle of ten or one group of ten and not just the digit 1, it means the child has started developing a sense of place value and the base-ten system (Beckmann, 2014). Various manipulatives such as craft sticks, base-ten blocks, Cuisenaire rods, etc. can help children develop an understanding of place value through activities involving the meaning of digits in a number.

Next, children learn about basic arithmetic that consists of various number operations, such as addition, subtraction, multiplication, and division. Most children use a variety of counting and external modeling strategies, such as physical objects, fingers, sounds, drawings, etc. to perform simple addition and subtraction problems even before they receive formal instruction in arithmetic (Carpenter & Moser, 1984). Over time, children rely on retrieval of answers from the memory over counting to solve addition problems (Geary,

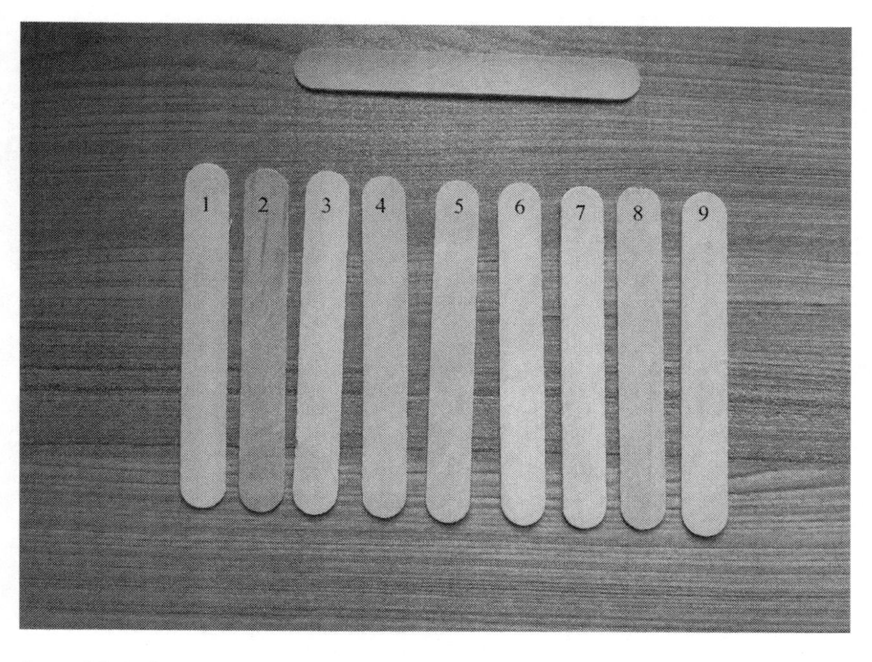

Figure 5.2 A Collection of Craft Sticks

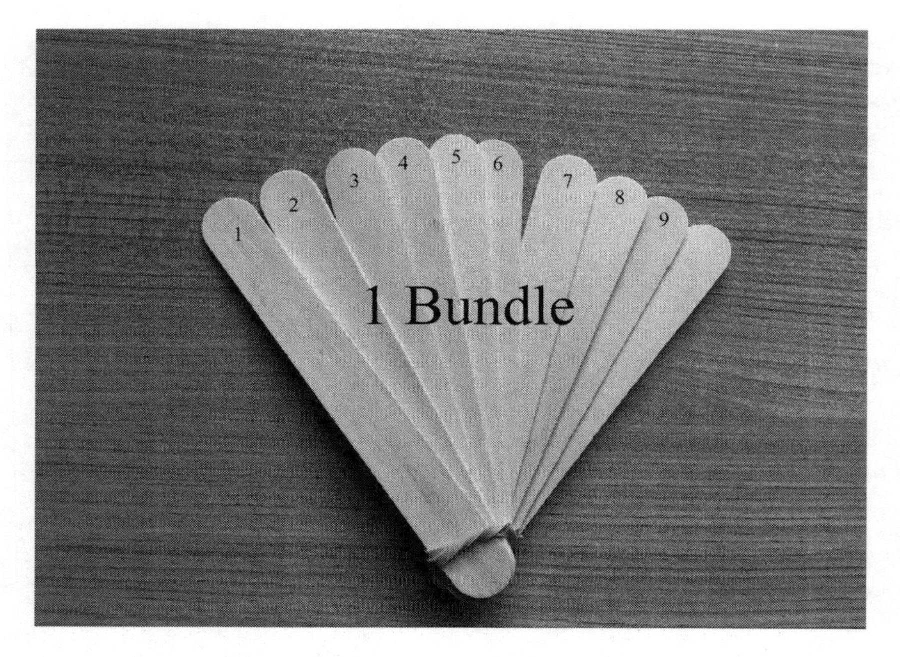

Figure 5.3 A Bundle of Craft Sticks

Brown, & Samaranayake, 1991). Knowledge of the place value is critical to doing arithmetic with two-digit numbers. Children also learn to compose and decompose numbers according to the place value and use it to understand various other number operations with single and multi-digit numbers, including some arithmetic properties of addition and multiplication, such as the commutative property, a + b = b + a, a x b = b x a.

Geometry

Putting it into Practice

"How much space does the yellow tile take up?" (see Figure 5.4) Sami asked Sun, her fifth-grader. Sun said *"2, 3, and 6."* Sami is wondering how Sun is visualizing the problem, and what those numbers represent for Sun.

Geometry is an important part of the elementary mathematics curriculum. It is the branch of mathematics that concerns properties and relationships of shapes and spaces. The mental representations of properties

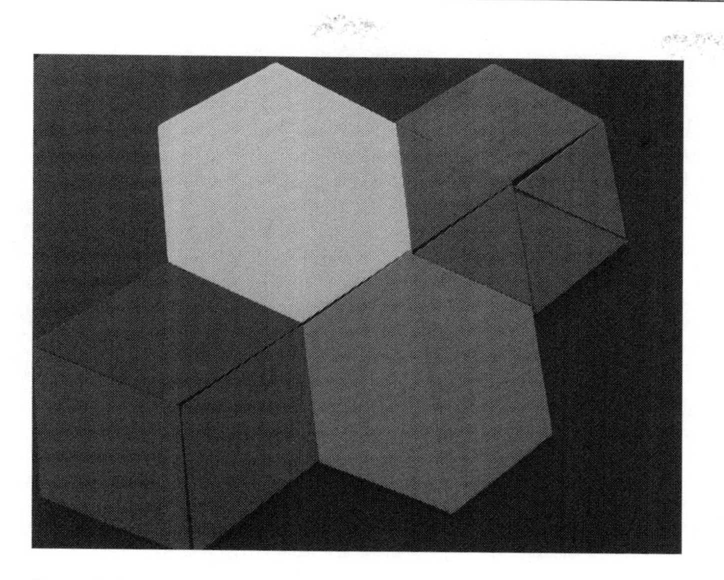

Figure 5.4 Area using Polygonal Tiles

and relationships of shapes constitute spatial thinking (Clements, 1999). Both geometry and spatial thinking are crucial in order to interpret and understand the world we live in (NCTM, 1989). They form the foundation of mathematical learning, including number and arithmetic skills (Arcavi, 2003; Clements, 1999).

A child's first conception of space is topological (Copeland, 1979), i.e., any shape is deformable by stretching or squeezing. Children of three to four years of age can distinguish closed and open features of a shape; older children can distinguish straight sides versus curved sides of a shape and also recognize shapes, even when shapes are rotated (Clements, 1999). Teachers can use visuals, manipulatives such as pattern blocks, geometric solids, Cuisenaire rods, wax craft sticks, etc. to promote flexible geometric and spatial thinking skills in children. Educators must provide children with various visual prototypes of geometric shapes as these shapes have a strong influence on children's thinking (Clements, 1999). For example, rectangles can be introduced by providing different examples and non-examples to help develop flexible geometric thinking in children (see Figures 5.5 and 5.6).

Kindergarteners can identify, compare, and compose shapes; around first grade, children learn about equal shares, and by second grade, children can divide simple polygons, such as rectangles and circles, into halves, thirds, fourths, etc. (National Governors Association Center for Best Practices, 2010). The concept of equal shares is visually represented through an equal amount of areas.

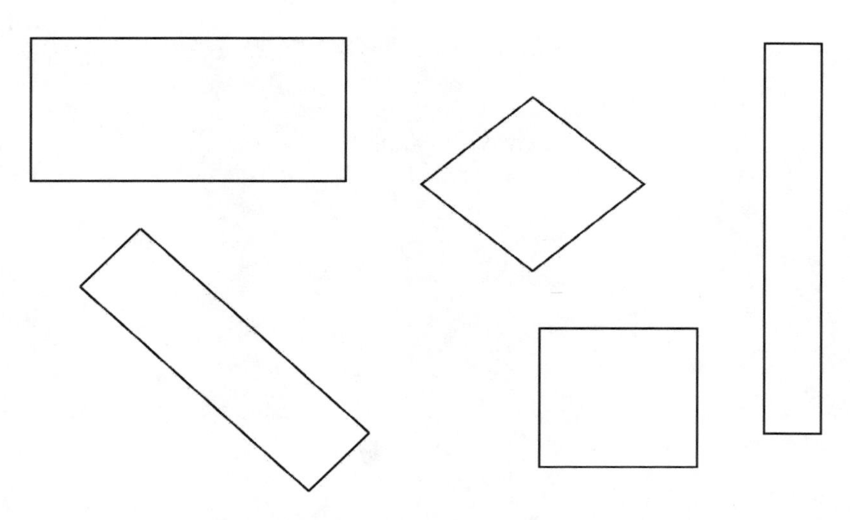

Figure 5.5 Examples of Rectangles

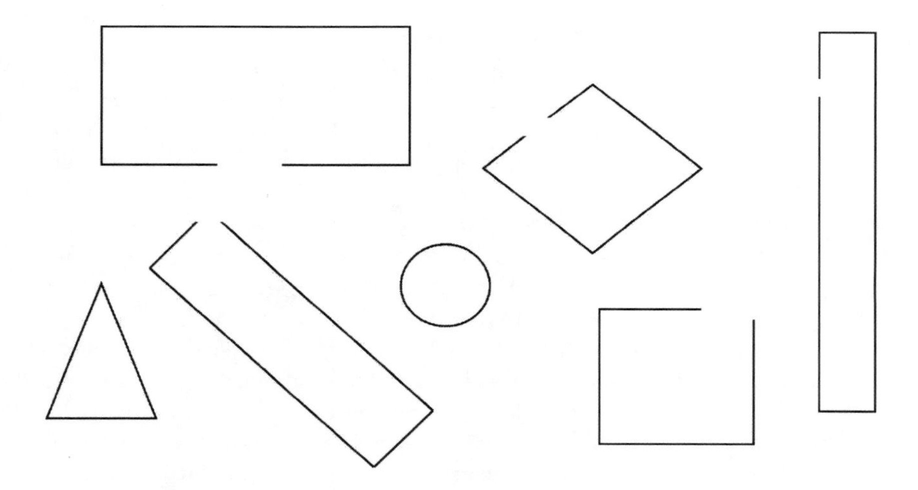

Figure 5.6 Non-examples of Rectangles

Area is one of the most important concepts in geometry. Area measurement is widely used in real-world applications, science, and technology (Martin & Strutchens, 2000), and more importantly, area measurement builds a foundation for understanding various foundational mathematical concepts such as fractions, multiplication, division, etc. (Clements et al., 2018). Area is the amount of two-dimensional (2D) space taken up by a 2D object. The concept of area is commonly quantified as the number of squares (the area-unit) that covers a planar figure without gaps or overlaps (Wheatley & Reynolds, 1996). For example, consider the 2D blue region in Figure 5.7; the area of the blue region is 35 square units. The figure shows some of the square tiles that have been used to cover the blue region.

The development of children's understanding of area measurement is a complex process that involves concepts of *covering*, *counting*, *subdividing*, and *spatial structuring* (Clements, Sarama, & Miller, 2017). Figure 5.7 illustrates these concepts. *Covering* involves iteration with an area-unit to cover the region physically or mentally (e.g., use of orange square tiles to cover the blue region); *counting* refers to the process of counting area-units (e.g., counting the number of orange

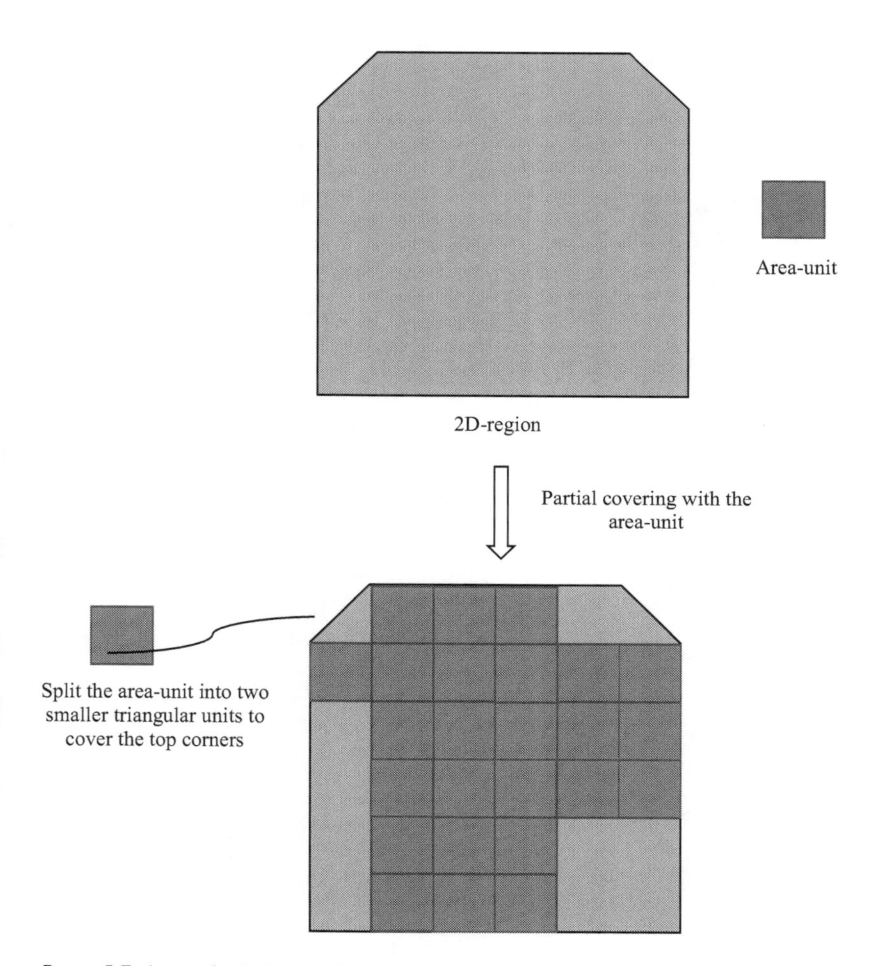

Figure 5.7 Area of a Polygonal Region

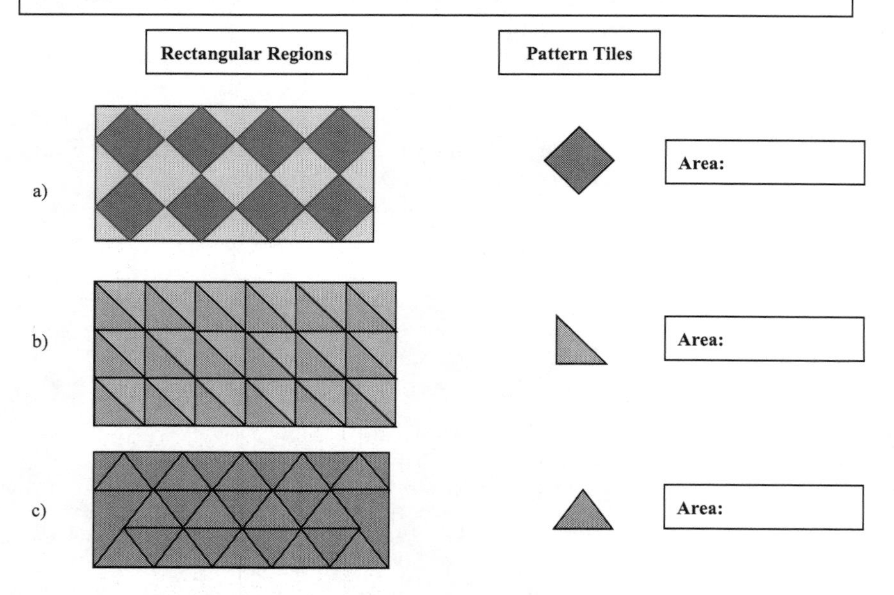

Figure 5.8 Area Using Square and Non-square Units

square tiles that covers the blue region without any gaps or overlaps); *subdividing* involves splitting area-units into smaller area-units (e.g., the orange square unit is divided into two triangular units to cover the top corners); *spatial structuring* is the act of forming a systematic physical, and ultimately mental, organization of a region into area-units (e.g., a systematic mental organization of the orange square tiles to cover the blue region). This understanding of area measurement involves conceptualizing area-units and its comparison with the given shape in consideration. Thus, children need to understand that any 2D object can serve as an area-unit. Teachers must provide area measurement tasks that include non-traditional square and non-square area-units as units of comparison (see Figure 5.8) to facilitate this understanding.

Putting it into Practice

Reflection: To understand Sun's understanding of the amount of space taken up by the yellow tile, Sami can ask Sun to show her the *2*, *3*, and *6* using the

Figure 5.9 Area Using Non-Square Tiles

colored tiles. Sami can ask Sun, "*2 of what? 3 of what? And 6 of what?*" The non-square tiles will help Sun to conceptualize area in terms of covering concept and to develop a sense of quantitative reasoning through comparison of non-square units and the 2D-shape.

Probability and Statistics

Putting it into Practice

Sami took Lalo, her eight-year-old, to go grocery shopping. They were in the cereal aisle when Sami asked Lalo, "*How many different varieties of breakfast cereals are there?*" Lalo walked along the aisle and identified nine different types of breakfast cereals. Sami is wondering what type of questions she should ask next to promote Lalo's understanding of data organization.

Figure 5.10 Varieties of Breakfast Cereals

Probability and Statistics are among the most applicable subjects of the twenty-first century. As early as pre-school and kindergarten, young children learn about classifying, sorting, and counting objects in categories (Leutzinger, 1990). Usually, by first grade, children learn to organize data in categories and compare data to answer which category has more or fewer data points (National Governors Association Center for Best Practices, 2010). A graphical representation of data points helps in the organization of the data. It may include charts, tables, or graphs with visuals and numerical information. A representation that uses real objects is called a real graph (Beckmann, 2014). Other examples of representation are a picture graph or pictograph, bar graph, double bar graph, multi-bar graph, line plot, etc. (see Figure 5.11). Graphing promotes inferential thinking that builds on the understanding of data comparison and relationships between data. Graphing in the elementary

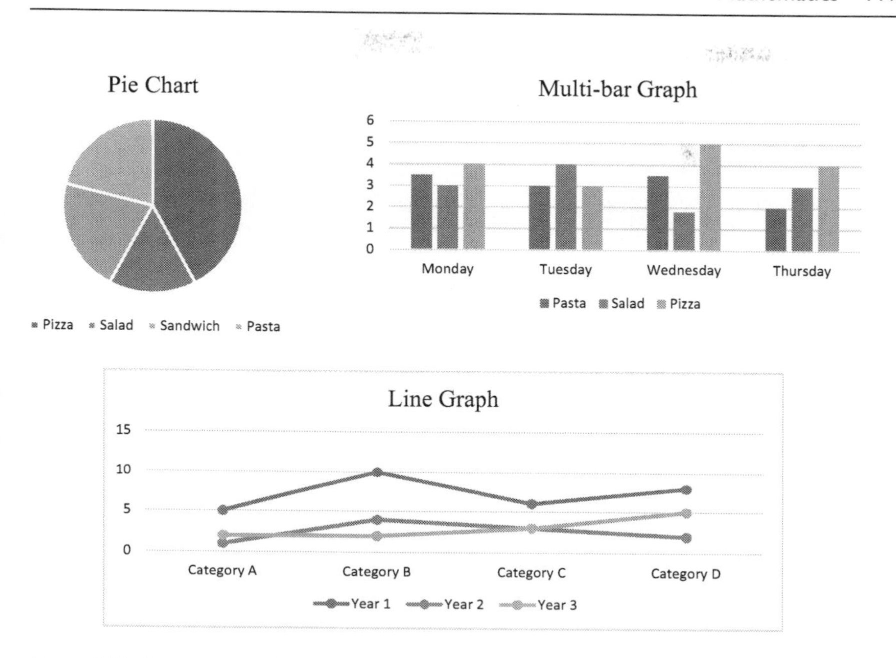

Figure 5.11 Examples of Different Graphs

mathematics curriculum provides an opportunity to integrate real-world problem-solving, as such graphing can be integrated with other subjects in an elementary school curriculum by assigning realistic projects (Leutzinger, 1990). Leutzinger further argues that graphing can be valuable if children create them in the context of solving real-world problems. These problems can come from science, social studies, language, or arts. Teachers can generate questions using information from their classroom and the local community. For example, how many different types of books are there in the classroom? How many different varieties of plants are there in the school's garden? How many different colored cars are there in the parking lot?

Graphs can also be useful to compute the probability of an event occurring (Leutzinger, 1990). The probability of an event is the likelihood of occurrence of the event, quantified by numbers between 0 and 1, 0 representing the impossibility of the occurrence, and 1 representing the definite occurrence of the event. The probability is connected with the concept of chance and predictions. Although understanding of the notion of chance develops in children around the age of 11 (Copeland, 1979), younger children can learn to use the words "likely," "more likely," "less likely," etc. in the context of everyday language (Leutzinger, 1990). Teachers can use small projects in the classroom to promote decision-making skills in children. For example, they can ask students from fourth to fifth-grade levels to predict about lunches that will be served in the cafeteria the next week from graphs displaying varieties of lunches served in the cafeteria for the past weeks. Children can learn to analyze these graphs and draw conclusions. They can use the words very likely, highly likely, less likely, etc. in response to the question. In this way, children can apply the knowledge of graphing to solve problems from day-to-day life. Teachers can also ask children to create questions and use the data to answer those questions.

Putting it into Practice

Reflection: Lalo is organizing the cereal data into different categories. Sami can ask questions that can involve data comparison, such as "*Which variety of breakfast cereal has more choices available in the store and how do you know that?*" or "*Are you going to buy that type of breakfast cereal? And why?*" These questions promote children's decision-making and reasoning skills.

Box 5.1 Common Core and Other Standards

Some Recommendations of NAEYC and NCTM for Mathematics Education for Three- to Six-Year-Old Children

Teachers and professionals should

- Provide ample opportunities for children to use their intuition and explore mathematical ideas, such as sorting, classifying, counting, comparing quantities, and noticing patterns in daily activities.
- Connect mathematical learning with children's daily experiences, informal knowledge, and backgrounds, including home, culture, and community.
- Foster children's problem-solving and reasoning skills using appropriate mathematics curriculum and teaching practices.
- Maintain a coherent curriculum that builds on what children know and need to learn progressing through a sequence of important mathematical ideas.
- Assess children's mathematical knowledge and skills regularly to support children's mathematical learning.

(NAEYC, 2010)

Some of the Common Core Mathematics Standards in Different Grade Levels for Numbers and Operations, Geometry, and Probability and Statistics

In the kindergarten's *Counting & Cardinality* domain of the Common Core State Standards, children learn number-names, count up to 100 using ones and tens, and understand the relationship between numbers and quantities, counting, and cardinality.

In the kindergarten through fifth grade *Number & Operations in Base Ten* domain of the Common Core State Standards, children learn to use place value, and understand properties of operations to perform arithmetic with whole numbers and decimals.

In the third grade *Geometry* domain of the Common Core State Standards, children learn to partition shapes into equal parts and use fractions to express the area of each part.

In kindergarten through fifth grade's *Measurement & Data* domain of the Common Core State Standards, children learn to classify and organize data into categories, draw various graphs such as pictures, bar and line plots, and infer from the data.

(National Governors Association Center for Best Practices, 2010)

Standards for Mathematical Practice

The following are examples of the mathematical practices that children are engaged in while learning about numbers and operations, geometry, and probability and statistics:

Make sense of problems and persevere in solving them: children can explain the problem to themselves and use various tools such as objects, graphs, tables to address the problem.

Reason abstractly and quantitatively: children can quantify objects and make sense of how many or how much of something there is.

Construct viable arguments and critique the reasoning of others: children can construct arguments in supporting their decisions using drawings, objects, graphs, etc. Children are engaged when they listen and ask questions to each other about those arguments.

Model with mathematics: children can relate real-world shapes with geometrical objects.

Use appropriate tools strategically: children can use objects, diagrams, and graphs to organize data to examine a problem.

Attend to precision: children can communicate their mathematical ideas with others.

Look for and make use of structure: children can use the area-unit as a measurement tool and look for the structure of the area-unit for quantitative comparison.

Look for and express regularity in repeated reasoning: children can tell the amount of space a two-dimensional shape takes up by looking at a partial covering of the shape by square units and can identify the same when the area-unit is one-half of the square or made up of two squares through reasoning.

(National Governors Association Center for Best Practices, 2010)

Tasks Promoting Right Mathematical Attitudes

Putting it into Practice

Sun used to be very good in mathematics through fourth grade. Lately, Sami is noticing her fifth-grader is struggling in mathematics and using the phrase, "*I am not good at math*" very often. Sun is giving up very easily, and getting frustrated. Sami is wondering what she should do to change Sun's attitude.

Mathematical learning and attitudes are deeply intertwined. Positive or negative attitudes about learning are often manifestations of the past experiences of the learners. For example, negative attitudes about mathematics are evident when children experience mathematical learning by memorizing rules instead of experiencing why such rules work and/or are needed (Willis, 2010). Prolonged negative attitudes may cause stress that can affect children's cognition, as one cannot use thinking skills when stressed (Willis, 2010). Teachers and professionals can promote children's cognition through proper guidance and quality instruction. One of the key features of quality instruction is the selection of cognitively demanding tasks (National Research Council, 2001). Various other studies describe critical characteristics of productive mathematical tasks (Hart, 2013; Mueller, Yankelewitz & Maher, 2010; Suzuka et al., 2009; Zaslavsky, Watson, & Mason, 2007). These characteristics include developing children's reasoning through multiple representations, methods and strategies, and multi-layered tasks, and providing connections to their experiences and opportunities for reconceptualizing previously learned content (Boaler & Staples, 2008; Stein, Smith, Henningsen, & Silver, 2009; Yackel, Underwood, & Elias, 2007). Productive mathematical tasks allow children to solve a problem via multiple representations, provide opportunities to each

Figure 5.12 Developing attitudes towards mathematics

learner to contribute using multi-layered tasks, and use children's existing knowledge and experiences.

This section focuses on the development of tasks that support children's mathematical cognition and discusses tasks that involve doubts, confusion, or some form of uncertainty that can promote children's mathematical competencies.

Tasks that Develop a Growth Mindset

Every individual has beliefs about their own learning and intelligence; some believe intelligence grows with hard work and others believe intelligence is fixed (Dweck, 2006). Dweck calls the former a *growth mindset* and the latter a *fixed mindset*. Several studies (Blackwell, Trzesniewski, & Dweck, 2007; Cury, Da Fonseca, Zahn, & Elliot, 2008; Good, Rattan, & Dweck, 2012) have shown that when one changes their mindset from fixed to growth, their learning outcomes and intellectual achievements grow.

A child's mindset is critical in their development as a mathematical thinker. Parents and teachers play an important role in shaping a child's mindset. Appropriate growth phrases should be used to praise a child's efforts rather than praising smartness or talent (Dweck, 2006). Boaler (2016) argues that anyone can be successful in learning mathematics in school when given proper guidance and teaching. In this endeavor, task selection is crucial. Educators should use rich mathematical tasks to engage children in meaningful learning. A rich mathematical task promoting a growth mindset must have the "five Cs"—*Curiosity*, *Connection-making*, *Challenge*, *Creativity*, *and Collaboration* (Boaler, 2016, p. 58). Teachers can integrate the five Cs into any task by engaging children in conversations about the mathematics they are learning, asking them about their approaches to solving a task, and encouraging them to listen to all the approaches being presented (Boaler, 2016). Teachers must welcome different ways of representing a problem and different approaches to solutions of the same problem, and must acknowledge different viewpoints. It is equally important that teachers create a classroom space where they can regularly discuss productive failures and struggles in learning with their students. Also, Boaler (2016) recommends that teachers add visualizations to problems, and ask students to connect the visualization with the mathematics involved. She also recommends providing tasks with a wide range of levels so that children have access to the problems at the very bottom level, where children can reason and then take the ideas to the highest levels. These types of problems, which Boaler calls "low floor and high ceiling" problems (p. 84), help in the development of the brain. Therefore, parents and teachers must engage children in these rich mathematical tasks to support children's curiosity, interests, and mathematical sense-making.

Tasks that Develop Uncertainty for Learners and Enhance Learning

The nature of tasks plays a significant role in teaching and learning (Kilpatrick, Swafford, & Findell, 2001; Sierpinska, 2004; Sullivan & Mousley, 2001). Elements of uncertainty can be embedded in creating tasks. This uncertainty, which may take the form of confusion, doubt, conflict, or perplexity, is generated when an individual's thought processes do not fit into the existing ideas and can lead the individual to generate new ideas and strengthen their understandings (Piaget, 1985). A critical part of teaching is to provide learners ample opportunities to struggle in order to motivate the learner to develop new knowledge (Hiebert & Grouws, 2007; NCTM, 2014). Zaslavsky (2005) describes three types of uncertainty in certain mathematical tasks: *competing claims*, *unknown path or questionable conclusion*, and *non-readily verifiable outcomes*. The first uncertainty—*competing claims*—refers to different viewpoints or conflicting arguments for the same mathematical situation (Zaslavsky, 2005). For example, the following task can challenge one's underlying conception of area-unit. The task has two competing answers and focuses: first, on two different area-units—a square unit and a rectangular unit; second, on understanding the connection between the area formula of a rectangular region and the idea of square units.

Area-Unit Task:

a) The area formula of a rectangular region is *length times width*. Turin used the area formula and said, "*the area of the rectangular region in (A) is 3 times 4, which is 12*". Do you agree with Turin? Why or why not?
b) Murin looked at the rectangular region in (A) and divided each of the small rectangular regions into halves as shown in (B). Then Murin said, "*the area of the rectangular region in (B) is 3 times 8, which is 24*". Do you agree with Murin? Why or why not?
c) Both the rectangular regions in (A) and (B) take up the same amount of space. Explain why Turin and Murin are getting two different answers for the area of the same rectangular region.
d) What is the area-unit, when one computes the area formula of a rectangular region using the area formula "*length times width?*"

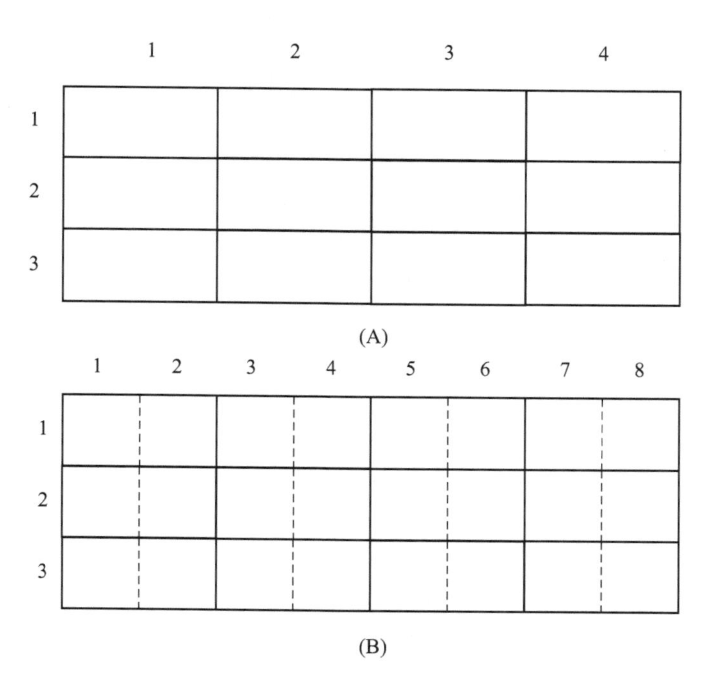

Figure 5.13 Area-unit Task

The second uncertainty—*unknown path or questionable conclusion*—arises from open-ended exploration tasks where the outcomes are unknown to the learners (Zaslavsky, 2005). For example, the following task can engage children in meaningful explorations and encourage them to make conjectures. This task supports multiple ways of arguing where each number lies. It allows children to experiment with different patterns and numbers, make conjectures, and refine their conjectures.

Spiral Picture Task:

a) On which sides in Figure 5.14 will the numbers 20, 28, 86, 99, 100, 177, 186, 1006 appear and why?
b) If we repeat using a similar triangular spiral picture and numeration (see Figure 5.15), can you determine on which side the numbers 44, 99, and 2001 will appear?

The third type of uncertainty—*non-readily verifiable outcomes*—arises due to the lack of confidence in verifying a solution to a problem (Zaslavsky, 2005). For example, a task asking how many rice grains are in a one-pound bag of rice might generate this uncertainty, as finding the solution just by counting is too tedious. This can lead learners to find multiple strategies to estimate the number of grains. For example, one strategy can involve dividing the rice grains into a few groups of almost equal size, estimating the number of rice grains in one group, and then estimating the number of grains in the bag by multiplication.

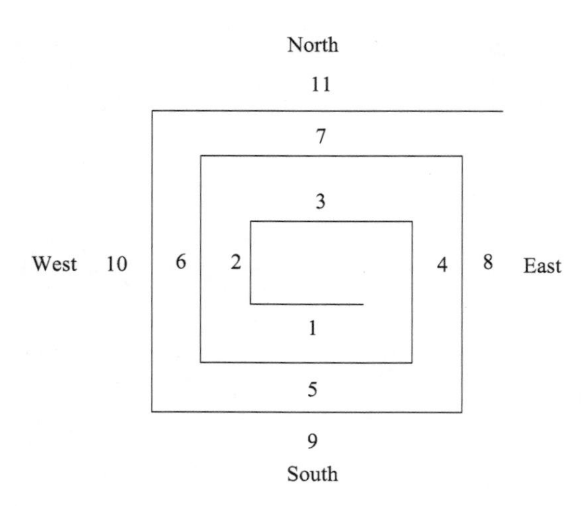

Figure 5.14 Rectangular-spiral Pattern Task

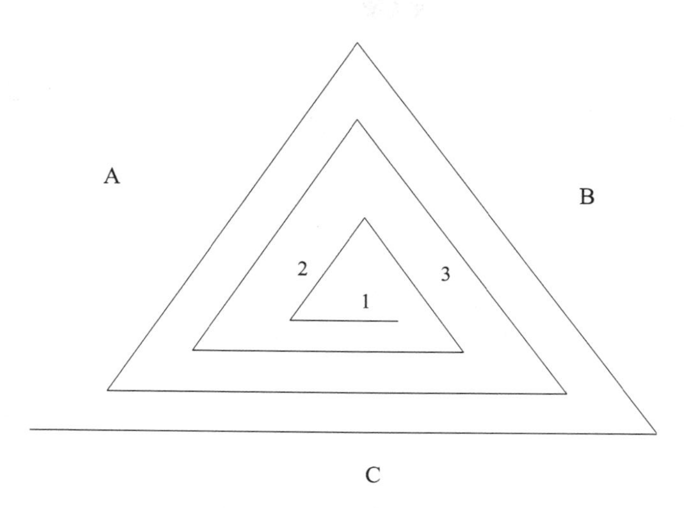

Figure 5.15 Triangular-spiral Pattern Task

These three different uncertainties are not mutually exclusive. Uncertainty of one type can trigger uncertainties of other types, and a task that generates uncertainty for one child might not generate uncertainty for another (Zaslavsky, 2005). These three different types of uncertainties help children to look for alternative solutions to a problem; as a result, these tasks have the potential to strengthen children's quantitative reasoning skills.

Importance of Errors, Uncertainties, and Struggles

All forms of learning errors, uncertainties, and struggles are crucial for children's cognitive development. They provide the learner an opportunity to grow. Each error, even without noticing, affects the growth of the brain (Boaler, 2016). There are two different types of neural signals—*error-related negativity* (ERN) and *error positivity* (Pe)—that can emanate from the brain. The former occurs when the brain experiences a conflict between correct and incorrect responses, and the latter occurs when a learner becomes aware of and consciously reflects on the error (Hughes & Yeung, 2011). In a study, Moser, Schroder, Heeter, Moran, and Lee (2011) found more enhanced neural signals in individuals when answers had errors than when answers were correct. They also found that growth-minded individuals have more neural signals compared to individuals with a fixed mindset. Their findings also corroborate with another study (Mangels, Butterfield, Lamb, Good, & Dweck, 2006) wherein individuals with a growth mindset were observed to have higher Pe signals compared to their counterparts. This means growth-minded individuals are more likely to reflect on their errors and correct them. Therefore, teachers must encourage children not to be afraid to make mistakes when learning (Boaler, 2016). Studies (Abiola & Dhindsa, 2011; Karni et al., 1998, Maguire, Woollett, & Spiers, 2006; Woollett & Maguire, 2011) have found that the brain can grow, change, and adapt within a short amount of time. Hence, it is important to teach children how the brain functions to promote their confidence in learning mathematics and increase their intelligence (Willis, 2010). In addition, Willis also suggests practicing relaxation techniques, such as breathing exercises and other wellness activities, before doing any mathematics problems; those relaxation techniques can help children to concentrate and reduce anxiety. Thus, tasks should be designed to provide opportunities for children to be challenged, grow intellectually, and develop a growth mindset.

Putting it into Practice

Reflection: Sami can talk to Sun about how the brain works and emphasize that with each mistake, one gets smarter. Sami can start giving *low floor tasks* that will give confidence to Sun and will reduce anxiety. Then she can add small complexities to the tasks. Sami can also give tasks that generate uncertainty for Sun. It can lead to a better mathematical understanding. Sami should regularly praise Sun for the efforts Sun is putting into the work and explore ways to connect mathematics with Sun's day-to-day experiences.

Selecting Mathematical Tasks with Context

Putting it into Practice

Mausam, a mother and elementary teacher, is planning to involve her children and students in problem-solving based on realistic contextual problems. Mausam is wondering which types of tasks she should select to promote children's mathematical thinking and interests.

Among other factors, mathematical task selection is one of the most important factors to determine children's development of mathematical thinking, mathematical sense-making, and engagement in the classroom. Mathematical tasks determine how children think and develop the cognitive processes involved in mathematics; tasks allow children to infer, reason, conjecture, and make decisions for their actions (NCTM, 1991; Stein, Grover, & Henningsen, 1996). The *Principles and Standards* (NCTM, 2000) and *Standards for Mathematical*

Practice (National Governors Association Center for Best Practices, 2010) call on mathematics educators to develop mathematical proficiency in children to solve problems from everyday life and society. This section discusses the selection of tasks with realistic, sociocultural contexts together with the challenges of selecting such contextual tasks.

Realistic Contextual Problem Solving

Mathematics is often treated as an isolated subject in school curricula. Classroom presentations are often too abstract, repetitive, and algorithmic, thereby making it an unrealistic subject for children, with no connections to real life (Peterson, 2012). This gives children the impression that mathematics is only needed to succeed in future mathematics classes with some applications only pertinent to some specific science, technology, engineering, and mathematics (STEM) disciplines. Thus, it is problematic to alienate the relevance of mathematics from daily lives of children.

Mathematics is everywhere. This is the message parents and teachers need to pass on to their children. This message can be illustrated by informing children about the use of mathematics not only in STEM-related disciplines but also in social sciences. Mathematics helps to solve social, ecological, and cultural issues. For example, plastic pollution is one of the challenges in today's world due to the improper dumping of plastic wastes (Chae & An, 2018). A small project using elementary mathematics, such as fractions, percentages, graphs, etc., to compute the weekly production of non-recyclable trash in one's household can bring awareness and can inform children how much non-recyclable trash is produced compared to biodegradable or recyclable trash.

Teachers can use realistic-contextual tasks to connect mathematics to students' lives. These contextual tasks provide mathematics learning opportunities within and outside the classroom (Tate, 2013). A *context* is where a problem is situated, and it often provides information that helps in solving the problem (Borasi, 1986). A context can motivate students to inquire and explore, apply mathematics, seek solution strategies, and deepen their mathematical understanding (Meyer, Dekker, & Querelle, 2001). Using contexts in the mathematics curriculum not only builds students' mathematical knowledge but also helps to anchor their understanding of society and social justice issues (Gutstein & Peterson, 2006). A high-quality contextual task must be real or at least relatable, must be mindfully crafted to include all groups, and must support modeling (Meyer et al., 2001). Teachers must acknowledge the very subjective nature of these contextual tasks. For some students, the tasks might be highly motivating and engaging, while for others they might be disengaging and non-contextual (Borasi, 1986). For example, consider the following word problem for division:

Figure 5.16 Trick or Treat

> Trick or Treat – This Halloween, you and your … (number of) friends visited … (number of) houses and collected … (number of) treats and placed all the treats in a bag. Now you want to share these treats equally among all of your friends, including yourself. How many treats will each of your friends get? Are there any leftover treats?

This problem assumes all students have celebrated Halloween and collected treats. Those students who have celebrated Halloween will bring personal experiences in completing the task, and for these groups of students, each number in the problem will relate to their memories of friends and family. For those students who did not go out to trick or treat, this task may serve as just a word problem task with some random numbers chosen by the teacher. Hence, this subjective nature of contextual tasks makes it challenging to incorporate it into the curriculum.

One common question is where to find these contextual tasks that are relevant to a specific classroom. There is no easy answer to this question. A good starting point is to be aware of the children's backgrounds. This helps teachers to design contextual tasks that foster children's understanding of themselves and their society and to connect classroom experiences with their life experiences. Gutstein and Peterson (2013) give some good advice on how teachers can integrate social justice ideas in their mathematics classes. They suggest that mindfully listening to students and having an awareness of current affairs are the keys to designing contextual tasks relevant to students' lives, their communities, and the world. A mathematically rich realistic-contextual task not only develops children's understanding and interests in mathematics but also provides them an opportunity to be aware of social and ecological problems and to get involved with society from an early age. Below is an example of a task to increase awareness about electricity consumption. This task is suitable for fifth- and sixth-graders.

Box 5.2 Theory and Research to Practice Connection

Electricity Consumption Awareness Project

Electricity is considered to be a clean form of energy.

Exploration 1: For what do you use electricity?

Do you know about 64% of total electricity generation in 2017 came from fossil fuels, namely coal, natural gas, petroleum, biomass, and industrial wastes?

(https://www.eia.gov/energyexplained/electricity/electricity-and-the-environment.php)

Exploration 2: What are fossil fuels and how they are formed?

These fuels, when burnt, produce harmful gases that have harmful effects on the environment and human health.

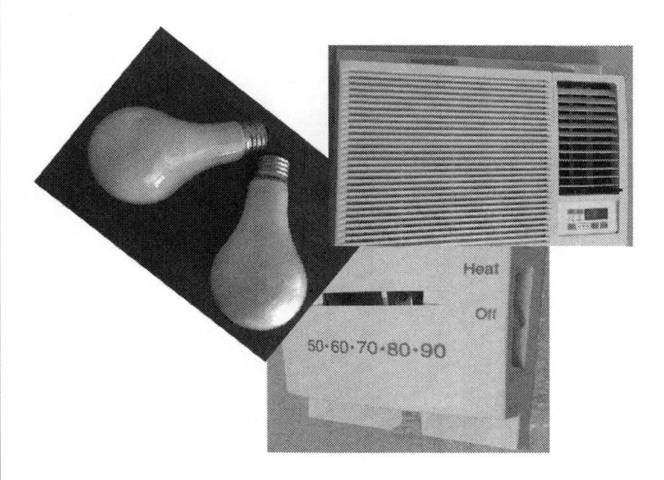

Figure 5.17 Household Appliances

Exploration 3: (Go to www.eia.gov) a) How much electricity is used in an American household?

b) Consider the electricity consumption at your home. Which appliances or devices use electricity? Make a table displaying the different categories and the number of hours used. Draw a bar graph displaying the data.

Appliances/ devices	Number of hours used	Teachers/parents provide info about finding wattage of the appliance/device	Daily electricity consumption: (wattage x hours/ day) ÷ 1000

d) Compute the total daily/monthly/annual electricity consumption.
e) Compare your numbers with others. Which devices consume electricity the most?
f) Discuss some strategies to optimally use electricity.

Tasks Reflecting Socio-Cultural Perspective

According to the National Center for Educational Statistics (2018), about 59% of three- to five-year-old children who were enrolled in preschool programs are from culturally and/or linguistically diverse backgrounds, and this percentage is expected to grow in the next few years. Hence, it is more important now than ever before for teachers to have the awareness and skills to support students from culturally diverse backgrounds. This requires teachers to implement teaching practices and curricula that are "culturally sensitive" and relevant to students' experiences (Durden, Escalante, & Blitch, 2015, p. 223).

Culturally-sustaining practice is a teaching pedagogy that centers around connecting students' classroom experiences with their home, culture, and language (Gay, 2000; Howard, 2003; Ladson-Billings, 2014; Paris 2012). Ladson-Billings (2014) argues that this practice fosters students' "intellectual growth," supports students in celebrating "their own cultures while gaining knowledge and fluency in some other culture," and helps students understand, recognize, "analyze and solve real-world problems" (p. 75). Paris (2012) argues that these practices not only need to be relevant to students' lives and experiences but also need to be sustained over time, which will allow all student diversity, including all languages, cultures, and individual differences. To create such classroom practices, teachers must have the intent to support students from both dominant and marginalized groups (Beauboeuf-LaFontant, 1999, as cited in Durden et al., 2015). As actions are guided by beliefs, it is critical that teachers hold a strong belief that these types of practices are important for a high-quality learning experience for culturally diverse students (Gay, 2000; Ladson-Billings, 2014; Paris, 2012).

With the amount of content to cover and with skills-focused curricula, teachers often have limited time to incorporate extra projects for students. The best way to incorporate is to start really small with tasks based on students' lived experiences, resonating with students' culture and community (Gutstein & Peterson, 2013). The choice of context in a task must be such that they are meaningful to students and make students feel included in the learning process. Allexsaht-Snider and Hart (2001) observe that the sense of inclusion or belonging is critical in mathematics learning as it promotes students' self-confidence and motivation to learn mathematics. They also discussed how sense of belonging is related to student engagement in the classroom, and how much it can relate to the culture and the language used in the classroom. Students will likely be engaged in the classroom if they are familiar with the context of the tasks being presented to them. It will also foster their sense of belonging in the mathematics community. Hence, educators need to be aware of children's cultural belonging, but also need to find ways to support children's learning with what each student brings in the class (Smith, Gilmore, Goldman, & McDermott, 1993).

It is also equally important that teachers create tasks to introduce global society, different cultures, and languages to children; such practices promote children's cultural and global competencies (Durden et al., 2015). Durden et al. (2015) suggest teachers can use resources such as books, family photos, etc. to engage children in learning about diverse societies around the world from a very young age. With careful consideration and thought, contextual tasks and culturally-sustainable teaching practices have the potential to support children's intellectual growth and understanding of the global society.

What Can Go Wrong in Selecting Contextual Tasks?

The usefulness of using contexts in the mathematics curriculum is well-studied (Meyer et al., 2001; Peterson, 2012; Tate, 2013). The most successful contexts are the ones that are based on students' home cultures and native languages. There are no doubts about the benefits of contextual tasks if implemented carefully. However, this needs serious consideration from teachers who plan to use contexts in their classrooms. Sullivan, Zevenbergen, and Mousley (2003) argue that first, teachers need to have an awareness of their students; next, they need to check for mathematical suitability of the context, relevancy, and meaningfulness of the context to the students; and finally, they need to be aware of the positive and negative impacts, if any, on the students. The negative impacts often include the exclusion of certain groups of students from mathematical learning.

Tate (2013) points out that most classroom experiences in American schools center around white history and perspectives. This puts students from other culturally diverse backgrounds in a disadvantageous position. Tate discusses one second-grade classroom experience where a student teacher used a context that was a barrier to mathematics learning for an African American child. The teacher used Thanksgiving pumpkin pie to situate a part-part-whole word problem. The teacher has asked the following problem: "*Joe has five pumpkin pies. Karen has six pumpkin pies. How many pumpkin pies do Karen and Joe have all together?*" (p. 46). Out of the five students, four white students were excited about the problem-solving process; one African American student was quiet. The teacher was under the impression that the African American child did not like math. Later on, after the researcher probed the teacher to ask the children if they ate pumpkin pie on Thanksgiving, they found that pumpkin pie was indeed the dessert for the white children, but not for the African American child. Thus, the context "Thanksgiving pumpkin pie" was completely irrelevant to the child who did not experience this at home. Even though the teacher had a good intention of using a context that was relevant to some students and she was indeed successful in connecting to those students, she failed to connect with a student whose experiences did not fit with the context. This suggests that the choice of mathematical tasks can lead to different outcomes if not chosen carefully.

In summary, contexts are useful in mathematics learning and should be used as an aid to help students learn mathematics. However, teachers need to have a clear "purpose" and well-considered "implications" for using contexts and must have multiple ways to make the context "clear and explicit" to the students (Sullivan et al., 2003 p. 111). Teachers need to take appropriate steps not only to make mathematics relevant, interesting, and engaging to students, but also not to exclude some students who are already marginalized in the process. Teachers need to choose a context that is appropriate for both the mathematical content and relevant to all students' experiences. Teachers need to pay extra attention to students' home culture and native languages so that the chosen context for a task is not foreign to them. There might be challenges while implementing contextual tasks in the classroom, but with appropriate measures and awareness, teachers can overcome those challenges. Below is a check-list for teachers to use while creating a contextual mathematical task.

Putting it into Practice

Reflection: Mausam can plan projects around children's daily experiences. Projects can involve calculating grocery expenses, calculating energy consumptions, current affairs, etc. Mausam should start small; Mausam needs to know her students really well and then pick topics that will generate interest among them.

Box 5.3 Social Justice and Diversity

Check-List for Teachers for Creating Contextual Mathematical Tasks

- What is the mathematical content?
- Who are the learners?
- What is the context?
- Is this context suitable for the content?
- Is this context suitable for the learners?
- Is the context relevant to all learners?
- What are the strategies to engage students in the problem-solving process?
- Is there any group that is excluded from using the context?
- Is the purpose of the context clear?
- What are the possible positive impacts of the context? What are the possible negative impacts of the context?
- What are some of the ways to reduce the negative impacts?

Cultivating Successful Mathematics Learners

Putting it into Practice

Genevi, a first-grade teacher, has a lot of anxiety when it comes to mathematics. As a student, she always struggled with mathematical concepts. Math has always been hard for her. Lately, she is noticing some children in her classroom, especially girls, are developing similar attitudes toward math. Genevi is trying to understand why this is happening in her class and is seriously looking for some solutions to address it.

What does it take to be a successful mathematics learner? This is a question many parents and teachers ask. Children's mathematical achievement depends on their understanding and knowledge of mathematics as well as their social and emotional experiences with mathematics. What can parents and teachers do to help children to be mathematically competent? To answer this question, this section looks at mathematical discourse in the classroom, with an emphasis on promoting social and emotional mathematical competence, supporting the development of a positive mathematical identity in students, and developing a classroom environment to promote learning and support students as mathematical problem solvers.

Developing Productive Mathematical Identity

Mathematics is associated with the myth that it is a set of rules and algorithms, and it is often perceived that computational fluency is the key to success in mathematics. However, this is not true. It is the growth mindset that can help students to get better in mathematics (Dweck, 2006; Boaler, 2016). These positive perceptions, such as having a growth mindset, and negative perceptions, such as believing the above myth about mathematics, can become a part of children's mathematical identities.

An identity within mathematics education has been well studied over the past two decades (Darragh, 2016). Martin (2006) defines a mathematical identity as a learner's dispositions and beliefs about their ability to engage and perform in mathematical activities. Martin further states that mathematical identity is dynamic and constantly changing; this identity refers to an individual's understanding of themselves, and how others perceive them when doing mathematics. This mathematical identity interferes greatly with learners' intellectual growth. A positive mathematical identity allows an individual to believe in their ability to perform well in mathematical tasks. A student's mathematical identity is linked to their sense of belonging to mathematics and is therefore a key to their intent to continue to pursue mathematics (Good et al., 2012). Good et al. (2012) argue that students maintain a high sense of belonging in regard to mathematics when they are around people who believe that one's mathematical abilities are acquirable, not inherited. This strongly suggests that parents and teachers must discuss the idea of a growth mindset regularly with children (Willis, 2010). Parents and teachers can influence how children think about themselves. It is crucial that parents and teachers first believe that anyone can grow their mathematical intelligence and promote the same in children so that children develop positive mathematical identities.

It is equally important that teachers believe in their own abilities as doers of mathematics, as their beliefs transfer to their students' mathematical beliefs. In a study, Beilock, Gunderson, Ramirez, Levine, and Smith (2010) argue that the mathematics anxiety of first- and second-grade female elementary teachers influences girls negatively, as young girls form a stereotype about "who is good at math," and this affects their achievements in mathematics. This suggests that young children, as early as five or six years of age, can be influenced by their teacher's mathematical identity.

Mathematical identity is closely connected with other forms of identity, such as gender, cultural, religious, ethnic, etc., that students develop and consider important in their own lives (Aguirre, Mayfield-Ingram, & Martin, 2013). Parents and teachers need to pay close attention to the type of mathematical identities their children are developing. Aguirre et al. (2013) suggest that teachers must attend to students' developing identities and must stay away from "negative stereotypes," such as "identifying black males as thugs" or "Asian children as illegal aliens" (p. 20), etc., and various other cultural, ethnic, demographic, and socio-economic labeling. They argue that teachers must attend to how students are making sense of these various labels and reflect on how and why students reject or accept these labels to understand why some students are engaged in mathematical tasks and some are not. Teachers must also acknowledge the different identities a child is developing through social and classroom interactions, reflect on how identities are interfering, and find ways to help develop a positive mathematical identity. A positive mathematical identity, influenced by teachers' classroom practices, encourages children to see themselves as doers of mathematics and engages them with mathematics in a meaningful way.

Promoting Mathematical Agency

The behavioral aspect of mathematical identity, i.e., the ability of students to see themselves as mathematical problem solvers and to participate in mathematical problem-solving, is referred to as "mathematical agency" (Aguirre et al., 2013). Learners either use procedural knowledge in problem-solving or thought processes to understand procedures conceptually. The former is called a disciplinary agency and the latter is called a conceptual agency (Gresalfi, Martin, Hand, & Greena, 2009). A mathematical agency can be used by students while working individually or working with classmates. Teachers must create opportunities inside and outside the classroom to assist students to develop their own mathematical agency. Aguirre and colleagues (2013) discuss that mathematical agency can also be *collective* when teachers and their students in a classroom are engaged in mathematical problem-solving. A collective mathematical agency can come in a variety of forms—some students can bring initial thoughts to solve a problem, some can bring strategies to solve the problem, some can engage in conversation about the problem in small groups and later feel comfortable contributing to the whole-class discussion, and some can ask clarifying questions in their small groups or during whole-class discussions (Aguirre et al., 2013). During this process, children must be comfortable sharing their developing ideas. Therefore, teachers must provide a safe space so children can feel welcomed to share ideas, reason, and argue professionally with each other. A positive mathematical agency fosters a positive identity in children and through proper teaching practices, teachers can help children to develop as competent problem solvers.

Box 5.4 Promoting Social and Emotional Competence

Strategies to Promote Collective Mathematical Agency

Below are some strategies that teachers can use in the classroom to promote collective mathematical agency:

Strategy 1: Establish classroom norms to create a safe space for everyone to participate and communicate respectfully with one another (Aguirre et al., 2013).
Strategy 2: Allow students to work in small groups to express themselves.
Strategy 3: Teach children to argue and reason professionally using statements such as *I agree with* ...; *Because I disagree with* ...; *Can you restate that for me?*, etc.
Strategy 4: Allow thinking time before letting students do group work.
Strategy 5: Create group norms for active participation and involve children in creating their own group norms as well.
Strategy 6: Assign talk times to each member of the group.
Strategy 7: Assign roles for each member of the group; one student can be the scriber, one student can be the spokesperson for the group, one student can restate the problems and the strategies discussed in the whole group, and one student can be the translator for English as a second language learners (Aguirre et al., 2013).
Strategy 8: Teach students to listen to mathematical arguments.
Strategy 9: Promote positive support and collaboration among peers.
Strategy 10: Allow students' mistakes for a richer discussion in the classroom.

Fostering Mathematical Problem Solving

Parents and teachers can teach children, from a very early age, appropriate problem-solving strategies so that children grow with the skills needed for making appropriate decisions, and can reason with valid and logical arguments. Also, children's development of mathematical understanding and skills can benefit from social interactions between peers as well as with the teacher in the classroom. Walker and Henderson (2012) argue that social interactions are very important for children's academic and social experiences. Children learn to think and apply their experiences and build new knowledge in the process.

Infants and young children acquire knowledge through their senses (Rowan & Bourne, 2001), then they progress through hands-on learning experiences and apply prior knowledge. Mathematical problem-solving is key to promoting such learning experiences in early childhood (Lopes, Grando, & D'Ambrosio, 2017). Mathematical problem-solving involves understanding the problem, planning, devising a plan, and making sense of the solution in the context of the problem (Polya, 1957). Teachers can use games and various classroom activities to develop children's mathematical problem-solving skills. Playful conditions help develop children's metacognitive and self-regulatory skills, which is critical for children's development of academic skills (Whitebread, Coltman, Jameson, & Lander, 2009).

Schwartz (2013) discusses six major contexts that promote mathematical problem-solving during children's developmental period. These contexts include channeling children's intuition towards formal mathematics as they follow their interests and promote curiosity about a problem. For example, a teacher can ask a child, who is drawing a square roof of a house, "is there a reason you chose a square over a triangle roof?" This question guides children to think about the features of the shapes and brings more consciousness to their choices and properties of shapes (Schwartz, 2013). The other contexts involve engaging children in planning playful activities, creating real models or crafts, or engaging them in realistic projects.

In summary, choosing activities or tasks that spark curiosity and interest and that guide children from informal intuitions to understanding formal mathematics can help children to be competent mathematical problem solvers, and thereby can promote positive mathematical identity and mathematical agency.

Putting it into Practice

Reflection: Genevi should believe in her own abilities to learn and teach mathematics. She needs to start thinking of herself as a mathematical problem solver and promote the idea of growth mindsets to her students. Genevi needs to tell her students about the importance of mathematics in the real world. She must pick activities or tasks that engage students and make them curious to learn more. She can involve students in planning for events so that they can take responsibility and learn by doing. She should develop a classroom environment that encourages thinking rather than quick mathematical calculations.

Chapter Summary

Mathematics is everywhere! This message highlights the importance of mathematics in the real world. Thus, mathematical literacy is essential in order to operate in today's world. Educators need to showcase the applications of mathematics to children from a very early age and create an environment for children so that they can see themselves as doers of mathematics. This chapter discussed four interconnected intertwined themes. The themes centered around core mathematical contents for TK–6 elementary pre-service teachers, and appropriate mathematical tasks selection that aimed to foster a growth mindset and a positive mathematical identity. The first section discussed the main elementary mathematical content areas—numbers and operations, geometry, and probability and statistics—as well as the NAEYC Program Standards for early childhood and the Common Core State Standards for mathematical practices and mathematics standards for K–6 classrooms. The second section featured the importance of the growth mindset in learning mathematics and the selection of appropriate mathematical tasks to promote growth mindsets in learners. This section also highlighted three types of learning uncertainties with example tasks that might provide learning opportunities for learners. The third section described the selection of tasks with realistic, socio-cultural contexts that have the potential to make mathematics more meaningful by raising awareness of social and ecological problems from an early age. This section also discussed the challenges of selecting such tasks and suggestions to overcome those challenges. The fourth section focused on how mathematical identities impact learners' mathematical interests and self-efficacy. It also discussed mathematical discourse in the classroom and ideas to develop a classroom environment to support students as mathematical problem solvers. This section listed strategies for promoting social and emotional mathematical competence to support the development of a positive mathematical identity in students.

This chapter has many sidebars that displayed scenarios at the beginning of each section highlighting issues that might arise during children's mathematical learning, as well as reflections at the end of each section addressing the issues.

References

Abiola, O., & Dhindsa, H. S. (2011). Improving classroom practices using our knowledge of how the brain works. *International Journal of Environmental & Science Education*, 7(1), 71–81.

Aguirre, J. M., Mayfield-Ingram, K., & Martin, D. B. (2013). *The impact of identity in K–8 mathematics: Rethinking equity-based practices*. Reston, VA: National Council of Teachers of Mathematics.

Allexsaht-Snider, M., & Hart, L. E. (2001). "Mathematics for all": How do we get there? *Theory into Practice*, *40*(2), 93–101.

Arcavi, A. (2003). The role of visual representations in the learning of mathematics. *Educational Studies in Mathematics*, *52*, 215–241.

Baroody, A. J., & Wilkins, J. L. M. (1999). The development of informal counting, number, and arithmetic skills and concepts. In J. V. Copley (Ed.), *Mathematics in the early years* (pp. 48–65). Reston, VA: National Council of Teachers of Mathematics.

Beauboeuf-Lafontant, T. (1999). The movement against and beyond boundaries. Politically relevant teaching among African American teachers. *The Teachers College Record*, *100*(4), 702–723.

Beckmann, S. (2014). *Mathematics for elementary teachers with activities* (4th ed.). Upper Saddle River, NJ: Pearson Education.

Beilock, S. L., Gunderson, E. A., Ramirez, G., Levine, S. C., & Smith, E. E. (2010). Female teachers' math anxiety affects girls' math achievement. *Proceedings of the National Academy of Sciences of the United States of America*, *107*(5), 1860–1863.

Blackwell, L., Trzesniewski, K., & Dweck, C. S. (2007). Implicit theories of intelligence predict achievement across an adolescent transition: A longitudinal study and an intervention. *Child Development*, *78*(1), 246–263.

Boaler, J. (2016). *Mathematical mindsets: Unleashing students' potential through creative math, inspiring messages and innovative teaching*. San Francisco, CA: Jossey-Bass.

Boaler, J., & Staples, M. (2008). Creating mathematical futures through an equitable mathematics approach: The case of Railside School. *Teachers College Record*, *110*(3), 608–645.

Borasi, R. (1986). On the nature of problems. *Educational Studies in Mathematics*, *17*, 125–141.

Carpenter, T. P., & Moser, J. M. (1984). The acquisition of addition and subtraction concepts in grades one through three. *Journal for Research in Mathematics Education*, *15*, 179–202.

Chae, Y., & An, Y. (2018). Current research trends on plastic pollution and ecological impacts on the soil ecosystem: A review. *Environmental Pollution*, *240*, 387–395.

Clements, D. H. (1999). Geometric and spatial thinking in young children. In J. V. Copley Ed.), In *Mathematics in the early years* (pp. 66–79). Reston, VA: National Council of Teachers of Mathematics.

Clements, D. H., Sarama, J., & Miller, A. L. (2017). Area. In D. H. Clements, & J. Sarama (Eds.), *Children's measurement: A longitudinal study of children's knowledge and learning of length, area, and volume* (pp. 71–82). Reston, VA: National Council of Teachers of Mathematics.

Clements, D. H., Sarama, J., Van Dine, D. W., Barrett, J. E., Cullen, C. J., Hudyma, A., Dolgin, R., Cullen, A. L., & Eames, C. L. (2018). Evaluation of three interventions teaching area measurement as spatial structuring to young children. *Journal of Mathematical Behavior*, *50*, 23–41.

Copeland, R. W. (1979). *How children learn mathematics* (3rd ed.). New York, NY: Macmillan Publishing, Co., Inc.

Cury, F., Da Fonseca, D., Zahn, I., & Elliot, A. (2008). Implicit theories and IQ test performance: A sequential mediational analysis. *Journal of Experimental Social Psychology*, *44*, 783–791.

Darragh, L. (2016). Identity research in mathematics education. *Educ Stud Math*, *93*, 19–33.

Durden, T. R., Escalante, E., & Blitch, K. (2015). Start with us! Culturally relevant pedagogy in the preschool classroom. *Early Childhood Education Journal*, *43*, 223–232.

Dweck, C. S. (2006). *Mindset: The new psychology of success*. New York, NY: Ballantine Books.

Fuson, K. C. (1988). *Children's counting and concepts of number*. New York, NY: Springer-Verlag.

Gay, G. (2000). *Culturally responsive teaching*. New York, NY: Teachers College Press.

Geary, D. C., Brown, S. C., & Samaranayake, V. A. (1991). Cognitive addition: A short longitudinal study of strategy choice and speed-of-processing differences in normal and mathematically disabled children, *Developmental Psychology*, *27*, 787–797.

Gelman, R., & Gallistel, C. R. (1978). *The child's understanding of number*. Cambridge, MA: Harvard University Press.

Good, C., Rattan, A., & Dweck, C. S. (2012). Why do women opt out? Sense of belonging and women's representation in mathematics. *Journal of Personality and Social Psychology*, *102*, 700–717.

Gresalfi, M., Martin, T., Hand, V., & Greena, J. (2009). Constructing competence: An analysis of student participation in the activity systems of mathematics classrooms. *Educational Studies in Mathematics*, *70*(1), 49–70.

Gutstein, E., & Peterson, B. (Eds.). (2006). *Rethinking mathematics: Teaching social justice by the numbers*. Milwaukee, WI: Rethinking Schools.

Gutstein, E., & Peterson, B. (Eds.). (2013). *Rethinking mathematics: Teaching social justice by the numbers* (2nd ed.). Milwaukee, WI: Rethinking Schools.

Hart, L. (2013). Pedagogical content analysis of mathematics as a framework for task design. In C. Margolinas (Ed.), *Task design in mathematics education. Proceedings of ICMI Study 22*, (pp. 337–345). Oxford, England, ICMI.

Hiebert, J., & Grouws, D. A. (2007). The effects of classroom mathematics teaching on students' learning. In F. K. Lester (Ed.), *Second handbook of research on mathematics teaching and learning* (pp. 371–404). Reston, VA: National Council of Teachers of Mathematics.

Howard, T. (2003). Culturally relevant pedagogy: Ingredients for critical teacher reflection. *Theory into Practice*, *42*(3), 195–202.

Hughes, G., & Yeung, N. (2011). Dissociable correlates of response conflict and error awareness in error-related brain activity. *Neuropsychologia*, *49*, 405–415.

Karni, A., Meyer, G., Rey-Hipolito, C., Jezzard, P., Adams, M., Turner, R., & Ungerleider, L. (1998). The acquisition of skilled motor performance: Fast and slow experience-driven changes in primary motor cortex. *PNAS*, *95*(3), 861–868.

Kilpatrick, J., Swafford, J., & Findell, B. (Eds.). (2001). *Adding it up: Helping children learn mathematics*. Washington, DC: National Academy Press.

Ladson-Billings, G. (2014). Culturally relevant pedagogy 2.0: a.k.a. the remix. *Harvard Educational Review*, *84*(1), 74–84.

Leutzinger, L. (1990). Graphical representation and probability. In J. N. Payne (Ed.), *Mathematics for the young child* (pp. 250–263). Reston, VA: National Council of Teachers of Mathematics.

Lopes, C. E., Grando, R. C., & D'Ambrosio, B. S. (2017). Experiences situating mathematical problem solving at the core of early childhood classrooms. *Early Childhood Education Journal*, *45*(2), 251–259.

Maguire, E., Woollett, K., & Spiers, H. (2006). London taxi drivers and bus drivers: A structural MRI and neuropsychological analysis. *Hippocampus*, *16*(12), 1091–1101.

Mangels, J. A., Butterfield, B., Lamb, J., Good, C., & Dweck, C. S. (2006). Why do beliefs about intelligence influence learning process? A social cognitive neuroscience model. *Social Cognitive and Affective Neuroscience*, *1*(2), 75–86.

Martin, D. (2006). Mathematics learning and participation as racialized forms of experience: African American parents speak on the struggle for mathematics literacy. *Mathematical Thinking and Learning*, *8*, 197–229.

Martin, W. G., & Strutchens, M. E. (2000). Geometry and measurement. In E. A. Silver, & P. A. Kenney (Eds.), *Results from the seventh mathematics assessment of the National Assessment of Educational Progress* (pp. 193–234). Reston, VA: NCTM.

Meyer, M., Dekker, T., & Querelle, N. (2001). Contexts in mathematics curriculum. *Mathematics Teaching in the Middle School*, *6*(9), 522–527.

Moser, J., Schroder, H. S., Heeter, C., Moran, T. P., & Lee, Y. H. (2011). Mind your errors: Evidence for a neural mechanism linking growth mindset to adaptive post error adjustments. *Psychological Science*, *22*, 1484–1489.

Mueller, M. F., Yankelewitz, D., & Maher, C. (2010). Promoting student reasoning through careful task design: A comparison of three studies. *International Journal for Studies in Mathematics Education*, *3*(1), 135–156.

National Association for the Education of Young Children. (NAEYC). (2010). *Early childhood mathematics: Promoting good beginnings*. A joint position statement of NAEYC and the National Council of Teachers of Mathematics (NCTM). http://www.naeyc.org/files/naeyc/file/positions/psmath.pdf

National Center for Educational Statistics. (2018). The condition of education. https://nces.ed.gov/programs/coe/indicator_cfa.asp

National Council of Teachers of Mathematics (NCTM). (1989). *Curriculum and evaluation standards for school mathematics*. Reston, VA: National Council of Teachers of Mathematics.

National Council of Teachers of Mathematics (NCTM). (1991). *Professional standards for teaching school mathematics*. Reston, VA: National Council of Teachers of Mathematics.

National Council of Teachers of Mathematics (NCTM). (2000). *Principles and standards for school mathematics*. Reston, VA: National Council of Teachers of Mathematics.

National Council of Teachers of Mathematics (NCTM). (2014). *Principles to actions: Ensuring mathematical success for all*. Reston, VA: National Council of Teachers of Mathematics.

National Governors Association Center for Best Practices. (2010). *Common core state standards*, Washington DC: Council of Chief State School Officers.

National Research Council. (2001). *Adding it up: Helping children learn mathematics*. J. Kilpatrick, J. Swafford, and B. Findell (Eds.). Mathematics Learning Study Committee, Center for Education, Division of Behavioral and Social Sciences and Education. Washington, DC: National Academy Press.

Paris, D. (2012). Culturally sustaining pedagogy: A needed change in stance, terminology, and practice. *Educational Researcher*, *41*(3), 93–97.

Peterson, B. (2012). Numbers count: Mathematics across the curriculum. In A. Wager & D. Stinson (Eds.), *Teaching mathematics for social justice, conversations with educators* (pp. 147–159). Reston, VA: NCTM.

Piaget, J. (1985). *The equilibration of cognitive structures: the central problem of intellectual development*. Chicago, IL: University of Chicago Press.

Polya, G. (1957). *How to solve it* (2nd ed.). Princeton, NJ: Princeton University Press.

Rowan, T., & Bourne, B. (2001). *Thinking like mathematicians: Putting the NCTM standards into practice*. Portsmouth, NH: Heinemann.

Sarnecka, B. W., Goldman, M. C., & Slusser, E. B. (2015). How counting leads to children's first representations of exact, large numbers. In R. C. Kadosh, & A. Dowker (Eds.), *Oxford library of psychology. The Oxford handbook of numerical cognition* (pp. 291–309). Oxford University Press.

Schwartz, S. L. (2013). *Implementing the Common Core State Standards through mathematical problem solving, Kindergarten-grade 2*. F. R. Curcio (Series Editor). Reston, VA: National Council of Teachers of Mathematics, Inc.

Sella, F., Berteletti, I., Lucangeli, D., & Zorzi, M. (2017). Preschool children use space, rather than counting, to infer the numerical magnitude of digits: Evidence for a spatial mapping principle. *Cognition*, *158*, 56–67. doi: 10.1016/j.cognition.2016.10.010

Sierpinska, A. (2004). Research in mathematics education through a keyhole: Task problematization. *For the Learning of Mathematics*, *24*(2), 7–15.

Smith, D., Gilmore, P., Goldman, S., & McDermott, R. (1993). Failure's failure. In E. Jacob, & C. Jordan (Eds.), *Minority education: Anthropological perspectives* (pp. 209–231). Norwood, NJ: Ablex Publishing Corporation.

Spaepen, E., Gunderson, E. A., Gibson, D., Goldin-Meadow, S., & Levine, S. C. (2018). Meaning before order: Cardinal principle knowledge predicts improvement in understanding the successor principle and exact ordering. *Cognition*, *180*, 59–81.

Stein, M. K., Grover, B. W., & Henningsen, M. (1996). Student capacity for mathematical thinking and reasoning: An analysis of mathematical tasks used in reform classrooms. *American Educational Research Journal*, *33*(2), 455–488.

Stein, M. K., Smith, M. S., Henningsen, M., & Silver, E. A. (2009). *Implementing standards-based mathematics instruction: A casebook for professional development*. New York, NY: Teachers College Press.

Sullivan, P., & Mousley, J. (2001). Thinking teaching: Seeing mathematics teachers as active decision makers. In F.-L. Lin and T. J. Cooney (Eds.), *Making sense of mathematics teacher education* (pp. 147–163). Dordrecht, The Netherlands: Kluwer Academic Publishers.

Sullivan, P., Zevenbergen, R., & Mousley, J. (2003). The contexts of mathematics tasks and the context of the classroom: Are we including all students? *Mathematics Education Research Journal*, *15*(2), 107–121.

Suzuka, K., Sleep, L., Ball, D., Bass, H., Lewis, J. M., & Thames, M. H. (2009). Designing and using tasks to teach mathematical knowledge for teaching. In D. S. Mewborn & H. S. Lee (Eds.), *Scholarly practices and inquiry in the preparation of mathematics teachers (AMTE monograph series, volume 6)* (pp. 7–23). San Diego, CA: Association of Mathematics Teacher Educators.

Tate, W. F. (2013). Race, retrenchment, and the reform of school mathematics. In E. Gutstein & B. Peterson (Eds.), *Rethinking mathematics: Teaching social justice by the numbers* (2nd ed.) (pp. 42–53). Milwaukee, WI: Rethinking Schools.

Walker, O. L., & Henderson, H. A. (2012). Temperament and social problem solving competence in preschool: Influences on academic skills in early elementary school. *Social Development*, *21*(4), 761–779.

Wheatley, G. H., & Reynolds, A. M. (1996). The construction of abstract units in geometric and numeric settings: Tiling the plane. *Educational Studies in Mathematics*, *30*, 67–83.

Whitebread, D., Coltman, P., Jameson, H., & Lander, R. (2009). Play, cognition and self-regulation: What exactly are children learning when they learn through play? *Educational and Child Psychology*, *26*(2), 40–52.

Willis, J. (2010). *Learning to love math- Teaching strategies that change student attitudes and get results*. Alexandria, VA: Association for Supervision and Curriculum Development.

Woollett, K., & Maguire, E. A. (2011). Acquiring "The Knowledge" of London's layout drives structural brain changes. *Current Biology*, *21*(24), 2109–2114.

Yackel, E., Underwood, D., & Elias, N. (2007). Mathematical tasks designed to foster a reconceptualized view of early arithmetic. *Journal of Mathematics Teacher Education*, *10*(4–6), 351–367.

Zaslavsky, O. (2005). Seizing the opportunity to create uncertainty in learning mathematics. *Educational Studies in Mathematics*, *60*, 297–321.

Zaslavsky, O., Watson, A., & Mason, J. (Eds.). (2007). The nature and role of tasks in mathematics teachers' education. *Journal of Mathematics Teacher Education*, *10*, 201–440.

Chapter 6

Social and Emotional Learning

Kimberly A. Gordon Biddle

This chapter relays how social and emotional learning (SEL) has been rediscovered in the last few decades, but is not necessarily a totally new concept and process. Social and emotional learning (SEL) is being intentionally taught with social and emotional development, behavior, and skills in order to display social and emotional competence. Social and emotional competence means displaying appropriate behavior and emotions in social settings in order to meet your needs or goals. The chapter continues by describing two major SEL frameworks and some strategies for implementing SEL in the elementary classroom. Next, there are descriptions of common elementary school curricula. The last section discusses the intersection of SEL with gender, socioeconomic status, and ethnic minority status.

(Re)Discovering the importance of Social and Emotional Learning

The National Association of Education for Young Children (NAEYC) has proposed for decades that educators, even in the elementary grades, should teach the whole child (NAEYC, 2015) and educators have agreed, for the most part (Jones & Kahn, 2018). This means fostering social and emotional development as well as cognitive development. Indeed, research demonstrates that social and emotional development has a close relationship with cognitive development and academic development (Jones & Kahn, 2018). Children with appropriate social and emotional development display social and emotional competence at various ages and developmental levels (Jones, Barnes, Bailey, & Doolittle, 2017). Social and emotional competence means displaying appropriate social and emotional regulation, behaviors, skills, and attitudes in the right contexts at the right age and developmental level (Jones & Bouffard, 2012). These behaviors and skills impact cognitive development and academic achievement (Jones & Kahn, 2018). These behaviors and skills also need to be fostered in children or taught to children (Jones, Barnes, Bailey, & Doolittle, 2017; Jones & Bouffard, 2012). Hence, researchers and educators are in the process of (re)discovering the importance of social and emotional learning, using teaching strategies and techniques to foster social and emotional competence in children (Jones, Barnes, Bailey, & Doolittle, 2017; Jones & Bouffard, 2012).

This is because when No Child Left Behind (NCLB) was passed in 2001, the emphasis within elementary education and all education became standard-based assessments and accountability. Standardized mathematics and English scores were focused on with a laser-like beam as the most important outcome of education endeavors to the detriment of other areas that make up the "whole child " (Billig, 1997; Shepard, Hannaway, & Baker, 2009). During this time period, a large number of education advocacy groups, educators, and employers still emphasized the benefits of educating the whole child (Jones & Kahn, 2018; NAEYC, 2015; National Network of Business and Industry Associations (NNBIA), 2015). However, NCLB remained the law that governed education practices in the United States until 2015 when the Every Student Succeeds Act (ESSA) became law and brought flexibility to educators and the education process in terms of standards, assessments, and accountability (Workman & Jones, 2016). ESSA specifically called for "well-rounded" education of students (US Department of Education, 2015; Workman & Jones, 2016); however, academics are still given the most weight when examining an elementary school or school district for effectiveness. Current research on social and emotional development and behavior does show a relationship between both of these areas (social and emotional) of a child's development and their academic performance (Jones & Kahn, 2018; Kulkarni & Sullivan, 2019). The teaching of appropriate social and emotional development, behavior, and skills has arrived once more as the process of social and emotional learning (Jones, Barnes, Bailey, & Doolittle, 2017). This new re-discovering of the importance of social and emotional development is not just happening in the United States. It is happening around the globe in places such as the United Kingdom, Europe, and other areas (Wood, 2018).

Some Useful Frameworks

Social and emotional learning is the teaching of appropriate social and emotional development, behavior, and skills, according to the author. These skills can be taught by parents, teachers, peers, or others. According to Taylor and Larson (1999), social and emotional learning (SEL) is the knowledge, tasks, and experiences one has to obtain or improve in their social and emotional competence, which means understanding, controlling, and appropriately expressing your emotions. Moreover, the need for teaching SEL skills in elementary schools, including Transitional Kindergarten (TK), has been recognized (CSEFEL, n.d; Jones, Bailey, & Jacob, 2014; Jones, Barnes, Bailey, & Doolittle, 2017; Wood, 2018). Learning these skills and learning them early has been shown to impact a child's mental and physical health, subsequent education, and teacher classroom management (Brown, 2013;

CSEFEL, n.d; Jones, Bailey, & Jacob, 2014; McCoy, Jones, Roy, & Raver, 2018; Tran, 2007). Indeed, the need for social and emotional learning in elementary schools and earlier is quite evident. This chapter, in conjunction with the entire text, focuses on TK through 6th grade in the area of social and emotional learning.

The CSEFEL Pyramid

CSEFEL is the Center on the Social and Emotional Foundations of Early Learning at Vanderbilt University. CSEFEL has created a research- and evidence-based model that is visually represented as a pyramid. See Figure 6.1. This pyramid has five levels that represent increasing levels of intervention concerning the enrichment of young children's emotional, social, mental, and behavioral skills and abilities (CSEFEL, n.d.). The bottom of the pyramid is the foundation of an effective workforce. The teachers of children from TK to 6th grade are very important. They should be educated and receive regular and routine training. Additionally, their own social and emotional behavior, skills, and abilities are important, because they teach and serve as models for young children (CSEFEL, n.d; Jones, Bailey, & Jacob, 2014). The next level of the pyramid contains "nurturing and responsive relationships." This level of the pyramid and of intervention is for all young children, especially in educational environments. All young children should have nurturing and responsive relationships. The third level of the pyramid, "high quality

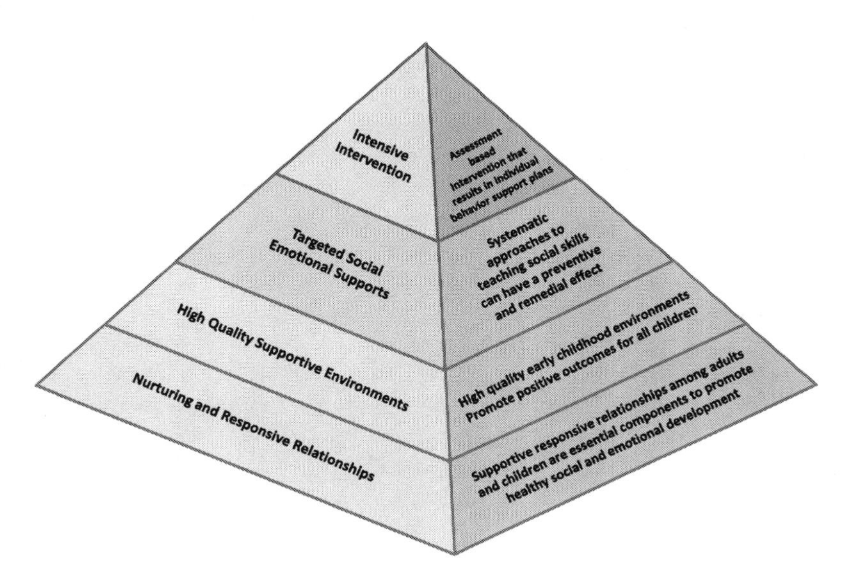

Figure 6.1 CSEFEL Teaching Pyramid. Source: Adapted from CSEFL website.

supportive environments," is also for all young children. This layer of promoting, fostering, and teaching all young children adds on to positive relationships. It includes the materials in the environment in addition to human beings. Indeed, even the routines, policies, procedures, and transitions in the environment can be considered part of a "high quality supportive environment." Levels two and three of the pyramid foster general social and emotional well-being for all young children. An example of these levels is the process of teaching young children to label their emotions. Level four of the pyramid contains "targeted social and emotional supports." These targeted social and emotional supports prevent behavioral issues in young children who show signs that they are at risk of displaying behavioral disruptions or inappropriate behavior in the social and emotional domains of development. Home visits and coaching of the teaching staff are examples of level four prevention methods. The last level of the pyramid is level five. Level five is for young children who display inappropriate social and emotional behavior in an educational setting. Level five contains "intensive intervention." This level is the provision of treatment or direct and targeted intervention with young children who display disruptive behavior. In some cases, level five support represents a crisis and the need for outside community specialists, such as mental health professionals (CSEFEL, n.d.).

Box 6.1 Common Core and Other Standards

The following is a list of states that have adopted the CSEFEL standards: California, Colorado, Hawaii, Iowa, Maryland, Massachusetts, Nebraska, North Carolina, Tennessee, Vermont, and Wisconsin. All of these states have adapted the standards to meet their needs and developed some of their own materials.

Tools and materials for fostering social and emotional competence in children have also been created by the CSEFEL team and teams of professionals who have adopted and adapted the CSEFEL standards in various states. Social and emotional competence means using appropriate and culturally acceptable methods for meeting your needs with emotional expression and behavioral regulation (CSEFEL, n.d.). The materials and tools supported by CSEFEL help with fostering cultural competence, finding tools to measure social and emotional competence in young children, connecting and referring children and families to community resources, and more. Cultural competence means relating to people from a culture that is different from yours. Some of the measurement tools suggested are the Ages & Stages Questionnaires: Social-emotional (Brookes Publishing Inc., 2002), Child Behavior Checklist (Achenbach, 2001), Infant-toddler Social Emotional Assessment (Pearson Assessment, 2005), and Vineland Social-Emotional Early Childhood Scales (Pearson Assessment, 2005). Although standardized assessments exist to measure social and emotional competence, it is actually a culturally influenced concept. Social and emotional competence varies in different cultures and different families and schools. The norms and definitions of social-emotional competence can vary for each student in the various contexts of home, school, and culture. This reality presents a challenge for children and families that are not from the dominant culture or whose home life is different from school life.

Box 6.2 Social and Emotional Competence

Differentiation between typical development and concerning or challenging behaviors is essential. Although standard assessments of social and emotional development exist, there remains an amount of subjectivity and judgment on the part of the adult who completes the assessment (CSEFEL, 2008). It is necessary to discern if the child is developing in a typical fashion or if their behavior truly is concerning or challenging. Questions to ask are as follows: how often does this behavior occur? What is the duration of the behavior? How intense is the behavior? Does the behavior happen in all settings or contexts or one particular setting or context? Do the culture of the adult observer and the culture of the child match? What is the child's developmental age? How is the child's health? Could the behavior be more acceptable in another environment in which the child finds him or herself during his or her day? Do other adults in the same environment or a different environment view the behavior as the same?

These questions are important to ask because labeling a child's behavior as problematic or slow in developing can impact his or her education and life success (McCoy, Jones, & Roy, Raver, 2018). Caregivers who aren't familiar with typical child development and milestones can mislabel a child's behavior. For instance, preverbal children often use mild aggression or assertiveness to get attention or to meet their needs (CSEFEL, 2008). These children could be seen as angry. However, it is typical for preverbal children to behave this way and the behaviors usually disappear on their own once the young children become able to express themselves verbally. This is why it is important to ask all of the questions mentioned here before labeling a child's behavior as inappropriate.

The previous information focused on a model for young children, including TK children. This model, CSEFEL, can be applied to all elementary school children. However, there are models of social and emotional learning that are specifically useful for and created with elementary schools in mind. One of the more prominent ones is the Jones elementary school framework for social and emotional learning (Jones, Bailey, & Jacob, 2014; Jones, Barnes, Bailey, & Doolittle, 2017).

The Jones Framework

The Jones framework defines social and emotional learning (SEL) as obtaining and displaying the skills necessary for successful education results, workplace results, relationships, and citizenship (Jones & Bouffard, 2012). Some of these skills are emotion regulation, effortful control, prosocial skills, communication skills, and more. As mentioned earlier in this chapter, these skills are related to cognitive development and academic achievement (Jones & Kahn, 2018). This is especially true in elementary schools, TK through 6th grade. However, these skills are acquired in broader contexts such as homes, peer groups, schools, and classrooms. Additionally, as Bronfenbrenner has taught us (Bronfenbrenner & Morris, 1998), there is an even broader context of culture.

Jones adapted her framework from the Collaborative for Academic, Social and Emotional Learning (CASEL). This framework contains the child in the middle, the school and classroom context, short and long-term developmental outcomes, teacher skills and competencies, and community contexts and school policies (see Figure 6.2). This is quite an elaborate and comprehensive

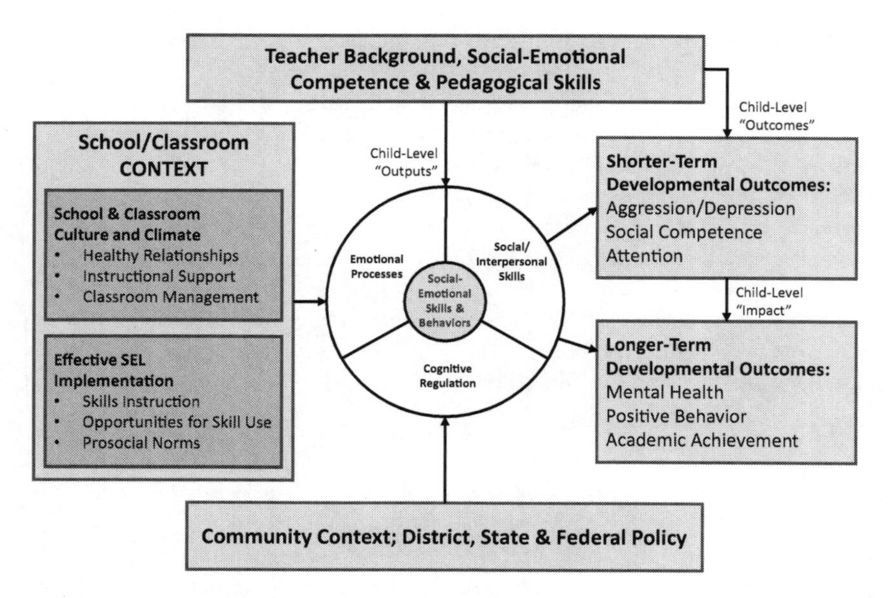

Figure 6.2 Organizing Framework for SEL. Source: Adapted from Jones and Bouffard (2012)

framework. Let's begin unpacking all of the aspects and elements of this framework.

Beginning with the child, there are certain social and emotional skills and behaviors that are labeled appropriate by a child's culture and context at certain ages and developmental levels. These skills are divided into three categorical groups by Jones: emotional processes, social/interpersonal skills, and cognitive regulation (Jones & Bouffard, 2012). Emotional processes include emotional knowledge, emotional expression, emotional regulation, behavioral regulation, empathy, and perspective-taking skills. Social/interpersonal skills are as follows: understanding social cues, interpreting others' behaviors, navigating social situations, interacting positively with age-mates and adults, and prosocial behaviors. Cognitive regulation contains executive functions such as attention control, the inhibition of inappropriate responses, working memory, and flexibility. These are skills that elementary school children have or must learn. These skills lead to outcomes.

The outcomes may be short-term or long-term. The outcomes are academic achievement, behavioral regulation and adjustment, and emotional well-being. Of course, a lack or slow development of these skills can impair academic achievement, behavioral regulation and adjustment, and emotional well-being. This leads to poor grades, dropping out of school, improper aggression or anger expressions, low-quality friendships, inattention, poor memory, and other outcomes. All of this depends on whether or not the child has learned or can learn to display social and emotional competence, a culturally defined construct.

The Jones framework takes culture and context into account. At the broadest level, a child's SEL in elementary school is impacted by education policies at the federal, state, and school district levels according to this framework. The laws and rules concerning education at the federal, state, and school district levels matter. Are there laws for supporting children with special needs and neurodiversity or children living in poverty? Does the school district even recognize the need for SEL? Which model and/or framework does the school district implement? How is cultural sensitivity taken into account at each level of policy-making? Answers to all of these questions impact a child's SEL. The community in which a child lives and the community in which a child's school is located also impact the child's SEL.

Community context is another aspect of the Jones framework. Is the community dangerous and violent? Is the community friendly, organized, and safe? Is the community rural, suburban, or urban? Is the community ethnically diverse? Is the community financially well-resourced and stable? These questions and more impact a child's SEL.

Moving closer to the child, the school/classroom context is another component of the Jones framework. What are the culture and climate? Are the culture and climate the same as the child's culture and climate in the child's community and home? How are the child's relationships in the school and classroom? Is there instructional support? How is the classroom managed? How is SEL implemented? In other words, how are skills taught and which skills are taught? Are there opportunities for the elementary school students to practice the skills? What are the school and class norms for prosocial behavior? All of these factors impact a child's SEL. There is one last component to discuss in the Jones framework: teachers.

Teachers play an integral role in the education of elementary students, especially a student's SEL. Does he, as a teacher, have good training? Is he, the teacher, socially and emotionally competent? In general, does he use good teaching techniques? Are the techniques he uses to teach SEL effective? Teachers have a very direct and impactful influence on a child's SEL.

Those are all of the components of the Jones SEL framework, a very comprehensive framework. The child's skills are at the center and lead to outcomes for them. The child's skills are impacted by other contexts, such as the child's community, the laws of the country and state, and the rules of the school district. The context and culture of the school and classroom are important, as well as the child's teacher. These all impact the child's SEL in elementary school, according to the Jones framework (Jones & Bouffard, 2012). So how do a school district, school, and teacher integrate the Jones SEL framework into education with practical applications and strategies?

Strategies for Educators

What are the necessary elements of techniques and strategies to more effectively implement SEL in the microsystems of elementary students? This section will explore and attempt to provide some answers to this question. According to Jones and Bouffard (2012), it is important to integrate SEL principles into the daily experiences of the classroom microsystem. Teachers can intentionally use emotion regulation techniques, activities to refine conflict resolution abilities and enrich attention skills, and democratic resolution of class problems or conflicts. Teachers can teach these techniques to students, place visual reminders of technique steps with words and images around the classroom, and make learning the techniques fun. In order to do this, teachers need training in SEL techniques and processes. Again, it is important for these techniques and processes to be used on a daily basis in the classroom as a part of everyday life for the students.

Pre-service teachers and in-service teachers need training in SEL knowledge, skills, and techniques. In other words, college students who are becoming teachers and teachers who are currently in the field both need SEL training. SEL training and exposure should be part of undergraduate and credential programs. Ideally, other elementary school personnel, such as counselors and principals, have SEL training, too. How to communicate and interact positively with students are important skills. Reacting effectively to challenges and conflicts are more SEL skills that are important for teachers to know.

It is important, also, to create a supportive and respectful environment in elementary school buildings and classrooms. The principal also needs training on these matters, because the principal's leadership impacts a student's SEL greatly. A principal's leadership also impact's a teacher's SEL skill learning and development. Without a large amount of effective SEL knowledge and skill, teachers cannot implement SEL. Teachers need their SEL enriched, as the elementary students do. All adults in elementary schools, including staff and principals, need SEL enrichment.

Teachers, other adult staff, and principals need supportive environments that work and operate using SEL principles. Teachers, especially, need support and a self-reflective attitude, as teachers are the main adult besides family members to interact with elementary school students. All elementary school staff should increase their SEL skills constantly, particularly teachers. This all leads to effective SEL implementation, positive relationships, and improved classroom management.

Federal and State Standards and Policies

Since we are in the time of ESSA and the emphasis is teaching the whole child, SEL skills should be written into all federal and state education policies. However, this is not the case. Some states have policies and some of those policies are more effective than others. At the federal level, there are currently not any country-wide SEL standards or policies in the United States as I write this chapter in the spring of 2020. However, rapid changes are occurring. What standards and policies do researchers recommend? Jones and Bouffard (2012) have some broad suggestions for all policy-makers and stakeholders from the federal, state, and local levels. These recommendations are as follows: establish adequate and flexible funding; strengthen standards; integrate SEL into administrator, teacher, and staff training; support assessment of SEL practices and skills; create opportunities for networking, learning, and continuous improvement; incentivize connections between SEL and academics; and support research strategies for integrating SEL into the school day. These broad suggestions are great for a start. What are the exact guidelines that states actually have? As an example, let's look at Illinois. According to Dusenbury, Zadrazil, Mart, and Weissburg (2011) the state of Illinois has comprehensive SEL standards for preschool to high school. At each level, there are benchmarks for the following standards: develop self-awareness and self-management skills to achieve school and life success; use social awareness skills to establish and maintain positive relationships; and demonstrate decision-making skills and responsible behaviors in personal, school, and community contexts. The guidelines in other states vary much from the Illinois model. Some states have a couple of guidelines in their social science frameworks and others do not mention SEL in their frameworks or guidelines at all. Obviously, more work and attention are needed concerning SEL policies and regulations.

Common SEL Curricula for Elementary School

There are many curricula that focus on SEL in elementary school. Some of them have been developed in the United States and other countries. The Collaborative for Academic, Social, and Emotional Learning (CASEL) (2020) has reviewed and evaluated many of the SEL curricula. Five of the commonly used ones are mentioned and described in this section, four of them are categorized as select programs, and one is categorized as a complementary program. The four select programs are listed here in alphabetical order and followed by the one complementary program.

Competent Kids, Caring Communities is the first curriculum to be described. This curriculum teaches students life skills and social-emotional competencies and offers strategies for fostering communication, collaboration, shared goals, and joint decision-making with education staff and family members. All lessons are accompanied by application activities. There are 35 lesson sets for kindergarten to 5th-grade students in addition to the family modules. At least one person from each school or district needs to attend a three-day training. This curriculum has limited research evidence from a medium-size quasi-experimental study. Improved academic outcomes were the result.

Promoting Alternative Thinking Strategies (PATHS) is another curriculum. PATHS is for preschool and elementary students, pre-K to 6th grade. PATHS teaches empathy and emotion regulation. It also teaches how to solve conflicts and make good decisions. There is a two-day training program; however, it is not required for implementing the curriculum. The number of lessons per academic year at each grade level ranges from 40 to 52. Each lesson is structured and comprehensive, with goals, guidelines for implementation, methods for engaging parents, answers to possible questions, activities, and more. The parents' materials come in Spanish and English. In contrast to the first curriculum, PATHS has lots of evidence from multiple randomized control trials. This adds to the evidence base of PATHS. The research was conducted in rural, suburban, and urban areas that varied in socio-economic status. The results included improved academics, social and emotional competence, and classroom climate, and lower incidents of conduct issues.

The third selected program is the "responsive classroom." This curriculum focuses on the teacher's behavior and not students' behavior. The responsive classroom should meet all of a student's needs, physical, emotional, social, and intellectual. There are ten teaching techniques and practices that accompany a responsive classroom, with additional suggestions for working with English Language Learners. These techniques are morning meetings, rule creation, interactive modeling, positive teacher language, logical consequences, guided academic discovery, academic choice, classroom organization, collaborative problem solving, and collaborating with parents and families. At least one teacher or staff member from a school or district needs to attend 30 hours of training. The evidence for this is approach is mostly a very big, three-year, quasi-experimental study. The study showed that this approach improved classroom climate and academic outcomes.

Box 6.3 Theory into Practice Connection

There have been a number of studies that show the responsive classroom works, including a three-year longitudinal study (Rimm-Kaufman, Fan, Chiu, & You, 2007). How can we take the techniques and apply them in real-life elementary classrooms? One issue common in elementary schools is bullying. Let us reflect on this situation and use responsive classroom techniques. There is a 5th-grade male student who is bullying another 5th-grade male student, verbally and emotionally. Perhaps the bully is taller and more physically mature. Maybe the victim is shorter, less physically mature, shy, and raised by a single mom. First, let us define bullying. Remember that not every act of aggression is bullying. Bullying is targeted, repeated, and occurs when the bully has some sort of power over the victim. What can be done here in this situation?

Logical consequences suggest that the bully should have to apologize and have another consequence, such as listening to how his behavior has impacted the victim, and other disciplinary acts. Also, have a way to support the victim and allow the bully to regain privileges. Morning meetings, collaborative problem-solving, and rule-making sessions are places where the incidents can be discussed, including talking about empathy and taking another's perspective. Ask students for solution suggestions. Spend individual time talking to the bully and the victim. The teacher can also talk to each set of parents individually. Be prepared to have evidence that the bullying actually occurred. Try to see what is happening in each home, as bullying behavior may be modeled or rewarded in the home of the bully. Share some of the classroom logic and rules with the parents. Let them know what rules their children are to follow when they are students in your classroom. Check to see if the families have any needs, such as counseling, mediation, food, shelter, or other needs. With the bully's family, the teacher wants to also communicate what the student is doing well. With the victim's family, the teacher wants to also communicate what supports they have to offer. All parties involved should be told what will happen if the incidences of bullying do not stop. Stronger, more consequential punishment can be given for physical bullying.

Second Step is another curriculum. Second Step focuses on teaching the students skills and not the teachers. It is for preschool to 8th grade. Skills taught in Second Step are emotion regulation and management, empathy, creating friendships, and problem-solving. Each grade has approximately 22 to 28 weeks of lesson plans. There are special lessons for helping preschoolers get ready for kindergarten. There are four key components to each lesson plan; fostering executive function, theme activities, activities to enrich the themes, and links to home. Training on Second Step is optional and voluntary. Training times vary from one to four hours. Second Step has both quasi-experimental and randomized research as evidence. The research shows that it reduces distress and conduct problems, but enriches social and emotional skills and positive behavior.

The next curriculum is Merrell's Strong Kids complementary program of ten lessons for pre-kindergarten through 5th grade. There are lessons for wide grade ranges and not for specific grades. That is why it is considered complementary. The grade ranges are Pre-K to K, K to 2nd, and 3rd to 5th. This program is integrated smoothly and is developmental in nature. The content of the lessons are empathy and perspective-taking; emotion recognition and regulation; management of anger, conflict, and stress; recognition of positive personal attributes; problem-solving; cognitive reframing; and goal-setting. Each lesson has certain components: ideas for student skill practice, reflections for teachers, mindfulness activities, and suggested children's books. No special training is needed for teachers or staff. Two evaluations for Strong Kids have occurred that are quasi-experimental. One study found enriched social-emotional skills and competencies and the other found fewer internalizing behaviors.

Gender, Socioeconomic Status, Ethnic Minority Status, and SEL

As with other elementary school initiatives and interventions, living in poverty, being a male, and being an ethnic minority matter (Camera, 2016; Jones, Bailey, & Jacob, 2014; Kulkarni & Sullivan, 2019; McCoy, Jones, Roy, & Raver, 2018; Porche, Grossman, Biro, MacKay, & Rivers, 2014). These issues arise in transitional kindergarten (TK) or even before that and can persist throughout elementary if there is not successful intervention. When considering, reflecting on, addressing, and researching these issues, it is important to keep in mind the comprehensive nature of SEL processes that were shared in Figure 6.1. The students have certain characteristics, skills, and abilities concerning SEL that contribute to student outcomes. The students' families, culture, ethnicity, and language use contribute to SEL and student outcomes. However, we also have to consider the school and classroom atmosphere and how it contributes to student outcomes. Additionally, the school and classroom policies impact student outcomes. Moreover, the teaching techniques, the strategies used to implement SEL curriculum, the teacher's self-reflection skills, and the teacher's own competence (social-emotional and cultural) all impact student outcomes. All of these factors come into play when determining student outcomes in elementary school.

In elementary school, TK to 6th grade, boys seem to fare worse (Camera, 2016; Jones, Bailey, & Jacob, 2014; Kulkarni & Sullivan, 2019; McCoy,

Jones, Roy, & Raver, 2018), especially impoverished ethnic minority boys. For these boys, and indeed all children, it is important how the classroom is managed (Jones, Bailey, & Jacob, 2014). For these boys, their journey through elementary school can impact later education and life outcomes (Camera, 2016; Kulkarni & Sullivan, 2019; McCoy, Jones, Roy, & Raver, 2018).

Box 6.4 Diversity and Social Justice: SEL and the Expulsion of TK Males of Color

Due to explicit and implicit bias and teachers' decision-making factors, TK males of color are often expelled and suspended, especially African American males (Alameda County Early Care and Education Planning Council, 2018; Gilliam, Reyes, & Chin, 2018; Wesley & Ellis, 2017). These precious little boys are often the recipients of inequitable discipline policies and practices that lead them straight to prison (Wesley & Ellis, 2017). Teachers of the young boys expected misbehavior, watched them longer, and had less empathy for these students and their family history. Wesley and Ellis (2017) state that this is a violation of the little boys' civil rights that causes them to miss foundational learning and causes undue stress to the boys and their families.

So, what can educators do? There are some general guidance and discipline guidelines that should exist in every TK and elementary school that involve administrators, teachers, other school staff, and parents (Alameda County Early Care and Education Planning Council, 2018). Administrators should have clear steps in their disciplinary policies; the steps should include a support plan and involvement of the child's caregiver. Administrators should clearly communicate the role of everyone (child, teacher, administrator, and caregiver) involved when a child deserves discipline. Possible reasons for program expulsion or suspension should be clearly outlined. One of the most important steps in this process is documentation of incidences, so these policies must also be stated very clearly.

Administrators and all staff, not just teachers, should have training in implicit bias and trauma-informed teaching in addition to typical staff training. Administrators should allow and fund an additional adult in every elementary classroom. These adults can be an ABA, a mental health professional, a developmental specialist, or a paraprofessional. This allows for some possibility for one-on-one support. Staff and teacher diversity should reflect student diversity in terms of gender, race, age, ethnicity, culture, temperament, and first language choice.

Additionally, teachers should understand challenging behavior, how to cope with it, and how to prevent it. Teachers also need to know how to relate to parents and families that are different from the teacher's lived experience. Recruitment of, intake of, communication with, engagement with, and relationships with these parents and families require cultural competence. There is even more that teachers can do, especially when teaching young TK males, according to Wesley and Ellis (2017). They can recognize their biases and cultural frames. They can learn about their students' culture. They can recognize and understand broader contexts, such as economics, social capital, and politics, that surround the classroom and elementary school and their reciprocal influences. They can be sensitive to and respectful of cultural differences and let this sensitivity impact their guidance methods. They can also develop caring and responsive classrooms.

Chapter Summary

For a couple of decades, social and emotional learning (SEL) has been a focus of elementary education, even though it is not a completely new phenomenon. Professional organizations and educators have advocated for teaching the whole child for even longer. In 2015 when the Every Student Succeeds Act (ESSA) was passed by President Obama, federal policy in the United States became more flexible and allowed for more focus on SEL in the classroom.

There exist some common SEL frameworks based on research and theory. One such framework is described by Jones and her colleagues. Another is supported by the Center for Social and Emotional Foundations of Early Learning at Vanderbilt University. Both of these frameworks are described in this chapter and are widely used, adopted, and adapted. Jones and her colleagues also describe some strategies for implementing SEL in the elementary classroom.

In addition to classroom strategies, there exist some curricula for overall elementary school implementation. A number of these curricula are described in the chapter with some helpful statistical and other information. The curricula described include the "responsive classroom" and Strong Kids.

This chapter ends with an examination of how demographic factors can impact SEL processes and procedures and, ultimately, student outcomes. These factors include gender, socioeconomic status, and ethnic minority status. SEL practices that are not implemented with cultural competence and awareness can disproportionately impact low-income males of color, particularly African American young males. The results can lead to poor outcomes for these young males and lead to a pathway from transitional kindergarten to prison.

References

Achenbach, T.M. (2001). *Manual for ASEBA school-age forms & profiles*. Burlington, VT: University of Vermont, Research Center for Children, Youth, &Families.

Alameda County Early Care and Education Planning Council (2018, July). *Guidelines for preventing preschool expulsion and suspension*.

Billing, S.H. (1997). Title I of the improving America's schools act: What it looks like in practice. *Journal of Education for Students Placed at Risk, 2*, 329–343.

Bronfenbrenner, U., & Morris, P.A. (1998). The ecology of developmental processes. In R.M. Lerner (ed.), *Handbook of child psychology: Theoretical models of human development* (5th Ed., vol. 1, pp. 535–584). New York: Wiley.

Brookes Publishing Inc (2002). *Ages & stages questionnaires: A parent-completed, child- monitoring system for social-emotional behaviors*, pbrookes.com.

Brown, K.M. (2013). *Relationships between a social-emotional learning program and emotional intelligence in middle school students*. Pro Quest LLC. Ph.D. Dissertation, Mississippi State University, p. 102.

Camera, L. (2016, June 22). *Boys bear the brunt of school discipline*. U.S. News & World Report. https://www.usnews.com/news/articles/2016-06-22/boys-bear-the-brunt-of-school-discipline.

CASEL (2020). Collaborative for academic, social, and emotional learning. *Casel.org*.

Duran, F., Hepburn, K., Kaufmann, R., Le, L., Allen, M.D., Brennan, E., & Green, B. (n.d.). *Research synthesis: Early childhood mental health consultation*. Center on the Social and Emotional Foundations for Early Learning, Vanderbilt University. http://csefel.vanderbilt.edu/documents/rs_ecmhc.pdf

Dusenbury, L., Zadrazil, J., Mart, A., & Weissberg, R. (2011). *State learning standards to advance social and emotional learning: The state scan of social and emotional learning standards, preschool through high school*. https://www.casel.org/wp-content/uploads/2016/01/state-learning-standards-to-advance-social-and-emotional- learning.pdf

Gilliam, W.S., & Reyes, C.R. (2018). Teacher decision factors that lead to preschool expulsion: Scale development and preliminary validation of the preschool expulsion risk measure. *Infants and Young Children, 31*(2), 93–108.

Jones, S.M., & Bouffard, S.M. (2012). Social and emotional learning in schools: From programs to strategies. *Social Policy Report, 26*(4), 1–22.

Jones, S.M., & Kahn, J. (2018). The evidence base for how learning happens: A consensus on social, emotional, and academic development. *American Educator, 41*(4), 16–21, 42–43. https://eric.ed.gov/?id=EJ1164389

Jones, S.M., Bailey, R., & Jacob, R. (2014). Social-emotional learning is essential to classroom management. *Phi Delta Kappan, 96*(2), 19–24. https://doi.org/10.1177/0031721714553405

Jones, S.M., Kargman, M., Kargman, M., & Bailey, R. (2014). *Preliminary impacts of SECURe PreK on child- and classroom-level outcomes*. Society for Research on Educational Effectiveness. https://eric.ed.gov/?id=ED562750

Jones, S.M., Barnes, S.F., Bailey, R., & Doolittle, E.J. (2017). Promoting social and emotional competencies in elementary school. *The Future of Children, 27*(1), 49–72.

Kulkarni, T., & Sullivan, A.L. (2019). The relationship between behavior at school entry and services received in third grade. *Psychology in the Schools, 56*(5), 809–823. https://doi.org/10.1002/pits.22231

McCoy, D.C., Jones, S.R., & Raver, C.C. (2018). Classifying trajectories of social-emotional difficulties through elementary school: Impacts of the Chicago School Readiness Project. *Developmental Psychology, 54*(4), 772–787. http://dx.doi.org/10.1037/dev0000457

NAEYC (2015). *Developmentally appropriate practice and the common core standards: Framing the issues*. Washington, DC: Author.

NNBIA (2015). *Work and learning in action: Successful strategies for employers*. Indianapolis, IN: Author.

Pearson Assessment (2005). *Brief infant-toddler social and emotional assessment.* Manual, Version 2.0.

Porche, M., Grossman, J., Biro, N., MacKay, N., & Rivers, S. (2014). *Collaboration to achieve whole school SEL across a large, urban district.* Society for Research on Educational Effectiveness. https://eric.ed.gov/?id=ED562719

Rimm-Kaufman, S.E., Fan, X., Chiu, Y.-J., & You, W. (2007). The contribution of the responsive classroom approach on children's academic achievement: Results from a three year longitudinal study. *Journal of School Psychology*, *45*(4), 401–421. https://doi.org/10.1016/j.jsp.2006.10.003

Shepard, L., Hannaway, J., & Baker, E. (eds.). (2009). *Standards, assessments, and accountability: Education policy white paper.* National Academy of Education, Washington, DC.

Taylor, H.E., & Larson, S. (1999). Social and emotional learning in middle school. *Clearing House*, *72*(6), 331–336. https://doi.org/10.1080/00098659909599420

Tran, L.T. (2007). Learners' motivation and identity in the Vietnamese EFL writing classroom. *English Teaching: Practice and Critique*, *6*(1), 151–163.

US Department of Education (2010). *A blueprint for reform: The reauthorization of the Elementary and Secondary Education Act.*

US Department of Education (2015, October 24). *Fact sheet: Testing action plan.*

Wesley, L., & Ellis, A.L. (2017). Exclusionary discipline in preschool: Young black boys' lives matter. *Journal of African American Males in Education*, *8*(2), 22–29.

Wood, P. (2018). 'We are trying to make them good citizens': The utilisation of SEAL to develop 'appropriate' social, emotional and behavioural skills amongst pupils attending disadvantaged primary schools. *Education 3-13*, *46*(7), 741–754. https://doi.org/10.1080/03004279.2017.133924

Workman, E., & Jones, S.D. (2016). *ESSA's well-rounded education.* Special Report. Washington, DC: Education Commission of the States.

Yates, T., Ostrosky, M.M., Cheatham, G.A., Fettig, A., Shaffer, L., & Santos, R.M. (2008). *Research synthesis on screening and assessing social-emotional competence.* Center on the Social and Emotional Foundations for Early Learning, Vanderbilt University, Nashville, TN.

Chapter 7

Movement, Visual, and Performing Arts

Lindy Valdez and Erin Miranda Morrison

Documents that Guide Instruction in Physical Education

There are four main documents that guide physical education instruction at an elementary school site. These physical education documents are the national standards, the state standards, the state framework, and the district curriculum standards. These documents guide the development and delivery of elementary physical education curriculum. The first of these documents that guide instruction in physical education is the National Standards. The Society of Health and Physical Educators (SHAPE) is the national organization that has defined excellence in physical education through the National Standards for K–12 Physical Education. The National Standards for K–12 Physical Education serve as the foundation for well-designed physical education programs across the country (National Standards for K–12 Physical Education, 2013). The National Standards for Physical Education are quoted as the following:

"Standard 1: The physically literate individual demonstrates competency in a variety of motor skills and movement patterns.
Standard 2: The physically literate individual applies knowledge of concepts, principles, strategies, and tactics related to movement and performance.
Standard 3: The physically literate individual demonstrates the knowledge and skills to achieve and maintain a health-enhancing level of physical activity and fitness.
Standard 4: The physically literate individual exhibits responsible personal and social behavior that respects self and others.
Standard 5: The physically literate individual recognizes the value of physical activity for health, enjoyment, challenge, self-expression, and/or social interaction."

State Standards

State standards vary by state. Each state in the United States of America sets its own standards for physical education. States and local school districts across the country often use the National Standards to develop or revise existing standards, frameworks, and curricula. Since each state has its own revision cycle, state standards may not match the current national standards. For example, in the authors' home state of California, the state standards were written in 2005 and matched the national standards at that time. The current national standards were written in 2013, resulting in the state standards being a mismatch.

State Frameworks

Many states additionally have state physical education frameworks that are guidelines for implementing the content standards adopted by the State Board of Education. State frameworks provide a more detailed curriculum guide on how to implement the state's content standards. Most often, the state framework gives guidance to teachers on what concepts and skills should be taught at each grade level. This information is particularly helpful to teachers in putting together their yearly plans for instruction for each grade level. Educators need to be mindful of these standards when planning their curriculum because failure to do this can result in legal risks if a child is injured in an activity that is in the state framework or content standards at a more advanced grade level.

School District Curriculum Guides

Most school districts also have their own curriculum guidelines. At their best, district curriculum guidelines match state frameworks, state standards, and national standards, and give more specificity for the district resources. Unfortunately, many district standards are written and then put on a shelf and not revised or updated on a regular basis. Many district curriculum standards then become outdated and often defer to state standards.

Other Supplemental Documents

There are additional professional documents that aid the teacher in understanding what quality instruction in elementary physical education looks like. One of those seminal documents in physical education is, "Appropriate Instructional Practice Guidelines, K–12: A Side-by-Side Comparison" (https://www.shapeamerica.org/uploads/pdfs/Appropriate-Instructional-Practices-Grid.pdf). This document, as it implies, assists the teacher to understand the key indicators of quality elementary physical education. This document lists both the appropriate practice and the most common inappropriate practice. Included in this document are areas of instructional importance including the learning environment; instructional strategies; curriculum; assessment; and professionalism. Neil Williams (PE Central, 2019) wrote a series of articles entitled the "PE Hall of Shame." He discusses physical education practices and games that should not be done in physical education classes. PE Central has added to this list of banned games and hosts an open forum to continue to look at inappropriate instructional practices (https://www.pecentral.org/professional/hos/).

Quality Physical Education

Quality physical education is both developmentally and instructionally relevant for all children. Appropriate instructional practices in physical education are those that recognize children's development and changing movement abilities, as well as their individual differences. Children's past motor skills, sports, cognitive and social experiences also are considered in this program design, lesson and delivery. Individual characteristics such as physical maturation and fitness, skill levels, and age are reflected in designing lessons and selecting instructional strategies. Appropriate instruction in physical education incorporates the best-known practices, derived from both research and teaching experiences, into a pattern of instruction that maximizes opportunities for learning and success for all children. To maximize the learning opportunities, those that need the most practice must be afforded the opportunities to receive equal practice. Movement practices that cause students to be eliminated from practice opportunities, such as Duck, Duck, Goose or musical chairs, eliminate the very children that need the most practice. Lines of students are another indicator that the activity is instructionally inappropriate. Lines, such as relay races, decrease practice opportunities by having children wait for their turn. There must be equipment for every student in order to ensure maximum practice opportunities. Educational practices that would be considered inappropriate in other subjects have often been a part of physical education. For example, educators would never have five math textbooks and put students into five lines to practice math after the book had been passed to them. This is a relay, which is a common practice in physical education. The standard for educational practices in physical education must be the same as for any other subject. If it is poor educational practice in other subjects, then it is poor educational practice in physical education. Good teaching is good teaching and bad teaching is bad teaching no matter where in the curriculum it occurs. Educational practice in any subject maximizes the students' opportunities to learn and practice those learned skills. Quality lessons and programs are designed to reflect the goals of national, state, and/or local standards for physical education. Teachers regularly assess student progress and adjust lessons and progressions accordingly. With increased teaching experience, this assessment process becomes more natural and a part of each lesson.

The most important indicator of quality physical education is that it is safe for the students. Putting students in unsafe or instructionally or developmentally inappropriate activities that compromise their safety is professionally irresponsible. As mentioned previously, the documents that guide instruction provide a template for appropriate instruction. The teacher must provide safety precautions for each lesson to students, have written lesson plans, and ensure they are in a position to observe all students while a lesson is in progress.

Movement Development

Importance of Play

Play is vital to the development of a child. The benefits of play include important contributions to the cognitive, physical, social, and emotional well-being of children. Play can provide opportunities to interact with parents and other children. With the onset of the digital age, outside play has been dramatically reduced. Play has often been the casualty of increased emphasis on academic activities (Ginsburg KR; American Academy of Pediatrics Committee on Communications; American Academy of Pediatrics Committee on Psychosocial Aspects of Child and Family Health, 2007). Play is so important to the physical development of the child that it can often predict adult educational attainment cross-culturally (Peet et al., 2015).

Outdoor versus Indoor Play

As mentioned previously, there has been a societal shift to less outdoor play. There is more availability of digital play or passive entertainment. Unstructured playtime is more valuable for a young child's developing brain than is electronic media. Young children are more likely to learn and remember information from a live presentation than they are from a video (Mayo Clinic Staff, 2019). Most American children spend about three hours a day watching TV. Added together, all types of screen time can total five to seven hours a day (Strasburger, Jordan, & Donnerstein, 2010). Time spent in outdoor play is diminishing, contributing to more sedentary lifestyles that are disconnected from the natural world and socialization opportunities (Bento & Dias, 2017). While fine motor development might happen during inside play, gross motor activities are largely unavailable inside. With a decline in outdoor play opportunities, there is a decline in children's gross motor physical development.

Theory and Research to Practice Connection

Teachers often experience difficulty transferring theoretical knowledge into practice. Effective teacher education programs seek ways to connect theory and practice in their pre-service teacher education programs. As the movement exploration discussion occurs in this next section, the theory is supported by research, and then suggestions are made to put this theory and research into practice.

Movement Exploration

The theory: When children participate in physical movement, it encourages the growth of locomotor and non-locomotor skills, and social skills by helping children to interact with one another. Children's cognitive development is stimulated during movement by experiencing problem solving and sensory awareness of their bodies in relationship to others and equipment. The transition from play to planned movement experiences starts with the exploration of a child's own environment. *The research*: Movement exploration is a way of teaching children which allows preschoolers and kindergartens to explore spatial relationships with objects and others (123 Expert, 2017). Movement exploration helps the child become aware of the joy of physical movement and the feelings that it brings to their bodies (Anderson et al., 2004). The movement exploration approach has shown an increase in creative confidence among early movers (Cheung, 2010). *The practice*: Movement exploration is less instructive and more, as the name indicates, explorative. Children are asked to move in the space around their bodies. This includes balancing on different body parts or moving like different animals. They can be introduced to different equipment such as bean bags or hula hoops to explore this equipment in safe ways they choose.

Movement Education

Movement Education is often described in literature as the "New PE." This is ironic as it has largely been derived from the work of Rudolf Laban, a Hungarian dance artist and theorist. Labanotation or Kinetography Laban is a notation system for recording and analyzing human movement that Laban formulated in *Schrifttanz* ("Written Dance") in 1928 (Laban, 1928). The basis of Laban movements is still in use today.

Movement Education is divided into two major categories: the concepts and the skills of movement. The concepts of movement are largely based on Laban's ideas of movement. They include spatial awareness, the dynamic quality of the movement, and the relationship of the body with movement. Spatial awareness addresses students exploring their self-space and the general space in an area that has a boundary. Students who are moving in their self-space or personal space learn that there are many movements they can do without leaving the space they are in. These movements include bending, twisting, jumping, and making different shapes out of their bodies. In the general space movement concept, the boundary is set by the teacher and can be as simple as the area in the cones, blacktop, grass, or court lines. Helping kids develop an awareness of their own space around themselves will make them move safely around others. Spatial awareness also includes moving in different directions, pathways, and levels. Two other movement concepts include relationships and the effort a movement takes. Relationships of movement include how a movement is done in relation to different body parts. There are surprisingly a lot of body parts to learn when you just begin to move. This movement concept also relates to the movements that occur in relation to another person. This is where partners begin to mirror or match other's movement patterns. The last of the movement concepts is the effort that a movement takes. The movement can be a sustained movement or a sharp or percussive movement. Effort can also take the form of a free movement, such as moving like an eagle, and a restricted movement, like moving as if there were a foot of mud on the ground.

The fundamental skills of movement include locomotor assessment, jumping and landing, chasing, fleeing and dodging, balance, transfer of weight, rolling, kicking, punting, throwing, catching, dribbling, volleying, striking, rhythm, dance, physical fitness, and cooperative activities. The previously discussed concepts of movement are modifiers of these movements. For example, when teaching throwing, students can be asked to throw the ball at different levels or in different directions, so the partner has to move to catch the ball. The students can be asked to throw and catch the ball in their self-space. In this way, the skill is modified by the concept of movement. Physical fitness is a byproduct of a quality physical education program where all students are moving with maximum participation. Games do not stand alone taught in isolation. Games provide an authentic assessment of the movement concept or skill. The teacher teaches a skill or concept and then uses a game that uses the skill or concept to determine whether the students have learned the application of the skill or concept. If the students demonstrate that they are able to use this skill or concept skillfully then the class is ready to move on to the next skill or concept. If the students are not using that skill or concept skillfully, then it is time to teach and reteach this skill or concept and provide more practice.

Like other subjects in school, kids develop physically at different timeframes. No two kids have identical developmental patterns. Still, there are some common developmental patterns that can be used to define physical movement (Valdez, 2017). Immature movements are those movements at the beginning stage of development. This is where children cannot replicate a movement and the movement is uneven and jerky. They are at the exploration stage of development. An example of this stage is throwing. In throwing at the immature pattern of movement, the child may put both feet together or the right foot forward or the left foot forward, often in successive throws. The throw is often pushed rather than thrown with the arm back. This illustration with throwing can be used in other movement skills to describe the immature pattern. The next pattern of physical development is the developing pattern. In the developing pattern of movement, the movement begins to look more uniform or consistent with greater concentration from the child. An example of this would be in catching, where the child has to be told to get ready to catch the ball and it needs to be thrown exactly to him and he catches it consistently. As the child progresses to the mature stage, the movement looks more automatic. In the previous examples, throwing and catching look consistent without the need for great preparation. The child can adjust their movement when the ball is slightly different. The practice or performance is in a static or unchanging environment. Very few children in elementary school progress beyond the mature level of movement. The mastery level is when children can perform a skill at a high level, in a dynamic or changing environment. The skill is often performed on the move with a defender in an ever-changing game situation. The mastery level is so rare at the elementary school level that it is not usually the focus of elementary school physical education curriculum. Students are most often at different skill levels in different skills. A student might be at the mature level in throwing and at the developmental level in jumping and landing.

Teaching and Planning for the Variety of Developmental Movement

In the planning stages for teaching physical education, the teacher must address each of the developmental levels they will encounter in the grade level they teach. At what grade levels will you see these different developmental patterns? From pre-kindergarten to kindergarten most students will be at the immature level of movement. In third grade, some students will be at the immature level, some at the developing level, and the rare students will be at the mature developmental level. In sixth grade, some students will be at the developing level and some students at the mature level of development. When the teacher plans a physical education lesson, in actuality it is one lesson with between one and three different accommodations for the differences in developmental skill levels.

As previously stated, no two students are at the exactly same developmental level. So how do you teach children that are at different developmental stages? The term most often heard in education is differential instruction. There are two educational strategies most often employed in teaching physical education to allow students to practice skills at their own developmental level. Firstly, give students a choice in practice that they feel is appropriate for their own level to succeed. This involves inviting students to decide what they can do to succeed at an 80% success rate. In implementation, it may be inviting the kids to throw against the wall as far back as they can and still hit the wall at least eight out of ten times. In this scenario, some students will be close up and some students are faraway. Every student is able to achieve success at their own distance. Since not all students will make the correct choice for them, the second strategy for differential instruction is for the teacher to decide where the student will move to ensure they are succeeding at the 80% success rate.

Teaching quality physical education takes careful preparation and planning. It takes time to teach a meaningful curriculum in any subject. Often physical education is unplanned and used as a break from learning. When this occurs, it is often recess that the teacher calls physical education, which confuses kids since recess is unstructured free time, which is the same thing that the teacher is now calling physical education. Physical education, as its name implies, has education as the core in its daily delivery. It has standards as a guide in determining what should be taught at each grade level. Physical education has structure and sequence as all other subjects in an elementary school have. The goal of physical education is to create lifelong lovers and participants of movement.

Social Justice and Diversity

A worthy goal in education has been to focus on and provide change to social inequities that our students, teachers, schools, and society experience. These inequities allow some individuals to have advantages over others. In physical education, we look for ways that we can promote more humane, socially just, and democratic forms of physical activity so that all people have opportunities to gain the benefits of physical activity. The strands of social justice center around race and ethnicity, age, gender, ability, sexual orientation, language, religion, and socioeconomic status (social class).

The following is a discussion of these strands of social justice as they apply to physical education curriculum and instruction. In looking at race and ethnicity the teacher examines their own practices concerning games they play that emphasize marginalized cultures. They must also make sure that discussions in class reflect a wide variety of athletes from different racial backgrounds. The goal of physical education is to create lifelong lovers of movement. This means that discussion and activities of movement should address all of the ages and stages in life, not just the current age of the student. Students should participate in games and activities they can do later in life. Students are often chastised for walking instead of running even though walking is the most common form of life-long activity. Inviting active, older adults to talk to students can help them gain insight and appreciation for others. There is an increasingly important discussion with students that they understand the difference between sex and gender. Sex is a biological classification (male, female, intersex, etc.). Usually, this is based on the external reproductive body parts (e.g. penis, vagina, etc.). Gender, on the other hand, has to do with the cultural meanings that are given to bodies (Lynch & Landi, 2018). Traditional stereotypes are less true than ever. Care has to be taken to ensure that skills and fitness are taught the same regardless of gender or identification. Classes, groups, and teams must reflect a mixed society and not be separated by gender. When students are grouped by ability, it can lead to students with disabilities being segregated from others. Physical education is most often trying to increase the skills of the students in the classes. As students gain skills this can widen the gap between some students and students with disabilities. Careful planning and reflection are required to make sure that there is full inclusion for all students. Disability awareness education examining barriers both in the school and community will help students to gain an appreciation of the challenges that others face. The teacher and school need to provide modification of equipment and tasks to ensure there is meaningful involvement for all students with disabilities in class activities. For many LGBTQIA (lesbian, gay, bisexual, transgender, queer/questioning, intersex, asexual) students, physical education can be a stressful place for learning. Cooperative learning activities often are preferred over a competitive learning environment. One of the advantages of physical education over other subjects is that language differences can be more easily accommodated. The physical nature of physical education allows for the demonstration of most tasks. This visual representation facilitates language acquisition in ways that less visual subjects struggle to provide. In preparing the curriculum and the learning environment, signs, exams, and cues must reflect the languages spoken in class to provide an effective learning atmosphere. There are many different religions practiced in the United States. As a teacher, it is essential you appreciate and acknowledge the beliefs of all students in your class. Being aware of the diverse religions in your own class will aid in planning for accommodations during certain months (e.g. Ramadan, etc.). Religious beliefs may also influence dress in physical education, such as a burka or burkini. Lastly, socioeconomic status is one of the major contributors to academic success and fitness opportunities. Students come from all different backgrounds. Resource access influences students' and parents' support outside of the school day. Opportunities to play outside or join sports teams are limited by financial support and transportation. For many students, physical education is their only opportunity to have movement experiences within their day. It is important to recognize the financial implications of activities that students are exposed to in physical education and whether this would limit their ability to pursue these activities outside of school. All of the areas discussed are considerations of social justice and creating equity and opportunity in physical education and schools.

Social Justice and Diversity

Equality versus equity: These terms mean different things but are often used interchangeably. Equity means providing everyone with an opportunity to be successful. Equality means fairness or treating everyone the same. In this next section, equality and equity will be applied in a teaching environment (Lynch et al., 2020).

The students are learning to bat a ball off a cone. The equipment available is cones (all the same height), plastic bats and balls, and boxes. Equality would be fulfilled by each student having their own cone, bat, and ball. Each student has equal equipment. This situation would not fulfill equity since there are different sized students in the class. Some students would need additional support and be allowed to modify their learning stations. Equity would be addressed by having students who do not need additional support stand on the ground and hit the ball. Those students who are shorter may need to stand on a box to hit the ball, while those who are tall may need to put the box under the cone to make it higher. These types of modifications recognize that not all students are the same or have the same needs. Providing additional support to those students who need it allows equity to be a principle for quality, reflective teaching.

Promoting Social and Emotional Competence

The Physical Education curriculum provides opportunities for students to learn and practice communication, problem-solving, and decision-making skills in partner and group situations. Movement is a potent means of learning and engaging in a variety of these personal, social, and cognitive skills (Ciotto & Gagnon, 2018). Because many of the activities in physical education require partner or teamwork, it is the perfect place for children to experience healthy social interactions, teamwork, and cooperation.

An example of a team-building, problem-solving cooperative game is River Crossing. Prior to the introduction of the game, instructions to the students are specific: that they must listen to each student team member prior to beginning a plan to accomplish the goal of the game. The goal of this game is for all members of the group to cross the river without falling or touching the water. Hula hoops work well for this activity. Ropes can be used to mark the river. Students are divided into groups of four or five. Each team has one more hula hoop than it has team members. The team must use the hoops to cross the river. The students and groups need to work together to stay in the hoops and take the back hoop to the front. If a player in the team is unbalanced and falls or touches the ground, then the whole team starts from the beginning. The first team to cross the river wins. Being a team game, River Crossing requires work and communication between members. The team players must discuss and understand all steps and actions, and time is given to pursue these discussions before the game begins.

Visual and Performing Arts

Visual and Performing Arts (VAPA) include drama, choir, band, art, dance, and other classes that involve movement and visuals. Most public schools in California offer these classes throughout K–12 education. In elementary school, these classes are usually supplemented into the classrooms throughout the week. VAPA teachers at the elementary level may not have a classroom, but go from classroom to classroom to meet the needs of students. At the middle and high school levels, these classes are usually chosen as elective classes by students. Secondary students often decide which elective they would like to take and these teachers often have their own classroom to support their students' creative needs. VAPA classes are important in the development of fine motor skills, creativity, social-emotional interactions, and much more. Each course under VAPA abides by different standards.

National Standards

Each state has its own set of standards for visual and performing arts. These standards can be found at https://www.nationalartsstandards.org/content/national-core-arts-standards-anchor-standards#creating. Standards are typically broken down into subject areas such as dance, media arts, music, theater, and visual arts. The National Art Standards serve as an overview for all Visual and Performing Arts standards. There are a few main concepts covered in all VAPA courses. These anchor standards include creating, performing/presenting/producing, responding, and connecting. These standards can be found on the National Arts Standards website. For each of these national standards, we will look at a general definition, core standards, and ideas for application and assessment of the standards in different VAPA classrooms (SEADAE, 2014).

Creating

Box 7.1 National Core Arts Standards

Anchor Standard #1: Generate and conceptualize artistic ideas and work.
Anchor Standard #2: Organize and develop artistic ideas and work.
Anchor Standard #3: Refine and complete artistic work.

Creativity is defined as conceiving and developing new artistic ideas and work. Application of creativity in a VAPA classroom is often easy for people to visualize. Students can be seen creating dances, exploring electronic art, making music, participating in plays or skits, or even making drawings, paintings, or sculptures. There are ideas for all educators to implement arts across curriculums. While these are often activities found within the walls of VAPA classrooms across the world, these activities don't have to be confined to an art room or band room. There are many opportunities for cross-curricular lessons. Cross-curricular VAPA lessons would be lessons taught in general education classes (math, science, history, English, etc.) that meet the Visual and

Performing Arts Standards. Let's take a look at each type of VAPA course and how these lessons can be taught in the everyday general education curriculum.

Dance

In order to meet the creativity standard, students can choreograph a dance. This could be implemented in a history, social studies, or geography lesson by having students research and share cultural dances from around the world. As there's more push for multicultural curriculum in schools, this would be a great opportunity for students to learn about other cultures through dance and movement. By engaging in dance, students get to experience different cultures and share what they learned with classmates by exploring movement.

Media Arts

Math might seem like a hard subject to incorporate VAPA standards with, but there are many chances for students to show their creativity. Students could create a sales sign which correlates to math problems dealing with percentages. This would give students the opportunity to figure out math problems, but also show creativity in deciding what they would sell and how they would show what percentage off their items were. Using computers, students would have to create sales signs using digital art. Signs would have to show what's being sold, be catchy to the eye, and accurately depict how much the sales item costs after a certain percentage is taken off. By applying math to a real-life event, such as a shopping sale, students engage in the lesson more and can have fun trying to advertise and sell items to classmates using visuals to make them appealing.

Music

Music is very creative and can give students the opportunity to express their knowledge in a different way than presentations can. Students could be given the task of making their own words to a song based on any subject area. A cross-curricular science lesson could be making a rap to remember the water cycle. By giving students a chance to share information in another method, more students will be engaged in the lesson and retain information later on.

Theater

Theater is a great performing art to incorporate into an English classroom where students explore character and plot development and travel to new worlds through literature. Students can write a short skit using book characters and personalities to describe book events. By creating a skit, students get to create new dialog between characters, show their understanding of the plot, and make connections to their personal lives by making the skit personal.

Visual Arts

There are endless ways to incorporate visual arts into different classes and subject areas. An art project could be as simple as drawing a picture of a new topic or a more difficult longer project such as creating a diorama. Many schools provide study skills classes, support classes, or an advisory class. One visual arts activity a teacher of these classes could incorporate is to have students draw a picture of themselves accomplishing a goal. While learning how to create goals it's important for students to keep in mind the end game. Goal writing can be incorporated into any subject area, but by adding in a visual arts drawing, students are able to visualize themselves succeeding and imagine how great they'll feel when they accomplish meeting their goal.

Performing/Presenting/Producing

National Core Arts Standards:

Anchor Standard #4: Select, analyze, and interpret artistic work for presentation.
Anchor Standard #5: Develop and refine artistic techniques and work for presentation.
Anchor Standard #6: Convey meaning through the presentation of artistic work.

There are three specific ways to display works of art, whether visual or performing. Works of art can either be performed, presented, or produced. The definition used for performing is "realizing artistic ideas and work through interpretation and presentation." Performances are used specifically for dance, music, and theater arts. Presenting, used for visual arts, is defined as "interpreting and sharing artistic work." Producing is typically used in the media arts and is defined as "realizing and presenting artistic ideas and work." Each different VAPA course will approach this standard differently depending on the class needs and projects/works being completed. Performances, presentations, or productions are common assessments used to grade students in VAPA classes so it's important to understand what the students are accomplishing in each project, performance, or work of art. Students are challenged to interpret other artists' works, develop their own style, and create meaning from works.

Application in VAPA Classrooms

Dance

To meet Standard 4, students can research different types of dance. They can research the history of the dance, compare it to other dances, and look up the importance or meaning of the dance. Students can then present this information to meet Standard 4. Students can then perform a sample of the dance to meet Standard 5. To take this project one step further and complete all three standards under performing/presenting/producing, students could then share their interpretation of the meaning of their dance or ask classmates to share what they believe the meaning is around the dance.

Media Arts

Producing unique business cards is a common project for media arts classes to incorporate into their lessons. In order to meet the three anchor standards, students could first start by researching different businesses and their advertising techniques. They can analyze what colors or imagery the company uses to sell its products and use this information towards creating their own projects to accomplish Standard 4. Standard 5 would be accomplished by then creating business cards and presenting their business ideas to their classmates. Finally, Standard 6 would be accomplished if students then share the meaning or purpose of their business cards or ask classmates to interpret why they used specific imagery or colors to sell their specific product.

Music

Many schools offer music classes to students, whether it's band, choir, or music appreciation, in order to provide well-rounded public education (CMA Foundation, 2017). Performing in a choir, band, or holiday music concert is common across schools in the United States. Concerts are performances that would meet Standard 5 under performing/presenting/producing, but there's more that goes into a performance than the end product that families and the community hear. Countless hours are typically spent at school and at home to perfect the music and make sure it's "performance ready." Standards 4 and 6 would usually happen in class as students are preparing for a concert or show. Music is selected specifically to meet the needs of students, whether beginning or advanced, but also music is usually chosen because it has a specific theme or meaning. Students in music courses often research different musicians or works throughout history or different cultures, which meets Standard 4. Students then derive meaning from these works, whether it is aesthetically pleasing to them or speaks to them on a personal level. Sharing these meanings or having discussions about the meaning behind different works in class would meet Standard 6.

Theater

Theater is a great way for students to be creative and share their passions with others. (Reeves, n.d.) Performing in a school play is the most common way to meet Standard 5, but there's a lot more to performances than just memorizing lines. Standard 4 is often met by learning about a specific play or musical that will be performed. It's common to discuss character development and settings, and interpret the meaning of the works throughout history or cultures, which meet Standards 4 and 6. Many plays have historical context that will help actors/actresses play the part. Theater arts also include costumes, set designs, and stage management. All of these jobs are important to make a performance run smoothly and be successful.

Visual Arts

Visual arts cover everything from drawing, painting, ceramics, sculpture, mixed media, digital art, and more. Holding an art show allows students to display completed works and share accomplishments with others. Students must plan their projects by researching other artworks or artists for inspiration. Students then need to produce artwork that will be shown. Holding an art critique in class would allow students to interpret works and better their pieces before showing the completed projects. Art shows allow viewers to interpret works and convey meanings.

Cross-Curricular Application

Though it's easy to present wos in VAPA classes, it would be easy to also incorporate any of the above ideas into other classes. Students share any of their creations from above in core classes by presenting works to their classmates or creating a video or PowerPoint to share. Presenting works allows students to express themselves in different ways and share understanding of topics in unique ways. There are endless ways to express knowledge other than taking tests. Proving understanding of a topic can be creative and memorable so students retain the information they learned (Aravindan, n.d.).

Responding

National Core Arts Standards:

Anchor Standard #7: Perceive and analyze artistic work.
Anchor Standard #8: Interpret intent and meaning in artistic work.
Anchor Standard #9: Apply criteria to evaluate artistic work.

Responding means understanding and evaluating how the arts convey meaning. There's important academic language for students to learn that helps guide discussions. Academic language is discipline-specific language, meaning vocabulary terms or phrases used in specific courses (Herr, n.d.). All

VAPA classes have a set of shared vocabulary that help guide discussions about works. Common terminology used across VAPA classrooms is the principles of design. "The principles of design describe the ways that artists use the elements of art in a work of art" (Getty, 2011). The principles of design can be used in any VAPA class and help interpret and evaluate works.

Principles of design:

1. Balance: Distribution of objects in a work to make them seem stable.
2. Emphasis: Making something in the work stand out from everything else.
3. Rhythm: Using elements in repetition to create organized movement.
4. Pattern: A repetitive design.
5. Proportion: Small parts related to larger parts.
6. Unity: Feeling of harmony between all parts of the work.
7. Variety: Using several different elements to create interest.

Application in VAPA Classrooms

VAPA teachers use class conversations and critiques to analyze work. "A critique is a formal analysis and evaluation of a text, production, or performance—either one's own (a self-critique) or someone else's" (Nordquist, 2019). Students often look at works to critique and analyze. In order to talk about works, students must learn terminology and use their academic language.

Cross-Curricular Application

English

English offers a great opportunity to incorporate academic language from other disciplines. Students can find the principles of design within literature. The principles of design can be used during poetry, especially when learning about patterns, balance, emphasis, or rhythm within writing. Students can listen to poetry to analyze the meanings of symbolism. To meet the standards, students would need to perceive meaning from the poem, interpret intent from the author, and critique the work using academic language.

Math

Learning new equations can be hard for students but applying an artistic viewpoint could help students understand and apply math in different ways. The principles of balance and pattern are used often in math, especially when balancing equations or finding number patterns. Humans naturally find patterns to better understand the world around them (Satell, 2015). Architecture uses math and art to create structures such as arches, domes, or pyramids. Students should view different mathematical equations or methods to find patterns.

Science

Science and art have been intertwined for centuries. Both scientists and artists are constantly looking for new discoveries and interpret the world around them (Maeda, 2013). Leonardo Da Vinci is a perfect example of an artist and scientist. Students often find patterns to reach conclusions in lab experiments. They can analyze experiments and discuss conclusions. Controversial beliefs would be a fun topic with which to analyze different conclusions of the same theory.

History/Social Sciences

There's endless variety in different cultures such as differences in the idea of beauty, food, or fashion. Students can find patterns in historical events or compare and contrast artistic elements from different times in history or places around the world. Teachers can incorporate the arts by having students view artworks, fashion, food, and dance, and listen to music of different cultures. Students can analyze the intent and meaning of the works and discuss how it relates to history or culture.

Connecting

National Core Arts Standards:

Anchor Standard #10: Synthesize and relate knowledge and personal experiences to make art.

Anchor Standard #11: Relate artistic ideas and works with societal, cultural, and historical context to deepen understanding.

Making connections is important in the process of learning and retaining information. Connecting means relating artistic ideas and work with personal meaning and external context. Finding personal connections to works will deepen student understanding by making new knowledge meaningful and memorable (FutureLearn, n.d.). Students are more willing to engage in topics they can relate to and retain the information learned through personal connections.

Multicultural Education

There's a push for multicultural education in public school education. Standard 11 incorporates the ideas of multicultural teaching. "Multicultural education refers to any form of education or teaching that incorporates the histories, texts, values, beliefs, and perspectives of people from different cultural backgrounds" (Great Schools Partnership, 2013). Equity in the classroom is created by incorporating ideas from all people. Connecting with works allows students to learn about different cultures, analyze works from around the world, incorporate different cultural aspects into their own works, and make personal cultural connections to works.

Chapter Summary

This chapter provides the basis for understanding what constitutes quality movement experiences for children. The documents that guide instruction in local, state, and national settings are examined. The importance of play is discussed in relation to the development of gross motor skills and interpersonal relationships. School-age experiences start with movement exploration and move to movement education. Movement concepts and skill development form the basis of elementary physical education. Key indicators of quality education include a curriculum that is developmentally and instructionally appropriate. Finally, differential instruction in physical education is focused on providing maximum learning opportunities for different skill levels that are prevalent in each grade level.

References

123 Expert (2017). Retrieved 9/27/17 from http://www.experts123.com/q/what-is-movement-exploration.html.

Anderson, L., Jones, M., Wright, D., Izumigawa, S., Iroz, A., & Cooper, R. (2004). *Movement exploration*. Retrieved from http://jgelfer.faculty.unlv.edu/ECE354/movement.doc.

Aravindan, S. (n.d.). *The importance of presentation skills in the classroom*. Retrieved from https://study.com/academy/lesson/the-importance-of-presentation-skills-in-the-classroom.html.

Bento, & Dias (2017). The importance of outdoor play for young children's healthy development. *Porto Biomedical Journal*, 2(5), 157–160.

Cheung, R. (2010). Designing movement activities to develop children's creativity in early childhood education. *Early Child Development and Care*, 180(3), 377–385, doi:10.1080/03004430801931196

Ciotto, C., & Gagnon, A. (2018). Promoting social and emotional learning in physical education. *Journal of Physical Education, Recreation & Dance*, 89, 27–33. doi:10.1080/07303084.2018.1430625

CMA Foundation (2017). *The status of music education in united states public schools – 2017. Give a note foundation*. Retrieved from https://www.giveanote.org/media/2017/09/The-Status-of-Music-Education-in-US-Public-Schools-2017_reduced.pdf

FutureLearn (n.d.). *Helping students make connections - the science of learning*. Retrieved from https://www.futurelearn.com/courses/science-of-learning/0/steps/40549

Getty (2011). *Principles of design*. Retrieved from https://www.getty.edu/education/teachers/building_lessons/principles_design.pdf

Ginsburg, K.R.; American Academy of Pediatrics Committee on Communications; American Academy of Pediatrics Committee on Psychosocial Aspects of Child and Family Health

(2007). The importance of play in promoting healthy child development and maintaining strong parent-child bonds. *Pediatrics*, 119(1), 182–191.

Great Schools Partnership (2013, August 29). *Multicultural education definition*. Retrieved from https://www.edglossary.org/multicultural-education/

Herr, N. (n.d.). *Academic language- defined by PACT*. Retrieved from https://www.csun.edu/science/ref/language/pact-academic-language.html

Laban, R. (1928). *Schrifttanz*. Wein: Universal.

Lynch, S., & Landi, D. (2018). *Social justice in physical education*. Retrieved 8/29/19 from https://blog.shapeamerica.org/2018/09/social-justice-in-physical-education/.

Lynch, S., Sutherland, S., & Walton-Fisette, J. (2020). The A-Z of social justice physical education: Part 1. *Journal of Physical Education, Recreation & Dance*, 91(4), 8–13.

Maeda, J. (2013, July 11). *Artists and scientists: More alike than different*. Retrieved from https://blogs.scientificamerican.com/guest-blog/artists-and-scientists-more-alike-than-different/.

Mayo Clinic Staff (2019). Screen time and children: How to guide your child. *Health Lifestyle: Journal of Children's Health*. Retrieved 11/04/19 from https://www.mayoclinic.org/healthy-lifestyle/childrens-health/in-depth/screen-time/art-20047952.

National Standards for K-12 Physical Education (2013). *SHAPE America – society of health and physical educators*. Reston, VA. Retrieved 10/08/19 from http://www.shapeamerica.org.

Nordquist, R. (2019, July 1). *What is a critique?* Retrieved from https://www.thoughtco.com/what-is-critique-composition-1689944

PE Central (2019). *PE hall of shame*. Retrieved 11/4/19 from https://www.pecentral.org/professional/hos/.

Peet, E.D., McCoy, D.C., Danaei, G., Ezzati, M., Fawzi, W., Jarvelin, M.-R., et al. (2015). Early childhood development and schooling attainment: Longitudinal evidence from British, Finnish and Philippine Birth Cohorts. *PLoS ONE*, 10(9), e0137219. https://doi.org/10.1371/journal.pone.0137219.

Reeves, J. (n.d.). *The importance of theatre education*. Retrieved from https://shearwaterproductions.com/2014/07/the-importance-of-theatre-education/.

Satell, G. (2015, May 10). *The science of patterns*. Retrieved from https://www.forbes.com/sites/gregsatell/2015/05/01/the-science-of-patterns/#b6af5f519004.

SEADAE (2014). *National core arts anchor standards*. Retrieved from https://www.nationalartsstandards.org/content/national-core-arts-standards-anchor-standards#creating.

Strasburger, V.C., Jordan, A.B., & Donnerstein, E. (2010). Health effects of media on children and adolescents. *Pediatrics*, 125(4), 756–767. PMID:20194281 www.ncbi.nlm.nih.gov/pubmed/20194281.

Valdez, L. (2017). *Movement education,(3 ed.) Stature books*. https://staturebooks.com/mved/

Chapter 8

Embracing Diversity to Humanize the Classroom Environment

Aletha Harven

Introduction

Teachers who embrace diversity are extremely thoughtful in how they humanize the classroom experience for themselves and their students. To humanize the classroom is to demonstrate vulnerability and authenticity, so as to create a safe space for students to do the same. When trust and honesty are built into the learning environment, along with a recognition and acceptance of students' lived experiences, teaching and learning become more meaningful for everyone. The question then becomes, *how do teachers engage in the challenging task of humanizing the classroom environment? Firstly*, we must agree upon a shared language surrounding what it means to embrace diversity, which is really the ability to recognize and respect people's differences. Our students' social identities, personalities, cognitive abilities, athletic abilities, socioemotional well-being, home environments, and the like will influence how they bring themselves to the classroom context. The challenges associated with student diversity, if viewed positively, can lead to the development of a more supportive and motivating classroom experience. *Secondly*, teachers must adopt the goal of creating an inclusive and equitable learning environment for their diverse students by sharing power. Inclusivity involves understanding and utilizing our knowledge of students' lived experiences and the communities to which they belong to connect with them and develop curricular activities that speak to their unique experiences. Inclusivity requires flexibility in pedagogy, flexibility in students' demonstration of knowledge, value given to students' voices, and curricular materials that emphasize diverse perspectives. When students feel seen and heard and are given agency in their learning, they are more likely to succeed in your classroom. Equitable learning environments feel fair to students, where no matter what is occurring in their lives, they can expect to receive the assistance they need to succeed academically. For instance, a student who has no transportation and little to eat in the mornings might require greater flexibility from his teacher in regard to his attendance and focus. To maintain her high expectations for the student, the teacher could devise a plan with the student to meet his basic and academic needs. To lower her standards, due to the student's life circumstances, would be unjust and inequitable. We must remember that inclusion and equity are about embracing student diversity and utilizing this knowledge to meet students' needs for success -—not lowering our standards out of sympathy or only maintaining high standards for students we feel are more educable.

Thirdly, as teachers, we must acknowledge how we bring ourselves to the classroom context. Take a moment to ponder the following questions: how might your appearance impact students' perceptions of you? How do your social identities intersect to influence your ability to understand and connect with students' lived experiences? Is your philosophical approach to teaching and learning rigid or fluid, and how might this approach impact student learning? How might the tone of your voice, your attitude, and your behavior shape the classroom context? How might your assignments, activities, grading standards, and general classroom policies impact student learning? How might your mental health and the extent to which you have healed from past trauma impact your classroom behavior? How might your implicit biases influence your interactions with students and the extent to which you challenge injustice? There are many more questions to consider in exploring how we bring ourselves to the classroom context, and it is our responsibility to engage in the challenging work of understanding how everything from our appearance to the intersection of our social identities, beliefs, and philosophies shape the lens in which we function in the classroom. *Fourthly*, teachers must learn to put words into action by bravely standing against injustice. Additional questions to consider include: how might accepting student diversity rather than tolerating it influence your interactions with students? Do you fully understand systems of privilege and oppression in our society? Do you understand how schools reproduce and maintain a system of injustice? Do you understand how to utilize your privilege to help those without a voice? Might your need to feel comfortable, by maintaining the status quo, further disadvantage your most vulnerable students? While there are many strategies to consider when embracing student diversity to humanize the classroom environment, the current chapter will expand upon the aforementioned strategies discussed here.

Embracing Student Diversity for a Humanizing Experience

How do we understand *diversity*? As previously stated, to embrace diversity is to recognize and respect people's differences. Our students walk into the classroom context with their own intersecting identities that shape their interactions with you and their classmates. Your job as an educator is to understand students' unique identities, in order to connect with them in meaningful ways. Please note that social identities are based on a number of factors such as national origin, race, ethnicity, sex, gender, sexual orientation, (dis)ability status, socioeconomic status, religious or spiritual affiliation, language, and the activities in which we engage. Here is an example of a young learner, who embodies many social identities: student, girl, Black, American, Christian, dancer, tutor, guitarist, daughter, sister, friend, middle-class, and able-bodied. Similarly, another young learner might embody the following social identities: student, boy, White, South African, Christian, son, brother, friend, artist, poet, autistic, and middle-class.

It is noteworthy that social identities can be derived from our status in different contexts, such as being a friend when playing with neighborhood children and being a son when at home with caregivers. Social identities can further be derived from the activities in which we engage, like being a gymnast, pianist, or painter. It is critical to note that specific social identities might be more salient (or important) in specific contexts, but not in others. For instance, the identity of a student might be salient in the school context but not in one's friendship circle, when the identity of friend takes on more importance while talking over pizza.

Students' social identities also intersect to give them a unique perspective on the world. To understand the intersection of social identities is to acknowledge *intersectionality*, which is a term coined by Kimberlé Crenshaw (1989) to bring awareness to how individual characteristics such as race, gender, socioeconomic status, and the like "intersect" to uniquely impact people's everyday lives. Harven and Perouse-Harvey (2020) stated that as educators, we must recognize that students' intersecting identities can either advantage or disadvantage them in the school context. That is, a Black female student, who is middle-class with educated parents who provide her with a lot of education at home, will likely have more cultural capital[1] than her classmates who have not been exposed to the same information. However, this student might experience a variety of barriers due to her intersecting social identities and people's stereotyped perceptions of who Black girls and women are supposed to be, which is typically not middle-class and well-rounded. An Asian American male who is low-income, whose parents speak little English, might be ignored in school due to stereotypes associated with Asian American children being "whiz kids" who need little assistance (Brand, 1987; Lee, 2015). This student might, in fact, need a lot of assistance with his homework completion, as his parents might not be able to assist him at home. Harven and Perouse-Harvey (2020) provided another example of how students with disabilities "might have a combination of low-privileged identities" that include their disability status, along with "being a person of color, a sexual minority, and being of a lower class," which could really alienate them in school (p. 1535), impacting their mental health and feelings of belonging.

To learn more, teachers should explore and use social identity wheels in their classrooms for meaningful conversations with students, or teachers could utilize these identity wheels to simply gain more knowledge on the advantages and disadvantages associated with diverse social identities (see Program on Intergroup Relations, 2020). By learning about students' intersecting identities, along with their home lives, mental health status, and personality traits, teachers will be armed with critical knowledge to meet students where they are—and to help each student to succeed in a way that works for them. Teachers could also use the knowledge they have on students to ensure that they all feel seen and heard and are represented in the curricular materials. Some questions to ponder include: are the images in your classroom texts and materials representative of your students? Do the pictures you present and/or display represent the diversity of your students? Do you bring in additional curricular materials that showcase diverse perspectives that relate to your students' lived experiences? Do you vary your teaching style to accommodate diverse learners? Do you allow your students to share their personal experiences (narratives) in unique ways? Do your students engage in pair and small group activities that allow for critical debates and perspective sharing? It is critical for teachers to address these questions to get the ball rolling on creating an inclusive classroom environment that embraces student diversity and humanizes the classroom.

Box 8.1 Theme: Social Justice and Diversity

When teachers reject the notion of being blind to students' differences, and instead acknowledge and embrace student diversity, they can begin to create an inclusive classroom environment that speaks to the unique needs of their students. As teachers, we must recognize our students' similarities and differences, so as to modify our pedagogical approaches to support the students we serve. In order to truly value the diversity of our students, we must take time to learn about them and bring that knowledge into the classroom environment. It is simply not enough to say that we care about social justice and diversity as it relates to our students; rather, we must act on that stance and show our students that we are truly here to support them and their success.

Sharing Power for Inclusive and Equitable Classroom Environments

As previously mentioned, teachers must adopt the goal of creating an inclusive and equitable learning environment for their diverse students, which includes the sharing of power. Inclusion is about finding ways to make all students, regardless of their differences, feel like they are part of the classroom environment. Research has consistently demonstrated that a sense of belonging is motivating for students (Roeser, Midgley, & Urdan, 1996; see also Gray,

Hope, & Matthews, 2018); therefore, teachers must create a trusting and safe environment for students to be exactly who they are while learning critical information and skills. A large part of inclusion involves equitable classroom practices, where students feel a sense of fairness in their classroom and are given numerous opportunities to succeed. To create a classroom environment that not only allows students to be actively engaged in the learning process but that also feels fair and supportive in nature, teachers have to share their power with students. Try not to think of sharing your power as a scary process, where you imagine relinquishing control to a group of chaotic students. Instead, try thinking of sharing your power as placing students' interests, voices, lived experiences, and needs at the center of the learning experience, where you act as a guide, co-constructing knowledge with students (Hardman, Jan, Hardman, & Frank, 2017). Harven and Soodjinda (2016) have suggested several ways for teachers to relinquish control and share power with their students for the development of safe, trusting, and inclusive classroom environments (see also Holley & Steiner, 2005; Stambler, 2013). I will present the suggestions here and elaborate on them for the purpose of this chapter.

Harven and Soodjinda (2016) suggested that teachers should modify the *physical seating* of their classrooms in thinking about the best structure for promoting personal connections among learners and a sense of belonging. Many teachers endorse traditional (or rote) teaching and learning philosophies, where they act as a Sage on the Stage, doling out information, while their students rush to take copious notes in seated rows that face the chalkboard. Non-traditional seating arrangements like circle seating or staging desks where students face each other in groups are suggested for effectively building a sense of community among learners. Sitting and facing one another, while sharing personal narratives and engaging in critical discussions, debates, and hands-on activities, can begin to bridge gaps between diverse students. Teachers should also join student circles and groups by sitting with students at their level, listening closely, and posing questions when appropriate, while letting students lead the discussion. Relinquishing control in this way can humanize the classroom experience by placing students' need for community at the center of learning, and you still maintain your status as teacher-facilitator. Harven and Soodjinda (2016) also suggested that teachers who want to embrace diversity and create an inclusive and equitable classroom environment should be "*knowledgeable and informative*" on social justice issues that impact diverse groups of students and their families, especially students with low-privileged or marginalized identities. This is where we, as teachers, must educate ourselves on how current events (e.g., immigration reform) might impact our students (e.g., undocumented youth) and their families. Research has demonstrated that children who experience trauma associated with the deportation of a caregiver often lose focus and motivation, experience mental health issues, and perform poorly in school (Gonzalez, Monzon, Solis, Jaycox, and Langley, 2016). Therefore, being aware of critical issues that impact students or even openly discussing or developing curricular activities to address these issues with students, will help make the curriculum more relevant to students' lived experiences, which feels humanizing.

Harven and Soodjinda (2016) further suggested that teachers be "*good models of effective participation*" by demonstrating vulnerability through sharing personal narratives with students. For example, teachers could share stories from their childhoods when appropriate and invite students to do the same in order to connect with students and make additional links to texts. Active listening is key when being an effective participant, for both teachers and students, where teachers must make a conscious effort to validate students' thoughts so they feel respected and valued. These behaviors do not take power away from teachers; in fact, they garner more respect from students because students feel their perspectives matter. Harven and Soodjinda (2016) endorsed active learning strategies for encouraging more engagement from students. *Active learning* strategies have continued to grow in popularity among educators, where the goal is to present critical information in a way that keeps students stimulated and excited about learning. Some active learning strategies that have been positively associated with critical thinking include inquiry-based instruction, which entails *questioning*, *written exercises*, and *discussions and debates* (Walker, 2003). These activities allow students to challenge their own thinking, as well as that of their classmates, while also encouraging them to find support for their arguments and to freely express their thoughts with others. Another great tool is *iClickers* or programs such as *poll anywhere*, where students can respond anonymously in real-time to questions that teachers pose and that the class can view (e.g., "what word describes your mood right now?"). Another technique is to encourage students to engage in mini-research activities, where they address critical questions for learning (see Sandoval & Harven, 2011 for an example).

Harven and Soodjinda (2016) have also stated the importance of teachers being *supportive of all opinions and non-judgmental* when trying to create a classroom environment that is inclusive of diverse opinions. Teachers must listen to and be willing to challenge students' opinions, especially if they are insensitive in nature. Questioning students is a great way to help them reflect on their thinking. Inviting their classmates to join in the discussion can be a powerful way to share the responsibility of addressing polarizing opinions. Teachers must also be *comfortable and calm* in challenging students' thinking by presenting opposing views and personal narratives from diverse voices (Harven & Soodjinda, 2016). Take some time to examine your curricular materials. Is your curriculum Eurocentric or White-centered, where the authors and scholars are primarily White, and perhaps male, which is typical of many curricular materials? If yes, you need to dismantle this need for Eurocentric or White-centered material and give voice to the diversity that exists among students' realities. One way to do this is to introduce diverse cultural frameworks into the classroom discourse when exploring various topics and issues. Upon diversifying your curricular materials, teachers should also provide background knowledge on diverse authors, scientists, scholars, and book characters, so students can possibly see themselves in the course material, which gives value to their experiences. As previously mentioned, encouraging students to share their own narratives will naturally lend itself to diverse perspective-taking among students. Lastly, Harven and Soodjinda (2016) suggested *maintaining high expectations* for students, which was mentioned earlier in this chapter. While inclusivity calls for teacher flexibility with students, teachers should never lower their standards or expectations for diverse groups of students, especially students from historically underserved communities. As educators, we must reject *deficit thinking*, where disadvantaged students are perceived as having deficits and/or being ineducable (see Garcia & Guerra, 2004 for a discussion on deconstructing deficit thinking). Teachers who endorse a deficit ideology are typically doing a disservice to historically underserved students, with low-privileged identities. Instead, teachers must maintain their high expectations and standards, while addressing students' individual needs for success. By doing this, teachers can create equitable learning environments.

The aforementioned suggestions allow for "*shared power*" in the classroom, which is so critical for creating an inclusive and equitable learning environment. Some additional suggestions for sharing power within the classroom include allowing students to modify and/or create the *classroom rules*, so they feel invested in the design and feel of the classroom environment. Teachers could also review their curricular language, such as the instructions on worksheets for tone. That is, language with an inviting tone is considered to be more inclusive than language that is demanding. For example, instead of instructions that read "write your opinion," teachers could modify the language to read, "*you are invited to share your opinion*" or "*please share your opinion.*" All in all, creating an inclusive and equitable classroom environment requires teachers to share power with their students, which breeds a sense of belonging and community among learners.

Box 8.2 Theme: Theory and Research to Practice

There is much research on school belonging, where a sense of belonging has been positively associated with higher levels of academic motivation (Neel & Fuligni, 2013). By sharing power with students, teachers can help students to feel like they are a part of the classroom structure and curriculum—and that their voices matter. Teachers must remember that sharing power is not about relinquishing control; rather, it is about inspiring students to become invested in the learning process by making them an integral part of the classroom environment.

Critiquing Our Presence in the Classroom

The way we bring ourselves to the classroom environment as educators can have a positive, negative, or even neutral effect on student learning. From the moment we walk into the classroom on the first day of school, the way we present ourselves will set the stage for how our students will perceive us and interact with us. To organize this section, I will address the questions posed in the introduction, so as to provide readers with food for thought.

Question 1: How might your appearance impact students' perceptions of you? Whether we like it or not, our appearance will influence our students' perceptions of us, as well as— their interactions with us. For instance, a White male teacher, who appears to be older in age, might be perceived as having more knowledge than a Mexican American female teacher, who is youthful in appearance. This perception could be associated with societal images of older White males in positions of power, as opposed to the portrayals of young women of color, who are typically not seen in similar positions. These perceptions might influence the extent to which students will listen to and challenge the teacher in the classroom, which we must be mindful of; however, young students and students of color might connect more with the youthful-looking Mexican American female teacher than with the teacher who is White, male, and older in appearance. Research demonstrates that students rate teachers higher who are similar to them, as opposed to teachers who present a racial mismatch in the classroom (McGrady & Reynolds, 2013). A racial or cultural mismatch between teachers and students can lead to negative learning outcomes, whereas matches between teachers and students can possibly lead to greater understanding and shared experiences and/or views (see van Kleeck, 2007; McGrady & Reynolds, 2013). *So what is a teacher to do?* Well, we cannot change our unique characteristics like our skin color, perceived race, ethnicity, age, (dis)ability status, and the like. However, we should acknowledge the reality of how our appearance might influence students' perceptions of us and work to connect with students in meaningful ways, so as to demonstrate authentic allyship. This is where teachers take time to build trust and safety with students by acknowledging their lived experiences.

Question 2: How might your social identities intersect to influence your ability to understand and connect with students' lived experiences? Similar to the discussion on acknowledging students' intersecting identities, we as teachers must acknowledge the impact of our intersecting identities on our teaching practices. For instance, a Japanese American male teacher, who teaches in a school with many Asian American students, might utilize the knowledge he has on different Asian ethnic groups to connect with his students in unique ways. However, if this same teacher was born and raised in an upper-class suburb and has extremely conservative political beliefs, then he might struggle to connect with his students, whose socioeconomic status and political views are very different from his. Regardless of teachers' differences in lived experiences, teachers are trained to endorse the status quo by embracing White middle-class values on teaching and learning, which advantages some and disadvantages others. Therefore, in understanding how we, as educators, bring ourselves to the classroom context, we must recognize that we operate from a place of privilege, *even if the privilege is not our own*. For instance:

- We come from a place of privilege when we assume that all students have home internet access, a working computer with a camera for teleconferencing, and a quiet place to study. Many students from underserved communities have difficulty working from home on schoolwork, for a variety of reasons, yet we penalize these students for not meeting our privileged expectations.
- We come from a place of privilege when we assume that all students have access to medical care if they get hurt or will visit the dentist if they chip their tooth or are having issues with teeth sensitivity, which is not the case for many students living in poverty.
- We come from a place of privilege when we require caregivers to attend teacher meetings at times that work with the school's schedule, which is unfair to caregivers who work two or three jobs or who start work in the afternoon for late shifts.
- We come from a place of privilege when we assume that all students will enjoy family holidays in the same way that many of us might, when in actuality, some students spend holidays, summers, and winter breaks avoiding being abused.

These are just a few examples of how teachers often endorse privileged beliefs, whether or not they are highly privileged, that turn into privileged expectations for students and their families. Therefore, it is critical for teachers to examine and dismantle these expectations in order to have a more flexible and understanding attitude with diverse student learners. Again, we must understand how our intersecting social identities, perspectives, political views, and privilege impact our expectations for students and their success in our classrooms.

Question 3: Is your philosophical approach to teaching and learning rigid or flexible, and how might this approach impact student learning? Rigid rules and expectations will ensure that some students will be left behind. However, flexibility in rules, pedagogy, assignments, activities, and classroom structure will ensure that most, if not all, students will perform well. For instance, in a class I currently teach, I allow students to tell me what they want to learn in the context of my course goals. I incorporate this information on students' interests into the course curriculum, so students are excited and invested in the course material. Elementary school teachers can also ask students what's important to them and find unique ways to address students' interests in the curriculum. Another idea is to allow assessments to vary by encouraging students to demonstrate their knowledge in a way that works for them. That is, teachers could give students options for demonstrating their knowledge on a particular topic such as (a) writing a reflective news article, (b) photo-journaling observations addressing a critical community-related issue, (c) creating a public service announcement (PSA) video to help other children, or (d) developing an idea for a software program, etc. Schools tend to focus heavily on testing, especially among young learners, but it is critical for teachers to create additional ways to assess students' knowledge by providing them with assessment choices that could aid them in test-taking. Flexibility also requires providing students with ample time to complete their assignments, as many students (a) do not work well under pressure, (b) might have a learning disability, and/or (c) might have study-related challenges at home that will require understanding from you. Your mode of instruction should also vary, so students can learn in a variety of ways. Thus, your philosophical approach to teaching and learning can either create an equitable learning environment or a learning environment that's based on survival of the fittest. Our goal as teachers should be to promote student learning, not to be gatekeepers who create inequitable learning environments.

Question 4: How might the tone of your voice, your attitude, and your behavior shape the classroom context? As previously mentioned, students watch our every move as teachers and instructors. Therefore, if your voice is consistently harsh, then students might perceive you in a negative way, especially if you're not a cultural match or they do not feel connected to you in some other way. Your positive or negative attitude will also impact the extent to which students enjoy learning from you. A positive attitude can make students feel excited about the class material, as opposed to a sour attitude coupled with a monotone voice. While joking with students can help them feel connected to you (Howard, 2001), jokes can sometimes go too far and become offensive. Teachers should avoid making any type of inappropriate comments when interacting with students, as hurtful comments can be demoralizing and dehumanizing. Many years ago, when I conducted focus groups with Black and Latinx students, they informed me of how their teacher, who happened to be an older White male, would get upset by their behavior, which would often spiral into a sparring match and end with the teacher telling the girls they would be pregnant school drop-outs, while the boys would end up in jail (Harven, 2004). Obviously, these race-specific comments were hurtful to students and the students expressed disengagement in that particular classroom. No matter how frustrating our students' behavior might be at times, it is our job to maintain a cool head and to make sure that our classroom environment feels comfortable for all students. Overall, teachers need to be mindful of tonality, attitude, and behavior and always maintain a professional stance.

Question 5: How might your assignments, activities, grading standards, and general classroom policies impact student learning? As previously mentioned, inclusive classroom environments are student-centered and active in nature, where teachers share their power with students. Co-constructing classroom rules with students and developing grading standards that are based on a variety of assessment types will help to create a more flexible and engaging learning environment.

Question 6: How might your implicit biases influence your interactions with students and the extent to which you challenge injustice? Implicit (or unconscious) biases refer to beliefs we unknowingly endorse. Greenwald and Krieger (2006) stated that implicit biases are "discriminatory biases based on implicit attitudes and stereotypes... they can produce behavior that diverges from a person's avowed or endorsed beliefs or principles" (p. 951). In other words, implicit biases are extremely problematic, because people who tend to endorse egalitarian values, believing themselves to be non-biased, unknowingly engage in discriminatory behavior. For instance, a male teacher might not be aware that he provides more assistance to his male students than his female students, suggesting a preference for boys. An able-bodied teacher might unknowingly call more on her able-bodied students than on her two students with physical disabilities, demonstrating her preference for able-bodied people. A teacher who provides very little help to Asian American students might endorse the model minority myth that Asian American students are naturally intelligent and do not need any assistance. A teacher who is always giving detention to Black and Latino male students might subconsciously believe that Black and Brown males are bad people. These are just some examples of how teachers' implicit biases can impact student mental health, motivation, and learning in a variety of ways. It is critical for teachers to explore their implicit biases. One way to do that is to take the Implicit Association Test (IAT), which was developed in 1995 by Anthony Greenwald, Mahzarin Banaji, and others and debuted on the internet in 1998 (Greenwarld, McGhee, & Schwartz, 1998). The IAT is comprised of a series of computer-based tests that employ association techniques to assist people in uncovering their unconscious biases (Adams, Devos, Rivera, Smith, & Vega, 2014). Some tests include the Skin-Tone IAT, which explores people's preference for lighter or darker skin tones. There is a RACE-IAT, a Gender-IAT, and additional tests designed to reveal people's attitudes toward diverse groups of people. As you begin to understand your implicit biases, you can start to effectively challenge them. If you do not understand your implicit biases, then you will likely interact with your students in discriminatory ways. I often hear teachers say that they believe in equality and care for all their students, yet are shocked and upset when students refer to them as racist or sexist. This is a perfect example of how these teachers might have implicit biases that are negatively affecting their interactions with students. Instead of invalidating students' perceptions, and becoming defensive because you believe yourself to be a good person, try to understand why students feel as they do. In sum, Harven and Soodjinda (2016) stated that teachers must "find comfort in disrupting biases, stereotypes, and embedded value systems that encourage oppressive practices" (p. 4). It is uncomfortable to embrace students' perceptions of us, but listening to students is key in understanding and valuing their lived experiences, even in our classrooms.

Question 7: How might your mental health and the extent to which you have healed from past trauma impact your classroom behavior? As teachers, we must monitor our mental health and heal from (or manage) past trauma, because that could play a role in our interactions with students. For instance, bipolar disorder, if not effectively treated, could lead to inconsistent and confusing behavior in the classroom, which could negatively impact student learning. A teacher who is stressed from personal issues might be distracted in the classroom and not focused on effectively delivering instruction. It is critical for us to take care of ourselves, so as to stay healthy for our students.

Box 8.3 Theme: Promoting Social and Emotional Competence

As teachers, we need to be aware of how we bring ourselves to the classroom context, especially in terms of our socioemotional functioning. If we begin to really embrace who we are and make modifications to how we bring ourselves to the classroom context, then we can help our students to embrace who they are and also increase their social and emotional well-being. Teachers should always demonstrate a high level of social and emotional competence, so students can model our behavior for their own adjustment. And if we, as teachers, can engage in the internal work necessary to understand ourselves, then we can help our students to do the same. As teachers, we should strive to work toward the same healthy goals as our students in being well-adjusted individuals.

Bravery in Advocating for the Voiceless

Teachers must learn to put words into action in bravely standing against injustice. As with the previous section, the questions posed in the introduction will serve as a guide.

Question 1: How might accepting student diversity rather than tolerating it influence your interactions with students? I have never liked the word *tolerate* when it comes to accepting people's differences, because *tolerate* has to do with the ability to endure; to sympathize with differences; and to allow for deviation from the standard (Merriam-Webster, 2020). It sounds painful to have to endure someone—and insensitive to "allow" students to be themselves. Instead, I have always liked the word *acceptance* because it is associated with having a favorable reception and a willingness to receive (Merriam-Webster, 2020). It is interesting how,when exploring both words, they had somewhat similar definitions regarding fairness and objectivity. Tolerating differences seems to be associated with maintaining one's implicit biases, whereas accepting people's differences requires exploration and rejection of one's implicit biases. To be inclusive and equitable in one's classroom practice is to willingly accept what makes us all different. Remember that acceptance and understanding can lead to a sense of belonging among students.

Question 2: Do you fully understand systems of privilege and oppression in our society? Do you understand how schools reproduce and maintain a system of injustice? Do you understand how to utilize your privilege to help those without a voice? These questions are critical, because as teachers we must first understand our own privilege, including how that privilege was obtained and is maintained. The power and privilege that a White male teacher has in the school context is different from the power and privilege that a Black male teacher possesses. However, male teachers tend to have more privilege than female teachers, but the intersection of race and gender further complicates the matter, as schools replicate societal norms. Given our intersecting social identities, how can you go about addressing inequality in your schools? It must be done in order for you and your students to function in an inclusive school environment. To care only about your classroom and ignore larger issues within the school context is to be complicit in an unjust system. Schools are institutions that reproduce the social order, and many teachers are complicit in maintaining the status quo. If you believe that institutions of learning are free of racism, sexism, and genderism, then you need to increase your understanding of the history of American schools and on how schools advantage some students while disadvantaging others. For instance, a large amount of scholarship demonstrates that more White students are enrolled in high-level classes and programs, which advantages them academically (Kerr, 2014; Toppo, 2012), whereas more Black and Brown students are overrepresented in low-level classrooms, which disadvantages them academically (Jordan, 2005; Ferri & Connor, 2005; Vallas, 2009; Wood, 2007; Moreno & Segura-Herrera, 2013). I urge you to explore the scholarship on *tracking* and the *hidden curriculum* to understand systemic racism in our schools (see Oakes & Lipton, 1992; Langhout & Mitchell, 2008, respectively). It is critical for us as teachers to not bury our heads in the sand, but instead, to become agents of change by being a voice for the voiceless.

Question 3: Might your need to feel comfortable by maintaining the status quo further disadvantage your most vulnerable students? Fitting into the school culture and maintaining one's job is critical; however, endorsing the status quo is more damaging to the very students we claim to care about. Advocacy looks different for everyone, and it is our job as teachers to confront the oppressive behaviors of our colleagues, including school administrators, and the oppressive school policies that impact our most vulnerable students. While a confrontation might seem scary, it does not have to dramatic. There are many ways to express our feelings about oppressive behavior and policies. Also, avoid waiting on someone else, like a more vocal colleague, to lead the way in creating change. As a teacher, your responsibility is to your students and to ensure that they are treated fairly in school. You should also not turn a blind eye to the discrimination and mistreatment of your colleagues. If you remain silent when your colleagues are being mistreated, because their situations do not directly affect you, then you are part of the problem. This goes back to my earlier point about teachers who endorse egalitarian values but behave in ways that are violent. Remember, remaining silent is considered an act of violence. As educators, we should strive to do what is right, even if it makes us feel uncomfortable. If confronting bigotry and discrimination is scary and uncomfortable to you, then sit with those feelings in order to understand them and challenge them.

Box 8.4 Theme: Common Core and Other Standards

In advocating for the voiceless, teachers must work with school administrators to obtain what they need to assist students in meeting curricular goals and standards. Also, teachers must find ways to increase students' sense of belonging, so as to inspire students to stay motivated academically. Advocating for students who might otherwise be ignored is what is necessary to ensure that students have what they need to be successful in school. It is crucial for teachers to not only work with their colleagues but to also work with caregivers, so students can achieve curricular goals.

In sum, teachers who embrace diversity for a humanizing classroom experience seek to (a) understand their students' lived experiences, (b) utilize students' experiences to create inclusive, equitable, and student-centered classroom environments, (c) understand how they bring themselves to the classroom context in unique ways that impact students, and (d) advocate for the dignity of their students (and colleagues) in fighting against injustice. Embracing diversity to humanize the classroom experience, so as to demonstrate an authentic level of care, is challenging work. It takes a real commitment to social justice to challenge yourself as a teacher to create real change. As teachers, we cannot always wait on a school administrator, a vocal colleague, or the creation of policies to begin to create inclusive learning environments for our students. The change we want to make truly starts with us.

Note

1 Cultural capital refers to an accumulation of knowledge, behaviors, and skills that are acquired from a variety of sources and speak to an individual's cultural competence and social status (Bourdieu, 1986; see also Huang, 2019).

References

Adams III, V.H., Devos, T., Rivera, L.M., Smith, H., & Vega, L.A. (2014). Teaching about implicit prejudices and stereotypes: A pedagogical demonstration. *Teaching of Psychology, 41*(3), 204–212.

Bourdieu, P. (1986). The forms of capital. In J. Richardson (Ed.), *Handbook of theory and research for the sociology of education* (pp. 241–258). New York: Greenwood.

Brand, D. (1987). The new whiz kids. *Time, 130*(9), 42.

Crenshaw, K. (1989). Demarginalizing the intersection of race and sex: A Black feminist critique of antidiscrimination doctrine, feminist theory and antiracist politics. *University of Chicago Legal Forum, 1989*, 139–167.

Ferri, B.A., & Connor, D.J. (2005). In the shadow of Brown: Special education and overrepresentation of students of color. *Remedial and Special Education, 26*(2), 93–100.

Garcia, S.B., & Guerra, P.L. (2004). Deconstructing deficit thinking: Working with educators to create more equitable learning environments. *Education and Urban Society, 36*(2), 150–168.

Gonzalez, A., Monzon, N., Solis, D., Jaycox, L., & Langley, A.K. (2016). Trauma exposure in elementary school children: Description of screening procedures, level of exposure, and posttraumatic stress symptoms. *School Mental Health, 8*(1), 77–88.

Gray, D.L., Hope, E.C., & Matthews, J.S. (2018). Black and belonging at school: A case for interpersonal, instructional, and institutional opportunity structures. *Educational Psychologist, 53*(2), 97–113.

Greenwald, A.G., & Krieger, L.H. (2006). Implicit bias: Scientific foundations. *California Law Review, 94*(4), 945–967.

Greenwald, A. G., McGhee, D. E., & Schwartz, J. L. (1998). Measuring individual differences in implicit cognition: The implicit association test. *Journal of Personality and Social Psychology, 74*(6), 1464–1480.

Hardman, J., & Hardman, F. (2017). *Guided co-construction in classroom talk*. https://doi.org/10.1007/978-3-319-02243-7_24.

Harven, A.M. (2004). *The primacy of perceptions: How teacher and student perceptions interact to maintain the Black-White test score gap*. Symposium presented at the Patterson Research Conference, Washington, DC.

Harven, A.M., & Perouse-Harvey, E. (2020). Instructing pre-and inservice teachers to support students with (Dis) abilities: Pillars, practical applications, and students' intersecting identities. In *Handbook on Promoting Social Justice in Education*. Switzerland: Springer International, 1533–1559.

Harven, A.M., & Soodjinda, D. (2016). Pedagogical strategies for challenging students' world views. In R. Papa, D. M. Eadens, & D. W. Eadens (Eds.), *Social Justice Instruction* (pp. 3–14). Cham: Springer.

Holley, L. C., & Steiner, S. (2005). Safe space: Student perspectives on classroom environment. *Journal of Social Work Education, 41*(1), 49–64.

Howard, T.C. (2001). Telling their side of the story: African-American students' perceptions of culturally relevant teaching. *The Urban Review, 33*(2), 131–149.

Huang, X. (2019). Understanding bourdieu—cultural capital and habitus. *Review of European Studies, 11*, 45. doi:10.5539/res.v11n3p45.

Jordan, K.A. (2005). Discourses of difference and the overrepresentation of Black students in special education. *The Journal of African American History, 90*(1–2), 128–149.

Kerr, R. (2014). "Advanced Classes? They're Only for White Kids": How one kansas school is changing the face of honors and advanced placement courses. *Action in Teacher Education, 36*(5–6), 480–489.

Langhout, R.D., & Mitchell, C.A. (2008). Engaging contexts: Drawing the link between student and teacher experiences of the hidden curriculum. *Journal of Community & Applied Social Psychology*, *18*(6), 593–614.

Lee, S.J. (2015). *Unraveling the "model minority" stereotype: Listening to Asian American youth*. New York, NY: Teachers College Press.

Merriam-Webster (2020). Dictionary. https://www.merriam-webster.com/dictionary

McGrady, P.B., & Reynolds, J.R. (2013). Racial mismatch in the classroom: Beyond Black-White differences. *Sociology of Education*, *86*(1), 3–17.

Moreno, G., & Segura-Herrera, T. (2013). Special education referrals and disciplinary actions for Latino students in the United States. *Multicultural Learning and Teaching*, *9*(1), 33–51.

Neel, C.G.O., & Fuligni, A. (2013). A longitudinal study of school belonging and academic motivation across high school. *Child Development*, *84*(2), 678–692.

Oakes, J., & Lipton, M. (1992). Detracking schools: Early lessons from the field. *Phi Delta Kappan*, *73*(6), 448–454.

Roeser, R.W., Midgley, C., & Urdan, T.C. (1996). Perceptions of the school psychological environment and early adolescents' psychological and behavioral functioning in school: The mediating role of goals and belonging. *Journal of educational psychology*, *88*(3), 408.

Sandoval, W.A., & Harven, A.M. (2011). Urban middle school students' perceptions of the value and difficulty of inquiry. *Journal of Science Education and Technology*, *20*(1), 95–109.

Stambler, L. G. (2013). *Critical literacy: Literacies for the digital age to teach in the k-12 classroom*. Presentation developed for the Pier Institute at Yale University, New Haven, CT.

Toppo, G. (2012, February 21). Report: Opportunity for AP classes uneven in USA. *USA Today*. http://www.usatoday.com/story/news/nation/2013/02/20/advanced placement-high-school-classes/1928913/

University of Michigan (2020, June 1). *Social identity wheel: Adapted by the program on intergroup relations and the spectrum center*. https://sites.lsa.umich.edu/inclusive-teaching/sample-activities/social-identity-wheel/

Vallas, R. (2009). The disproportionality problem: The overrepresentation of black students in special education and recommendations for reform. *Virginia Journal of Social Policy & the Law*, *17*, 181.

van Kleeck, A. (2007). Home talk and school talk: Helping teachers recognize cultural mismatch. *The ASHA Leader*, *12*(13), 23–24.

Walker, S.E. (2003). Active learning strategies to promote critical thinking. *Journal of Athletic Training*, *38*(3), 263.

Wood, M.R. (2007). ESL and bilingual education as a proxy for racial and ethnic segregation in US public schools. *Journal of Gender Race & Justice*, *11*, 599.

Chapter 9

Developmental Diversity in the Classroom

Cindy Collado

Introduction

The United States is increasingly moving toward inclusive environments whereby students with a range of developmental abilities, including those with the most significant medical, intellectual, and developmental delays and disabilities, are considered full members of their neighborhood schools and classrooms (Young, Herring, & Morrison, 2017). As such, teachers must be equipped with mindsets and tools to support all students in inclusive classrooms as they build community, plan units of study and lessons with all students in mind, and provide individualized supports and interventions to promote access to learning. While it is important to have a foundational understanding of disabilities and how students with disabilities are supported by federal and state laws, Dr. Steven Shore infamously said, "If you've met one person with Autism, you've met one person with Autism." Hence, this chapter will provide foundational knowledge about disabilities and then dive deep into how students with different abilities and experiences can be supported in today's 21st-century classrooms where they are expected to engage in the Common Core State Standards' (CCSS) rigorous grade-level expectations through problem-solving, collaboration, communication, and creative thinking. Readers will be left with a belief that all children can learn and with the knowledge to support all children in a developmentally diverse inclusive classroom.

What Is a Developmentally Diverse Inclusive Classroom?

Inclusion

> means that everybody that is in my classroom is getting access to grade-level materials and materials at their own level. So, for instance, my student who is in 6th grade has Down syndrome, and he is probably performing at kindergarten level, but he still comes to the carpet to do notes for math, and then he will do kindergarten level math work. So, it is just making sure that every student that is here is getting the best quality education for their circumstances.
>
> (Jocelyn, 5th/6th-grade inclusion classroom teacher)

As this classroom teacher highlights, within a *developmentally diverse inclusive classroom*, students are recognized as unique learners at various stages of development including social and emotional, cognitive, physical, language, and communication. Development is understood as varied within and across students. A developmentally diverse inclusive classroom honors students as unique individuals who all have the potential to learn and develop in their own ways and at their own pace while learning and engaging with their same-age peers. These classrooms embrace diversity including students who differ according to ability, culture, language, gender, sexual orientation, religion, and socioeconomic status, to name a few factors. For example, see Figure 9.1 for a sample of students in Ms. Muran's developmentally diverse inclusive classroom:

Notice how different yet dynamic students may be in an inclusive classroom. Inclusive classrooms are often successful because educators plan with all students in mind and create a welcoming classroom community that celebrates both what students share in common as well as what makes them unique. When challenged to think beyond teaching the elusive average student, educators find their instruction improves, relationships are strengthened, and the classroom learning environment is more conducive to learning (Rao, Ok, & Bryant, 2014; Spencer, 2011; Friesen, 2010; see Shelley Moore's "Five Moore Minutes" at www.fivemooreminutes.com). This is because learning is seen as a community experience as students learn together through dialogue, meaningful activities, collaboration, exploration, and practice. In inclusive classrooms, "students with disabilities are supported members of chronologically age-appropriate general education classes in their home schools, receiving the specialized instruction delineated by their [Individualized Education Plans] IEPs, within the context of the core curriculum and general activities" (Halvorsen & Neary, 2009, p. 1). This is quite different from what schools may be used to since historically students with disabilities have been taught in separate classrooms or even separate schools. Interestingly, research has found that inclusion is beneficial to both students with and without disabilities. Including students with disabilities in regular education classrooms has been found to benefit students with disabilities in particular, as their teachers' strategic and collaborative planning led to higher expectations for learning, greater access to grade-level curriculum, increased student engagement and participation, higher work completion, and improved academic performance (Rao, Ok, & Bryant, 2014; Spencer, 2011; Friesen, 2010; Dessemontet & Bless, 2013; Dessemontet, Bless, & Morin, 2012; Kurth, Lyong, & Shogren, 2015; Sauer & Jorgensen, 2016). Contrary to what some believe, inclusion also benefits (or has a neutral impact on) students without disabilities as they have also shown increased engagement and work completion (Sauer & Jorgensen, 2016). In an "All Means All" approach to inclusion (see the SWIFT education center: www.swiftschools.org/), all students regardless of ability,

Atiqua is highly verbal and physically active. Emotionally, she struggles to understand her own and her friends' feelings, so socially and emotionally it can be hard for her. It helps to teach her problem-solving strategies and co-regulate with her when she is upset. She loves outside recess and is a creative artist. Academically, she is learning at grade level across subject areas.

Joseph is very artistic and loves to draw. He has a great sense of humor and makes the other students (and the teacher) laugh with his unassuming jokes and unique artwork. He is working at grade level in all academic areas and is particularly motivated during science lessons. He has autism and receives special education services. The special education teacher works with him on using calming strategies when he struggles to communicate, identifying emotions, and interacting socially.

Lis is a leader in the classroom with her quick wit and high vocabulary and reading level. She also speaks Hmong as her home language and uses a voice output device to communicate, which is an iPad set up with the Proloquo2Go app, because her cerebral palsy makes it hard for her to speak. With alternative ways to engage and express her ideas, she is successful academically.

Jane excels during math and science lessons. She loves to help her peers during these subjects. At times, she struggles to regulate her body and needs opportunities to move and get her wiggles out. Reading is hard for her as she has a reading disability (dyslexia), but with the help of audiobooks she comprehends at grade level. She also works with a special education teacher on learning to use reading strategies to decode words.

Antonio is quiet and a hard worker. Graphic novels are his favorite. He has a good group of friends who help him in the classroom as he just returned after a few months in the hospital for leukemia. It is hard for him to concentrate, and he has lost some of his motor and cognitive skills due to chemotherapy, for which he receives special education services. Also, it is hard for him to say goodbye to his mom so sometimes she stays as a classroom volunteer.

Maxwell is a ball of energy and loves to talk about and act out video games. He is working at grade level for math and struggles with reading comprehension, as he is reading materials one grade below grade level. His family is also going through a divorce, so he has been more energetic lately. It helps him to have a calming space to relax when he feels overwhelmed.

Figure 9.1 A Sample of Students in Ms. Muran's Developmentally Diverse Inclusive Classroom. Images source: Sofia Mercedes Collado, 9 years old.

race, language, culture, experience, gender, class, or sexual identity attend their neighborhood school with their peers and siblings and are considered full members of the regular education classroom with their chronologically same-age peers. See Box 9.1 for more insight. Given the proven benefits of including students with disabilities in regular education classrooms, continue on to learn how teachers create such an inclusive classroom environment within their schools and centers for students like Joseph, Antonio, Jane, and Lis mentioned above.

Box 9.1 Social Justice and Diversity: What We Mean by "All Means All" in an Inclusive School

Over the years, inclusion has had varied meanings and has been used synonymously with mainstreaming or integration. To be clear, there are key differences between these three terms (Gee, 2002). *Inclusion* means students with disabilities are full members of the regular education classroom that they would have attended if they did not have a disability. They spend the majority of their day in the regular classroom and peers see them as classmates. Sometimes, instruction is modified during the lesson, so they may be learning the same subject but at a different level, or targeted instruction might be provided one-on-one or in a small group within the classroom or nearby where anyone might be pulled to learn. In an inclusive school, the general education teacher collaborates and plans with the special education teacher and related service providers (e.g., speech and language pathologist, occupational therapist, etc.) to ensure students with mild to significant support needs are meaningfully participating in daily activities and are engaged in learning alongside their peers. This differs from *integrated schools* where students spend a lot of time in the regular education classroom, but often only with the support of a paraprofessional or for some subjects like physical education or art. These students receive subject-specific instruction in a separate classroom. This also differs from *mainstreaming schools* where students visit the regular education classroom for part of the day but sit separately from peers and do not feel like a meaningful part of the classroom, as peers may or may not know them (Gee, 2002). In an inclusive school all children, including those with developmental delays and disabilities:

- participate in developmentally appropriate curriculum, activities, and environments with their same-age peers with and without disabilities,
- attend their neighborhood school with their siblings and community peers,
- feel like they belong in their classroom, school, and neighborhood,
- receive tiered levels of increasingly more intense and frequent supports to meet their needs, with these supports and services changing and evolving over time, and
- learn a growth mindset within a strengths-based approach.

What Does a Strengths-Based Inclusive Classroom Look Like?

When you walk into an inclusive classroom that is working like a well-oiled machine, you simply know it. There are some key aspects you notice right away with respect to the environment, the adults, and the students. Environments like Kya's K/1 inclusion classroom, seen in Figure 9.2 (or the preschool inclusion classrooms featured on the Seeds of Partnership website: www.seedsofpartnership.org/preschoolLREpartB.html) catch your eye for these reasons:

- *organization*: there are clear spaces such as a group meeting space and academic specific areas like a writing or reading area where materials are labeled and easily accessible by students with clear expectations for how to engage with them;
- *family- and student-centered atmosphere*: families and students are front and center with their pictures and work hung throughout the room, in picture frames on shelves, and on bulletin boards; inspiring strengths-based quotes and pictures may be on the wall but they are kept to a minimum to reduce clutter; rules and expectations are posted that were created with (and at times signed by) the students;
- *welcoming spaces*: it feels like home with soft spaces such as a calm-down corner and pillows or beanbags in the library or group area, carpets, alternative seating like pillows at a low table or stools at a high table, plants, mirrors, and non-fluorescent lighting such as lamps, window lighting, or fluorescent light covers.

Then you notice the students who are smiling, interacting, working close to and with each other, making eye contact, using active listening skills,

Figure 9.2 Kya's Classroom. Source: photo taken by Cindy Collado with permission from Kya (pseudonym), K/1 inclusion classroom teacher

providing positive encouragement, commenting on one another's strengths and accomplishments, supporting one another, respecting one another, and flexibly moving about the room. You realize that these classrooms work so well because there are strong relationships built among the students and with the adults. Everyone feels like they belong, that they have a place in this community, that they can take risks, that their strengths are appreciated, and that their needs are supported. Community is built through practices such as class meetings, person-centered and family-centered planning activities where teachers learn more about them as individuals, group work, project-based child-directed learning, growth mindset discussions focused on learning from mistakes and the importance of effort, and consistent discussions about shared similarities and differences in the classroom.

This kind of classroom represents a strengths-based approach, drawn from the theory of positive psychology. Positive psychology moves away from a focus on illness or diagnosis; rather it is "the scientific study of ordinary human strengths and virtues... with an interest in finding out what works, what is right, and what is improving" (Sheldon & King, 2001, p. 216). This strengths-based approach aligns well with a growth mindset (Dweck, 2006; Armstrong, 2012), such that educators convey the message that what is important is growth rather than accuracy, mistakes are critical for learning, and everyone is working on improving by learning and practicing new strategies and skills (Young, Herring, & Morrison, 2017). The strengths-based perspective honors all students as diverse human beings who are unique in their interests, experiences, motivations, friendships, families, resources, academic and social-emotional strengths, areas of need, and strategies that work or don't work for them (Armstrong, 2012). The role of the teacher then is to create a classroom community that recognizes the diversity within one another. For more insight into what it means to be a strengths-based inclusive teacher see Box 9.2.

Box 9.2 Theory to Practice Spotlight: Strengths-Based Inclusive Teacher

In the classroom, a *strengths-based teacher* is guided by four elements: (1) child- and family-focused, (2) asset-based, (3) access-focused, and (4) progress-focused (National Council of Teachers of English, 2016). Being child- and family-focused means the teacher believes the child (not the curriculum) is the focus since learning happens within the interactions with others surrounding the child including direct interaction with family and friends and then in the classroom and neighborhood (Bronfenbrenner, 1977). This belief leads the teacher to cater the curriculum to the students rather than allowing the curriculum to drive daily activities. An asset-based teacher sees each student as a whole child, and makes a concerted effort to help every student realize his or her strengths and motivations as well as areas of need and what works for them. With a focus on access, teachers realize there are many barriers within the classroom learning environment and curriculum because students process the world in many different ways. By creating a classroom that includes multiple ways to understand the concepts, interact with them, and express ideas, the strengths-based teacher is breaking down these barriers (Rapp, 2014; Eredics, 2018). Finally, focusing on progress is critical as each child is seen as an individual such that assessment information identifies current skills and next steps in development rather than focusing on deficits or labeling students as delayed or below grade level. See Figure 9.3.

For example, Ms. Muran, in her second-grade inclusive classroom, starts off her year (and then revisits these ideas intermittently) with each child exploring their individuality during an age-appropriate activity such as using a mirror to draw themselves with their favorite things or activities (whereas in the older grades students may fill out a graphic organizer about themselves; for example, see these student profiles on the FACT Oregon website: https://factoregon.org/person-centered-plan-samples/). Then her students share their drawings during class meetings in that first week of school, thereby celebrating similarities and differences within one another. During subsequent class meetings, Ms. Muran also engages her students in disability awareness activities and simulations, for example practicing what it feels like to not be able to speak in order to build students' empathy (for some ideas, see how this teacher team created a disability awareness curriculum: www.inclusionstartsnow.com). Finally, Ms. Muran uses children's literature about differences and disabilities as a key vehicle to open the door to meaningful discussions (see this booklist: https://iris.peabody.vanderbilt.edu/resources/books/).

Child/Family-centered	Asset-based	Access-focused	Progress-focused
•The child/family is the center of education (not the curriculum) with strong network of supports (Bronfenbrenner's Ecological Model of Development).	•Everyone is capable and competent. •Everyone has unique strengths, talents, and interests (funds of knowledge).	•People learn, engage, and express themselves in multiple and different ways (Universal Design for Learning approach). •People have different ways of processing and understanding the world (learning styles, Multiple Intelligences).	•Assessments focus on learning progress and what is presently working for the child/family (not a long list of deficits or issues). •Focus is on how to support learning and next steps in development.

Figure 9.3 Strengths-Based Education Perspective. Source: based on the Equity and Early Childhood Education: Reclaiming the Child research policy brief by the National Council of Teachers of English (NCTE) (2016)

How Do Teachers Develop an Inclusive Strengths-Based Perspective?

While teachers may aspire to be inclusive educators, their underlying unconscious biases may not be aligned. Historically, our society has segregated students with disabilities and viewed them as less valuable (Yell, 2019; Boroson, 2017). Since inclusion is just beginning to spread across the United States, teachers have grown up in schools where they were exposed minimally to individuals with disabilities, especially those with more extensive support needs like intellectual disabilities or multiple disabilities (e.g., cerebral palsy and intellectual disability). Experiences and exposures help our minds process the world and create schemas to reduce the amount of effort put forth on a daily basis. Common schemas developed in the minds of young children who learn in segregated schools where students with disabilities are taught in separate classrooms are that students with disabilities are not as smart, not the same as everyone else, and ultimately not deserving of an equal education (Wilson, 2017).

Such ableist beliefs often stem from the different ways students with disabilities communicate, behave, and process the world. Now these students are our teachers who carry these implicit schemas to their work, and as adults assume a disability means one cannot achieve success and can only learn in a specialized environment. These assumptions are far from reality as everyone can learn when given a chance. For example, many students with more extensive support needs, such as a student with cerebral palsy and autism, may not use words to communicate (sometimes described as nonverbal), but instead communicate through gestures, behaviors such as hitting when frustrated, or an Augmentative Alternative Communication (ACC) device such as an iPad that speaks (like that used by Lis in Ms. Muran's class). Assuming that an individual cannot learn based on atypical ways of communicating is harmful and lowers our expectations for learning (Donnellan, 1984). Research has found that teachers that have a negative bias toward individuals with disabilities tend to have low expectations for them (Forlin, Tait, Carroll, & Jobling, 1999), whereas those with a positive attitude have higher expectations. Educators have an ethical obligation to their students to assume they can learn, assume they can connect with others and build relationships, and assume positive outcomes into adulthood, even if it is not always easily observed (Donnellan, 1984). In fact, humans are social beings who are wired for connection and learning with others. So, to assume individuals with disabilities who display challenging behaviors or are nonverbal are better off in isolated settings is an inequitable perspective and leads to diminished outcomes. In developing a strengths-based perspective, teachers must confront their explicit (known) and implicit (unconscious) biases towards students with disabilities and students of color (Staats, 2016). This distinction is critical so that one's actions are aligned with one's explicit beliefs.

What Does the Law Say About Educating Students with Disabilities in School?

Only within the last 50 years have students with disabilities been afforded an equal opportunity to learn in our public schools. Before laws required public schools to accept students and provide a Free and Appropriate Public Education (FAPE), young children and youth with disabilities were kept at home with their families or sent to institutions where they were treated inhumanely (Gardner, 2006; Pelka, 2012). Ableist policies such as denying students with disabilities a public education discriminated against them, as they were believed to be of less worth than individuals without disabilities and disruptive to the learning of others (Coates, 1989; Kavale & Forness, 2000; Sauer & Jorgen, 2016). Such beliefs and practices are socially constructed beliefs that there is somehow a "normal" or "average" way of being in our society that is more desirable than the celebration of diverse ways of thinking and being (Wilson, 2017).

Along with other movements of the civil rights era in the 1960s and 1970s, the disability rights movement came to a head. Families were and have always been the catalyst for advocating for the rights of their children with disabilities to be educated at their local public schools. Following the seminal court case ruling that separate schools for black students were indeed not equal in the 1954 Brown v. Board of Education Supreme Court case, key Supreme Court cases addressed the rights of children with disabilities to an equal education. Namely, two class-action lawsuits, Pennsylvania Association for Retarded Children (PARC) v. Pennsylvania (1972) and Mills v. Board of Education (1972) in the District of Columbia found the denial of public education for children and youth with disabilities unconstitutional according to the equal protection clause of the 14th Amendment to the Constitution (Yell, 2019). The courts agreed with the families on the basis that all children and youth, regardless of disability, have the capacity to learn. These and other seminal cases shaped what later became the first federal law outlining requirements for the education of students with disabilities in public school systems.

The Individuals with Disabilities Education Improvement Act (IDEIA). In 1975, the first law in support of students with disabilities was passed, the Education for All Handicapped Children Act (EAHCA). The law has since been reauthorized (1986, 1990, 1997, 2004) and over time expanded coverage to children and youth from birth to 21 years old and included greater protections for young children and youth with disabilities and inclusion of their families in their educational progress. In 1990, the name of the law was changed to the Individuals with Disabilities Education Act (IDEA) to reflect more inclusive people-first language and in 2004 with the last reauthorization it was renamed again to the Individuals with Disabilities Education Improvement Act (IDEIA). Across these reauthorizations, the following six principles for students with disabilities covered under IDEIA have remained stable (Yell, 2019):

1) a Free and Appropriate Public Education (FAPE),
2) appropriate and non-discriminatory evaluations for services,
3) an Individualized Education Program (IEP) for students aged 3–21 and Individualized Family Service Plan (IFSP) for children from birth to 3 years old,
4) an education provided in the Least Restrictive Environment (LRE),
5) parent and student participation throughout the program decision-making process, and
6) clear procedural safeguards for schools and families when they disagree.

With each new reauthorization of the original Public Law 94-142: EAHCA of 1975, the law has evolved and court cases have shifted the focus from ensuring access to public education to a focus on high expectations and accountability, and currently to focus on what it means to provide a quality inclusive education (Boroson, 2017). Other influential laws for students with disabilities include Section 504 of the Rehabilitation Act of 1973 which made it illegal for federally funded institutions to discriminate against individuals with disabilities. To this day, students who require supports (e.g., medication at school) or accommodations (e.g., preferential seating, assistive technology, etc.), but not intervention services from a special education teacher or related service provider (e.g., speech and language pathologist, occupational therapist, physical therapist) are provided a 504 plan that identifies necessary accommodations to be provided across the school day. Such a formal plan can be developed by the school's Student Success/Study Team (SST) after meeting with the family to discuss a student's strengths, interests, needs, and what has been working to support them. For more information about IDEIA, see https://sites.ed.gov/idea/ and for more on special education law see https://www.wrightslaw.com/.

The Least Restrictive Environment (LRE). Students with disabilities have continued to remain some of the most segregated students in our education system. Since inclusion is not mentioned in IDEIA, schools enact inclusion in different ways. The most important principle of those in IDEIA in support of inclusive education is the Least Restrictive Environment (LRE) (Gardner, 2006). Historically, districts have inappropriately used this principle to support the segregation of students with disabilities, particularly those who are not meeting grade-level expectations and/or present with behavioral or communicative challenges (Kavale & Forness, 2000; Kunc, 2000). However, the LRE is grounded in the belief that special education is not a place, even though people often call rooms where students with special needs are supported as the "special ed room." Instead, special education is "specially designed instruction, at no cost to the parents, to meet the unique needs of a child with a disability" (§300.39, IDEIA, 2004) and provided by specially trained education specialists (special education teachers) and related service providers such as speech and language pathologists, occupational therapists, physical therapists, and others. The LRE in the Individuals with Disabilities Education Act (IDEIA,

2004) states that an individual with disabilities can only be removed from a general education classroom if (and only if) "the nature or severity of the disability is such that education in regular classes with the use of supplementary aids and services cannot be achieved satisfactorily" (§300.114, IDEIA, 2004). This means that the school has first attempted inclusion with peers without disabilities before considering placement in separate settings. What happens in reality, however, is IEP teams preemptively decide that a child with a disability most likely will not succeed in the classroom learning environment due to the child's disability, and therefore decide to place the student in a separate classroom without ever having tried supports and services in an inclusive classroom. What we know, however, from longitudinal research is that when students with significant support needs are effectively included, they can successfully learn, be engaged in academic tasks, develop friendships, and reduce their challenging behaviors (Lee, Wehmeyer, Soukup, & Palmer, 2010; Kurth et al., 2015).

How Do We Define Students with Disabilities?

People First language. There are a variety of ways we understand individuals with disabilities. First and foremost, they are individuals with dreams, goals, friends, family, and learning styles. This strengths-based perspective of individuals sees them as people first and thus our language when we speak about individuals with disabilities must match such a view. Aligning our language with our viewpoint may take deliberate attention as we shift how society considers and addresses these individuals. For example, by using such language as "handicapped" or "disabled," we prioritize the disability, hence taking a deficit-minded perspective. Their disability only impacts them because our society is not universally set up for them. Instead, we should be using People First language by saying first the individual and then the disability identity; for example, "the child with Down syndrome" (not "the Down's kid") or "the student with an IEP" (not "the special needs student"). This same rule also applies to avoiding damaging labels for students that highlight negative aspects about them and instead describing the child and their behaviors in understandable terms. For example, "when Maxwell is overstimulated, he tends to leave the classroom in order to regulate himself" (not "Maxwell the runner"). Our language matters because it affects how we view people, which then impacts how we treat them. For some individuals with disabilities, they prefer identity-first language, which means they believe their disability is a primary identity that defines them, including those in the Deaf community as well as some in the autistic community. As with any individual, it is important to respect their individual identities and adjust your language when requested.

IDEIA 2004 disability categories. In the American educational system, students with disabilities or developmental delays must first be found eligible under a primary disability category before they can be provided services. Therefore, labels are necessary for these purposes. The Individuals with Disabilities Education Improvement Act (IDEIA, 2004) defines disabilities for school-age children according to 13 disability categories, with developmental delays as an additional category for students aged 3–9 years old (see Table 9.1). A student identified as meeting criteria for at least one of the 13 IDEIA identified disabilities can receive services through an Individualized Education Program (IEP) if, in addition, it is found that the student's disability adversely affects their educational performance.

The developmental delay category for young students is utilized as a key strategy for avoiding mislabeling students before an accurate disability diagnosis can be made. These students within this age range may use this label for three years, upon which a reevaluation will determine eligibility and primary category for further services. Once found eligible for special education services under IDEIA, the IEP team (or IFSP team for infants and toddlers) develops the IEP (or IFSP) with annual learning goals targeted to their individual needs, accommodations that provide necessary supports, and relevant services to be updated every year and re-evaluated every three years. As most students are complicated and diverse individuals, they may have additional secondary disabilities that are comorbid. In the case of autism, studies have found about one-third of individuals with autism also have Attention-Deficit/Hyperactivity Disorder, about 13–42% also have an anxiety disorder, and a smaller percentage also have other disabilities including depression, behavioral disorders, Obsessive-Compulsive Disorder (OCD), or Intellectual Disability (ID) (Belardinelli, Raza, & Taneli, 2016). Keep in mind human beings have intersectional identities including disabilities, races, nationalities, cultures, gender identities, sexualities, ages, experiences, and histories. Seeing the student as developmentally diverse is critical to successfully building relationships and collaborative programs of support.

The range of impact of the disability: mild to significant support needs. As education systems move toward inclusive education, districts and states are changing their language from disability labels as indicators of services to the level of support needed to be successful. Hence, students' Least Restrictive Environment (LRE) is first thought in terms of what works to support the student in inclusive settings. Some students may need support in one aspect of development such as in cognitive (academic), social/emotional, motor, health, language, or adaptive skills, while other students may need supports across multiple areas of development. The amount of support needed ranges from mild to moderate to extensive support needs. Disability labels alone are no longer helpful for determining services and supports because every disability has a range of ways a child may be impacted. For example, a student with autism who has mild support needs such as Joseph in Ms. Muran's class may only need support for adaptive skills such as following a routine or developing self-regulation skills for calming down and using mindfulness skills. In

Table 9.1 The 13 Disability Categories + Development Delay in IDEIA 2004

Specific Learning Disability (SLD) "A disorder in one or more of the basic psychological processes involved in understanding or in using language, spoken or written, that may manifest itself in the imperfect ability to listen, think, speak, read, write, spell, or to do mathematical calculations, including conditions such as perceptual disabilities, brain injury, minimal brain dysfunction, dyslexia, and developmental aphasia."	**Other Health Impairment (OHI)** "Having limited strength, vitality, or alertness, including a heightened alertness to environmental stimuli, that results in limited alertness with respect to the educational environment, that is due to chronic or acute health problems such as asthma, attention deficit disorder or attention deficit hyperactivity disorder, diabetes, epilepsy, a heart condition, hemophilia, lead poisoning, leukemia, nephritis, rheumatic fever, sickle cell anemia, and Tourette syndrome."
Speech or Language Impairment (SLI) "A communication disorder, such as stuttering, impaired articulation, a language impairment, or a voice impairment."	**Autism Spectrum Disorder (ASD)** "A developmental disability significantly affecting verbal and nonverbal communication and social interaction."
Intellectual Disability (ID; formerly Mental Retardation, MR) "Significantly subaverage general intellectual functioning, existing concurrently with deficits in adaptive behavior and manifested during the developmental period."	**Emotional Disturbance (ED)** "A condition exhibiting one or more of the following characteristics over a long period of time and to a marked degree... an inability to build or maintain relationships... inappropriate types of behaviors... a general pervasive mood of unhappiness or depression... a tendency to develop physical symptoms or fears."
Multiple Disabilities "Concomitant impairments (such as intellectual disability-blindness or intellectual disability-orthopedic impairment)."	**Hearing Impairment** "Impairment in hearing, whether permanent or fluctuating."
Orthopedic Impairment "A severe orthopedic impairment... includes impairments caused by a congenital anomaly, impairments caused by disease (e.g., poliomyelitis, bone tuberculosis), and impairments from other causes (e.g., cerebral palsy, amputations, and fractures or burns that cause contractures)."	**Traumatic Brain Injury (TBI)** "An acquired injury to the brain caused by an external physical force, resulting in total or partial functional disability or psychosocial impairment, or both."
Visual Impairment (VI) "Including blindness means an impairment in vision... includes both partial sight and blindness."	**Deaf-Blindness** "Concomitant hearing and visual impairments, the combination of which causes such severe communication and other developmental and educational needs."

(*Continued*)

Table 9.1 Continued

Deafness	Developmental Delay (DD)
"A hearing impairment that is so severe that the child is impaired in processing linguistic information through hearing, with or without amplification."	"Children aged three through nine... who is experiencing developmental delays... in one or more of the following areas: Physical development, cognitive development, communication development, social or emotional development, or adaptive development."

Source: Individuals with Disabilities Education Improvement Act of 2004, Public Law 108–446, U.S. Department of Education, Washington, D.C.

contrast, another student who also has autism and requires extensive support needs may need similar support in developing self-regulatory skills as well as require a voice output device to support communication, targeted intervention for reading comprehension that is three grades below grade level, and social skills instruction.

How Do We Teach Students with Disabilities in the Classroom?

Many districts and classrooms in the United States are keeping up with an increasingly heterogeneous student body by appreciating the positive impact a diverse set of learners brings to a classroom community. Teachers, as a result, have transformed into masterful designers of environments, communities, and instruction as well as instructional performers. To manage this pressure to be a master of all things, teachers approach their classroom using tiered levels of planning, teaming, and delivering (Eredics, 2018). Both academic skills and social-emotional skills are the focus since we know that children must first feel like they belong in the classroom and feel regulated before they can be expected to learn. Through a multi-tiered system of supports (MTSS), teachers create a classroom community and support students' academic learning through Response to Intervention (RTI) and support social and emotional learning through Positive Behavioral Intervention Supports (PBIS).

A joint statement on inclusion by the Division for Early Childhood of the Council for Exceptional Children (DEC) and the National Association for the Education of Young Children (NAEYC) (2009) identified three factors that made inclusion effective: (1) *access* to grade-level learning by breaking down barriers in the curriculum, interactions, and instruction using the principles of Universal Design For Learning (UDL); (2) *participation* in daily learning activities with peers without disabilities using embedded instruction that is thoughtfully and strategically planned by the general and special education teachers; and (3) *supports* for teachers and staff with regard to training, resources, and opportunities to collaborate.

In inclusive classrooms, it can easily be overwhelming to think about all the balls you must hold in the air such as creating a classroom community, connecting and building relationships with students, planning units and lessons, individualizing instruction, collecting student data, engaging students, and supporting them in times of need. However, the tiered approach is a helpful framework that begins with teachers establishing universal practices (Tier 1) that build the foundation upon which two additional tiers of increasingly more intense supports and interventions can be provided to some of the students in class that require it (Sandall, Schwartz, Joseph, & Gauvreau, 2019; Grisham-Brown & Hemmeter, 2017).

In Tier 1 of MTSS, universal instruction, environments, and assessments are established as the foundation for all students. Teachers begin with organizing their classroom environment to be inclusive and supportive of their students. Academically, they plan units and lesson plans that account for all students while also considering how individual students can be supported. With regard to behavior and social-emotional planning, they develop relationships with all students, build a class community, create clear behavioral expectations and teach social skills; see Chapter 2 on "Positive Behavior Interventions and Supports" for a more in-depth explanation.

When planning instruction with all children in mind, teachers follow the principles of *Universal Design for Learning (UDL)*. As such, teachers understand every student is different in how they receive information, process it, and express it. Some students are better visual learners while others learn best when hearing information or engaging with it through movement. Teachers that create effective learning environments anticipate the barriers to learning for individual students that may be created by the curriculum, environment, or instruction (Spencer, 2011; Rapp, 2014). Another way to describe this is planning for the low floor, high ceiling, and wide walls (Resnick & Robinson, 2017). In other words, teachers develop a map in their minds of the progression of skills in, let's say, math by studying the Common Core standards below and above grade level, which subsequently establishes the low floor and high ceiling for learning in the specific math skill. This way, the lessons allow multiple entry and exit points for learning across that vertical learning progression that increase access to learning throughout the unit (Young, Herring, & Morrison, 2017). Then they consider the wide-walls, which are the multiple pathways within those lessons since students' brains think using different strategies and approaches to solve and learn (Resnick & Robinson, 2017).

Kya, a K/1 inclusion classroom teacher, explained, "UDL makes me as a teacher more thoughtful, more intentional, and reminds me I have to reach each learner every day." See Figure 9.4 for guiding questions teachers may ask themselves as they engage in the UDL planning process. Units and subsequent lessons begin with UDL-aligned learning goals that are broad enough to capture all types of learners and connected to skills and concepts that can be applied over a lifetime (Nelson, 2015). For example, instead of a traditional

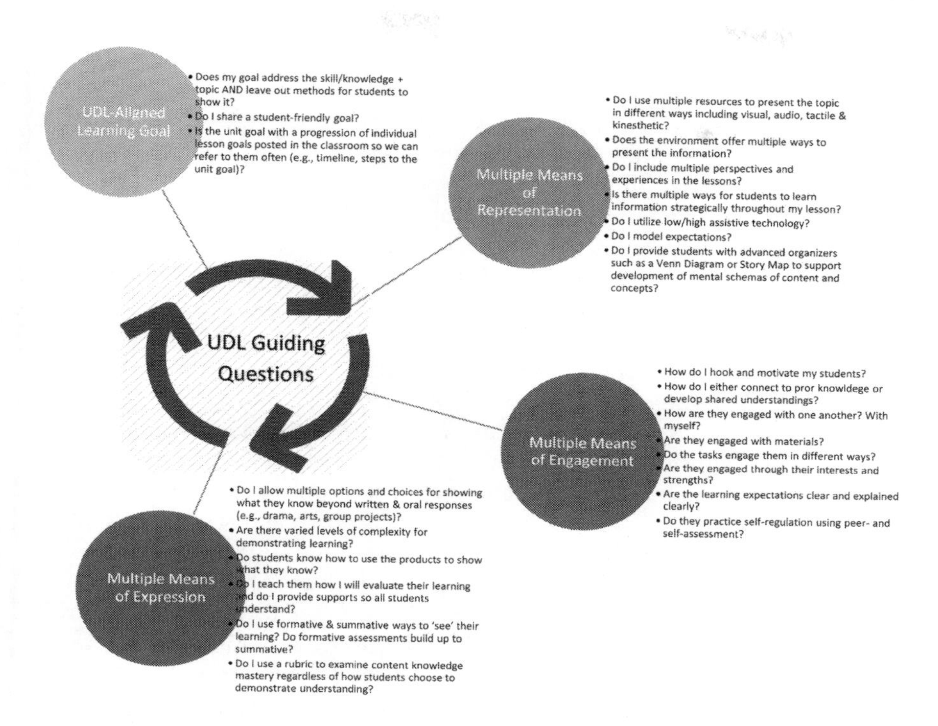

Figure 9.4 Universal Design for Learning (UDL)-Aligned Questions Teachers May Consider When Planning Inclusive Units and Lessons

learning goal tied to *how* students will perform (e.g., *Students will be able to write a persuasive essay about the story read*), a UDL-aligned goal could be focused on *what* they will show they have learned: *Students will be able to persuade the audience about the impact of the story on the reader*. Once the UDL-aligned learning goal is identified, teachers may consider different ways to represent the information, such as through reading text, examining visual representations (e.g., story maps, pictures, comic strips), and listening to audiobooks. Secondly, there are multiple levels of processing and engaging with the content that can be planned to help students interact with the information such as through reflection, group discussions, visual representations, and connecting to prior experiences. Finally, multiple means for expression is key for ensuring all students have the opportunity to demonstrate what was learned, such as through a simulated debate or choice of persuasive outlet like podcast, essay, video, dramatic demonstration, or artistic poster, to name a few. It is important for teachers to use formative assessments throughout the daily instruction as quick checks for understanding (e.g., exit tickets, discussions, student interviews, independent work) so that immediate adjustments to learning can be made.

Using UDL principles challenge teachers to find ways to break down barriers in the environment, materials, instruction, and expression (Rapp, 2014). See http://www.cast.org/ for more information on UDL.

In Tier 1, teachers must also strategically plan for supports that are available to all students as well as individual students. Supports are referred to as *adaptations*, which are adjustments to support access to learning and participation in activities (Eredics, 2018). "Adaptations can be made to the materials, activities, expectations, and level of assistance from adults or peers" (Barton, Reichow, Wolery, & Chen, 2011, p. 10). One type of adaptation is an accommodation. An *accommodation* is an adjustment to how students receive information (e.g., audiobooks, visuals), express and communicate their ideas (e.g., speech-to-text software, outline, verbal explanation), materials (e.g., pencil grip, graph paper, number line, calculator), environment (e.g., wiggle seat, seat at the front of the room), or learning strategies (e.g., use of a visual schedule or checklist, mnemonics) without changing the grade-level expectations or content. For example, alternative seating like wiggle seats, tall stools, open seating, and bean bag chairs are planned with the student with Attention-Deficit/Hyperactivity Disorder (AD/HD) in mind who needs to move or the student with autism spectrum disorder (ASD) who needs different sensory input; however, teachers begin to realize many students in the classroom benefit from the choice to sit in a space that is most conducive to their own personal learning. When teachers have equity as the driving force in the classroom, adaptations are viewed as every student getting what they need rather than everyone getting the same thing. By adjusting the environment, instruction, or relational interactions, access to learning is increased. As with anything new, students need to be taught clearly the purpose of the adaptation (e.g., alternative seating or fidgets), taught how to engage with it (e.g., clear step-by-step explanation using demonstration and role-play), and practice using it with adult feedback. Teachers might find it silly to teach students how and when to hold a stress ball, but these expectations are not always clear to students, so it is best to be proactive and not expect students to simply know.

Many adaptations are a type of *Assistive Technology* (AT) that helps the students access learning content and instruction. AT is typically considered along a continuum from low-tech tools to high-tech devices and software. Low-tech AT are tools teachers can use in their typical classrooms, such as pencil grips for a student with fine motor (writing) difficulties, fidgets, graph paper for organizing computation problems for ease of solving, or graphic organizer worksheets for visually displaying information in an organized manner. High-tech AT requires a formal evaluation by a specialized provider to determine what advanced technology or software could support the student's learning and/or communication in the classroom, including an Augmentative or Alternative Communication (AAC) device (e.g., Dynavox, iPad with Proloquo app, Picture Exchange Communication [PECS] system), computer, or computer software (voice-to-text or text-to-voice program). See www.understood.org/ and www.ctdinstitute.org/.

Some helpful accommodations according to need are:

- for a student who needs to move: fidgets, multiple learning spaces, alternative seating, TheraBand tied to the chair or table legs;
- for a student who is minimally verbal or nonverbal: computer to type responses, Augmentative or Alternative Communication (AAC) device, drawn responses;
- for a student who needs self-regulation support: calming space, visual guide with steps for calming down, fidgets, break card;
- for a student who needs organizational support: advanced organizers, visual schedules or activity checklists, pictures of what a clean desk looks like, homework folder system, calendar with assignment due dates;
- for a student who needs reading support: audiobooks, whisper phone, advanced organizers for processing what is read, color overlays, viewfinders or a ruler to track reading, strategy or cue cards as a reminder to use strategies.

When planning instruction across the school day, teachers plan with all students in mind using UDL principles as well as plan for individual students by considering specific accommodations that may be helpful to increase access to learning. See Box 9.3 for an example of inclusive classroom planning when creating class meetings.

Box 9.3 Social-Emotional Competence: Process for Creating Successful Inclusive Class Meetings

In any classroom, the classroom community is the most important foundation. When students feel supported, connected to the teacher and peers, and understood, they flourish. One way to begin the year building a strong community is through class meetings. These are quick meetings (5–10 minutes or longer towards the middle and end of the year) at the start or end of the day (or both) where teachers plan to greet all students, check in emotionally with them, and set the stage for learning or reflection. According to Responsive Classroom, these class meetings typically involve a greeting between students, sharing or check-in, a group activity to stimulate interaction and connection, and a message to kickstart the learning for the day (Rimm-Kaufman, Fan, Chiu, & You, 2007). Teachers in inclusive settings are faced with the challenge of bringing all students with such a variety of abilities and interests into a productive meeting (see www.responsiveclassroom.org/tag/special-needs/). Meetings can serve a variety of purposes such as building community in the classroom, reflecting on learning, or problem-solving class challenges (see Positive Discipline for a problem-solving class meeting format: www.positivediscipline.com/articles/what-does-positive-discipline-class-meeting-look). Inclusive class meetings must be planned purposefully using the principles of Universal Design for Learning (UDL) to break down barriers in the curriculum and instruction so that all children feel like they are included and supported and then individual students are provided with targeted adaptations to ensure meaningful participation. While pre-planning can be effective, often teachers must respond in the moment to make necessary adjustments as well as reflect on the success of the overall meeting for students and the success of individual adaptations for specific students with disabilities. To address ability diversity, teachers can proceed through the following thoughtful and reflective steps.

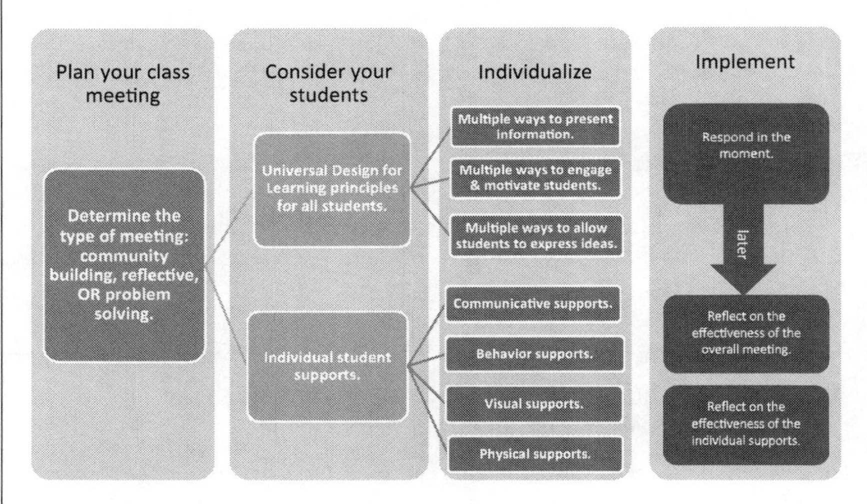

For example, Ms. Muran planned a community-building class meeting at the beginning of the year to set a positive tone for the day and check-in after a long weekend. She planned for students to gather in a circle and begin with greeting their neighbors using a special elbow-to-elbow handshake decided by the students. Then for partner sharing, they turned to their neighbor to share about their weekend. Finally, they engaged in Simon Says as a community-building activity. Using UDL principles, the teacher created a visual schedule of the class meeting to help students stay on task and know what was going to happen next, modeled how to do the handshake and talk with a peer, and ensured the meeting included different ways to engage and move. For four students with more support needs, the following accommodations were planned:

Student	*Meeting Supports*
Jane struggles with staying on task and attending during meetings.	An activity visual schedule is provided to Jane to follow along with each part of the morning meeting. As each part is completed, she is taught to look at her schedule and check off when completed by reading a social story written with her about the steps in the meeting and expectations for behaving and interacting. Ms. Muran also set up a cue of tapping her shoulder to remind her the class is moving onto the next part. See: www.responsiveclassroom.org/extra-support-with-transitions/
Antonio struggles with transitioning from home due to the trauma he has experienced with chemotherapy.	When Antonio arrives, give him time to adjust in the calming space, draw a picture or write words about how he feels, and the choice to share these during the meeting. Ms. Muran lets him know his peers will be sharing about their weekends so he may like to draw about something that happened this weekend. See: www.responsiveclassroom.org/morning-meeting-is-for-everyone/
Lis is nonverbal and communicates using her iPad voice output device.	The speech and language pathologist and special education teacher created a "What I did this weekend" section in the Proloquo2Go app on her iPad voice output device to use during the Monday morning meeting sharing time, then taught Lis how to use it. See: www.responsiveclassroom.org/morning-meeting-is-for-everyone/
Joseph has difficulty interacting with his peers.	Ms. Muran chose Joseph to be the leader during Simon Says to build his confidence and create positive interactions with his peers. See: www.responsiveclassroom.org/planning-morning-meetings-for-students-with-asd/

For some students who are learning below grade level, accommodations that increase their access to learning are not enough, so a different type of adaptation is necessary to make the content understandable. *Modifications* change the curriculum, assessment, or outcome for a student with a disability to their level of understanding with regard to age-appropriate Common Core standards. The IEP team meets to plan these modifications and writes them into the student's IEP (Eredics, 2018). Notably, IDEIA of 2004 states "a child with a disability is not removed from education in age-appropriate regular classrooms solely because of needed modifications in the general education curriculum." Therefore, modifications are strategic ways to ensure a student in the general education classroom or other setting is learning the grade-level CCSS at an appropriate learning level, which may be one or more grade levels below. In an inclusive classroom, students with significant support needs who need modifications are learning at their level of understanding within subject-specific activities alongside their peers. For example, while Ms. Muran is teaching a whole-class math lesson on subtracting three-digit numbers, Antonio, who has regressed in math skills due to chemotherapy, may be learning number identification while participating in the group lesson. See Box 9.4 to learn how collaboration is key to the learning success of students with significant support needs.

Box 9.4 Common Core: Participation and Support Plans for Students with Significant Support Needs

The Common Core State Standards (CCSS) for literacy and math are high grade-level expectations to prepare students for college and careers. Students with disabilities are no exception. In fact, IDEIA 2004 requires school teams to develop Individualized Education Programs (IEPs) that are aligned with the student's grade-level CCSS. This ensures high expectations and age-appropriate IEP goals. In inclusive classrooms, teachers believe all students can learn, and thus learning must be modified to ensure the progress of students with significant support needs that may struggle significantly with grade-level concepts. Collaborating with a special education teacher trained to embed instruction and interventions into daily instructional activities is critical so that there is a strategic plan in place for the student to learn and be successful. Such plans are called Participation and Support plans (Gee, 2017; Jorgensen & Lambert, 2012), or Planning Worksheets if using the Building Blocks model in early childhood (Sandall, Schwartz, Joseph, & Gauvreau, 2019). In Ms. Muran's inclusion classroom, she finds time each week to meet with Mr. Joe, the special education teacher, to create a plan for Jane, who has a significant reading disability, as well as Lis, who has cerebral palsy. During this meeting, Ms. Muran shares insight into the unit and lesson activities planned for the week, especially those that may be challenging for Jane, as they require her to read, or Lis, as they may require the use of her voice output device. Then Mr. Joe is able to identify if and how the activities can be modified for each student with significant support needs, like Jane and Lis, to ensure both participation in the activities with peers and learning. With Bronfenbrenner's (1977) ecology model in mind, one way to increase access to learning is through the support of peers in the classroom. Peers are powerful resources that can help a student with learning needs by learning how to support the student and then engaging them throughout the activity and day (Ruppar, Allcock, & Gonsier-Gerdin, 2017). Oftentimes these plans pull from a variety of resources including peer supports, accommodations, advanced UDL strategies, and assistive technology. See the flowchart below for how decisions are made to create a Participation and Support Plan and an example of a collaboratively created plan.

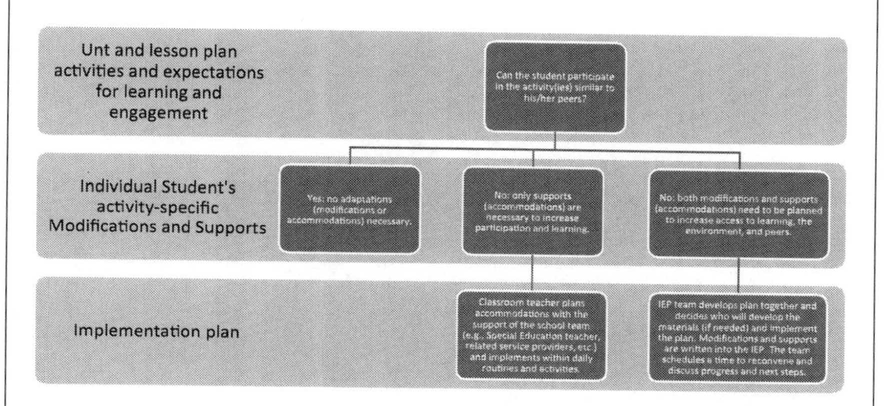

Participation and Support Planning Worksheet for Jane and Lis (see profiles above)

Student: Activity/ Routine	*Expectations for all students*	*Individualized adaptations (accommodation or modification) for this student*
Jane: Arrival, independent reading time.	Put away things, choose a book from class library, find a spot to sit and read independently. Independent reading books are labeled with reading levels for ease and every two weeks students choose new books for their book bin.	• Teacher greets her at door, walks her through the visual schedule for the day, and guides her to her peer buddy (Mr. Joe creates visual schedule and trains peer buddy). • Peer buddy helps her find a book from her personal book bin and they read together (Ms. Muran helps Jane choose books for her book bin).

Lis: Science lab	Gather materials, complete experiment, discuss with peers, record observations and results.	• Lis assigned role of leader during lab (Ms. Muran creates collaborative group role necklaces). • Key unit vocabulary added to her voice output device (by Mr. Joe). • Digital version of class worksheet added to her device to record her observations and results (by Mr. Joe).

In an MTSS model, once a strong foundation has been established, Tier 2 small group interventions are critical for any student with or without disabilities that may continue to struggle. For example, in Ms. Muran's class, if Maxwell continues to fall further behind in reading or if Atiqua struggles more with self-regulation, she may begin to talk to their families about brainstorming ways to support them more. This brainstorming for some students usually occurs with the school's Student Success/Study Team (SST) who meets with the family (and student if appropriate) to discuss strengths, challenges, and helpful supports and interventions. It is important for the team to have a discussion about the underlying reason for the student's difficulties so that additional supports and interventions are addressing the actual need in order to be effective. If the team suspects a disability might be impacting the student's success, then the team can immediately refer for an educational evaluation; it is a myth that a student needs to proceed through all three tiers of MTSS before qualifying for an evaluation. If the team decides to proceed with Tier 2 interventions, then these are attempted in small timeframes like six to eight weeks. For example, the team found that Atiqua developed good self-regulation skills by participating in a social skills group with the school counselor and through class meetings led by Ms. Muran on teaching all students to develop self-regulation. However, Maxwell continued to struggle with reading even after five weeks of an intense small group reading program. In Tier 2, small groups of students are provided with targeted interventions for math, literacy, or behavior and social-emotional skills. Three renowned websites for planning interventions are helpful: Intervention Central (https://www.interventioncentral.org/), RTI Action Network by the National Center for Learning Disabilities (www.rtinetwork.org), and the Center on Response to Intervention at American Institutes for Research (https://rti4success.org/). PBIS World is also a great tool for determining tiered levels of intervention for common challenges, like a student who is often out of seat or has anxiety (https://www.pbisworld.com/). These small group interventions for three to five students often focus on teaching strategies for learning, such as for solving word problems, reading words (decoding), or dealing with strong emotions. To determine if any of these interventions were effective, collecting data is key. Data is often reported from assessments as numbers on a math or reading test or as reductions in challenging behavior, but it can also be descriptive data such as observational notes from a teacher about the student's performance or behavior that gives context to the numbers. Progress monitoring data is collected on the student's progress and the results are brought back to the team to discuss the next steps. They may decide to continue as planned due to success (such as in Atiqua's case), or if unsuccessful, then try out new interventions and/or supports or move to Tier 3.

If small group interventions have not been successful, then the team may decide to move the student to Tier 3 interventions (such as in Maxwell's case). These are for a few students who need more intense interventions to determine the underlying cause of the learning challenges and to make frequent assessments to track progress and make needed adjustments. These interventions are often more intense, requiring more effort from the general education and/or special education teachers (e.g., Video Modeling, Social Stories, Token Economy), and are provided to one to two students at a time. If the student continues to not make progress, then the team may refer the student for a full educational evaluation by the school Multidisciplinary Team, which involves specialists relevant to the student's needs, such as a special education teacher, speech and language pathologist, psychologist, occupational therapist, social worker, nurse, and more. For example, after a full educational evaluation, Maxwell was found to be eligible for a learning disability (specifically for reading) and Other Health Impaired (for AD/HD). At this tier, individualized accommodations are critical as universal planning may not fully increase access to learning for the student. Additionally, two key points are important to remember in a school that implements MTSS for both academics and behavior. Firstly, the tiers are cumulative, such that *all* students are in Tier 1 receiving UDL-aligned instruction in academics and behavior within supportive inclusive environments and positive relationships. Some students need additional Tier 2 interventions and support, while a few will then need Tier 3 support as well. Secondly, movement throughout the tiers of support is fluid, as students move between them based on decisions made by the SST in collaboration with the student's family. The SST must discuss progress every six to eight weeks and make necessary adjustments so that the student does not continue to fail and disconnect from the classroom and school.

Chapter Summary

In summary, effective inclusion is based on a strengths-based approach utilizing a growth mindset that celebrates all students as learners in the classroom community. General and special educators collaborate to ensure units and lessons are planned using the principles of Universal Design for Learning (UDL) and then strategically plan for how some individual students with more support needs will require adaptations, including accommodations and/or modifications to increase participation, engagement, and learning. The MTSS framework is a wonderful way for schools to build their capacity for inclusive education. Without high-quality instruction and relationships in place, it would be hard to know if students in the classroom are struggling due to an unpredictable and unsupported learning environment, or if it was indeed related to developmental delays or disabilities. If individualized supports at the highest tier were targeted without ensuring the child was learning in a high-quality developmentally appropriate classroom, then those interventions would be ineffective and the inverted tiers would topple. What it would look like in the classroom is intense supports for one or two students through a one-on-one paraprofessional or repeated corrections of a child's behavior that continued to be ineffective. We must be careful that these instances do not become examples of the ineffectiveness of inclusion, but rather that the team takes a look at the system to ensure the teachers and students are appropriately supported at all tiers. In an inclusive classroom, access to the curriculum and embedded individual learning goals are critical for the success of students with disabilities. Finally, inclusive teachers believe all individuals can learn and ensure students have alternative ways to perceive information, process ideas even at higher levels of thinking, and express that learning in their own way that capitalizes upon their strengths.

References

Armstrong, T. (2012). *Neurodiversity in the classroom: Strength-based strategies to help students with special needs succeed in school and life*. Association for Supervision & Curriculum Development (ASCD): Alexandria, VA.

Barton, E., Reichow, B., Wolery, M., & Chen, C. (2011). We can all participate! Adapting circle time for children with autism. *Young Exceptional Children*, *14*(2), 2–21.

Belardinelli, C., Raza, M., & Taneli, T. (2016). Comorbid behavioral problems and psychiatric disorders in autism spectrum disorders. *Journal of Childhood & Developmental Disorders*, *2*(2), 1–9.

Boroson, B. (2017, April). Inclusive education: Lessons from history. *Educational Leadership*, *74*(7), 18–23.

Bronfenbrenner, U. (1977). Toward an experimental ecology of human development. *Journal of the American Psychological Association*, *32*, 513–529.

Coates, R.D. (1989). The regular education initiative and opinions of regular classroom teachers. *Journal of Learning Disabilities*, *22*(9), 532–536.

DEC/NAEYC (2009). *Early childhood inclusion: A joint position statement of the Division for Early Childhood (DEC) and the National Association for the Education of Young Children (NAEYC)*. Chapel Hill: University of North Carolina, FPG Child Development Institute.

Dessemontet, S.R., & Bless, G. (2013). The impact of including children with intellectual disability in general education classrooms on the academic achievement of their low-, average-, and high-achieving peers. *Journal of Intellectual and Developmental Disability, 38*(1), 23–30.

Dessemontet, S.R., Bless, G., & Morin, D. (2012). Effects of inclusion on the academic achievement and adaptive behaviour of children with intellectual disabilities. *Journal of Intellectual Disability Research, 56*(6), 579–587.

Donnellan, A.M. (1984). The criterion of the least dangerous assumption. *Behavioral Disorders, 9*(2), 141–150.

Dweck, C. (2006). *Mindset: The new psychology of success*. New York: Ballantine Books.

Eredics, N. (2018). *Inclusion in action: Practical strategies to modify the curriculum*. Baltimore, MD: Paul H. Brookes.

Forlin, C., Tait, K., Carroll, A., & Jobling, A. (1999). Teacher education for diversity. *Queensland Journal of Educational Research, 15*(2), 207–225.

Friesen, S. (2010). Raising the floor and lifting the ceiling: Math for all. *Education Canada, 48*(5), 50–54.

Gardner, P. M. (2006). Creating inclusive schools for all learners. In E. Durán (Ed.), *Teaching English learners in inclusive classrooms*. (pp. 3–49). Charles C. Thomas Publisher.

Gee, K. (2002). Looking closely at instructional approaches: Honoring and challenging all children and youth in inclusive schools. In W. Sailor (Ed.), *Whole school success and inclusive education*. New York: Teacher College Press.

Gee, K. (2017). Designing and adapting the curriculum. In F.P. Orelove, D. Sobsey, & D.L. Giles (Eds.), *Educating students with severe and multiple disabilities: A collaborative approach* (5th ed.). Baltimore, MD: Paul H. Brookes.

Grisham-Brown, J., & Hemmeter, M.L. (2017). *Blended practices for teaching young children in inclusive settings* (2nd ed.). Baltimore, MD: Paul H. Brookes.

Halvorsen, A.T., & Neary, T. (2009). *Building inclusive schools: Tools and strategies for success* (2nd ed.). Boston: Pearson Education.

Individuals with Disabilities Education Act, 20 U.S.C. § 1400 (2004).

Jorgensen, C.M., & Lambert, L. (2012). Inclusion means more than just being "in": Planning full participation of students with intellectual and other developmental disabilities in the general education classroom. *International Journal of Whole Schooling, 8*(2), 21–35.

Kavale, K.A., & Forness, S.R. (2000). History, rhetoric, and reality: Analysis of the inclusion debate. *Remedial and Special Education, 21*(5), 279–296.

Kunc, N. (2000). Integration: Being realistic isn't realistic. *Electronic Journal for Inclusive Education, 1*(3), 1–10.

Kurth, J., Lyon, K.J., & Shogren, K.A. (2015). Supporting students with severe disabilities in inclusive schools: A descriptive account from schools implementing inclusive practices. *Research and Practice for Persons with Severe Disabilities, 40*(4), 261–274.

Lee, S., Wehmeyer, M.L., Soukup, J.H., & Palmer, S.B. (2010). Impact of curriculum modifications on access to the general education curriculum for students with disabilities. *Exceptional Children, 76*(2), 213–233.

National Council of Teachers of English (NCTE) (2016). *Equity and early childhood education: Reclaiming the child research policy brief*.

Nelson, L.L. (2015). *Five steps to get started with UDL*. Lawrence, KS: SWIFT Center.

Pelka, F. (2012). *What have we done: An oral history of the disability rights movement*. University of Massachusetts Press.

Rao, K., Ok, M.W., & Bryant, B.R. (2014). A review of research on universal design educational models. *Remedial and Special Education*, *35*(3), 153–166.

Rapp, W.H. (2014). *Universal design for learning in action: 100 ways to teach all learners*. Baltimore, MD: Paul H. Brookes.

Resnick, M., & Robinson, K. (2017). *Lifelong kindergarten: Cultivating creativity through projects, passion, peers, and play*. Cambridge, MA: MIT Press.

Rimm-Kaufman, S.E., Fan, X., Chiu, Y., & You, W. (2007). The contribution of the responsive classroom approach on children's academic achievement: Results from a three-year longitudinal study. *Journal of School Psychology*, *45*, 401–421.

Ruppar, A.L., Allcock, H., & Gonsier-Gerdin, J. (2017). Ecological factors affecting access to general education content and contexts for students with significant disabilities. *Remedial and Special Education*, *38*(1), 53–63.

Sandall, S.R., Schwartz, I.S., Joseph, G.E., & Gauvreau, A.N. (2019). *Building blocks for teaching preschoolers with special needs* (3rd ed.). Baltimore, MD: Paul H. Brookes.

Sauer, J.S., & Jorgensen, C.M. (2016). Still caught in the continuum: A critical analysis of least restrictive environment and its effect on placement of students with intellectual disability. *Inclusion*, *4*(2), 56–74.

Sheldon, K.M., & King, L. (2001). Why positive psychology is necessary. *American Psychologist*, *56*(3), 216–217.

Spencer, S.A. (2011). Universal design for learning: Assistance for teachers in today's inclusive classrooms. *Interdisciplinary Journal of Teaching and Learning*, *1*(1), 10–22.

Staats, C. (2016). Understanding implicit bias: What educators should know. *American Educator*, *39*(4), 29–33.

Wilson, J.D. (2017). Reimagining disability and inclusive education through universal design for learning. *Disability Studies Quarterly*, *37*(2). DOI: http://dx.doi.org/10.18061/dsq.v37i2

Yell, M.L. (2019). *The law and special education* (5th ed.). Boston: Pearson Education.

Young, K. S., Herring, T. J., & Morrison, A. D. (2017). Conceptual strategies for culturally sustaining and inclusive education. *Kappa Delta Pi Record*, *53*(4), 174–178.

Chapter 10

Assessment and Evaluation

Arlene Ortiz

Vignette

Mark is a second-grade teacher who recently got a new student, Isabel, assigned to his class. Isabel recently moved from another state and Mark does not have much information regarding her academic skills. Mark is a strong proponent of individualized instruction and divides his class by reading level for literacy instruction. In order to assign Isabel to an appropriate reading group, he administers a brief curriculum-based measure that measures reading accuracy and fluency. Isabel's score on this measure falls well below second-grade benchmarks and her decoding is at a kindergarten level. Her performance concerns Mark and he is uncertain whether Isabel may have a learning disability in reading or if she simply lacks appropriate instruction in reading. Given his concerns, he consults with the reading specialist, who agrees to work one-on-one with Isabel daily for four weeks to help her remediate her reading skills. The reading specialist provides explicit phonics instruction and assesses Isabel's decoding and fluency skills weekly. At the end of the intensive four-week intervention, Isabel is able to read at a first-grade level. Although Isabel still has work to do to meet grade-level benchmarks, she can now join her class for reading instruction. Given the significant progress made during the intervention period, Mark no longer suspects that Isabel may have a learning disability.

This chapter focuses on the assessment and evaluation of children within pre-kindergarten and elementary school settings. Readers will gain an understanding of the utility of assessment and learn best practices in assessment for this population. An emphasis will be placed on distinguishing between formative and summative assessment practices used to inform instruction and help identify students who may require specialized instruction. To accomplish this goal, the chapter is divided into five sections: 1) Introduction, 2) Assessment of the Whole Child: Formative and Summative Practices, 3) Referring Children for Special Education Testing, 4) Assessing Special Populations, and 5) Measuring Quality in Elementary School Settings.

Introduction

Novice educators often spend a large amount of time planning lessons; each lesson has its own set of goals. Given the time and energy spent on planning, it is imperative that teachers have knowledge related to the effectiveness of their work. Similarly, it is important for educators to know whether target goals have been met for the classroom and for individual students, to identify children who may be at risk for a disability, and to obtain information related to areas of strengths and weakness of their own teaching practices. Assessment is a critical component to help answer these concerns. *Assessment* is defined as the systematic collection and analysis of information that is used in order to gain information related to student and teacher performance. Often, assessment is not sufficient to answer the concerns noted above. *Evaluation* is defined as the process of using data obtained from the assessment process to form judgments and identify relationships to determine an outcome. In other words, when a teacher needs to determine whether a child is making adequate grade-level progress in reading, she may identify various assessments related to reading to gain information about the child's skills in this area. The teacher engages in evaluation of the child's reading skills when she uses the results from various assessment tools to identify patterns and form a conclusion about whether the child meets grade-level expectations in reading.

There are two major assessment categories identified in the literature: summative and formative assessments. Summative assessment practices tend to be more traditional and include paper-and-pencil exams, such as standardized state tests. Formative assessment practices align better with modern classrooms and teaching pedagogy as they focus on providing students with multiple ways of communicating knowledge and skills. Although both summative and formative assessment practices are valuable, a developmental perspective is critical when selecting assessments. For example, it may not be helpful to assess a four-year-old child's knowledge of basic verbal concepts through a paper-and-pencil test. Other developmental factors to consider when selecting assessments include a child's attention span, distractibility, sensory needs, motor skills, receptive and expressive language skills, experience in formal testing environments, temperament, and other social and emotional variables.

Purpose of Assessment

In modern pedagogy, assessment is an essential component of the learning process. As previously mentioned, assessment is the systematic collection and analysis of information to gain information related to student and teacher performance. Assessment may be used to inform many aspects of the learning process and includes teacher planning and instruction, identification of children who may be at risk, program quality, and policy development.

Assessment guides teacher planning. Knowledge of development across the grade levels typically guides teacher planning; however, skills and abilities from students from one year to the next may vary and require teachers to modify their practices. As such, information about student performance may be used to identify student strengths and weaknesses, which in turn can be used to inform instructional design and set SMART goals for students. Specifically, SMART goals are *S*pecific, *M*easureable, *A*chievable, *R*elevant, and *T*ime-bound. Assessment results can be used to help the classroom teacher identify patterns in academic performance across students. For example, a teacher may give a reading assessment and identify students who may need to focus on decoding skills while other students need to focus on reading fluency. The teacher can use this information to divide the classroom into small groups, some that focus on providing evidence-based instruction for decoding and some that focus on fluency. In this manner, assessment can also be used to help select evidence-based strategies and curriculums that are specific to the needs of students. Selecting evidence-based curriculums is only effective if the child's needs are accurately identified, which is challenging to do without assessment. Finally, a component of instruction that may be overlooked is student interest and engagement. Children demonstrate more motivation and engagement when lessons incorporate student interests. Assessment can also be used to gather information related to student interests. For example, a kindergarten teacher may read aloud stories about dinosaurs during storytime after most children have expressed an interest in the topic in a graph completed during a morning meeting.

Assessment helps identify children at risk or with delays. For many parents, educators are the first professionals who provide them with expert feedback on their child's development. This is inclusive of positive statements related to acquisition of developmental milestones and acquisition of grade-level content, but may also include sentiments of concern for developmental delays and learning problems. Educators do not want to worry parents unnecessarily and often express concerns for delays only when they have sufficient evidence, such as continuous progress monitoring data. Assessment serves to inform educator decisions about whether a child may be at risk. There are a variety of assessment methods, which will be discussed later in this chapter, that may be employed to understand a child's strengths and weaknesses. When children are identified as at-risk, they may be referred for additional assessment to determine whether delays are due to a disability and whether they may be eligible for special education services. Generally, the school professional completing these diagnostic assessments is the school psychologist. A school psychologist is an educational professional with expertise in developmental and behavioral disabilities and psychoeducational assessment. Additionally, a school psychologist is able to implement social-emotional, behavioral, and academic interventions.

Assessment helps inform program quality and policy. Assessment may also serve to promote program quality and inform policies relevant to child development and education. A school administrator working at a school that recently adopted a new math curriculum may want to know whether teachers were provided with sufficient training to appropriately implement the curriculum or whether they may need additional professional development support. Assessment tools may be used to help this administrator answer their question. As such, the administrator collects data related to curriculum fidelity to determine whether teachers are implementing the curriculum as designed. Results of the assessment may be used to determine whether additional training or consultation is needed. Similarly, schools may conduct assessments to determine the school climate in order to gain information related to staff, teacher, and student attitudes toward school.

Data collected on a large scale, such as school-wide or district-wide data, can be helpful in identifying strengths and weaknesses within systems. Consistent data patterns may be used to inform policy at various levels. For example, several parents in a school district complain that their children are not receiving enough physical activity. As such, the school administrator for the district leads an effort to collect data that measures the relationship between the amount of recess and physical education and the academic grades for children in elementary schools within the district. Results suggest that in schools where more time is allotted to physical activity, students perform better in reading and math. These results help inform the school administrator's decision to have all schools within the district allocate a minimum amount of time for physical activity.

Standards for Learning

Learning standards define the knowledge, concepts, and skills that students should acquire at each grade level. In other words, learning standards are the goals for what students should know and be able to do at each grade level. Students who demonstrate acquisition of grade-level goals are considered proficient. Generally, each state establishes its own definition of proficiency. In an effort to have consistency in learning standards across the nation and help ensure all students are prepared to graduate from high school with the skills they need to succeed, numerous states and territories adopted a set of standards known as the Common Core State Standards (Common Core State Standard Initiative, n.d.). Forty-one states, the District of Columbia, four out of five territories, and the Department of Defense Education Activity have adopted the Common Core State Standards for English language arts/literacy and math. As of 2019, Alaska, Florida, Indiana, Minnesota, Nebraska, Oklahoma, Puerto Rico, South Carolina, Texas, and Virginia have not adopted the Common Core State Standards. Whether or not educators work in a state that has adopted Common Core State Standards, having clear learning standards is a critical component of assessment, because they serve as unbiased outcome variables for education. Having concrete and well-defined expectations, such as learning standards, allows educators to work backward and design the most effective tools to measure the intended outcome, such as grade-level proficiency. All teachers should be familiar with their respective state learning standards as well as summative assessment practices used within the state to assess for proficiency of these standards. Additionally, teachers should develop their own formative assessment practices to obtain ongoing information related to student progress towards these standards.

Box 10.1 Common Core and Other Standards

Concerns and Opportunities: Common Core State Standards for Young Children

Common Core standards continue to be debated, especially for young children in preschool and kindergarten. Many early childhood educators fear that standards may be too rigorous and not developmentally appropriate, forcing teachers to reduce play and enriching classroom experiences. Similarly, some believe that instruction may become drill focused, reducing opportunities for naturalistic, language-rich conversations, leading children to become less engaged in their learning. However, some educators argue that developing curriculums that align with Common Core standards lead to noticeable increases in students' abilities to think critically and work collaboratively. Although educators will likely continue to debate on this topic, what seems to be a common factor for educational success is extensive resources allocated to professional development to help teachers.

Assessment Practices

As previously mentioned, it is important to identify the purpose of assessment in order to select appropriate methods of assessment. Similarly, it is important to consider the target behavior, skill, or ability as well as developmental factors. There are many methods of assessment, including observations, direct tests, and rating scales. Each of these methods is discussed in detail in the second section of this chapter. It is advised that various methods be used, as some students may perform differently depending on the assessment method. Consider a second-grade student who has test anxiety; that student is likely to perform poorly on direct tests of reading, but may do better when observed by the teacher during paired reading time in class. Conversely, a child with ADHD may appear to be off-task and not have mastered specific math skills based on teacher observations during small group instruction; however, when given a direct test of math skills in a one-on-one setting, the student may perform exceptionally well. Although the student with ADHD may be hyperactive and have difficulty directing his attention to complete academic tasks in larger groups, a one-on-one setting reduces the amount of distracting stimuli in the environment and may allow the student to better direct his attention to academic tasks.

In addition to determining the method of assessment, timing of assessment should also be considered. Assessment can be conducted at various time intervals; the frequency of assessment should be guided by the purpose and goals of assessment. Being familiar with development and research related to the time it takes to develop specific skills may also help guide the frequency of assessment. Assessment can be most helpful when it is administered at consistent intervals; however, these intervals may vary and include daily, weekly, quarterly, or annually. Consider a struggling reader who just moved to the school, and is very far behind peers in regards to sight word recognition skills. The education team selects an intervention strategy to help him catch up to his peers. Given the importance of this skill, the child's ability, and knowledge of age-appropriate expectations for words read correctly per minute, the team selects to assess sight word recognition skills daily. In contrast, a child with special needs receiving a six-week social-skills intervention may be assessed prior to the intervention and during the last week of the intervention to determine gains in social skills.

Challenges of Assessing Children

Assessing children across developmental domains can be challenging due to factors such as limited attention span, anxiety, motivation, familiarity with formal testing, variation in reading skills, and inconsistency in performance across days. Assessing preschoolers' learning can be particularly challenging, as this developmental period is marked by uneven and rapid growth. Most young children have limited attention spans; therefore, there may be wide variations in child performance on any given day. Given these limitations, great care should be taken when making decisions about assessment design and implementation. Furthermore, the technical adequacy of test results, including reliability and validity, often come into question when working with children, especially young children. This is discussed further in the next section. Given various challenges, multiple sources of information and approaches across time and settings are recommended to yield a comprehensive analysis of a child's strengths and weaknesses.

Assessment of the Whole Child: Formative and Summative Practices

This section provides an overview of contemporary assessment practices used in primary educational settings, including formative and summative assessments. Learning in the classroom can take various forms; therefore, it is important for educators to be familiar with different assessment practices in order to best assess specific learning goals.

Formative Assessment Practices

Teachers in a modern classroom utilize ongoing data collection to inform instruction. Figure 10.1 demonstrates the formative learning cycle (Moss & Brookhart, 2009), which incorporates formative assessment. Formative assessment is "a planned, ongoing process used by all students and teachers during learning and teaching to elicit and use evidence of student learning to improve student understanding of intended disciplinary learning outcomes and support students to become self-directed learners" (Formative Assessment for Students and Teachers State Collaborative on Assessment and Student Standards, 2018).. Assessment is formative when students and teachers use assessment data to figure out where students are in relation to intended learning standards and what they need to do next to make progress. Formative assessment practices have been linked to improved academic outcomes for all

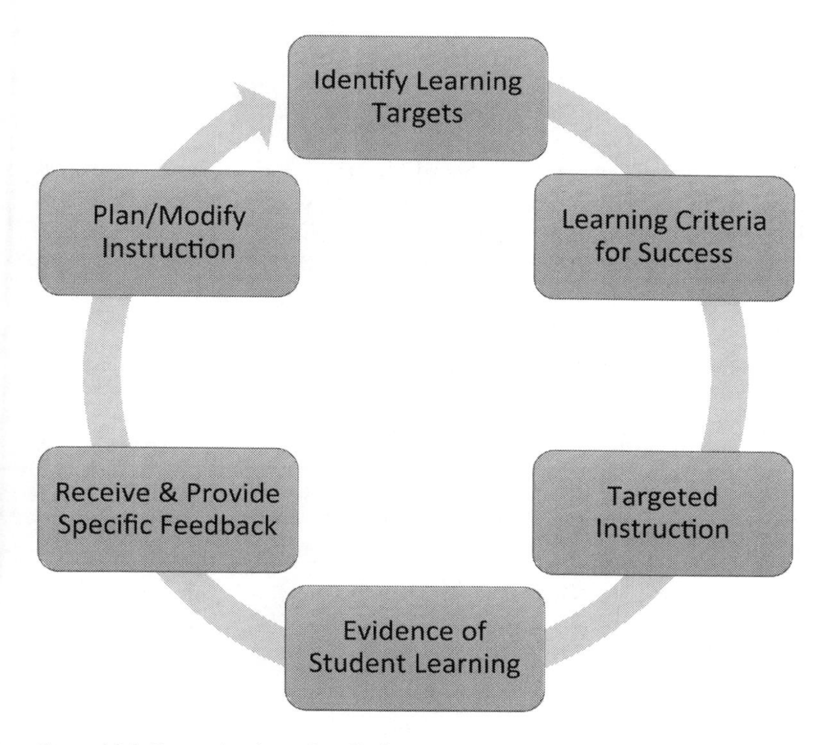

Figure 10.1 Formative Learning Cycle

students, including struggling learners (Black, Harrison, Lee, Marshall, & Wiliam, 2003).

Teachers consider three key questions for formative assessment: Where do I want my students to go? Where are they now? What do I need to do next to get students where I want them to be? In order for formative assessment to be effective, clear and meaningful learning goals and criteria for success should be communicated to students. Learning should be evaluated and students should receive immediate feedback related to their performance based on predetermined criteria. Feedback should be directly related to goals, constructive, ongoing, varied, and consistent. Students should have a clear understanding of what they need to do to move closer toward goal attainment. Additionally, evidence and feedback should be used to adjust learning strategies, goals, or instruction as needed. Analyzing student work, checklists, round-robin charts, strategic questioning, three-way summaries, think-pair-share, classroom polls, exit/admit tickets, and one-minute papers are some examples of informal formative assessment types. For the purposes of this chapter, observations and progress monitoring are considered formal methods of formative assessment and are described below.

Observation-based assessment for learning-related behaviors. At times, children display behaviors in the classroom that make learning challenging, such as difficulties with emotion regulation or attention. It may become necessary to establish behavioral goals for students, which can be monitored using observation-based assessment. Additionally, information related to skill acquisition may be assessed through observation. For example, fine motor development may be observed through a child's ability to use scissors, color in between the lines, and use a fork and spoon independently. Observations can also be helpful in understanding how students respond to transitions, deal with challenging tasks, and respond to limits. Table 10.1 outlines specific behaviors that may be assessed across domains of functioning.

Table 10.1 Behaviors to Assess When Observing Students Across Developmental Domains

Cognitive	*Communication*	*Social and Emotional*	*Sensorimotor*
• Attention Span	• Pragmatics	• Temperament	• Muscle Strength
• Planning/ Organization	• Discourse Skills	• Attribution Style	• Tone
• Problem-Solving Approaches	• Listening Comprehension	• Social Interactions with Others	• Reactivity to Sensory Input
• Type of Play: Symbolic and Representational	• Semantic and Syntactic Understanding	• Coping Strategies/ Self-Regulation	• Endurance
	• Phonology	• Play Themes	
	• Imitation/Echolalia		

Table 10.2 Special Education Eligibility Criteria and Red Flags for Risk

Eligibility Category	*Main Components of IDEA Definition*	*Red Flags*
Specific Learning Disability	A disorder in one or more of the basic psychological processes involved in understanding or in using language, spoken or written, that may manifest itself in the imperfect ability to listen, think, speak, read, write, spell, or to do mathematical calculations, including conditions such as perceptual disabilities, brain injury, minimal brain dysfunction, dyslexia, and developmental aphasia. Specific learning disability does not include learning problems that are primarily the result of visual, hearing, or motor disabilities, intellectual disability, emotional disturbance, or environmental, cultural, or economic disadvantage.	• Problems with memory, such as difficulty remembering multi-step directions or routines • Poor grades despite significant effort and intervention • Require constant, step-by-step guidance to complete academic tasks • Difficulty deriving meaning from information heard or read • Difficulty with rapid letter recognition • Difficulty reading sight words • Difficulty applying phonics skills to sound out unknown words • Taking significantly longer than peers to read grade-level reading passages • Difficulty applying phonics skills to spell words • Difficulty applying basic rules of grammar • Difficulties with automaticity of basic math facts • Using immature strategies to solve problems such as using fingers to count long after peers have stopped
Speech and Language Impairment	A communication disorder, such as stuttering, impaired articulation, a language impairment, or a voice impairment that adversely affects a child's educational performance.	• Trouble with articulation • Frequent mispronunciation of words • Trouble using correct verb tenses, plurals, or pronouns when speaking • Trouble rhyming and/or playing sound or word games

(*Continued*)

Table 10.2 Continued

Eligibility Category	*Main Components of IDEA Definition*	*Red Flags*
Other Health Impairment	Having limited strength, vitality, or alertness, including a heightened alertness to environmental stimuli, that results in limited alertness with respect to the educational environment, that: 1) is due to chronic or acute health problems such as asthma, attention deficit disorder or attention deficit hyperactivity disorder, diabetes, epilepsy, a heart condition, hemophilia, lead poisoning, leukemia, nephritis, rheumatic fever, sickle cell anemia, and Tourette syndrome; and 2) adversely affects a child's educational performance.	• Difficulty sustaining attention to instruction or assigned work • Impulsive behaviors, such as interrupting others and difficulty waiting their turn • Hyperactive behaviors such as difficulty sitting in their seat and constantly moving • Difficulty organizing materials • Difficulty planning for projects • Losing or forgetting materials and forgetting to turn in completed assignments
Autism	A developmental disability significantly affecting verbal and nonverbal communication and social interaction, generally evident before age three, that adversely affects a child's educational performance. Other characteristics often associated with autism are engagement in repetitive activities and stereotyped movements, resistance to environmental change or change in daily routines, and unusual responses to sensory experiences. Autism does not apply if a child's educational performance is adversely affected primarily because the child has an emotional disturbance. A child who manifests the characteristics of autism after age three could be identified as having autism if the criteria detailed here are satisfied.	• Difficulty communicating needs with appropriate words or gestures • Delayed language development • Persistent repetition of words or phrases • Avoidance of interactions with peers • Difficulty demonstrating or understanding their own feelings or other people's feelings • Avoidance of eye contact • Difficulty changing activities or handling disruptions to routines • Unusual or intense reactions to sounds, smells, tastes, textures, lights and/or colors

Authentic assessment refers to the systematic recording of developmental observations over time related to children's behaviors and competencies that occur in their natural environments, such as the classroom; familiar and knowledgeable caregivers collect these data in order to provide context to the behaviors observed (Bagnato, Goins, Pretti-Frontczak, & Neisworth, 2014). This type of assessment focuses on data collection of functional skills, which are real behaviors relevant to the child's current daily functioning. In order to ensure that specific skills are observed as well as to ensure that information collected is reliable, multiple observations across settings are essential. If necessary, the professional may choose to manipulate the environment so that specific skills can be observed.

Various observation methods can be utilized to collect information related to student behavior, such as ABC charts (event sampling), time sampling, checklists, and behavior rating scales. An ABC chart is a direct observation tool that can be used to collect information about events occurring within a student's environment. "A" refers to the antecedent (event or activity) that immediately precedes a target behavior. The "B" refers to the observed target behavior, and "C" refers to the consequence, the event that immediately follows a response. Table 10.3 provides an example of an ABC chart. Time sampling, shown in Table 10.4, is a method of collecting data in which a student is observed for a specific amount of time and whether or not a target behavior or activity took place is recorded. Rating scales can be used to evaluate performance by rating the frequency with which target behaviors occur across multiple criteria, which are then added together. For example, a teacher may rate the frequency a child raises their hand during class instruction as Never

Table 10.3 ABC Chart

Date	*Time*	*Antecedent*	*Behavior*	*Consequence*	*Possible Function*
				Description: ☐ Reinforcing ☐ Not Reinforcing	☐ Attention ☐ Escape ☐ Sensory ☐ Tangible Object
				Description: ☐ Reinforcing ☐ Not Reinforcing	☐ Attention ☐ Escape ☐ Sensory ☐ Tangible Object
				Description: ☐ Reinforcing ☐ Not Reinforcing	☐ Attention ☐ Escape ☐ Sensory ☐ Tangible Object

Table 10.4 Time Sampling Chart

Date	*Time*	*Length of Each Interval*	*Interval Number*				
			1	*2*	*3*	*4*	*5*

Instructions: Mark an X if behavior occurred based on the method of time sampling selected.
Method of Time Sampling: ☐ Whole Interval Recording ☐ Partial Interval Recording ☐ Momentary Time Sampling

Table 10.5 Rating Scale of Classroom Behaviors

Date	*Activity/ Lesson*	*Rate the Frequency of Each Behavior*			*Total*
		Raises Hand Quietly	*Waits to be Called on Before Speaking*	*Eyes on Teacher or Materials*	
	e.g., math	0 1 2 0 1 2	0 1 2 0 1 2	0 1 2 0 1 2	

Instructions: Please rate the frequency the student engages in each behavior during whole-class instructional periods using the following scale: 0 = Never, 1 = Sometimes, 2 = Often.

(0 points), Sometimes (1 point), or Often (2 points). This method may be less time consuming for teachers to assess the frequency of behaviors, but is also more subjective (see Table 10.5).

Box 10.2 Promoting Social-Emotional Competence

Spotlight on New York Public Schools: Using Positive Behavioral Intervention and Supports to Monitor Social-Emotional Well-Being

Positive Behavioral Intervention and Supports (PBIS) is a multi-tiered system of supports to create and maintain positive school climates.

PBIS emphasizes the prevention of behavioral and school discipline problems by teaching, modeling, and recognizing appropriate behavior in schools. PBIS is a systems framework that guides the selection and implementation of evidence-based practices for improving behavioral and social-emotional outcomes for all students. Each school in New York sets three to five behavioral expectations for all students and staff across settings. These expectations are taught to students and school personnel so that everyone knows what those expectations are. Students are consistently acknowledged for meeting expectations and provided with positive corrective feedback when expectations are not followed. Students may also receive additional support to encourage and/or teach the expected, positive behavior. PBIS can be a part of a multi-tier system of supports model, which is explained in detail on this page.

Screening and progress monitoring to inform instruction. Multi-Tier System of Supports (MTSS) is a service delivery model supported by IDEIA that incorporates the use of universal screening tools to identify students at risk for academic and behavioral difficulties who may benefit from additional specialized interventions (Fuchs & Fuchs, 2006). A screener is a brief and low-cost procedure used to obtain preliminary information about a wide range of behaviors for large groups of children (Gridley, Mucha, & Hatfield, 1995), and may be helpful at identifying children who may be at risk or who may require additional support to meet specific goals. An example of a screener used to assess literacy skills is the Dynamic Indicators of Basic Early Literacy Skills (DIBELS), currently in its eighth edition. DIBELS assesses for key areas of early literacy known to be predictive of reading challenges, such as reading rate and accuracy. The screener is designed to be administered three times during the school year as a way to monitor progress. Each period of assessment has established benchmark criteria to help the professional determine which children may require additional support in reading. Children identified as at-risk and needing additional support should be monitored closely through continuous progress monitoring. Progress monitoring is used to quantify a student's rate of improvement or responsiveness to instruction and to evaluate the effectiveness of instruction.

Summative Assessment and High-Stakes Testing

Summative assessment, such as paper-and-pencil tests, is an efficient and objective assessment approach that allows quick and reliable results. The goal of summative assessment is to evaluate student learning at the end of a specified period or event, such as at the end of an instructional unit. Summative assessment includes direct testing and may include the following question types: multiple-choice, matching, true or false, fill-in-the-blank, short answer, or a combination of these. Other examples of summative assessment include a final paper or a music recital. Although this approach can be informative, when used in isolation, it may not assess the development of the whole child.

Summative assessments are often high-stakes, which means that they have a high point value. Given the high point value, there can be significant consequences for students if they do not perform well. Although summative assessment practices can be less time-consuming than formative assessment methods, some children may learn to associate negative feelings such as fear with tests, which may lead to test anxiety. Therefore, teachers are encouraged to create friendly and low-stress environments when testing, such as playing relaxing music, giving tests fun names, and allowing children to participate in high-interest activities following tests.

When administering summative assessments, it is important to consider whether students need accommodations. Testing accommodations are changes to the regular testing environment and auxiliary aids and services that allow individuals with disabilities to demonstrate their knowledge (U.S. Department of Justice Civil Rights Division, n.d.). Examples of testing accommodations include extended time, testing in a distraction-free room, use of scribes, having the test read aloud when reading is not being assessed, and physical prompts such as redirection.

Judging the Quality and Utility of Assessments

Given that assessment instruments are used to inform instructional and diagnostic decisions, it is imperative that practitioners select quality instruments that demonstrate adequate psychometric properties. Reliability and validity are the two main psychometric properties.

Reliability is the ability to reproduce a result consistently. Three common forms of reliability include internal reliability, test/re-test reliability, and inter-rater reliability. *Internal reliability* assesses the consistency of scores across items within a test. Salvia, Ysseldyke, and Witmer (2017) recommended a minimum internal reliability standard of .80 when making screening decisions and a reliability standard of .90 when making diagnostic decisions. *Test-retest reliability* is obtained by administering the same test twice to the same individual over a period of time. *Inter-rater reliability* is used to assess the degree to which scores across items for different raters are similar. Inter-rater reliability is especially important when assessment involves observations of behavior, including rating scales, because observers may not interpret items the same way.

Validity encompasses the extent to which scores reflect what the test is designed to measure. The three main forms of validity include face validity, construct validity, and criterion-related validity. *Face validity* helps answer the question of whether the instrument appears to be assessing what it is designed to measure, and may include expert consensus. *Construct validity* assesses whether the instrument measures the construct it is designed to measure and not some other construct. For example, an assessment instrument designed to assess disruptive behavior should actually assess disruptive behavior and not reading skills or intelligence. Construct validity can be assessed by analyzing the relationship of scores between two or more assessment instruments (Messick, 1995). Messick (1995) suggested that both convergent and discriminant correlation patterns are important to investigate when exploring construct validity. Convergent patterns indicate a correspondence between measures of the same construct, whereas discriminant patterns indicate distinctness from measures of other constructs (Messick, 1995). Finally, *criterion-related validity* is used to predict current or future outcomes. Concurrent validity refers to a comparison of scores between the instrument and some outcome at the same time while predictive validity refers to a comparison of scores between the instrument and some later outcome.

When selecting quality instruments for both formative and summative assessment, it is insufficient to have adequate reliability, and test scores must also demonstrate adequate validity. When reviewing assessments, these properties may typically be found in the technical portion of the test manual. Additionally, the Mental Measurements Yearbook is a resource that includes test reviews, including measures of reliability and validity. By selecting quality tools, professionals may have confidence that the tools they are using are useful for obtaining information related to a specific area.

Referring Children for Special Education Testing

The third section will highlight Child Find policy and introduce contemporary models of assessment for learning disabilities, such as Multi-Tiered Systems of Support (MTSS) as well as methods for applying cognitive test results to inform classroom instruction.

A disability is any condition of the body or mind that makes it more difficult for the individual to do certain activities and interact with the world around them (Center for Disease Control, 2019). According to the World Health Organization (2001), disability has three dimensions: 1) impairment in a person's body structure or function, or mental functioning such as loss of a limb or memory loss, 2) activity limitation, such as difficulty seeing or problem-solving, and 3) participation restrictions in normal daily activities, such as working and engaging in social activities. Children with disabilities often require specialized instructional practices or equipment to learn. Therefore, it is important that assessment practices are put into place within school systems to identify students in school who may have disabilities and identify necessary supports.

Child Find Policy

Prior to 1975, millions of children with disabilities were denied appropriate access to public education due to their disability status (Katsiyannis, Yell, & Bradley (2001)). In 1975, the Education for All Handicapped Children

Act (Public Law 94-142), now known as the Individuals with Disabilities Education Act (IDEA), was signed into law. IDEA is a federal law that mandates that all children with disabilities receive a free appropriate public education (FAPE) to meet their specialized needs. Child Find is a legal requirement under IDEA and requires all school districts to identify and evaluate all children suspected of having a disability. The Child Find mandate applies to all children and youth from birth through age 21 who reside within a state, regardless of the severity of their disability. This includes children who attend public and private schools, migrant children, and homeless children (20 U.S.C. 1412(a)(3)). IDEA mandates general public notice obligations. For example, school districts may send out notices to inform and educate community members about the need to locate and identify children with disabilities.

During the 2017–2018 school year, 14% of children in public schools received special education services under one of the 13 IDEA eligibility categories (McFarland et al., 2019), which are: intellectual disability, specific learning disability, speech or language impairment, autism, other health impairment, emotional disturbance, orthopedic impairment, traumatic brain injury, hearing impairment, visual impairment, deaf-blindness, and multiple disabilities. Table 10.2 provides federal definitions for the most prevalent disability categories. Additionally, states and local education agencies may elect to include developmental delay as an eligibility category for children who are between the ages of three and nine. In the United States, the most prevalent disabilities in public schools include specific learning disability (34%), speech and language impairment (19%), other health impairment (14%), and autism (10%) (McFarland et al., 2019).

When to Refer Children for Special Education Testing

Within the school setting, teachers are often the first to see signs of potential delays in children because they spend the most time with children and frequently assess their development and performance. As such, educators must be aware of behaviors that may be indicative of potential disabilities in order to comply with the Child Find mandate under IDEA. Teachers may consult with appropriate school staff, such as the school psychologist or administrators responsible for special education decisions, to determine the appropriate steps for making a formal referral as these practices vary from school to school. A referral is a process taken to determine the need for additional support for students that may be completed by a teacher when they believe a student needs some type of specialized intervention to help them overcome presented challenges and be successful within the school setting. Typically, teachers must specify their concerns and identify interventions attempted and the outcomes of those interventions when completing a referral. As such, documentation of challenges and teacher response to those challenges is beneficial as it helps establish a pattern in behavior, which helps to justify the need for the referral. Prior to making the referral, teachers should also discuss their concerns with parents and gain insight into the child's history that may be impacting their school performance, such as recent changes in family dynamics. Table 10.2 displays red flags for the top four special education eligibility categories.

Special Education Eligibility Testing Through a Multi-Tiered Systems of Support Framework

Multi-Tiered System of Supports (MTSS) is a framework that helps educators organize levels of academic, behavioral, and social-emotional supports and resources based on intensity of needs in order to help all children be successful. In this way, educators take on a proactive approach to identifying students with potential disabilities. The key components of MTSS include universal screening of all students, continuous progress monitoring, tiers of interventions, school-wide approach to expectations and supports, and parent involvement. A conceptual representation of the model is a pyramid divided into three tiers and is shown in Figure 10.2. Please refer to Box 10.3 to learn more about MTSS.

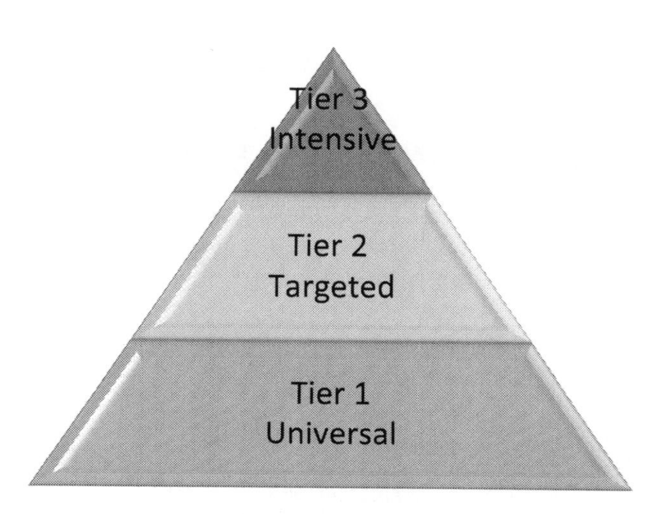

Figure 10.2 Multiple-Tiered System of Supports (MTSS) Framework

Box 10.3 Theory to Practice Connection

Spotlight on the PA-MTSS Model: Using Continuous Progress Monitoring to Inform Instruction and Identify Students with Learning Disabilities

One popular MTSS model is Pennsylvania's Multi-Tiered System of Support (PA-MTSS). It is a framework that aligns with learning standards related to academics, behavioral, and social-emotional functioning with the goal of enhancing academic, behavioral, and social-emotional outcomes for all students. PA-MTSS utilizes a three-tiered model shown in Figure 10.2. Tier 1 is the largest tier and sets the foundation for the framework. In order for this MTSS model to work effectively, evidenced-based instructional strategies for academic, behavioral, and social-emotional learning must be provided to all students at this level. Examples of Tier 1 interventions include a phonics-based reading curriculum and a classroom behavior management token economy system. Some students may not respond to Tier 1 interventions and may require additional support to meet academic, behavioral, and/or social-emotional goals. Students who fail to respond to Tier 1 supports receive Tier 2 targeted supports where the intensity varies across group size, frequency and duration of intervention, and level of training of the professionals providing instruction or intervention. These services and interventions are provided in small-group settings in addition to instruction in the general curriculum. For example, children having difficulty sustaining attention during reading instruction may be given a Tier 1 reading curriculum in a smaller group setting of three students or they may receive a more specialized reading curriculum designed for struggling readers. It is estimated that between 10% and 25% of students will require Tier 2 interventions. Many children will respond positively to targeted supports provided in Tier 2; however, some children may make limited progress toward their goals and continue to exhibit challenges. These struggling children will require individualized supports such as assistance from outside agencies or special education services. It is estimated that fewer than 10% of all students will require Tier 3 interventions. Students who do not achieve the desired level of progress in response to these targeted interventions are then referred for a comprehensive evaluation and considered for eligibility for special education services. The data collected during Tiers 1, 2, and 3 are included and used to make the eligibility decision.

Understanding Cognitive Test Results

Most students who fail to respond to Tier 3 supports are tested by the school psychologist to gain a better understanding of students' learning potential as well as strengths and weaknesses, which may be used to design goals and individualized supports. Although evaluation results may be used to inform practice, many teachers fail to incorporate evaluation results into their day-to-day practice with students. Teachers who understand the utility of psychoeducational testing results may be better able to translate scores into practices that may support student needs.

Across the states, learning potential is estimated based on general intelligence or overall cognitive functioning and has to do with an individual's ability to acquire and apply knowledge and skills, and is made up of several specific cognitive abilities. Although measures of intelligence or overall cognitive ability can be useful in identifying children who may have intellectual or learning disabilities, they are less helpful in developing goals or instructional supports for children. Specific cognitive abilities used to derive overall intelligence may be more helpful in designing goals. Although cognitive abilities used to define intelligence vary slightly depending on the theoretical model used by test developers, most tests include measures of verbal ability, nonverbal reasoning, spatial reasoning, and memory. Verbal ability generally has to do with a child's ability to listen to a question, draw upon learned information, reason through an answer, and express thoughts aloud and may include vocabulary knowledge and understanding of conceptual relationships. Children who have deficits in this area may have difficulty with listening and reading comprehension. Nonverbal reasoning has to do with a student's ability to examine a problem, identify common themes, and create and implement solutions when presented with visual information. A deficit in this area can make many aspects of learning challenging as children have difficulty detecting patterns and relationships. For example, they may have difficulty learning multiplication even though they have mastered addition because they struggle to understand that multiplication is a form of repeated addition, or they may have trouble making inferences for stories they read. Spatial reasoning is the ability to examine visual information and integrate visual-motor and spatial skills to solve problems. Children with deficits in spatial reasoning may have difficulty organizing multistep math problems, understanding concepts of geometry, and writing. Memory is often subdivided into working memory and long-term memory. Working memory has to do with the ability to hold information in immediate awareness and then use it within a few seconds to complete a task. Children with deficits in working memory may have difficulty following multi-step directions or decoding long words. Similarly, deficits in long-term memory may impact all areas of learning. In this case, children may be able to demonstrate mastery of a task for a short period, but may have difficulty retrieving learned information at a later time, resulting in inconsistent performance.

Generally, intelligence and cognitive ability scores are obtained by administering norm-referenced, standardized tests. Standardized tests are administered in the same way to each child in order to be able to compare scores from one child of the same age or grade to another. A test is considered norm-referenced when it was administered to a large group of children who resemble the characteristics of the general school-age population. Standardized tests are typically given in a one-on-one setting with minimal distractions. Scores on these tests are generally reported as standard scores, which have an average score of 100 and a standard deviation of 15, which means that students who obtain an intelligence standard score between 85 and 115 can be said to have average intelligence or learning potential. Similarly, a child with a reading comprehension score between 85 and 115 can be said to have average reading comprehension skills relative to the specific norm group, such as other students of the same age or in the same grade. A child who obtains a score below 85 is considered to be performing below peers of similar age and may signal that the student is at risk for learning delays. A child who scores 70 or below on an overall measure of cognitive ability may have significant learning delays as well as a potential intellectual disability.

Implications for Teaching and Learning

Teachers who adopt a growth mindset believe that intelligence and cognitive abilities can be developed (Dweck, 2007) and strengthened with experience. As such, teachers can implement strategies to support student strengths and help develop areas of weakness. Although strategies should be individualized based on multiple sources of data, strategies for the four main areas of intelligence are discussed. Teachers can help students develop verbal ability by explicitly teaching vocabulary across the curriculum and providing students with multiple opportunities to express their ideas orally and in writing. Nonverbal reasoning ability can be targeted by explicitly stating the connections between concepts. Additionally, teaching through thematic units helps children see the interrelationships across subjects, and can help them generalize skills to other areas of learning. Teachers can support development of spatial ability by allowing students to use manipulatives when working with abstract concepts and providing opportunities to integrate motor movements with visual information; this may include copying or completing puzzles. In regard to memory, teachers may facilitate storage and retrieval of information by explicating teaching memory strategies known to facilitate learning, such as chunking large quantities of information into smaller pieces that are related, helping students associate new information with previously learned information, incremental rehearsal strategies, and providing visual cues to serve as reminders for multi-step tasks.

Assessing Special Populations

The fourth section of this chapter focuses on assessment considerations for special populations of minority students: dual language learners and children with low-incidence disabilities.

Dual Language Learners

A dual language learner (DLL) is an individual who is in the process of acquiring two or more languages simultaneously. DLLs in schools have particularly unique instructional needs as a result of cultural and linguistic differences and require specialized instruction that takes into account these differences. There were 4.9 million DLLs enrolled in U.S. schools in 2016, representing approximately 10% of the K–12 population (National Center for Education Statistics, 2019). Although most DLLs speak Spanish, there are over 400 languages spoken by DLLs in U.S. public schools.

DLLs are considered either simultaneous or sequential bilinguals. Simultaneous bilingual students acquire English prior to the age of three, whereas sequential (i.e., successive) bilinguals begin to learn English after the age of three (McLaughlin, 1995). Although simultaneous bilinguals generally meet speech and language milestones similarly to monolinguals, sequential bilinguals go through five unique stages of language acquisition, including preproduction, early production, speech emergence, intermediate fluency, and advanced language. Figure 10.3 describes each of these stages.

There are many benefits for children who can speak multiple languages that often go unrecognized. Research studies consistently demonstrate the cognitive, social, and economic benefits of bilingualism (e.g., Bialystok, 1999). However, a lack of understanding of the strengths and needs of DLLs has resulted in poor educational outcomes, disproportionality for those students in special education (Hosp & Reschly, 2004). Fewer DLLs graduate high school relative to their peers and at similar rates to students with disabilities. Furthermore, during the 2014–2015 school year, the overall proportion of students with a specific learning disability was higher for DLLs (49.7%) than for monolingual children (37.5%) (U.S. Department of Education, n.d.). Knowledge of bilingual language acquisition and acculturation must be embedded in current instructional and assessment practices to move towards

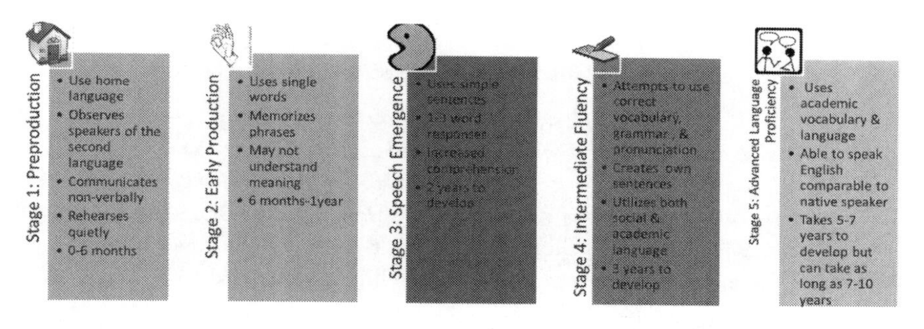

Figure 10.3 Language Acquisition Stages for Sequential Bilingual Children

more equitable outcomes for DLLs. Goals and criteria for reaching those goals should be informed by knowledge of second language development.

Few remedial services were available for DLLs in schools prior to 1960. Since that time, case law involving the education of DLLs noted the legal obligations public schools have to provide a free and appropriate education that includes both English language development and acquisition of content knowledge (Rios v. Read, 1978). In other words, schools must adopt, implement, and evaluate an educational program for DLLs based on sound educational theory and appropriate instructional practices. The Every Student Succeeds Act of 2015 (ESSA) and its predecessors require states to develop standards and accountability systems for all students, including DLLs. Specifically, ESSA requires all states to develop English-language proficiency standards and align those standards to assessment measures used for accountability purposes. As such, in addition to assessing learning outcomes related to academic standards, educators must also assess student outcomes related to English acquisition. In this way, DLLs who may require additional language and/or academic support may be provided this support early to remediate any deficits early and reduce the achievement gap between this population and monolingual English speakers.

When assessing students, it is important to select methods that will result in information related to the intended target area and not a student's English proficiency. In other words, a math assessment should give a teacher information related to student math skills and not level of English proficiency. It may become necessary to adapt assessments to ensure the validity of assessment results. Consider giving DLLs extra time to complete assessment tasks, providing tests in the child's dominant language, reduce language demands of assessments, allow translators if available, review key vocabulary prior to assessment, provide visuals and pictures to provide context, and provide direct instruction related to test-taking skills.

Box 10.4 Social Justice and Diversity

Disproportionate Representation of Minority Youth in Special Education: Why Considerations of Language and Culture Matter

As a bilingual psychologist, I was contracted to complete an independent educational evaluation for a child who was a dual language learner, which is a private evaluation parents may request from the school district when they disagree with the results of evaluations for special education referrals completed by district personnel. Upon reviewing prior testing records for the child, who was in third grade, I noticed that many of his intelligence standard scores were in the 60s, suggesting the child was intellectually disabled. In fact, the child had been identified in kindergarten as a child with an intellectual disability and placed in a special class where only children with significant learning needs were placed, limiting the child's access to appropriate language models. As a psychologist trained to work with culturally and linguistically diverse students, I first assessed the child's language proficiency in both English and his primary language and discovered that his language abilities across languages were significantly delayed. As such, instead of assessing his intelligence with a traditional test, which the prior assessor had done, I chose to utilize a less traditional measure of intelligence. The test I selected was administered with gestures and did not require any expressive language communication from the student. The child's overall intelligence score was a standard score of 100, which is considered average. Unfortunately, this meant that for three years teachers had not been challenging the student sufficiently, and did not provide him with adequate language supports. Additionally, when the measure of adaptive functioning was elevated, the scores reflected the student's level of acculturation and language differences and not deficits in adaptive functioning.

Children with Low-Incidence Disabilities

Low-incidence disabilities are impairments that affect a small number of individuals who generally require support from staff who have highly specialized skills and knowledge in order to receive FAPE. Children with low-incidence disabilities may have challenges with communication, mobility, social relationships, memory, generalization of skills, and self-care. According to IDEA, a low-incidence disability includes: 1) a visual or hearing impairment, or simultaneous visual and hearing impairments; 2) a significant cognitive impairment; or 3) any impairment for which a small number of personnel with highly specialized skills and knowledge are needed in order for children with that impairment to receive early intervention services or a free appropriate public education (IDEA Part D §1462 C3). Examples of low-incidence disabilities include deafness, visual impairment (including blindness), deaf-blindness, hearing impairment, multiple disabilities, severe orthopedic impairment, and traumatic brain injury. Generally, low-incidence disabilities are further defined by the expected incidence rate of less than 1% (30 EC 56026.5).

Assessing children with low-incidence disabilities can be challenging, because many assessments designed for typically developing children may not accurately reflect the skill or ability they are designed to measure. Instead, traditional assessments produce results that reflect the student's impaired sensory and communication skills. Traditional tests require children to hear, understand directions, and have adequate vision and fine motor skills (Sattler &

Dumont, 2004). As such, special considerations need to be taken when selecting and designing assessments for children with low-incidence disabilities. Formative assessment is especially helpful when working with children with low-incidence disabilities. Additionally, authentic and alternative assessments are often necessary to be able to assess student learning. Ecological inventories, assessment of adaptive and life skills, and functional behavior assessment should be considered when working with this population (Gresham, Watson, & Skinner, 2001).

Similar to assessing DLLs, adaptations to traditional assessments are often necessary when working with children with low-incidence disabilities. Accommodations and modifications are examples of such adaptations. Testing accommodations include changing some aspect of the test format, content, or administration procedures in order to make the test accessible to students. Testing accommodations do not change the construct being measured. At times, testing accommodations may not be sufficient, and educators may need to consider testing modifications for students with low-incidence disabilities. A testing modification is a change to the test that may alter the construct being measured. Generally, modification for a physical disability such as orthopedic impairment is considered less problematic than those for visual or auditory disabilities (Lezak, Howieson, Bigler, & Tranel, 2012). Examples of accommodations and modifications include changing the presentation format of the assessment, changing the response format, changing the time requirements, changing the test setting, using only parts of the original test, and using alternative procedures. Children with a low-incidence disability who qualify for special education or 504 services have access to specialized school funds to support their access to the curriculum, such as interpreters, transcribers, sensory aids, and large print or braille materials which should be utilized by teachers.

It is also important to keep in mind the nature of the student's physical, medical, and mental health conditions and consult with other experts, such as a vision specialist, prior to testing a child with a low-incidence disability. Similarly, it is imperative that the child's communication needs and preferred mode of communication be taken into consideration prior to assessment. Other considerations that may be important include whether the student requires an interpreter and an environment that minimizes distractions and background noise. When assessing students, make sure they have glasses and/or hearing aids if used, provide tactile and symbolic representations of concepts, do not place time limits, and incorporate the use of any assistive technology if used.

Measuring Quality in Elementary School Settings

The final section of this chapter focuses on the assessment of instructional variables such as classroom climate and fidelity of evidence-based instructional programs.

School and Classroom Climate

School and classroom climate strongly influences students' motivation to learn and improve academic achievement while also reducing bullying and aggressive behavior (Thomas, Bierman, & Powers, 2011). Learning increases when school staff and students feel safe, valued, cared for, respected, and engaged. When students learn and educators work in an environment that is safe, supportive, and connected, they are more likely to develop the social and emotional competencies they need to be successful (CASEL, n.d.). Classroom factors such as student–teacher relationships have more influence on students' perceptions of the school environment than school-specific variables (Koth, Bradshaw, & Leaf, 2009).

Classroom climate refers to the quality of the students' social learning environment (McRobbie & Fraser, 1993). Teacher support for student success and classroom structure are factors that contribute to classroom climate. Conditions that facilitate the motivation, academic achievement, and social development of students are also important factors (Altaf, 2015). Altaf (2015) identified three broad domains of classroom experiences that contribute to classroom climate: 1) interpersonal relationships, 2) goal orientation, and 3) system maintenance and change. Interpersonal relationships have to do with the nature and intensity of personal relationships and the extent to which they support and help each other. Goal orientation has to do with basic directions along which personal growth and self-enhancement may occur. System maintenance and change have to do with the extent to which the environment is orderly and clear in expectations, maintains control, and is responsive to change. In classrooms with a positive climate, teachers and students are enthusiastic about learning and respectful of one another; they have positive relationships with each other and enjoy spending time together in the classroom (Stuhlman, Hamre, Downer, & Pianta, n.d.).

Classroom climate is typically measured by gathering information related to teacher and student perceptions and may include interviews, checklists, and rating scales completed by individuals in a particular classroom or school. Secondly, an external observer's ratings and systematic coding are often employed. This may include having school administrators complete a structured observation that targets examples of the three broad domains of classroom climate (Freiberg, 1999).

An example of an observation-based measure used to assess classroom climate is the Classroom Assessment Scoring System (CLASS) (Pianta, La Paro, & Hamre, 2008). The CLASS describes dimensions of teaching that are linked to student achievement and development. The CLASS can be used to reliably assess classroom quality to help teachers become more effective. A trained observer conducts a series of four, 15-minute classroom observations in order to rate specific behaviors and responses. Areas assessed include social and emotional supports (e.g., teacher sensitivity, regard for student perspectives), organizational and management supports (e.g., behavior management, productivity, strategies for engaging students), and instructional supports (e.g., strategies to foster content knowledge and quality of feedback). Use of the CLASS or other empirically supported tools to measure classroom climate can inform teaching effectiveness and increase positive student outcomes.

Fidelity of Instructional Practices

Fidelity of implementation is the delivery of instruction in the way it was designed to be delivered (Gresham, MacMillan, Beebe-Frankenberger, & Bocian, 2000). Fidelity of formative assessment, such as screening and progress-monitoring procedures, serves to address the integrity of these methods. Instructional techniques and interventions that are evidence-based undergo substantial research to conclude that they are effective for most students (Abry, Hulleman, & Rimm-Kaufman, 2015). In order to increase the likelihood that selected evidence-based interventions will be successful in the classroom, it is important to implement it as intended, with fidelity (Harn, Parisi, & Stoolmiller, 2013). Interventions implemented with higher fidelity tend to be more effective (Quinn & Kim, 2017).

Both formative and summative assessment techniques may be used to assess fidelity of instruction and student assessment. Many evidence-based interventions include fidelity checklists to help educators monitor and self-assess the level of implementation fidelity. Five elements of fidelity have been proposed that should be considered when designing or selecting fidelity measures (O'Donnell, 2008), and include adherence, exposure, quality of delivery, program specificity, and student engagement. Adherence has to do with how well the plan, curriculum, or assessment is followed. Exposure has to do with the frequency and duration of the intervention. Quality of delivery has to do with how well the intervention, assessment, or instruction is delivered. Program specificity has to do with how well the intervention is defined and unique to other interventions. Student engagement has to do with the level of student engagement and involvement. Fidelity is another essential element to effective teaching and learning.

Redefining Assessment in Modern Classrooms

In the modern classroom, teachers are mindful and deliberate in their teaching practices and instruction. They engage in continuous reflection and analysis of data obtained from multiple sources to help design individual and classroom goals related to student behavior and academic outcomes. Teachers also use data to help inform their own professional development. Innovative formative assessment practices in combination with summative assessment help to define the modern classroom. These practices provide critical information that helps educators determine what students understand and areas of weakness. In order to respond to the individual needs of students and ensure assessments reflect a student's actual knowledge and skills, multiple types of data should be collected. Teachers then work to triangulate the various results to form opinions and inform future directions in order to improve student outcomes.

According to Frey (2014), modern classrooms also incorporate the use of performance-based assessment and authentic assessment into their practice. These practices can be especially helpful when working with DLLs and low-incidence populations. Performance-based assessment is defined as an assessment that requires students to produce a product or deliver a performance for the purpose of evaluating a skill or ability (Frey, 2014). Performance-based assessment is a format where students are able to demonstrate their knowledge, skills, and abilities through a performance or the construction of a product. Examples of performance-based assessments can be participating in a debate, conducting an experiment, making a painting, or creating a short story. The purpose of performance-based is to assess more than knowledge.

Authentic assessment is an assessment that aligns with real-world tasks and expectations (Frey, 2014), and may include performance-based assessment. Authentic assessment grew out of the need for classroom learning to be generalized into a student's day-to-day functioning outside of the classroom. As such, authentic assessment strives to move away from artificial testing environments to incorporate tasks that are more in line with real-world challenges and expectations. By designing tests that keep in mind ecological validity, educators focus on the knowledge and skills that best prepare students to be successful in the real world. An example of authentic assessment for assessing literacy skills is having students write an email to their parents about why they deserve a specific product (e.g., toy, video game). A rubric can be created to assess similar skills and knowledge that would be targeted on a multiple-choice exam.

Teachers in today's classroom focus on identifying educational goals related to learning and development and they are mindful and deliberate when selecting assessments to address the unique needs of their students.

References

Altaf, M. (2015). Exploring classroom environment through perception- An overview of various inventories. *International Journal of Novel Research in Education and Learning*, *2*, 23–32.

Bagnato, S.J., Goins, D.D., Pretti-Frontczak, K., & Neisworth, J.T. (2014). Authentic assessment as "best practice" for early childhood intervention: National consumer social validity research. *Topics in Early Childhood Special Education*, *34*, 116–127. doi:10.1177/0271121414523652

Bialystok, E. (1999). Cognitive complexity and attentional control in the bilingual mind. *Child Development*, *70*, 636–644. doi:10.1111/1467-8624.00046

Black, P. Harrison, C., Lee, C., Marshall, B., & Wiliam, D. (2003). *Assessment for learning: Putting it into practice*. Maidenhead: Open University Press.

Center for Disease Control (2019, September). *Disability and health overview*. Retrieved from https://www.cdc.gov/ncbddd/disabilityandhealth/disability.html.

Common Core State Standards Initiative (n.d.). *What are educational standards?* Retrieved from http://www.corestandards.org/faq/what-are-educational-standards/

Dweck (2007). *Mindset: The new psychology of success*. New York: Ballantine Books.

Every Student Succeeds Act, Pub. L. 114–95, Stat. 1177 (2015).

Formative Assessment for Students and Teachers State Collaborative on Assessment and Student Standards (2018). Revising the definition of formative assessment. Retrieved from https://ccsso.org/resource-library/revising-definition-formative-assessment

Freiberg, H. (1999). *School climate: Measuring, improving, and sustaining healthy learning environments*. Philadelphia: Falmer Press.

Frye, B.B. (2014). *Modern classroom assessment*. London: SAGE Publications. doi:10.4135/9781506374536

Fuchs, D., & Fuchs, L. S. (2006). Introduction to response to intervention: What, why, and how valid is it? *Reading Research Quarterly*, *41*(1), 93–99. https://doi.org/10.1598/RRQ.41.1.4

Gresham, F. M., MacMillan, D. L., Beebe-Frankenberger, M. E., & Bocian, K. M. (2000). Treatment integrity in learning disabilities intervention research: Do we really know how treatments are implemented? *Learning Disabilities Research & Practice*, *15*(4), 198–205. https://doi.org/10.1207/SLDRP1504_4

Gresham, F. M., Watson, T. S., & Skinner, C. H. (2001). Functional behavioral assessment: Principles, procedures, and future directions. *School Psychology Review*, *30*(2), 156–172.

Gridley, B. E., Mucha, L., & Hatfield, B. B. (1995). *Best practices in preschool screening*. In A. Thomas & J. Grimes (Eds.), Best practices in school psychology III (pp. 213–225). Washington, DC: National Association of School Psychologists.

Harn, B., Parisi, D., & Stoolmiller, M. (2013). Balancing fidelity with flexibility and fit: What do we really know about fidelity of implementation in schools? *Exceptional Children*, *79*(3), 181–193.

Hosp, J.L., & Reschly, D.J. (2004). Disproportionate representation of minority students in special education: Academic, economic, and demographic predictors. *Exceptional Children*, 70, 185–200.

Katsiyannis, A., Yell, M., & Bradley, R. (2001). Reflections on the 25th anniversary of the individuals with disabilities education act. *Remedial and Special Education*, *22*, 324–334.

Koth, C.W., Bradshaw, C.P., & Leaf, P.J. (2009). Teacher observation of classroom adaptation—checklist: Development and factor structure. *Measurement and Evaluation in Counseling and Development*, *42*, 15–30. doi:10.1177/0748175609333560

Lezak, M. D., Howieson, D. B., Bigler, E. D., & Tranel, D. (2012). *Neuropsychological assessment* (5th ed.). Oxford University Press.

Messick, S. (1995). Validity of psychological assessment: Validation of inferences from persons' responses and performances as scientific inquiry into score meaning. *American Psychologist*, *50*(9), 741–749. https://doi.org/10.1037/0003-066X.50.9.741

McFarland, J., Hussar, B., Zhang, J., Wang, X., Wang, K., Hein, S., Diliberti, M., …& Barmer, A. (2019). *The condition of education 2019 (NCES 2019–144)*. Washington, DC: National Center for Education Statistics. Retrieved from https://nces.ed.gov/pubsearch/pubsinfo.asp?pubid=2019144

McLaughlin, B. (1995). Fostering second language development in young children: Principles and Practices. National Center for Research on Cultural Diversity and Second Language Learning. Retrieved from https://escholarship.org/uc/item/23s607sr

McRobbie, C.J. & Fraser, B.J. (1993). Associations between student outcomes and psychosocial science environment. *Journal of Educational Research*, 87, 78–85.

Moss, C. M., & Brookhart, S. M. (2009). *Advancing formative assessment in every classroom.* Alexandria, VA: ASCD.

National Center for Education Statistics (2019, May). *English language learners in public schools.* Retrieved from https://nces.ed.gov/programs/coe/indicator_cgf.asp

O'Donnell, C. L. (2008). Defining, conceptualizing, and measuring fidelity of implementation and its relationship to outcomes in k–12 curriculum intervention research. *Review of Educational Research, 78*(1), 33–84. https://doi.org/10.3102/0034654307313793

Pianta, R. C., La Paro, K. M., & Hamre, B. K. (2008). *Classroom Assessment Scoring System™: Manual K-3*. Paul H Brookes Publishing.

Quinn, D. M., & Kim, J. S. (2017). Scaffolding fidelity and adaptation in educational program implementation: Experimental evidence from a literacy intervention. *American Educational Research Journal, 54*(6), 1187–1220. https://doi.org/10.3102/0002831217717692

Ríos v. Read, 480 F. Supp. 14 (E.D.N.Y. 1978).

Salvia, J & Ysseldyke, J. & Witmer, S. (2017). *Assessment in special and inclusive education* (13th ed.). Boston, MA: Cengage Learning.

Sattler, J., & Dumont, R. (2004). *Assessment of children: WISC-IV and WPPSI-III supplement*. San Diego, CA: Jerome M. Sattler.

Stuhlman, M.W., Hamre, B.K., Downer, J.T., & Pianta, R.C. (n.d.). *What should classroom observation measure?* Retrieved from https://curry.virginia.edu/sites/default/files/uploads/resourceLibrary/CASTL_practioner_Part2_single.pdf

Thomas, D.E., Bierman, K.L., & Powers, C.J. (2011). The influence of classroom aggression and classroom climate on aggressive–disruptive behavior. *Child Development, 82*, 751–757. doi:10.1111/j.1467-8624.2011.01586.x

U.S. Department of Education (n.d.). *Our nation's English learners*. Retrieved from https://www2.ed.gov/datastory/el-characteristics/index.html#four

World Health Organization (2001). *International classification of functioning, disability and health (ICF) external icon*. Geneva: WHO.

Chapter 11

Parent, Families, and Community Engagement

Elizabeth Ferry-Perata

Benefits of Family Engagement

Relationship Between Educators and Families

The connection between a family and their child's education has been an ongoing topic for many years. Schools are challenged with balancing a child's school day between their formal education, such as academics and standards, and incorporating the informal curriculum such as rules or norms. Schools are charged with developing a critical and essential relationship between educators and families. When the school is successful, the child will have the tools required to become a successful individual within society.

Effective engagement involves recognition of the distinct contributions educators and families provide. Additionally, engagement has benefits for both educators and families. When considering engagement, reflection may occur on the following questions:

- Are educators intent on finding ways to involve children's families in the children's school experiences?
- Are educators interested in understanding children's families?
- Do educators consider a family's contribution to their child's education to be of value?
- When a child's family enters a school or classroom, are they interested in understanding how they can become involved in their child's school experiences?
- Are a child's family interested in understanding educators' approaches to teaching and expectations for children's learning?

What does the term family engagement actually mean? Researchers have defined family engagement in various ways. Epstein (2019) developed a framework to address different ways to partner with families so that they are involved in their children's education. These approaches include parenting, communicating, volunteering, learning at home, decision-making and collaborating with the community. See the section "School, Family and Community

Partnership Model" under "Theoretical Frameworks Contributing to Engagement" for further information. Other researchers have defined family engagement as parental expectations and aspirations for their children's academics (Hall et al., 1997). Grolnick and Slowiaczek (1994) stated that "parent involvement is defined as the dedication of resources by the parent to the child within a given domain" (p. 238). Families may foster and support the education of the children within the home–school partnership. When thinking about family engagement, it includes the bridge between the school and the home settings and the activities that occur within.

Research has shown that over the past few years, there has been an increase in the engagement of families within the school setting. In fact, 89% of families have attended a general meeting, parent–teacher conference or school event (Child Trends, 2018). More than likely, educators will encounter the mothers more than the fathers because mothers are often the primary caregivers that socialize their children at an early age (Laursen & Collins, 2009.) It is key for educators to understand the dynamics of the family in order to better serve them. This could also mean that the expectations that educators practice and ask of families in early elementary school grades need to meet with their children's developmental levels within the classroom.

When thinking about the engagement of families, one must consider how relationships are established. Relationships need to be established and continuous, not just a one-time contact. Epstein (2019) indicates that a key factor of relationships and the establishment of partnerships with families is communication. Families need to be made aware of their children's progress and education. Some examples of family communication include conferences, language translators, technology usage and folders with the student's work that may travel back and forth between the home and school. Again, see the section "School, Family and Community Partnership Model" under "Theoretical Frameworks Contributing to Engagement" for further information. By utilizing different means of communication, relationships are established. This creates a multi-directional connection between a family and their child's school. The outcome is powerful because not only are families aware of their children's progress, but educators are able to understand the way families operate.

Educators need to keep in mind family practices when establishing relationships. Families are diverse, and that includes the varieties of how they raise their children. Researchers have identified four different types of parenting styles: authoritative, authoritarian, permissive and uninvolved (Clarke-Steward & Parke, 2014; Berger, 2008). Authoritative parenting style is when parents set expectations and are responsive to their child's individual needs. Authoritarian parenting style is when parents are not responsive to their child's individuals needs and put a lot of expectations on the child. Permissive parenting style is very warm and responsive to their child's individual needs; however, no expectations are set for the child. Uninvolved parenting style is when the parent is not warm or responsive to their child's individual needs and no expectations are placed upon the child. It is important to understand the different child-rearing practices in order to interact with each family appropriately (Laursen & Collins, 2009).

Educators and families understand a child in different ways due to the unique context of their interaction with the child. Educators' contributions involve perspectives on the child in the context of an educational setting (Koralek et al., 2004). An educator may know a child's:

- Interest areas in the classroom;
- Strengths regarding learning;
- Interactions with others;
- Reactions to change in the environment;
- Sharing of events that occur away from school; and
- Daily activities and learning opportunities.

Short-Term Benefits for the Child

Parental engagement has been associated with both short-term and long-term benefits for children. Specifically, family engagement research has shown a significant impact on a child's academic success. A study of 21,000 kindergarteners reported significant gains in overall academic efforts when the child's family is involved in the early school years of the child (Galindo & Sheldon, 2012). In the same study, it was found that when families are involved in school activities, their children tend to outperform their counterparts who do not have any family engagement in all areas of the educational curriculum.

More importantly, when parents begin the conversation with their children at home about the importance of academic success, children tend to do better in reading and math (McWayne, 2004). The earlier that families have this conversation, the better. When families discuss the importance of academic achievement upon the child's entry into kindergarten, their math and reading skills improve in the first year of school (McWayne, 2004; Galindo & Sheldon, 2012; Kim & Bryan, 2015).

The involvement of families has been linked to the increase in positive behavior among early elementary school children. When families are involved in their children's education, it is less likely the children will have any behavioral issues (Sheldon & Esptein, 2002; Hoglund et al., 2014). "When children demonstrated less academic and social competence and more aggressive behaviors, their parents were particularly likely to engage in more subsequent homework assistance" (Hoglund et al., 2014, p. 528). Schools that encourage family engagement tend to reduce disciplinary actions with students in that school setting (Sheldon & Esptein, 2002). It is important to note that the correlation between children who demonstrate high social competence and less aggressive behavior results in receiving more support from their family at home.

Family empowerment has also been linked to short-term benefits for a child's academic success (Kim & Bryan, 2017; McWayne, 2004). When 9,982 parents were surveyed, they said they are more likely to voice any concerns about their child's education because the teacher found ways to connect with them. When parents are made aware of the happenings in their child's education, it results in them feeling more empowered and they will be more likely to help their child at home (Kim & Bryan, 2017; McWayne, 2004).

Long-Term Benefits for the Child

Research has shown the long-term benefits that family engagement has on a child. Particularly, a child's performance in the early years of schooling is predictive of later achievement. A long-term study showed that the more involved the family is, the less likely a child will be to drop out of school (Barnard, 2004). Specifically, it was found that if a child has a parent who participates in their education for three years, there is a lower chance of them dropping out of school. The more years a parent is involved in their child's schooling, the more likely a child will be to continue their schooling and graduate from high school.

Long-term benefits of family engagement have been linked to the success of interpersonal relationships. Nokali et al. (2010) followed 1,364 children over a long period of time and found that children have better social skills when parents are involved in their schooling. It was further found that a child's social skills improved more between first and fifth grade when parents were involved. Cooperative learning programs have also been linked to better interpersonal relationships (Santos Rego et al., 2018). When children participate in cooperative learning activities, they have better study habits and are more inclined to ask for help from fellow students.

Family engagement has been linked to motivation in children, particularly their self-efficacy in achieving academic success. A long-term study found that the involvement of parents has been linked to higher levels of literacy performance between the first and fifth grades (Dearing et al., 2006). Children with high levels of family engagement are more motivated to want to continue to adopt literacy activities later in their schooling. Levpuscek and Zupancic (2009) found that a child entering the eighth grade will be motivated to continue with math, depending on how involved the parents were in the early part of the child's education.

Educators should consider family engagement a valuable resource regarding the success of a child. Not only is family engagement tied to educational outcomes, but it is also tied to the social competency of the child. See "Promoting Social and Emotional Competency" for further demonstrating on this topic.

Box 11.1 Promoting Social and Emotional Competence: NAEYC Message in a Backyard

The home–school partnership is important to consider for a child's success. The success of a child includes their social and emotional well-being. The National Association for the Education of the Young Child (NAEYC) developed some resources for educators to give to the families and communities that they serve.

Resource Overview

The NAEYC developed one-page informational sheets to help families understand their children's social and emotional development. Each one-page overview has a variety of topics including helping children understand responsibility, transitions, fun ways to incorporate math into the home setting, making mealtimes fun and much more. Each one-page sheet is easy to use and developmentally appropriate for children. Each one-page resource is available in several languages. The articles are designed to have educators make copies and give them to the families they serve.

How This Activity Can Be Used in the Classroom

Many of the topics are connected to a child's social and emotional development. Educators can print out the material and give it to the children in their classroom. The teacher can talk to the children, incorporate each topic daily and connect it to the informal curriculum. These activities are geared towards early education and can be used up to the third grade.

For further information:
https://www.naeyc.org/resources/topics/message-backpack

Diversity of Families and Attitudes about Schooling

Cultural Backgrounds of Families

As previously discussed, educators need to keep in mind varying parenting practices. It should also be noted that family engagement might vary across cultures (Cheung & Pomerantz, 2011; Huntsinger & Jose, 2009). Families that have adopted collectivistic values emphasize the accomplishments one makes as a reflection of one's own family; whereas, in individualistic families, the belief is that when one succeeds, it is based solely on one's own efforts (Santrock, 2019). Collectivistic families typically include Latinx and Asian families and individualistic families typically include European families.

The expectations that educators put on family engagement should match up with the cultural beliefs of the families within the classroom. For example, white, middle-class parents volunteer in the school system more than Asian Americans during the early grades (Mau, 1997). Chinese parents use more workbooks and practice drills, and typically do not interact with the teacher (Huntsinger & Jose, 2009).

As children progress in their education, cultural differences have been found in the expectations that families put on their children's success. Some families use more psychological control as opposed to more independence during a child's education. Cheung and Pomerantz (2011) found that the "American parents' involvement was associated less with their control and more with their autonomy support than was Chinese parents'" (p. 13). Studies show that Asian Americans are more involved in their children's education than White Americans. Some studies have shown that immigrant families are not as involved in their children's education regardless of ethnicity. Mau (1997) found that "parents of recent immigrants typically are less fluent in English and have little knowledge about the school environment, which may limit their school involvement" (p. 275). This can influence how successful a child could become in their education. Mau (1997) also found some parents put stringent expectations on their child's education, and even though they don't want to get involved with their child's education due to cultural beliefs, they end up getting involved anyway. This is important to know because many families have immigrated to the United States and have adopted a bicultural orientation. They want to adopt the customs of the United States, but still continue to practice their heritage.

Socioeconomic status doesn't seem to have an effect on family engagement. When parents put expectations on their child's schooling and achievement, then a child may be more likely to be successful in their educational endeavors (Halle et al., 1997). Some families that educators encounter may struggle to ask for ways to support their children's education, but if teachers provide literacy activities to be used in the home environment, family involvement will increase.

Family Structures

The structure of the American family is varied and continues to change over time. Individuals are choosing to get married later in life in order to finish their education and begin their careers. The decision to become a parent is one that requires communication between partners. Questions such as when to have children and how many should be discussed, as well as who will stay home, and whether childcare will be utilized. It is estimated that raising a child could cost more than $227,000 just to provide basic needs of housing, food, clothes, health care and transportation (Knox et al., 2014). The pregnancy rate for women between the ages of 15–29 has declined over the years, and more women are choosing to have children in their thirties.

In the United States, more than half of the children under age five have both parents in the workforce (Santrock, 2019). For some of these families, they are working multiple jobs in order to make ends meet. There is debate on whether women should work outside the home and contribute to the family. The research is not clear on the long-term effects of both parents working outside of the home (Parke-Stewart & Clark, 2014). Educators should keep in mind that it might be difficult to meet with some parents during the school day if both parents are working.

The American family does not consist of a mother, a father and children anymore. According to Santrock (2019), 23% of American households with children under the age of 18 are single-parent households, making the United States the highest of all industrial countries. There are several reasons for the high rates of single-parent households in the United States. Personal choice is a predominant reason; 40% of births are to unmarried women (Parke-Stewart & Clark, 2014). Modern reproductive technologies have given women more opportunities to expand their families, and also the ability to wait longer to start a family. Since 1978, roughly 50 million families in the world have used technology to conceive a child (Parke-Stewart & Clarke, 2014). Another explanation for single-parent households is the death of a spouse. In the United States, 11.4 million women are widows (Knox & Schacht, 2016). The third highest reason for single-parent households is divorce.

Even though the divorce rate among American families has gone down steadily since the 1980s, the United States still faces the highest divorce rate in the world. It is estimated that 40–50% of all marriages will result in divorce (Parke-Stewart & Clarke, 2014; Knox & Schacht, 2014). Santrock (2019) points out that "40 percent of children born into married parents in the United States will experience their parents' divorce" (p. 186). When divorce occurs, financial upheaval affects the mother more. Experts estimate that a woman who gets a divorce loses between one-fourth and one-half of her income after the fact, compared to fathers, who only face about a one-tenth loss in their income (Santrock, 2016).

When divorce occurs, single parents might seek out the companionship of others. When two families come together and blend their respective households, also known as blended families, some members of the family might need time to adjust. With time, families can accept the changes and learn how to cope. Blended families are the fastest-growing type of family in the United States (Knox & Schacht, 2014). About 5.3 million children under the age of 18 are living with both a biological parent and another adult, either through remarriage or cohabiting (Knox & Schacht, 2014). Approximately three-quarters of divorced couples will remarry (Kreider & Fields, 2011), while others might choose to forgo marriage and live together instead.

Families can choose adoption in addition to or in place of having biological children. There are several ways adoption can occur including private, public, kinship, independent choice and stepparent (Knox & Schacht, 2014). The cost of adoption varies depending on the route chosen. It is estimated that these costs can range between $5,000 and $40,000. Families make the choice to adopt for various reasons which include not being able to conceive biologically, wanting to give a child an opportunity for a stable home or not wanting to contribute to the overpopulation. Some adoptive parents started out as short- or long-term foster parents and then decided to give the child a permanent home.

A growing number of American families include parents in same-sex relationships. An estimated 37% of gay and lesbian families have had a biological child of their own (Gates, 2013). Gates (2013) estimates that "nearly half of LGBT women (48%) are raising a child under age 18, along with a fifth of LGBT men (20%)" (p. 1). Same-sex couples are six times more likely to be raising a child that has been adopted than their heterosexual counterparts.

Rates of interracial marriages in the United States have nearly doubled since 1980 (Knox & Schacht, 2016). "Of the 3.8 million adults who married in 2008, 9% of Whites, 16% of Blacks), 26% of Hispanics and 31% of Asians married someone whose race or ethnicity was different than their own" (Passel et al., 2013). Approximately 63% of people are okay with choosing a partner outside of their culture (Knox & Schacht, 2014). An increasing number of couples are looking outside of their cultural and ethnic heritage to begin families of their own.

Every family is unique with different attitudes about learning, discipline and social interactions. Oswald et al. (2018) found that "lower parental involvement among divorced parents may reflect the fact that single parents are more likely to have limited time to participate in school activities or to support their child's education with home and community activities" (p. 321). What about stress and family engagement? See "Social Justice and Diversity: Incarcerated Parents" at the end of this section for further information. Educators should be sensitive to the varying, unique and sometimes sensitive structure of a family unit. Family engagement could be happening on multiple levels, and it is important that an educator understands the family structure in order to facilitate what is best for each student.

Box 11.2 Social Justice and Diversity: Incarcerated Parents

It is estimated that more than 2.5 million children in the United States have a parent currently incarcerated (Wakefield, 2015). Research has indicated that parental incarceration is linked to harmful outcomes in a child's social and emotional development.

Research Study Overview

In this article, three different data sets were gathered from Project on Human Development in Chicago Neighborhoods (PHDCN) between 1994 and 2002.

There were roughly 6,000 children between the ages of three and 15. The focus for this article was mainly the second data set about parental quality and home environment dynamics including conflict resolution.

Article Findings

This study showed "little evidence that parental incarceration increases positive parenting or increases warmth between parent and child" (Wakefield, 2015, p. 921). It was further found that with the presence of an observer, parents are likely to be more involved or show physical signs of warmth. This establishes that parental incarceration increases negative parenting behavior and proposes that parenting behaviors are very complex. The relationship the child and the parent had before the parent was incarcerated will influence the dynamics of the two based on the age of the child when the parent left the home.

How This Research Study Can Be Used in the Classroom

Although poverty and socioeconomic status are tightly linked to parental incarceration and parenting behaviors due to the financial stress and hardships that might arise within the family, it could be pointed out that educators need to be more understanding about these hardships when addressing family engagement. When stress arises within the family, the expectation of family engagement might not be considered important. Educators could ask families to participate in smaller activities that reinforce the concepts of family engagement but do not add stress to the family unit. Educators could support positive behaviors between family members and children such as cuddling or verbal encouragement.

For further information:

Wakefield, S. (2015). Accentuating the positive or eliminating the negative? Paternal incarceration and caregiver-child relationships quality. *The Journal of Criminal Law & Criminology, 104* (4), 905–927.

Community/Neighborhood and School Climate

The impact of family engagement can vary across certain communities and neighborhoods. Leventhal, Dupere and Brooks-Gunn (2009) indicated that a neighborhood may consist of 3,000 to 8,000 individuals living in an area with "major streets, railroads, ethnic divisions, and the like" (p. 412). Contributing factors that can have an impact on family engagement include: social demographic, employment, racial composition and the social organization and institutions of the area.

Research points out that individuals living in neighborhoods with high social economic statushave higher school success rates (Leventhal et al., 2009), whereas, it has been reported that in urban areas with high poverty, the high school dropout rate can exceed 40% (Alexander et al., 2003). Poor school attendance, low grades and behavioral problems in the school setting have been linked to the amount of violence an individual is exposed to in their community (Sheldon & Epstein, 2002). Adolescents living in low-SES neighborhoods have more social, emotional and behavioral problems including higher rates of sexual behavior among adolescent teen girls (Leventhal et al., 2009).

Community attitudes regarding school and learning may impact different families' views of family engagement. Some families view the teacher as the expert and feel that if they interfere it could disrupt the educational process (Barnard, 2004). Some parents feel that if they get involved in their child's education it will cause tension. Eccles and Roeser (2009) pointed out that the expectations set by private schools are completely different than those set by public schools. "A school environment that reduces the amount of disconnect between students' lives within and outside of school could reduce the potential for violence" (p. 9). Research indicates that if schools change their climate and create more academic goal structures, then this can in turn influence the motivation of parents, students and teachers.

The way to change perceptions is to educate. Communication is the best way to educate families about what is expected of them and their students. Communicating with the family and asking for involvement to support educational and social issues may help produce a safer and more productive school environment. When schools draw on the involvement of the family to support educational and social issues, it may help produce the desired result and create a safer school environment (Sheldon & Epstein, 2002; Leventhal et al., 2009).

Theoretical Frameworks Contributing to Engagement

Ecological Systems Theory: Urie Bronfenbrenner

When a family undergoes a change, the systems around that family can shift. As families take on these changes, the experiences that a child has vary across each context and environment (Berger, 2008). In order to understand the changes in a child's life, Urie Bronfenbrenner developed a theory, called the Ecological Systems Theory, to explain how the development of a child occurs (Berger, 2008; Berk & Meyers, 2016; Bronfenbrenner & Morris, 2006). The child is the center of this system, also known as the microsystem, and the direct interactions they have with their parents are the biggest and most direct influence on the child (Berger, 2008). The mesosystem is the interactions that the child has on a more formal level. These include with peers, or in school or childcare settings. Places and experiences that a child visits infrequently are part of the exosystem. This might include the parent's employment, religious institutions and even community organizations. The macrosystem is the "outermost level of Bronfenbrenner's model that consists of cultural values, laws, customs and resources" (p. 28). Each society has laws and norms that the communities within it follow. Typically, a child is socialized based on beliefs within these communities.

With this theory, time plays an important role; as a child gains experience interacting with others, they learn more about themselves and what they enjoy. The more they learn, the more their development changes and shifts. "The life course of an individual is embedded in and shaped by the historical times and events they experience over their lifetime" (Bronfenbrenner & Morris, 2006, p. 821). This theory explains the interrelated pieces all working together to form this complex system (Berk & Meyers, 2016).

Family Systems Theory

Each family functions differently. Within each family, there is a hierarchical structure (Cox & Paley, 1997). There are questions to consider:

- Who is the head of the household?
- What is the role of the siblings?
- How does the family interact within their personal community?
- How does employment influence the structure of the family within the community?

How a family works is answered by the above questions. When everyone has a specific role within the family, it determines how the individuals will interact with one another (Knox & Schacht, 2016). This is known as the Family Systems Theory. Within each family, there are boundaries set and members must understand these in order to interact appropriately in the family unit. For instance, if there is a conflict among the siblings, the parental figure within the household might set the rule that the siblings need to figure out how to resolve the issue. Larger issues, such as family budget or legal matters, might be dealt with by the adults; however, in some families, they might choose to also include the children. Other examples might include children helping with grocery shopping, chores and family nights.

Each individual has a role that functions differently in that family unit (Knox & Schacht, 2016; Cox & Paley, 1997). "In healthy families, individuals are allowed to alternate roles rather than being locked into one role" (Knox Schacth, 2016, p. 29). Roles that are determined within a family can affect the functionality of the family. When marital discord arises, the parent–child relationship could be affected (Cox & Paley, 1997). Within the Family Systems Theory, families should be adaptive to any changes that might happen. This allows families to be flexible and adjust as needed. When flexibility doesn't occur, dysfunctionality can occur. Rules and boundaries should be clear and understood within a family. The employment of parents is an example of this. If one family member commutes, the family needs to adapt to this change so that the family may function. Older siblings might have to take on the caregiver role for the younger siblings until the parent returns home, or the family might need to seek out additional childcare if both parents are working outside of the home.

Within each family unit, family engagement is also determined. "Parental involvement in schooling and support teaching style was found to be positively linked to students' achievement" (Levpuscek & Zupancic, 2009, p. 545). Even when there are positive outcomes, each family is structured differently, and expectations can vary. The family sets the expectations about social interactions and involvement with schooling. See the section below, "Theory and Research to Practice Connection: Support for Learning Case Study", for further information.

Box 11.3 Theory and Research to Practice Connection: Support for Learning Case Study

The need for educators and parents to work together is imperative. Mary Scanlan developed an activity that models the home–school partnership where the child takes the lead role in the process.

Case Study Overview

29 early elementary children were given a shoebox to take home over the winter break. The children were instructed to collect items that would be beneficial and motivational for them to write about. Once the children collected their items, parents were told to ask the child why they chose that specific item, and how the item would be used in their own personal writing. After the children brought their shoeboxes back to school, they were given the opportunity to present their items during circle time. After presenting their items, the children were then told to write a short story using the items from home. All the children wrote short stories and were given the opportunity to illustrate them. The teacher collected these short stories, bound them together and had each child write a narrative.

Findings

The teacher reported that they were able to see the improvement in the children's writing, and the children were more motivated to want to write, especially among the boys of the classroom. It is important to note that when the parents were interviewed after this activity, they were very positive about it because they were asked to be included in their child's education. This activity was successful for two reasons: the children had the opportunity to reflect on why they were motivated by sharing their items in class and also were able to share the activity with their parents.

How This Activity Can Be Used in the Classroom

Educators can duplicate this activity in the classroom. Explain or illustrate to the family why their participation is important. Let them know that it is crucial the child is able to discuss their choices and tell why they chose them. Tell the family that the child will be given the opportunity to write a short story and draw illustrations about the items they picked. This is a great activity for family engagement. Parents are able to play an integral part in the child's assignment.

For further information:

Scanlan, M. (2012) 'Cos um it like put a picture in my mind of what I should write': An exploration of how home-school partnership might support the writing of lower-achieving boys. *Support for Learning, 27*(1), 1–10.

School, Family and Community Partnership Model: Joyce Epstein

Families' contributions involve knowledge of a child's history and perspective on the child in a home environment (Koralek et al., 2004). A family may know a child's:

- Health and growth history;
- Food allergies and medical concerns;
- Favorite activities at home;
- Relationship with other family members;
- Reactions to change in routines;
- Fears;
- Ways to find comfort when upset;
- Lifestyle with family; and
- Recent activities in the evenings, on weekends and during vacations.

With effective engagement and communication, contributions from the family can be beneficial for educators and the child (Driscoll & Nagel, 2008; Epstein et al., 2018). Benefits for educators include improved morale, stronger communication between educator and family, assistance from families in the classroom and with resources, understanding of students' families, helpful approaches to homework, parental involvement in conferences and a better connection with families and the community. Epstein et al. (2018) distinguished benefits based on six types of involvement:

1. Parenting (e.g. supportive home environments);
2. Communicating (e.g. variety of methods for exchanges);
3. Volunteering (e.g. organizing assistance at school, home and other locations);
4. Learning at home (e.g. resources for homework and activities);
5. Decision-making (e.g. representation on school committees); and
6. Collaborating with the community (e.g. incorporation of resources and services from the community).

Understanding parenting practices benefits educators because there is an understanding of the families' backgrounds and concerns, respect for families' strengths, appreciation of student diversity and recognition of their skills. Utilizing different communication methods increases the contact between educators and families, the appreciation for parental networks and the ability to understand family perspectives on educational programs. Communicating with families includes encouraging volunteering. When a teacher communicates with a family, the family is more likely to volunteer, which is a benefit for the student and the classroom. Educators can learn more about individual talents and ways to develop novel volunteer opportunities. Having more volunteers in the classroom results in an increase in individual student attention. When an educator understands how learning occurs in the home, they can use that information to develop homework assignments and activities that benefit the child and their family, which leads to more family support and appreciation of family time. When decision-making occurs between families and educators, an increased awareness about parent perspectives on policies occurs, and the acknowledgment of what values the families share are represented on committees. Collaboration between the community and educators benefits families because there is an expanded awareness of how community resources may benefit the curriculum, strengthen partnerships with community members and improve the ability to provide referrals for special services.

Application of Practices

Communication between Educators and Families

Verbal communication between educators and families is very important. As an educator, observe who does the drop off in the morning and who picks up in the afternoon. Consider this when planning your communication to engage the parent. Making an effort to talk to a family member before or after school is an integral part of building a working relationship that will benefit you as an educator, the child and the family unit. When educators take the time and talk to families, either when picking up or dropping off, it shows an effort is being made. Often when a child isn't behaving appropriately, a teacher wants to have a discussion with the family in order to address it. Discussing behavioral problems is necessary, but taking the time to share something positive about the child is extremely beneficial. Positive communication builds a foundation with the family so that if a negative issue does arise, the parent is more open to discussion. Positive communication establishes a connection. If the opportunity to have a short discussion about the child doesn't present itself, consider alternate ways to communicate with the family such as a progress report, a short email or a handwritten note on an assignment the child is taking home.

With the increased use of technology, more families are relying on alternative ways to communicate such as email or texting. It is important to ask families at the beginning of the school year how they would prefer to get their information regarding their child. Some schools and educators have developed groups on social media so that families can stay connected and informed about class or school activities and events.

Ways to Participate

As stated earlier, family engagement varies from family to family. Regardless of the amount of family engagement, all families want their children to succeed. The culture of the school helps to dictate the amount of family involvement. When families are asked to participate, "families respond based on their past experiences and their current situations" (Berger, 2008, p. 133). When educators incorporate family engagement in both class activities and homework, it can increase the empowerment of families, and they will be more likely to support their child's learning at home. Think about family engagement as multiple layers so that families are encouraged to be involved.

Collaborative methods between home and school could be organized in a multitude of ways. Here are some suggested ways based on Epstein's research:

- Explore the various skills and knowledge that families already have about their child and ask them about it.
- Communicate with parents through multiple means. This might include telephone calls, emails, text messages and one-on-one contact which could include collaborative problem-solving.
- Encourage families to volunteer or contribute. This could be either in or outside of the classroom. Some families may not be able to volunteer in the classroom but could contribute in other ways such as donations. Pose an open-ended question asking parents in what ways they feel they are able to contribute to the classroom. Some may have ideas or skills that you haven't thought of.

- Provide strategies for families to use when doing homework or projects with their children. See "Theory and Research to Practice Connection: Support for Learning" for an idea of this one.
- Involve parents in decision-making.
- Provide families with information on community resources and services.

Support for Families

Providing support for families is critical for the child's educational success (Berger, 2008). Some activities that promote support could include:

- Back-to-school nights: teachers can communicate (or share) classroom expectations. Berger (2008) pointed out that some families have different work schedules that might prevent them from attending evening events. Offering either a one-on-one meeting during the weekend, before or after school or on your staff development day will give families more opportunities to meet with you.
- Parent networks: parenting networks provide parents with the opportunity to problem-solve and share with each other. Additionally, as children progress in their education, so does their development. By providing developmental information to parents, educators can effectively communicate with families about the students' interests and needs (Epstein, 2019).
- School–home activity packets: many educators send activities home that correspond with the curriculum taking place in class. Consider the amount of time required to complete the activity at home and remember that some families have less time than others for home projects and homework (Berger, 2008). Instead, send home small positive and fun activities that encourage family involvement.
- Home visits: see the section titled "Common Core and Other Standards: Home Visits" for further information on this topic.

Box 11.4 Common Core and Other Standards: Home Visits

Home visits have been identified as a key component for connecting with families. When educators show they care by meeting families in their own personal environment, parents tend to be more willing to get involved in their child's education.

Research Study Overview

In a five-year follow-up, 29 teachers who taught kindergarten through second grade were asked to fill out a questionnaire in a school-wide initiative in a midwestern school district. This questionnaire included information such as "students' attendance, attitude and academic performance, parent's attitudes toward school, the teacher and the parent's involvement" (Meyer et al., 2011, p. 193). Additionally, there were four open-ended questions asking teachers to describe their personal experience, what they learned about their students, the communication they used with the child's parents, and how parents were impacted as a result of the home visit.

Findings

The results were very positive: 89% of the teachers said that the home visits helped the student's school attitude, 100% said that it helped parents' school attitude and 97% said that the home visits helped parents' attitudes toward the teacher. What this research study found about home visiting is that the teachers were able to understand the child's basic needs, such as coming to school hungry or being tired at school. Teachers also stated that home visits provided more of a personal connection with families.

How This Research Study Can Be Used in the Classroom

When schools are willing to support home visits, educators are given the opportunity to establish personal relationships with families. When home visits are conducted early in a child's elementary schooling and early in the school year, a partnership is established. Parents might be more willing to ask the teacher about their child's educational progress over the school year and teachers can share what the educational goals of the school year will be. When home visits are conducted, it has been shown that children have a higher attendance rate and end up reading at or above grade level.

For further information:

Meyer, J.A., Mann, M.B., & Becker, J. (2011). A five-year follow-up: Teachers perceptions of the benefits of home visits for early elementary children. *Early Childhood Education*, *39*, 191–196.

Understanding the dynamics and differences of each family provides an opportunity to improve communication efforts and engagement. These are a few suggestions. Use your own ideas or experiences to get to know your families so a home–school connection can be made for the children in your program.

Chapter Summary

This chapter addressed the importance of parent, family and community engagement in early care and education. The first section examined the benefits of family engagement with a focus on the relationship between educators and families, the short-term benefits for the child and the long-term benefits for the child. The second section provided information on differing cultural backgrounds of families, considering family attitudes about schooling and their influence on engagement. In addition, an overview of diverse family structures was discussed and the impact of community/neighborhood and school climate on engagement was presented. The third section described the theoretical frameworks contributing to family engagement, including the Ecological Systems Theory, the Family Systems Theory and the School, Family and Community Partnership Model. This model is critical to understanding family engagement. The fourth section presented the application of practices, focusing on methods of communication, ways in which families can participate and how educators can support families.

References

Alexander, K.I., Entwisle, D.R., & Dauber, S.L. (2003). *On the success of failure: A reassessment of the effects of retention in the primary school globes* (2nd ed.). Cambridge University Press: New York.

Barnard, W.M. (2004). Parent involvement in elementary school and education attainment. *Children and Youth Services Review*, *26*, 39–62.

Berger, E.H. (2008). *Parents as partners in education: Families and schools working together* (7th ed.). Pearson: Upper Saddle River, NJ.

Bronfenbrenner, U., & Morris, P.A. (2006). The bioecological model of human development. In R.M. Lerner & W. Damon (Eds.), *Handbook of child psychology: Theoretical models of human development* (pp. 793–828).: John Wiley & Sons Inc: Hoboken, NJ.

Cheung, C.S., & Pomerantz, E.M. (2011). Parents' involvement in children's learning in the United States and China: Implications for children's academic and emotional adjustment. *Child Development*, *82*(3), 932–950.

Child Trends (2018). *Parental involvement in schools.* Child Trends. Retrieved 18 July 2019, https://www.childtrends.org/indicators/parental-involvement-in-schools

Clarke-Stewart, A., & Parke, R.D. (2014). *Social development* (2nd ed). Wiley: Hoboken, NJ.

Cox, M.J., & Paley, B. (1997). Families as systems. *Annual Review of Psychology*, *48*, 243–267.

Dearing, E., Simpkins, S., Kreider, H., & Weiss, H.B. (2006). Family involvement in school and low-income children's literacy: Longitudinal associations between and within families. *Journal of Educational Psychology*, *98*(4), 653–664.

Eccles, J.S., & Roeser, R.W. (2009). Schools, academic motivation, and stage-environment fit. In R.M. Lerner & L. Steinberg (Eds.), *Handbook of adolescent psychology: Individual bases of adolescent development* (pp. 404–434). John Wiley & Sons Inc: Hoboken, NJ.

Epstein, J.L. & Associates (2019). *School, family, and community partnerships: Your handbook for action* (4th ed). Corwin: Thousand Oaks, CA.

Galindo, C., & Sheldon, S.B. (2012). School and home connections and children's kindergarten achievement gains: The mediating role of family involvement. *Early Childhood Research Quarterly*, *27*, 90–103.

Gates, C.J. (2013, February). *LGBT parenting in the United States*. Los Angeles. Williams Institute, U.C.L.A.

Grolnick, W.S., & Slowiaczek, M.L. (1994). Parents' involvement in children's schooling: A multidimensional conceptualization and motivational model. *Child Development*, *65*, 237–252.

Halle, T.G., Kurtx-Costes, B., & Mahoney, J.L. (1997). Family influences on school achievement in low-income, African American children. *Journal of Educational Psychology*, *89*(3), 527–537.

Hoglund, W.L.G. Brown, J.L., Jones, S.M., & Aber, J.L. (2014). The evocative influence of child academic and social-emotional adjustment on parent involvement in inner-city schools. *Journal of Educational Psychology*, *107*(2), 517–532.

Huntsinger, C.S., & Jose, P.E. (2009). Parental involvement in children's schooling: Different meanings in different cultures. *Early Childhood Research Quarterly*, *24*, 398–410.

Kim, J., & Bryan, J. (2017). A first step to a conceptual framework of parent empowerment: Exploring relationships between parental empowerment and academic performance in a national sample. *Journal of Counseling & Development*, *95*, 168–179.

Knox, D., & Schacht, C. (2014). *Choices in relationships: An introduction to marriages & the family* (12th ed.). Cengage: Boston, MA.

Kreider, R.M., & Fields, J.M. (2011). *Current population reports*. U.S. Census Bureau: Washington, DC.

Laursen, B., & Collins, W.A. (2009). Parent-child relationships during adolescence. In R.M. Lerner & L. Steinberg (Eds.), *Handbook of adolescent psychology: Contextual influences on adolescent development* (pp. 3–42). John Wiley & Sons Inc: Hoboken, NJ.

Leventhal, T., Dupéré, V., & Brooks-Gunn, J. (2009). Neighborhood influences on adolescent development. In R.M. Lerner & L. Steinberg (Eds.), *Handbook of adolescent psychology: Contextual influences on adolescent development* (pp. 411–443). John Wiley & Sons Inc: Hoboken, NJ.

Levpuscek, M.P., & Zupancic, M. (2009). Math achievement in early adolescence: The role of parental involvement, teachers' behavior, and students' motivational beliefs about math. *Journal of Early Adolescence*, *29*(4), 541–570.

Mau, W. (1997). Parental influences on the high school students' academic achievement: A comparison of Asian immigrants, Asian-Americans, and White Americans. *Psychology in the Schools*, *34*(3), 267–277.

Mcwayne, C.M., Hampton, V., Fantuzzo, J., Cohen, H.L., & Sekino, Y. (2004). A multivariate examination of parent involvement and the social and academic competencies of urban kindergarten children. *Psychology in the Schools*, *41*(3), 363–377.

Meyer, J.A., Mann, M.B., & Becker, J. (2011). A five-year follow-up: Teachers perceptions of the benefits of home visits for early elementary children. *Early Childhood Education*, *39*, 191–196.

Nokali, N.E., Bachman, H.J., & Votruba-Drzal, E. (2010). Parent involvement and children's academic and social development in elementary school. *Child Development*, *81*(3), 988–1005.

Oswald, D.P., Zaibi, H.B., Cheatham, D.S., & Brody, K.G. (2018). Correlates of parental involvement in students' learning: Examination of a national data set. *Child Family Study*, *27*, 316–323.

Passel, J.S, Wang, W., & Taylor, P, (2013). *Marrying out: One-in-seven new U.S marriages is interracial or interethnic*. Pew Research Center. Retrieved 18 July 2019. https://www.pewsocialtrends.org/2010/06/04/marrying-out/

Santos Rego, M.A., Ferraces Otero, M.J., Godas Otero, A., & Lorenzo Moledo, M.D. (2018). Do cooperative learning and family involvement improve variables linked to academic performance. *Journal of Education & Research*, *30*(2), 212–217.
Scanlan, M. (2012). 'Cos um it like put a picture in my mind of what I should write': An exploration of how home-school partnership might support the writing of lower-achieving boys. *Support for Learning*, *27*(1), 1–10.
Sheldon, S.B., & Epstein, J.L. (2002). Improving student behavior and school discipline with family and community involvement. *Education and Urban Society*, *35*(1), 4–26.
Wakefield, S. (2015). Parental incarnation and caregiver-child relationships quality. *Journal of Criminal Law & Criminology*, *104*(4), 905–927.

Chapter 12

Educational Policy in Context

Alicia Herrera

The Importance of Context

Understanding the far reach of educational policy provides an important foundation for teachers who wish to create classrooms that support developmentally appropriate experiences for every student under their care. This chapter provides an overview of education policies and initiatives in the United States with a focus on viewing policies in the context of interacting levels of the educational system.

This chapter will help answer these important questions from the classroom teacher's perspective:

- What is the purpose of educational policy and how is it enacted?
- What are some historical federal policies with lasting impacts?
- How can teachers employ state policies to support developmentally appropriate practices?
- How is policy personally meaningful to teachers and students?
- How can classroom teachers develop a critical lens for viewing and interpreting policy?

Educational Policy: Purpose and Process

Educational policy is a term that refers to the collection of laws, rules, and norms that guide the systemic operation of education. Policy-making seeks to define the purpose of education and the outcomes it seeks to enact in society, as well as the mechanisms for measuring the policy's successes and failures. Policy can be understood as a kind of mirror that reflects something about the community with which it interacts. The goals of policy are nested in the values of the society in which they exist, as interpreted through the lens of policymakers, the public, educators, and multiple interest groups (Atherton, 2000; Morgan, 2016; Secretary's Commission on Achieving Necessary Skills, 1991).

Educational policy operates at various levels: federal, state, and local. What teachers experience at the local level, such as school rules, content-area standards, state-adopted textbooks, curricula, and overall school climate, all have

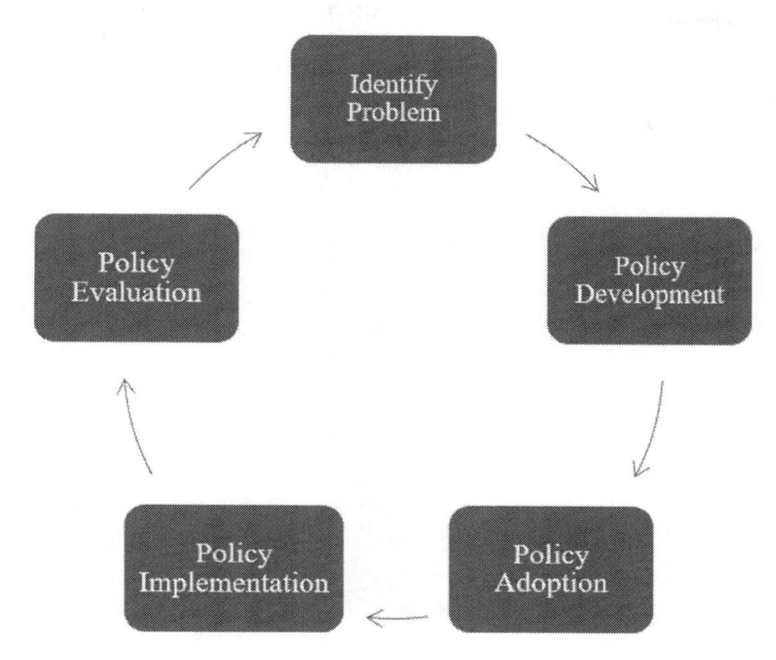

Figure 12.1 The Policy-Making Process

meaningful connections to the larger context of federal, state, and local education policies.

The policy-making process is launched when an idea, concept, or problem is identified, and then individuals begin to address options for solutions (Morgan, 2016; see Figure 12.1). For example, the idea that elementary students should have opportunities to formally experience social-emotional learning in school is one that many teachers, parents, educational policy-makers, and the media have addressed. At the policy development level, policy-makers take input from experts and are informed by various stakeholders, and they may create committees to explore the topic and collect feedback in the form of recommendations. At the policy adoption level, all of these ideas are written as policies that become laws, rules, and regulations. After some time, at the policy evaluation level, policies are examined for effectiveness and areas of possible improvement. If new problems, or unintended consequences, are identified, then the policy-making process can begin anew (Atherton, 2000; Morgan, 2016).

Educational Policy Ecosystem

A meaningful way to approach understanding educational policy is by placing the student experience in the classroom within the larger context of the

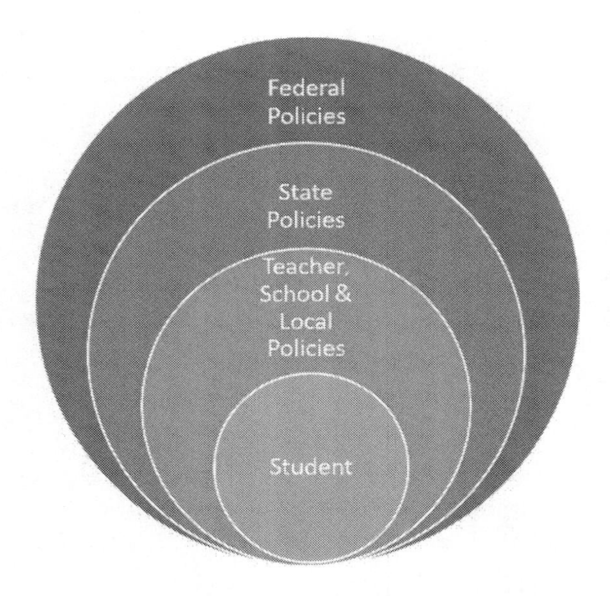

Figure 12.2 The Educational Policy Ecosystem

Table 12.1 Timeline

Year	*Policy and Event*
1965	Elementary and Secondary Education Act (ESEA)
1965	Education for the Disadvantaged, Title I
1966	Migrant Education Act
1968	Bilingual Education Act
1972	Indian Education Act
1978	Indian Welfare Act
1983	A Nation at Risk: The Imperative for Educational Reform released
1990	Individuals with Disabilities Education Act (IDEA)
1994	Improving America's Schools Act (IASA)
2001	No Child Left Behind Act (NCLB)
2002	Partnership for 21st Century Learning formed
2002	Bilingual Education Act repealed and replaced with NCLB
2004	Individuals with Disabilities Education Improvement Act (IDEA 2004)
2007	Common Core State Standards Initiative development process begins
2010	Common Core State Standards (CCSS) released for adoption
2010	Obama proposes reforms to NCLB (flexibility waivers)
2013	Next Generation Science Standards published
2015	Every Student Succeeds Act (ESSA)
2017	Trump Administration revises ESSA

interrelationships among all areas of their development and the educational policies and practices that support them (Darling-Hammond & Cook-Harvey, 2018; see Figure 12.2). By viewing how all layers of educational policy interact to impact a child's educational experience, a teacher can contextually organize their thinking about how the educational system supports—or does not support—any particular child's growth and development. This practice will allow a teacher to become more attuned and responsive to the ways in which the educational system meets the needs that students bring to the classroom.

Box 12.1 Theory and Research to Practice Connection: The Community School Model of Integrated Student Supports

An example of developmental theory and research enacted into policy can be seen through the growing popularity of the use of integrated student supports across the country. What is currently called the Community School Model is one such example, in which, in addition to traditional academics, a collection of community partnerships are also established at the site to support the development of the whole child. These schools are a place where supports that positively interact with the whole child's ecosystem are organized and integrated into the purpose of the school itself. Schools become hubs of the community and are open to the extended families of students as well as other members of the neighborhood. Many community schools operate all day and year-round, often providing individualized academic enrichment, health and social services, youth and community development opportunities, case management coordinators, and a variety of other services that address learning barriers for students (Coalition of Community Schools, 2019; Bronstein & Mason, 2016).

Sufficient evidence exists to qualify the community schools approach as "evidence-based intervention" under ESSA (Every Student Succeeds Act), as there are several community school models that had met the criteria of having at least one well-designed study that supports the practice. The kinds of integrated student supports that community schools provide are associated with positive student outcomes in multiple domains of development (Maier, Daniel, & Oakes, 2017).

Historical Federal Policies in Context

Paying attention to the historical trajectory of major policy reforms can help teachers create a current learning environment with intention, accessing a holistic sense of policy while advocating for developmentally appropriate experiences for students in the present moment. In this section, the reader will be able to explore and connect how various iterations of the Elementary and

Secondary Education Act (ESEA) and its subparts may have contributed to current educational contexts that directly impact elementary school settings.

Elementary and Secondary Education Act

The Elementary and Secondary Education Act of 1965 (ESEA) has been the most widespread federal legislation impacting the way education is understood at the national level (U.S. Congress, 1965). President Lyndon B. Johnson passed ESEA as part of his larger War on Poverty campaign, during a time when public scrutiny of the government's role in the well-being of underserved populations was heightened. In the spirit of the civil rights movement, the act emphasized equal access to education, providing federal mechanisms to address educational inequities in the system. Before ESEA, federal legislation dealing with education was limited and written with the intention of giving states the ability to make most curricular and managerial decisions regarding schools (Halperin, 1975).

The ambitious central goal of the ESEA in 1965 was to improve the educational opportunities and outcomes for children from lower-income families. This goal was addressed through the creation of policies that changed the balance of the role of the federal government in relation to state and local control. The federal government would gain more direct involvement through the creation of new programs, and funding opportunities would be put in place at the local level to express a federal investment in equalizing educational opportunities across the nation (U.S. Congress, 1965).

The Breadth of ESEA: A Key Understanding

ESEA has many subparts, called Titles. A version of ESEA has been reauthorized many times since 1965, and at the time of reauthorization, the name of this legislation has changed along with key features inside the policy itself. Clinton's Improving America's Schools Act of 1994, Bush's No Child Left Behind Act of 2001, and Obama's Every Student Succeeds Act of 2015 are all examples of iterations of ESEA (U.S. Congress, 1965, 1994, 2001, 2015). Each reauthorization provides an opportunity for current political and educational leaders to potentially change course. Policy can be written or adapted to reflect the dominant views on the purpose of education at the time, including ideas about how developmentally appropriate learning occurs within the context of schools. In this way, educational leaders' ideas about the value of equitable public education for all children in the United States are revealed through their policy. By following the trajectory and changes of ESEA over the course of its history, you can see an evolving document that reflects public discourse around education of the time (Atherton, 2000; Morgan, 2016). The first version of ESEA in 1965 ushered in many new programs that are still operating in one form or another today, including Title I and Special Education, both discussed in this chapter.

Title I

Title I was a significant subpart of the original version of ESEA in 1965, meant to provide financial assistance to local educational agencies (LEAs) for the education of children from low-income families (U.S. Congress, 1965). Title I has been amended over the years to reflect the expressed needs of LEAs and the values of the educational policy-makers of the era (Atherton, 2000; Morgan, 2016).

All versions of Title I express the intent of providing federal funds to local educational agencies (LEAs) and schools that serve economically disadvantaged students by way of providing various grants (U.S. Congress, 1965). Funding formulas for these grants are based primarily on census poverty estimates and are created with the intent to counter-balance the complex social and economic conditions that contribute to poverty and the resulting disparate academic achievement levels of children from low-income families' curricula (U.S. Department of Education, 2018). The original iteration of Title I took the form of funding for pullout programs. Later versions of Title I sought to create more nuance in the funding formula and have included a variety of accountability measures to track student progress as a requirement for securing funds. In more recent years, the grants have moved toward a focus on school-wide programs (U.S. Department of Education, 2018).

Title I fund usage continues to be widespread. As of the 2015–2016 school year, more than 55,906 public schools in the United States received grants curricula (U.S. Department of Education, 2018). This funding continues to provide academic support for more than 26 million children experiencing gaps in opportunities to meet state standards in core academic subjects (U.S. Department of Education, 2018). Funds provide important developmental support, for instance, extra instruction in reading and mathematics, as well as special preschool, after-school, and summer programs to extend and reinforce the regular school curriculum (U.S. Department of Education, 2018). Teachers can familiarize themselves with the personal impact of Title I by exploring how these monies are allocated by their LEAs.

Bilingual Education Act

The passing of the Bilingual Education Act (BEA) reflected a growing national awareness of the importance of guided linguistic development policy for school-aged English language learners (Petrzela, 2010). At that time, the BEA was the first federal legislation that targeted English learners, providing funding in the form of federal grants. Prior to the act, some individual states were already providing language development programs for English language learners (ELLs), but the passing of legislation at the national level acknowledged that ELLs have special educational needs, and in the interest of equal educational opportunity, a federal funding structure was used to implement widespread bilingual programs (Stewner-Manzanares, 1988). Additionally, funds were devoted to the research of language acquisition and programs that would best support students' linguistic development (Stewner-Manzanares, 1988).

Bilingual education remains a topic of debate in the United States despite overwhelming empirical evidence showing the cognitive benefit of speaking two or more languages (Marian & Shook, 2012). The perceived value of bilingualism itself has historically fluctuated in the eyes of policy-makers and reflects changes in cultural perspectives on diversity and immigration as well as the level of understanding of linguistic development of those charged with writing and enacting bilingual educational policy (Petrzela, 2010; Stewner-Manzanares, 1988). Teachers can take a close look at linguistic policy and programs offered in local public school settings that are funded by state and federal dollars, and reflect on how they embody the values of educational leaders and the communities they serve.

Migrant Education Act

The Migrant Education Act was added as an amendment to ESEA, Title I, in 1966 and prompted the creation of the Office of Migrant Education Program (MEP). The MEP established the initial call to meet the unique educational and social needs of school-aged children of workers in the agricultural and fishing industries. Children of migrant workers struggle to achieve the same level of access to high-quality public education as their non-migratory peers. Without policy and programmatic structures in place to accommodate for the educational needs of those who frequently relocate, disruptions in services occur for migrant students, contributing to slower progress through school and, ultimately, higher push-out rates (Kuenzi, 2006). Additionally, traditional academic calendars have been at odds with seasonal relocation, creating negative social barriers for migrant students, including disconnection from school culture and challenges in making lasting relationships with teachers and peers (Martinez & Cranston-Gingras, 1996). Ideally structured for state-level advocacy, the creation of the MEP allowed states greater flexibility in program development by increasing federal funding and creating partnerships that resulted in far-reaching interstate coordination efforts for migrant education services, most notably the Migrant Student Records Transfer System, a national student database that stores educational and health information that follows students with each move (Branz-Spall & Wright, 2004). Teachers can familiarize themselves more with these programs by exploring how the MEP is structured in their community.

Indian Education Act

The 1972 Indian Education Act focused national attention on the distinct educational, cultural, and linguistic needs of Indigenous children and adults and how federal policy might support a comprehensive approach toward meeting those needs. In 1974, the act was amended to add a teacher training program and a fellowship program. A subsequent amendment in 1988 allowed schools to apply for formula grants and created an authorization for Gifted and Talented education.

To view the Indian Education Act in context as part of a larger system with many interacting policies, also consider the Indian Child Welfare Act of 1978 (ICWA). Although not an educational policy, the ICWA shifted power and responsibility between the United States federal government and native governments concerning custody proceedings that involved Indian children. These changes potentially impacted the school–home relationship for many students. Before the ICWA, between 25 and 35 percent of all Indian children were being forcibly removed from their homes and placed in non-Indian communities by state and county social service agencies (Johnson, 1999; Jones, 1995; S.S., n.d, U.S. Department of the Interior Indian n.d). This was often done by courts that showed clear preference for placing native children with non-native families (Jones, 1995). Through the ICWA, Congress recognized that the interests of cultural heritage were important considerations in supporting the overall developmental well-being of native children and declared that it would protect and promote tribal stability through policy (Barsh, 1979). Teachers might consider exploring local educational policy history regarding Indigenous populations and how it may be impacting their current school climate.

Education for All Handicapped Children Act

When ESEA passed in 1965, it did not mandate access to a free and appropriate public school education within the least restrictive environment for students with special needs. At that time, many individual states had laws that excluded children with certain types of disabilities from attending public school, including children who were handicapped, blind, deaf, and children labeled with cognitive and emotional diagnoses. More than one million students with special needs did not have access to the public school system at all (Bursztyn, 2007; Valero-Kerrick, 2013). The passing of the Education for All Handicapped Children Act of 1975 brought increased awareness of our national and local public policies that provided support—or lack of support—to students with special needs. With each amendment of this legislation, such as the Education of the Handicapped Act of 1986 and the Individuals with Disabilities Education Act of 1990 (IDEA), we can trace the development of policies and programs in our country. These changes reflect a changing public understanding of human development and the developmentally supportive role educational law can play, as special education did not always exist in the United States and has undergone dramatic changes in both policies and the values that support them since its inception (Keogh, 2007). For a more comprehensive overview of policies and programs that serve students with special needs, see Chapter 9.

Improving America's Schools Act

In 1994, the Clinton administration significantly revised the ESEA, renaming it the Improving America's Schools Act (IASA). The IASA emphasized high and rigorous standards for all students, sustained and intensive teacher education and professional development, expanded school choice and accountability, and closer partnerships between families, schools, and communities (Riley, 1995). Among these many changes, this version of the ESEA specifically reauthorized increased funding for bilingual education and, notably, included a provision for accountability measures for Title I students. Because of the reframing of Title I to include a direct link to measurements of effectiveness, funds would become a lever for federal oversight and an integral part of state accountability reform efforts, rather than an add-on program (Billig, 1997). Ultimately, the IASA ushered in standards-based reforms that would be carried forward in earnest under the Bush administration with the No Child Left Behind Act (NCLB) of 2001, and it continues to be controversial among educational experts, political leaders, and the general public to this day (Billig, 1997; Shepard, Hannaway, & Baker, 2009).

No Child Left Behind

In the wake of the September 11, 2001 attacks, the Bush Administration passed No Child Left Behind (NCLB) quickly with overwhelming bipartisanship. This controversial reauthorization of ESEA played an important role in how the nation reframed the issue of what improving student performance and accountability would look like at the policy level, while creating significant challenges for institutions and educators dedicated to sustaining developmentally appropriate practices for all students (Darling-Hammond, 2007). Structurally, NCLB held four overarching reform principles: 1) accountability, 2) emphasis on scientifically-based research, 3) school choice for parents, and 4) expansion of local control within the frame of specific federal accountability measures (U.S. Department of Education, 2001).

NCLB aimed to improve educational equity through local accountability by reorganizing the way that the federal government motivated schools to perform (U.S. Congress, 2001). High-stakes, one-size-fits-all standardized testing at many grade levels created serious consequences for schools that failed to meet adequate yearly progress (APY) benchmarks (Abedi, 2004; Hursh, 2004). For instance, schools were required to meet APY goals that eventually had 100 percent of all children on grade level by 2014, but didn't have a mechanism in place to give schools credit for helping students make academic growth while still performing below standardized benchmarks (Abedi, 2004). The NCLB accountability measures that focused on proficiency vs. growth masked the progress of schools that were facilitating tremendous holistic growth for students but were still technically below grade-level in the tested subject matter areas (Abedi, 2004; Darling-Hammond, 2007; Hursh, 2004).

No Child Left Behind (NCLB) included strict accountability measures in order to provide transparency and a move towards equity of academic outcomes for underserved populations, but did not deeply focus on other systemic issues, such as the unequal allocation of resources serving wealthy and poor students, and the increasing teacher shortage in high-need areas. By closely linking accountability measures to student performance on high-stakes tests, NCLB undermined the expertise of educational professionals dedicated to developmentally appropriate instructional practices in preference for one-size-fits-all standardization (Hursh, 2004). Accountability for student performance was largely focused at the individual and institutional levels, putting the emphasis on reducing the "achievement gap" between subgroups of students vs. an emphasis on the structural inequities in place that set the stage with "opportunity gaps" that contributed to disparate student outcomes (Abedi, 2004; Hursh, 2004).

In 2009, in lieu of a direct effort to pass the next iteration of ESEA, the Obama Administration began offering waivers to many states for schools that showed growth but had failed to meet proficiency standards under the NCLB (Wong, 2014; McGuinn, 2016). These waivers required schools to link teacher evaluations to student outcomes, implement several school improvement measures, and adopt approved academic standards such as the Common Core State Standards (CCSS). Many states chose to take advantage of the waivers in 2011, and by 2012 CCSS adoption was taking place in several areas of the country (Wong, 2014; McGuinn, 2016). The CCSS are explored in depth later in this chapter.

Every Student Succeeds Act

The Every Student Succeeds Act (ESSA) was signed by President Obama in December of 2015, in the final years of his administration. ESSA is the most current version of the 50-year-old Elementary and Secondary Education Act (U.S. Congress, 2015).

ESSA builds on key areas of progress in recent years through the relative loosening of requirements for annual testing, accountability, and school improvement. These most visible changes directly impact teachers, who must navigate policy in order to create what ESSA describes as a "well-rounded education" for their students (Workman & Jones, 2016). Also essential, the law largely shifts control from the federal government back to states and school districts regarding accountability and school improvement activities (Rentner, Kober, & Frizzell 2017).

ESSA modified heavily but did not eliminate provisions relating to the periodic standardized tests given to students under No Child Left Behind (Walker, 2015). ESSA still requires states to annually test elementary-aged students in reading and math in grades 3–6. States must also test students once in science during the elementary school years. The law encourages states to get rid of unnecessary duplicate state-level testing, and provides funds for them to audit their current testing policies and procedures (U.S. Congress, 2015). ESSA stipulated that assessments must be high quality, worthwhile, time-limited, fair and transparent, just one of multiple measures, and tied to learning (U.S. Department of Education, 2015).

However, in a move toward more holistic evaluation, states now measure school performance based on several components, rather than tests alone. Most factors are still academic and tied to standardized test scores, but schools must include at least one non-academic factor that measures school quality. Many states choose to focus the required non-academic component on issues such as chronic absenteeism, school safety, and student or parent surveys. Academic factors are still given the greatest evaluative weight in ESSA's vision of a well-rounded education (Workman & Jones, 2016). More can be read about enacting this policy in the Promoting Social and Emotional Competence box later in this chapter.

After evaluating and comparing the overall performance of schools, states must identify the schools that are comparatively struggling after considering both academic and at least one non-academic factors and move forward with comprehensive support. The definition of this support is driven by each state as they design their own accountability plans. Paying close attention to who designs these plans and what role individual schools play in them will give a sense of how much flexibility teachers have in determining tailored, developmentally informed instructional practices in their own classroom settings.

Uncertain Times: Suspension of Accountability Requirements under ESSA

Shortly after inauguration, the Trump Administration froze and delayed implementation of certain new regulations passed during the Obama administration, including parts of ESSA (Devos, 2017). In 2017, lawmakers used the Congressional Review Act to eliminate ESSA's accountability regulations (Brown, 2017; Goldstein, 2017). This further loosening of federal accountability rules gives states even more control and increased responsibility to support the improvement of educational outcomes for every student in their care (Devos, 2007). State and district educational leaders currently find themselves in a moment of both great change and great opportunity, as the focus pivots from compliance with federal regulations toward a broader focus on supporting local districts and schools. For many advocates of educational equity, it is also a moment of deep uncertainty as states have more freedom in choosing their focus. States may continue to devote significant energy and resources to equity issues, or they may refocus energy elsewhere, weakening their commitment to the improvement of educational experiences for under-resourced students (Weiss & McGuinn, 2017). While ESSA repealed the AYP framework in NCLB and replaced it with a state-determined accountability system based on multiple measures, the future of ESSA's new accountability measures remains uncertain under the Trump administration (Welner, Kim, & Biegel 2017).

Box 12.2 Promoting Social and Emotional Competence

Enacting Social-Emotional Learning Policy

Through ESSA, individual states have the responsibility to guide curriculum, accountability systems, and state funding. The policy that is enacted at state, school district, and school levels can focus the system on developmental supports for children. To ensure developmentally healthy school environments, teachers can interpret their current school policy through the examination of:

- *Accountability and Improvement Systems*: Are there measures of school climate, social-emotional supports, and school exclusions as part of the school's evaluation process? Increased awareness of the many interacting domains of the educational ecosystem and developmentally focused policy can guide improvement at the classroom level.
- *SEL Standards*: Does the school climate and culture prioritize social, emotional, and cognitive learning? Seek opportunities to integrate the kinds of competencies students should be helped to develop and the kinds of curricula and pedagogical approaches that can help them accomplish these goals.
- *Discipline Policies*: There are ample data to support the removal and replacement of zero-tolerance discipline policies with the explicit teaching of social-emotional strategies and restorative discipline practices. Consider what kinds of discipline support young people in learning key skills and developing responsibility for themselves and their community.
- *Professional Development*: Model what you encourage in your own students. Be a lifelong learner and seek opportunities to increase understanding of social, emotional, and cognitive development, as well as restorative practices.
- *Funding Advocacy*: Oftentimes there are funds available at the site and district levels meant to support school climate. Social-emotional learning and restorative justice programs can be framed as impactful investments. Establishing multi-tiered systems of support, integrated student services, extended learning, and professional learning for educators enables social-emotional development within schools.

Source: adapted from Darling-Hammond, L., & Cook-Harvey, C. M. (2018). *Educating the whole child: Improving school climate to support student success*. Palo Alto, CA: Learning Policy Institute.

Current State Initiatives and Policies in Context

The development and implementation of the Every Student Succeeds Act of 2015 (ESSA) bridged two dramatically different administrations. This time of great change has posed many challenges for teachers, including understanding the philosophical underpinnings of ESSA and how they interact with various state policies and initiatives, as well as how to then best make use of the state- and district-level policies that are the most visible in the daily lives of teachers and guide learning experience for children. Let's explore several state-level policies and initiatives that are most likely to play a role in a classroom teacher's daily life.

The Common Core State Standards

In 2007, the Common Core State Standards for K–12 (CCSS) were under development to create a consistent national framework of what students are expected to learn in English language arts and mathematics subject areas. The idea of state education standards had been in existence since the 1990s, and by the early 2000s, every state had developed and adopted its own learning standards specifying what students should be able to do at certain grade levels. Every state also had its own definition of proficiency, which was generally defined as the level at which a student is determined to be sufficiently educated at each grade level and how prepared a student is upon graduation from high school. An acknowledgment of the lack of national agreement about graduation expectations for students and standardization at each prior grade level was one reason the CCSS were launched by most states in 2009 (National Governors Association, 2010).

The CCSS were conceived during the No Child Left Behind era, launched in 2009, and are still in use today. Federal policies generally have supported ways to adopt and use the CCSS at the state and local levels and are currently adopted at the state level in 41 of the 50 U.S. states (National Governors Association, 2010; Ravitch, 2014).

The CCSS development process was conceived and funded by governors and state school chiefs, along with the Pearson Publishing Company, the Bill and Melinda Gates Foundation, and various other public and private stakeholders (Ravitch, 2016; Saltman, 2016). The development process of the actual content of the standards was also guided in part by these stakeholders. The standards were initially chosen or derived from other state standards already in use and meant to provide a universal framework of consistent benchmarks for all students regardless of where they lived in the United States. A subsequent industry of CCSS-approved curricula and assessment tools was designed to support implementation of the CCSS (Ravitch, 2014; Saltman, 2016; Strauss, 2014).

Among the CCSS' many goals were to have fewer, clearer, and consistent standards that were mapped through backward design from the outcome goal of each student having particular college- and work-readiness traits through the acquisition of progressive K–12 grade-level goals. The standards were designed to be relevant to the real world, reflecting the knowledge and skills that young students would eventually need for success in college, careers, and competition in a global economy (National Governors Association, 2010).

The standards were initially divided into two categories:

- *College- and career-readiness standards*: These standards address what students are expected to know and understand by the time they graduate from high school, according to the developers.
- *K–12 standards*: These standards address expectations for elementary school through high school, and would provide a clear map to college and career readiness.

The Common Core State Standards have drawn both support and criticism from those in educational leadership and from the general public. Let's take a look at the CCSS through the lens of developmentally appropriate practice, applying some essential considerations for educators tasked to implement CCSS-related curriculum and assessments.

A Developmentally Informed Common Core State Standards Approach

Implementation of the CCSS aligns with developmentally appropriate practices in many ways. Teachers benefit from having guidance in the process of interpreting what is both challenging and attainable for young learners (NAEYC, 2015). Standards and developmentally appropriate practices can work well together in that standards provide a goal and developmentally appropriate practices bring the methods to scaffold learning experiences that will promote growth towards that goal (Goldstein, 2008).

For this reason, it is critical for teachers to develop the capacity to participate fully in an ongoing review process of the CCSS (NAEYC, 2015). Teachers are in the unique position of having direct contact with the standards and the ways in which they impact students' learning experiences across multiple domains of development. The importance of professional development for teachers is explored later in this chapter.

An initial consideration is that the CCSS were conceived with standards in only two subject areas—mathematics and English language arts—which comprised the high-stakes standardized testing at play during NCLB (NAEYC, 2015). Having widely adopted and narrowly defined expectations for students can prove to be problematic in an era laden with standards created by many stakeholders with diverse perspectives on desired outcomes at the societal, institutional, and student levels. These stakeholders' expectations may be held without a deeper understanding of the most recent developmental research. A focus on standards limited to only reading and math can be potentially concerning for educators who are committed to teaching with the whole child in mind, and who have a deep appreciation for the complex interaction among all domains of development within the context of the learning environment.

More specifically, standards have traditionally been aligned with accountability systems and have sometimes been used as part of program evaluations (Mathis, 2010). If local administrators do not have an understanding of developmentally appropriate practices, CCSS can be linked to assessment design in ways that do not support balanced instructional practices (NAETC, 2015). Additionally, *what* is chosen to be assessed can provide indications of importance and thus become the focus in educational settings, even formally or informally tied to teacher evaluations (McDaniel, Isaac, Brooks, & Hatch, 2005). A narrow emphasis on two subject matter standards can create overwhelming pressure for both teachers and students, leading to potentially problematic teaching practices in order to meet expectations (Mathis, 2010). Since the inception of CCSS, the challenge for policymakers has been to develop additional standards that provide a more holistic view of children's needs (NAEYC, 2015). For instance, in recent years, some groups have worked to develop science and social-emotional learning standards and frameworks for state adoption, both explored later in this chapter.

When looking closely at the CCSS in English language arts and mathematics, it is possible to appreciate the degree to which they may tend to encourage (or discourage) developmentally appropriate practices. Though the standards focus on outcomes, not processes, there are several indications of flexibility in the standards language regarding the choice of instructional strategies in order to meet grade-level goals.

English language arts (ELA). The language used in CCSS for English language arts (ELA) leaves much room for interpretation at the teacher level regarding instructional decision-making. The ELA standards documents offer broad guidance at each grade level without dictating specific practices. The introduction to the standards states that the standards will define what students are expected to learn, not how teachers should teach (NAEYC, 2015; National Governors Association, 2010). The standards indicate that instruction should be differentiated for diverse learners and that teachers must offer guidance and support. Teachers may guard against a one-size-fits-all approach to reading instruction by aligning developmental theory with the CCSS. It is important to note that after kindergarten, less specific language in the CCSS is aligned with developmentally appropriate practices, and should be closely evaluated by educators attuned to the unique developmental needs of their students (Ivrendi & Johnson, 2002; NAEYC, 2015).

Mathematics. As with the ELA standards, the CCSS mathematics standards are organized around themes that provide some support for developmentally appropriate practices (NAEYC, 2015). The mathematics standards recognize that mathematical understanding follows a progression, and content builds from one grade level to the next (National Governors Association, 2010). The content standards are linked, however, to grade-level expectations and teachers may need to closely evaluate if research supports the age–grade alignment for each individual standard and each individual student. Expectations for children should be responsive to the needs of the whole child in context (NAEYC, 2015).

Ultimately, it is the teacher who takes responsibility for stimulating and supporting children's development and learning by providing experiences each child needs. Ongoing professional development can help teachers connect assessment standards as a means of monitoring children's progress and informing future teaching (NAEYC, 2015). By placing the CCSS in the larger context of an era of using standards-based student assessment data for high-stakes decisions, classroom teachers can remember that the issue of finding ways to ensure developmentally appropriate practices extends beyond the reach of the CCSS (Copple & Bredekamp, 2009; NAEYC, 2015). Evaluating the nature of support that policy provides at the classroom level is an ongoing issue that is a part of the job.

Next Generation Science Standards

The Next Generation Science Standards (NGSS) were completed in 2013 through a collaborative, state-led process, in part to coordinate with the CCSS, which were limited to ELA and mathematics (Lee, Quinn, & Valdés, 2013). Having a new set of K–12 science standards available for state adoption would address an additional subject matter left unaddressed by the CCSS. The idea for national science standards was timely, in that it had been nearly two decades since the research that informed the last set of standards was produced. NGSS identified scientific and engineering practices, crosscutting concepts, and core ideas in science that all K–12 students should be guided to master in order to prepare for success in college and 21st-century careers (NGSS Lead States, 2013).

The spirit behind the NGSS acknowledges that future graduates from high school will obtain jobs that require more skills in science, technology, engineering, and mathematics (STEM) than in the past. Developing a deeper understanding of science beyond fact memorization is required for success (National Research Council, 2012). The NGSS demands that students integrate knowledge across disciplines, as well as have education experiences in K–12 applying knowledge to solve complex problems.

Five NGSS Teaching Innovations

1) *Three-Dimensional Learning*: Curricula designed under NGSS should a) connect the dimensions of science and engineering, b) integrate these concepts, and c) include discipline-specific core knowledge.
2) *Integrated Three-Dimensional Progression*: Scaffolded standards build on the integrated knowledge from previous grade-levels.
3) *Phenomena and Design Engagement*: Learning is rooted in real-world phenomena and design solutions that utilize Three-Dimensional Learning.
4) *Additional Integration of Engineering and the Nature of Science*: Some aspects of engineering are incorporated, such as problem-solving. Scientific theories are used to frame the NGSS.
5) *Math and Literacy Integration*: The NGSS urges meaningful and substantive overlapping of skills and knowledge with both mathematics and ELA (NGSS Lead States, 2013).

Like the CCSS, the NGSS are standards, not curricula. This lack of curricula presents a challenge and also an opportunity for local districts, schools, and classroom teachers, as they must determine what is taught throughout the year and how it is taught. The integrated nature of the NGSS lends itself to developmentally appropriate practices in the classroom and compliments 21st-century learning and project-based learning, both covered in this chapter.

21st-Century Learning

Until the approach of the 21st century, education systems across the United States tended to focus on preparing their students by teaching content knowledge (Care & Anderson, 2016). Schools focused on language arts and mathematic instruction, as these skills were perceived to be essential for success in the real world (Care & Anderson, 2016). Meanwhile, in the last several decades, technological developments have made foundational content increasingly accessible to all.

In part because of this change in information accessibility, ideas about the role of education in the U.S. shifted and, in 1983, the U.S. government released a seminal report titled *A Nation at Risk: The Imperative for Educational Reform* (National Commission on Excellence in Education). A compelling case was made to policymakers that in order for the United States to remain globally competitive, students emerging from educational systems would need the ability to respond to pressing technological, demographic, and socioeconomic changes. Educational leaders proposed a shift toward providing students with a range of skills that relied not only on cognition, but also on the interaction of cognitive, social, and emotional characteristics (National Commission on Excellence in Education, 1983).

The case was made that the workplace of the future would require a workforce that had a new mixture of fundamental skills: foundational knowledge, the ability to critically apply that knowledge, personal skills and attributes, and workplace competencies (Secretary's Commission on Achieving Necessary Skills, 1991).

Some of the 21st-century attributes identified were skills and abilities, such as:

- Enthusiasm for the process of learning,
- Deep understanding,
- Ability to apply learning,
- Inquiry, critical thinking, and reasoning,
- Communication,
- Cultural, social, and environmental understanding,
- Technological proficiency, and
- Diverse integrated learning across subject areas.

Schools today across the United States are still grappling with how to implement these 21st-century learning goals in an educational system originally designed for the industrial age. Creating educational systems that are responsive to the demands of the rapidly changing world continues, as educators guide students in preparation for an increasingly global society and a technologically interconnected world (Whetzel, 1992).

To communicate this change in thinking about the role of education, many school districts have created graduate profiles based on 21st-century learning skills. Additionally, in 2010, the CCSS Initiative called for the integration of 21st-century learning skills into K–12 curricula across the United States (National Governors Association, 2010).

Box 12.3 Common Core and Other Standards

Common Core and Other Standards: Integrating Standards through Project-Based Learning

Project-based learning (PBL) is the term used to describe a kind of experiential learning arranged in thematic units in which several different subject matter content inquiries occur simultaneously. By design, PBL places learning standards in context by challenging students to use their skills to think creatively and work cooperatively. Students are guided to identify a real-world problem and then collaboratively research (and cooperatively develop) a solution based on their research. PBL often culminates in some kind of multimedia presentation derived from CCSS or 21st-century learning goals (Jenkins, Clinton, Purushotma, Robison, & Weigel, 2006).

Project-based learning typically is grounded in the following elements:

- Role-playing,
- Applied scenarios,
- Blended writing genres,
- Multiple reading genres,
- Authentic assessments,
- Authentic audiences,
- Outside guest expertise brought into the classroom,
- Units that assess multiple standards,
- Units that require integration of multiple subjects,
- Student choice,
- Sophisticated collaboration, and
- A variety of communications, including writing, speaking, visual presentations, and publishing (Wolpert-Gawron, 2015).

For example, a group of third-graders might be guided to redesign their own school (or create a new design for a school) including new content areas, grading, collaboration, and community involvement. Through a PBL unit, the teacher could address many areas of the CCSS for third grade, including but not limited to:

CCSS.ELA-Literacy.RL.3.1
Ask and answer questions to demonstrate understanding of a text, referring explicitly to the text as the basis for the answers.

CCSS.Math.Content.3.MD.C.6
Measure areas by counting unit squares (square cm, square m, square in, square ft, and improvised units).

Through PBL, students are able to demonstrate their learning as they journey through the inquiry process with their peers, reflecting on their own growth along the way. Teachers are also able to conduct formative assessments in cognitive and social-emotional growth as students interact with lessons and collaborate with their peers. Although the experience often culminates in a multimedia presentation, PBL is built upon the appreciation of the student as a whole child embedded in a real-world context, and the idea that there is more value to integrated, thematic learning than can be measured through a single summative assessment at the end of each unit.

The Practitioner in Context

How are federal and state policies visible at the local and personal levels? This final section highlights some considerations for navigating and applying policies in the classroom, specifically the ways federal, state, and local policies may interact with the curricular and pedagogical decision-making process for elementary teachers. Making connections between various policies and one's own ideology is an important component of intentional teaching.

Policy and the Teacher Certification Process

Research shows that children benefit from having teachers who are well prepared for thclassroom experience (Harowitz & Darling-Hammond, 2005; Darling-Hammond & Bransford, 2007). In this way, ongoing public questioning of teacher competency can be interpreted to go hand-in-hand with concerns about student performance. To address these concerns, every state has developed some form of teacher certification process for beginning teachers in order to monitor teacher quality.

According to the NAEYC (2009), a highly qualified practitioner should be able to:

1) Promote child development and learning.
2) Build family and community relationships.
3) Observe, document, and assess.
4) Use developmentally effective approaches to connect with children and families.
5) Use content knowledge to build meaningful curriculum.
6) Become a professional.

States vary widely in their definitions of quality and their approaches to the issue, but all seek to create a certification process that balances the ever-present demand for classroom teachers with the need for a well-prepared teacher workforce in the public school system (Cochran, Mayer, Carr, Cayer, & McKenzie, 2015).

Pathways to Teacher Certification

One place to begin understanding the policies that have informed teacher certification programs is by exploring a state education department's requirements for working in the public school system. Most certification programs will require an application, content-area assessments, and a Bachelor's degree. Some accelerated intern programs are designed to earn a Bachelor's degree at the same time as completing teaching certification. There are many options to consider in becoming a professional (Corcoran, 2007). Students prepared in programs grounded in child development can use their understanding of children's characteristics, needs, and multiple interacting environmental factors to create healthy, supportive, and challenging learning environments for the children in their classrooms (NAEYC, 2009).

Critically examining programmatic features of any given teacher certification pathway can indicate what societal needs and policies may be driving that particular option. Just as with national and state policy, comparing teacher preparation programs and their educational coursework will give you a sense of the degree of developmental perspective within them (Corcoran, 2007).

Examining Educational Coursework

A careful look at teacher certification program components also matters personally because thinking about the field of education and one's role within it will be shaped by curriculum and experiences in any given preparation program. Regardless of the type of teacher education program, most prospective teachers should encounter certain types of education classes in a comprehensive program (National Research Council, 2010):

- *Child development or developmental psychology*: These courses highlight the use of developmentally effective approaches used to connect with children and families.
- *Curriculum and instruction*: These courses support the use of content knowledge to build meaningful, culturally responsive curricula.
- *Methods*: These courses focus on pedagogy, including developmentally informed practices for the classroom.
- *Assessment*: These courses provide theory and practice observing, documenting, and measuring growth and proficiency in multiple domains of development and will likely be tied to current state standards.
- *Special education*: All teachers must understand special education policy to some extent, as well as have an understanding of the differentiation and inclusion considerations at play in all classrooms.
- *Field experience*: This programmatic feature provides some type of teaching practicum and guidance in a setting with real, live children. Multiple, diverse field experiences provide a broad developmental view of the field. Single and/or lengthier experiences provide focus and depth of knowledge of a particular context.

Continuing Professional Development

Once certified and teaching in a classroom setting, teachers continue their learning through what is commonly called professional development. Formalized professional development is often embedded in the policies of school districts to meet the federal and state criteria for maintaining highly qualified teachers. It is important to remember that, although the criteria for what is considered a "highly qualified teacher" change when new policies are enacted, the issue of staying knowledgeable of the current learning standards for both teachers and students is ever-present and part of being a professional teacher (Corcoran, 1995, 2007; Darling-Hammond & Bransford, 2007).

Differing strategies have been used to address professional development for current teachers. For instance, some school districts hold regular staff meetings during which a site administrator will facilitate learning about the latest in content area standards or statewide assessment measures. Local educational agencies often have various workshops to offer teachers, and participation may be incentivized through federal- or state-mandated teacher recertification requirements, additional one-time pay, or acquiring the needed college credits to increase salary permanently.

When taking a critical look at the features of optional professional development opportunities, it becomes essential that potential participants take a developmental view of their own learning and are clear about what their ideology is (or wish it to become) as well as what kind of skills they would like to see developed (Gorski, 2016). Regardless of the specific program options in question and where one is in their teaching career, those concerned with the development of children should simultaneously have a sense of their own intentions for their own development as professionals in the field (Gorski, 2016; Sensoy & DiAngelo, 2017).

No matter where one is in their career, teachers concerned with the healthy development of children should not only have a deep understanding of child development in relation to their goals for students, but should also simultaneously have a clear sense of their own intentions for their own development as professionals in the field (NAEYC, 2015).

Articulating Personal Ideology

Explicitly placing one's own personal view of teaching within the larger context of the educational ecosystem is a powerful way to gain clarity and a sense of purpose (Goodyear & Allchin, 1998; Sensoy & DiAngelo, 2017). One practical way to accomplish this is through the creation of a working developmental education philosophy (Chism, 1998. A working developmental education philosophy is a document that gives structure to a teacher's thinking when encountering and interpreting policies that are part of everyday school life. Additionally, most credential programs and employers will request some iteration of this document, so having a working version of current thinking about development and the purpose of education becomes a useful way to frame beliefs and values when communicating with others (Corcoran, 2007; Goodyear & Allchin, 1998).

A developmental philosophy is a self-reflective statement that combines an ideological statement with concrete examples of what is done in the classroom to support those beliefs (Chism, 1998). It is usually written from the first-person perspective and conveys a professional image of how theory, policy, and personal values translate into action. If well developed, this document will provide a way to purposefully assess one's own teaching approach in context (Goodyear & Allchin, 1998). Most philosophy statements are one to three pages long and cover ideas about the following topics:

- Purpose of education.
- Concepts of teaching and learning.
- The framing of goals for student development in context.
- Teaching methods that support healthy development.
- Ideas about the nature of relationships with family and community.
- Beliefs about assessments.
- Goals for professional and personal development.

Why call it a "working" developmental education philosophy? Inevitably a reflective teacher will grow to develop a more nuanced philosophical view as more professional experience is acquired. New experiences will integrate with the old and refine ideologies. By maintaining a reflective working document, a teacher acknowledges that they are also mindfully engaged in continuous learning, demonstrating a commitment to lifelong learning (Corcoran, 2007; Gorski, 2016; Goodyear & Allchin, 1998; Sensoy & DiAngelo, 2017).

Developing a Critical Policy Lens

After articulating current thinking through a working developmental education philosophy, a teacher can evaluate how their beliefs about how children grow and learn interact with the policy and programmatic experiences offered through various learning opportunities in teacher education programs, school districts, individual schools, and the interpersonal relationships within an individual school with which they will be working most closely.

By honing an ability to critically examine one's knowledge of development in relation to policies and programmatic language, it is possible to see how the language of policy frames both teacher and child (Sensoy & DiAngelo, 2017). Ultimately, policy is a pervasive factor in determining the goodness of fit between the child and the educational context. Teachers serve as an intermediary between policy and the children in their classrooms, and can make efforts to ensure the context will support all domains of the child's development. Developing a critical lens for viewing educational policy is an important part of being able to advocate for a developmentally appropriate learning environment for all children in our nation's schools (Gosrski, 2016; Sensoy & DiAngelo, 2017).

Box 12.4 Social Justice and Diversity

Going Deeper: Policy Evaluation as Social Justice

It is important that classroom teachers look beyond the superficial rhetoric of educational policies and programmatic language to see the underlying ideology and the historical context in which they were created (Gillborn, 2005; Sensoy & DiAngelo, 2017). This can be done by developing a critical lens through which one can view how policy reflects and reinforces both desirable and undesirable societal values (Gorski, 2016). For instance, asking critical questions like:

- What does this policy say about the learning expectations for a diverse range of students?
- What does it say about the explicit or implicit cultural values of the educational community?
- How can classroom teachers use policy to best support learning for all students?
- Who will be held accountable for the implementation of this policy, and how will success or failure be measured?

What beliefs and values are embedded into policy becomes personal for teachers and for students in the classroom in that policies dictate the curriculum adopted, the standards chosen, and how and for what purpose resources will be spent (Gillborn, 2005; Sensoy & DiAngelo, 2017). Upon implementation, it should be apparent that policies directly support the well-being of children's cognitive, social-emotional, and physical development, as well as being responsive to the cultural context in which these domains interact (NAEYC, 2015). For these reasons and many more, teachers are an important part of the ongoing policy review process, as they experience what policies look like in practice, in real classroom settings, with real children. Teachers' evaluations and experience with outcome data can inform the policy-making process moving forward (NAEYC, 2015).

Chapter Summary

This chapter provides the classroom teacher a foundational understanding of educational policies and initiatives in the United States by placing various policies in the context of interacting levels of the educational policy ecosystem. Understanding the purpose of educational policy and how it is enacted and interacts at local, state, and federal levels gives the classroom teacher a frame through which to view the broader educational community. Making sense of how the goals of policy spring from the values of the society in which they exist, as interpreted through the lens of policy-makers including the public, educators, and multiple interest groups, can help teachers work for positive systemic change within their own spheres of influence. Federal policies, such as iterations of ESSA, the Bilingual Education Act, and the Indian Education Act are placed in a historical context that demonstrates their underlying ideology and everyday implications for the classroom teacher at state and local levels. Policy impacts the classroom teacher both indirectly and directly through all phases of their own education and professional experience in the field, including the teacher certification process and subsequent professional development. Finally, teachers are encouraged to develop a critical lens in order to view how policy reflects and reinforces both desirable and undesirable societal values so that they may be aware and advocate for developmentally appropriate experiences that support the growth of all children in their care.

References

Abedi, J. (2004). The No Child Left Behind Act and English language learners: Assessment and accountability issues. *Educational Researcher*, *33*(1), 4–14.

Atherton, H. (2000). We the people... Project citizen. *Education for Civic Engagement in Democracy: Service Learning and other Promising Practices*, pp. 93–102.

Barsh, R.L. (1979). The Indian Child Welfare Act of 1978: A critical analysis. *Hastings Law Journal*, *31*, 1287.

Billig, S.H. (1997). Title I of the improving America's Schools Act: What it looks like in practice. *Journal of Education for Students Placed at Risk*, *2*, 329–343. doi:10.1207/s15327671espr0204_3

Branz-Spall, A., & Wright, A. (2004). *A history of advocacy for migrant children and their families: More than 30 years in the fields*. Retrieved from ERIC database. (ED481635).

Bronstein, L.R., & Mason, S.E. (2016). *School-linked services: Promoting equity for children, families, and communities*. New York: Columbia University Press.

Brown, E. (2017, March 27). Trump signs bills overturning Obama-era education regulations. *The Washington Post*. Retrieved from https://www.washingtonpost.com/news/education/wp/2017/03/27/trump-signs-bills-overturning-obama-era-education-regulations/?noredirect=on

Bursztyn, A. (Ed.). (2007). *The Praeger handbook of special education*. Westport, CT: Greenwood Publishing Group.

Care, E., & Anderson, K. (2016). *How education systems approach breadth of skills*. Skills for a Changing World. Retrieved from https://www.brookings.edu/wp-content/uploads/2016/05/brookings_how-education-systems-approach-breadth-of-skills_v2-1.pdf

Chism, N.V.N. (1998). Developing a philosophy of teaching statement. *Essays on Teaching Excellence*, *9*(3), 1–2.

Coalition for Community Schools. (n.d.). *What is a community school?* Retrieved from http://www.communityschools.org/aboutschools/what_is_a_community_school.aspx

Cochran, C.E., Mayer, L.C., Carr, T.R., Cayer, N.J., & McKenzie, M. (2015). *American public policy: An introduction*. Scarborough, ON: Nelson Education.

Copple, C., & Bredekamp, S. (2009). *Developmentally appropriate practice in early childhood programs serving children from birth through age 8*. Washington, DC: National Association for the Education of Young Children.

Corcoran, T.B. (1995). *Helping teachers teach well: Transforming professional development*, CPRE Policy Brief. Consortium for Policy Research in Education. University of Pennsylvania School of Education. Pennsylvania, PA.

Corcoran, T.B. (2007). *Teaching matters: How state and local policymakers can improve the quality of teachers and teaching*. Consortium for Policy Research in Education. University of Pennsylvania School of Education. Pennsylvania, PA, https://repository.upenn.edu/cpre_policybriefs/36/.

Darling-Hammond, L. (2007). Race, inequality and educational accountability: The irony of 'No Child Left Behind'. *Race Ethnicity and Education*, *10*(3), 245–260. doi:10.1080/13613320701503207

Darling-Hammond, L., & Bransford, J. (Eds.). (2007). *Preparing teachers for a changing world: What teachers should learn and be able to do*. Hoboken, NJ: John Wiley & Sons.

Darling-Hammond, L., & Cook-Harvey, C.M. (2018). *Educating the whole child: Improving school climate to support student success*. Palo Alto, CA: Learning Policy Institute.

DeVos, B. (2017). *Key policy letters signed by the education secretary or deputy secretary*. Washington, DC: US Department of Education. Retrieved from https://www2.ed.gov/policy/elsec/guid/secletter/170313.html

Gillborn, D. (2005). Education policy as an act of white supremacy: Whiteness, critical race theory and education reform. *Journal of Education Policy*, *20*(4), 485–505.

Goldstein, D. (2017, March 9). Obama education rules are swept aside by congress. *New York Times*. Retrieved from https://www.nytimes.com/2017/03/09/us/every-student-succeeds-act-essa-congress.html

Goldstein, L.S. (2008). Teaching the standards is developmentally appropriate practice: Strategies for incorporating the sociopolitical dimension of DAP in early childhood teaching. *Early Childhood Education Journal*, *36*, 253–260.

Goodyear, G.E., & Allchin, D. (1998). Statements of teaching philosophy. *To Improve the Academy*, *17*(1), 103–121.

Gorski, P.C. (2016). Poverty and the ideological imperative: A call to unhook from deficit and grit ideology and to strive for structural ideology in teacher education. *Journal of Education for Teaching*, *42*(4), 378–386.

Halperin, S. (1975). ESEA ten years later. *Educational Researcher*, *4*(8), 5–9; *Education for Teaching*, 42, 378–386.

Horowitz, F.D., Darling-Hammond, L., Bransford, J., Comer, J., Rosebrock, K., Austin, K., & Rust, F. (2005). Educating teachers for developmentally appropriate practice. In L. Darling-Hammond & J. Bransford (Eds.), *Preparing teachers for a changing world: What teachers should learn and be able to do* (pp. 88–125). San Francisco: Jossey-Bass.

Hursh, D. (2004). No child left behind. In J. O'Donnell, R.C. Charvez, & M. Pruyn (Eds.), *Social justice in these times* (pp. 172–179). Greewich, CT: Information Age Publishing.

Ivrendi, A., & Johnson, J.E. (2002). Kindergarten teachers' certification status and participation in staff development activities in relation to their knowledge and perceived use of developmentally appropriate practices (DAP). *Journal of Early Childhood Teacher Education*, *23*(2), 115–124.

Jenkins, H., Clinton, K., Purushotma, R., Robison, A.J., & Weigel, M. (2006). *Confronting the challenges of participatory culture: Media education for the 21st century*. Chicago, IL: The John D. and Catherine T. MacArthur Foundation.

Johnson, T.R. (1999). The state and the American Indian: Who gets the Indian child? *Wicazo Sa Review*, *14*(1), 197–214.

Jones, B.J. (1995). Indian Child Welfare Act: The need for a separate law. *Compleat Lawyer*, *12*(4), 18–23.

Keogh, B.K. (2007). Celebrating PL 94–142: The Education of All Handicapped Children Act of 1975. *Issues in Teacher Education, 16*(2), 65–69.

Kuenzi, J.J. (2006). *The federal migrant education program as amended by the No Child Left Behind Act of 2001*. Washington, DC: Congressional Research Service, the Library of Congress.

Lee, O., Quinn, H., & Valdés, G. (2013). Science and language for English language learners in relation to Next generation science standards and with implications for common core state standards for English language arts and mathematics. *Educational Researcher, 42*, 223–233.

Maier, A., Daniel, J., Oakes, J., & Lam, L. (2017). *Community schools as an effective school improvement strategy: A review of the evidence*. Palo Alto, CA: Learning Policy Institute.

Marian, V., & Shook, A. (2012). The cognitive benefits of being bilingual. *Cerebrum, 2012*, 13.

Martinez, Y.G., & Cranston-Gingras, A. (1996). Migrant farmworker students and the educational process: Barriers to high school completion. *High School Journal, 80*(1), 28–38.

Mathis, W.J. (2010). *The "Common Core" standards initiative: An effective reform tool?* National Education Policy Center. University of Colorado. Boulder, CO., https://nepc.colorado.edu/publication/common-core-standards

McDaniel, G.L., Isaac, M.Y., Brooks, H.M., & Hatch, A. (2005). Confronting K-3 teaching challenges in an era of accountability. *Young Children, 60*(2), 20–26.

McGuinn, P. (2016). From No Child Left Behind to the Every Student Succeeds Act: Federalism and the education legacy of the Obama administration. *Publius: The Journal of Federalism, 46*(3), 392–415.

Morgan, L.A. (2016). Developing civic literacy and efficacy: Insights gleaned through the implementation of Project Citizen. *i.e: Inquiry in Education*, 8(1), 3.

National Association for the Education of Young Children (NAEYC) (2009). *NAEYC standards for early childhood professional preparation* [Policy statement]. Retrieved from https://www.naeyc.org/sites/default/files/globally-shared/downloads/PDFs/resources/position-statements/2009%20Professional%20Prep%20stdsRevised%204_12.pdf

National Association for the Education of Young Children (NAEYC) (2015). *Developmentally appropriate practice and the common core state standards: Framing the issues*. Washington, DC: Author.

National Commission on Excellence in Education (1983). A nation at risk: The imperative for educational reform. *The Elementary School Journal, 84*(2), 113–130.

National Governors Association (2010). *Common core state standards*. Washington, DC: Author.

National Research Council (2010). *Preparing teachers: Building evidence for sound policy. National academies press. Crosscutting concepts, and core ideas*. Washington, DC: National Academies Press.

National Research Council. (2012). *A framework for K-12 science education: Practices, crosscutting concepts, and core ideas*. National Academies Press. Washington, D.C.

NGSS Lead States. (2013). *Next generation science standards: For states, by states*. Washington, DC: National Academies Press.

Petrzela, N.M. (2010). Before the federal bilingual education act: Legislation and lived experience in California. *Peabody Journal of Education, 85*, 406–424.

Ravitch, D. (2014). Everything you need to know about common core. https://dianeravitch.net/2014/01/18/my-speech-about-common-core-to-mla/.

Ravitch, D. (2016). *The death and life of the great American school system: How testing and choice are undermining education*. Basic Books: New York, NY.

Rentner, D.S., Kober, N., & Frizzell, M. (2017). *Planning for progress: States reflect on year one implementation of ESSA*. Washington, DC: Center on Education Policy.

Riley, R.W. (1995). The Improving America's Schools Act and elementary and secondary education reform. *Journal of Law & Education, 24*, 513.

Saltman, K.J. (2016). Corporate schooling meets corporate media: Standards, testing, and technophilia. *Review of Education, Pedagogy, and Cultural Studies, 38*(2), 105–123.

Secretary's Commission on Achieving Necessary Skills (1991). *What work requires of schools: A SCANS report for America 2000*. Washington, DC: US Department of Labor.

Sensoy, O., & DiAngelo, R. (2017). *Is everyone really equal?: An introduction to key concepts in social justice education*. Teachers College Press: New York, NY.

Shepard, L., Hannaway, J., & Baker, E. (2009). *Standards, assessments, and accountability*. Journal of Education Policy White Paper. Washington, DC: National Academy of Education (NJ1).

Social Security (n.d.). *Compilation of the social security laws: The Indian Child Welfare Act 1978*. Retrieved from https://www.ssa.gov/OP_Home/comp2/F095-608.html

Stewner-Manzanares, G. (1988). *The bilingual education act: Twenty years later* (Vol. 6, No. 5). Washington, DC: National Clearinghouse for Bilingual Education.

Strauss, V. (2014, January 18). Everything you need to know about common core—Ravitch. *The Washington Post*. Retrieved from https://www.washingtonpost.com/news/answer-sheet/wp/2014/01/18/everything-you-need-to-know-about-common-core-ravitch/

U.S. Congress (1965). Elementary and secondary education act of 1965. *Public Law*, 89–10, https://www.govinfo.gov/content/pkg/STATUTE-79/pdf/STATUTE-79-Pg27.pdf#page=1.

U.S. Congress (1994). Improving America's Schools Act. *Public Law, 103*(383), 103–227.

U.S. Congress (2001). No child left behind act of 2001. *Public Law, 107*, 110.

U.S. Congress (2015). Every student succeeds act. *Pubic Law*, 114–195, https://www.congress.gov/114/plaws/publ95/PLAW-114publ95.pdf.

U.S. Department of Education (2015, October 24). *Fact sheet: Testing action plan*. Retrieved from https://www.ed.gov/news/press-releases/fact-sheet-testing-action-plan

U.S. Department of Education (2018). *Title I, part A program*. Retrieved from https://www2.ed.gov/programs/titleiparta/index.html

U.S. Department of the Interior Indian Affairs. (n.d.). *Indian Child Welfare Act*. Retrieved from https://www.bia.gov/bia/ois/dhs/icwa

Valero-Kerrick, A. (2013). *Early childhood education: Becoming a professional*. Thousand Oaks, CA: SAGE, 424–446.

Walker, T. (2015, December 9). With passage of Every Student Succeeds Act, life after NCLB begins. *NEA Today*. Retrieved from http://neatoday.org/2015/12/09/every-student-succeeds-act/

Weiss, J., & McGuinn, P. (2017). *The evolving role of the state education agency in the era of ESSA and Trump: Past, present, and uncertain future*. University of Pennsylvania. Retrieved from https://files.eric.ed.gov/fulltext/ED586782.pdf

Welner, K., Kim, R., & Biegel, S. (2017). *Legal issues in education: Rights and responsibilities in US public schools today*. West Academic: Saint Paul, MN.

Whetzel, D. (1992). *The secretary of labor's commission on achieving necessary skills*. Retrieved from ERIC database. (ED339749).

Wolpert-Gawron, H. (2015). *DIY project based learning for ELA and history*. United Kingdom: Routledge.

Wong, K. (2014). *Education waivers as reform leverage in the Obama administration: State implementation of ESEA flexibility waiver request*. In APSA 2014 Annual Meeting Paper.

Workman, E., & Jones, S.D. (2016). *ESSA's well-rounded education*. Special Report. Washington, DC: Education Commission of the States.

Index

Page numbers in **bold reference tables.
**Page numbers in *italics* reference figures.

Made in the USA
Las Vegas, NV
07 September 2023